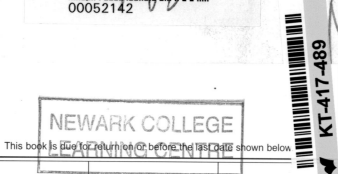

# Illustrated Dictionary
# of Practical Pottery

# Illustrated Dictionary of Practical Pottery

Robert Fournier

Photographs by John Anderson
Diagrams by Sheila Fournier

**VNR** VAN NOSTRAND REINHOLD COMPANY
New York Cincinnati Toronto London Melbourne

Dedicated to the memory of
DORA BILLINGTON
For the sound basis of knowledge and
appreciation that her training gave
me and many others.

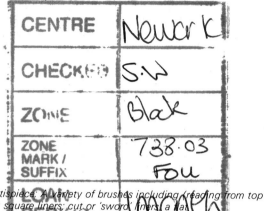
*Frontispiece: A variety of brushes including (reading from top
left): square liners; cut or 'sword' liners; a flat
liner; several Japanese brushes; a one-stroke or flat
duster, a goathair mop, and a hake brush. (Photograph:
Wengers.)*

Van Nostrand Reinhold Company Regional Offices:
New York   Cincinnati   Chicago   Millbrae   Dallas
Van Nostrand Reinhold Company International Offices:
London   Toronto   Melbourne
Copyright © Robert Fournier 1973
Library of Congress Catalog Number 78–39886
ISBN 0 442 29950 8

Designed by Rod Josey.
This book is printed in Great Britain by Jolly and Barber Ltd., Rugby
and bound by Webb Son and Co. Ltd.,
Ferndale, South Wales
Published by Van Nostrand Reinhold Company Inc.
450 West 33rd Street, New York, N.Y. 10001 and Van Nostrand
Reinhold Company Ltd., 25-28 Buckingham Gate, London SW1E 6LQ
Published simultaneously in Canada by Van Nostrand Reinhold
Company Ltd.
16   15   14   13   12   11   10   9   8   7   6   5   4   3   2   1

# INTRODUCTION

This dictionary collects into an easily available form much of the practical information now open to craft potters. It stays strictly within the scope of its title: aesthetics are considered only where inseperable from discussion of the entry, while historical references are kept to a minimum. Similarly industrial or archaic terms have been omitted, entertaining though these often are (I have been unable to resist just one old term!). All the material included will, it is hoped, be of practical use to all potters — student, amateur, and professional alike.

Materials and equipment which you may encounter in merchants' catologs have been covered together with terms used in books on ceramics. Some duplication of information has been inevitable in order to avoid constant cross-reference by readers. Charts have been compiled where necessary to make facts as accessible as possible. Sources are mentioned where appropriate and a bibliography will be found on page 254.

The factual nature of the book has imposed severe restraint on the author, but some counter-balance has been introduced by the illustrations of completed work which help to keep the craftsman's ultimate goal in sight — the production of fine and individual pots.

# THREE NOTES

### Analyses
The analyses by weight included in this dictionary have been arranged with the various oxides in their RO. $R_2O_3$. $RO_2$ columns, i.e. in a similar way to glaze formulas. It is hoped that this will give potters a more immediate picture of the material than the normal listing which places the highest percentage first. It has been carefully stated in each case that the analysis is by weight, not molecular parts as would be represented in a formula.

### Italicization, and bibliographical referencing
The words printed in italics in this dictionary indicate a reference to another entry which would help to clarify the definition or the discussion. Minerals and oxides have not been treated in this way, it being understood that each has its own entry to which reference can be made if required.

The initials in the text (e.g. A.RE., B.TGH.) are abbreviated bibliographical references and the full titles will be found on page 254. The same applies to films mentioned in the dictionary.

### Atomic and molecular weights
The number immediately following any element, oxide, or mineral mentioned in the dictionary indicates the atomic or molecular weight of that material to the nearest whole number or decimal point.

# A

## ABRASIVE

A hard rough material used for cutting, grinding or polishing. The usual abrasives for pottery are *silicon carbide* (carborundum) and *fused alumina*. The latter avoids carbide contamination in the surface of biscuit which can cause glaze scum. The 'Cintride' range of abrasive blocks is also useful although the base metal to which the tungsten fragments are attached is too soft. A small high-speed electric grinding wheel can be used on minor glaze faults. There is a wide range of wheel qualities and bonding materials which are listed in detail in D.DC.

Dry clay or soft biscuit will respond to medium glass paper or alumina pad. To level unstable pots, clip the abrasive paper to a whirler or wheel head and rotate it while holding the pot firmly in the center.

David Leach uses car engine grinding-in paste (a waterbound carborundum) for settling wobbly lids into the flanges of teapots, etc. It has a high cutting power and will deal with stoneware and porcelain.

A pot which needs a lot of grinding after glazing is usually a 'second' anyhow, and prevention is better than the cure.

## ABSOLUTE TEMPERATURE SCALE

A scale on which 'absolute zero' ($-273°C.$) becomes $0°$ Kelvin, symbol K. The boiling point of water—$100°C.$—thus equates with $373°$ K. It is used to determine *gas expansion*, essential data in kiln design, and approximate *sintering* temperatures. See also *temperature conversion table*.

## ABSORPTION

The taking up of liquid into the pores of a pot. The water absorption of a ceramic material is an indication of its degree of *vitrification*. It is expressed as a percentage of the weight of the dry material.

If a pot weighing one kg. absorbs 150 gm. of water it has an absorption of

$$\frac{150}{1000} \times \frac{100}{1} = 15\%$$

A rough test is to weigh a pot after thoroughly drying it in an oven, then to immerse it in water for twelve hours and reweigh it. Absorption can also refer to the taking up of gases, light or heat. (See also *porosity*.)

## ACID, acidic oxides

Among potters, the term 'acid' is used rather loosely. Strictly speaking an acid is a compound containing hydrogen which will combine with a base to form a salt, releasing the hydrogen in the form of water ($H_2O$) and rendering each material chemically neutral.

Example: $HCl + NaOH = NaCl + H_2O$.

Where an acid contains oxygen, the abstraction of water $H_2O$ will leave the acidic oxide; and it is this acid oxide which is referred to when 'acid' is mentioned in this book. For instance, silica $SiO_2$, and not the true silicic acid $H_2SiO_3$, is listed under the heading *acid* in *glaze formulas*.

It is useful to know to which main chemical group an oxide belongs, for this will give some indication of its behavior in the kiln. The principal acid oxides used in pottery are silica and the oxides of boron, antimony, tin, chromium, titanium and zircon. Two others of less importance are phosphorus and germanium which, together with the first three listed above, act as *glass-formers*. In general, acids are refractory; *boric oxide* is an exception. (See also *chemistry of pottery*.)

## ACID RESISTANCE

It is essential that glazes used on wares which will come into contact with chemically active substances should be stable and well-balanced. Vinegar, wines (especially if fermented in the vessel) and some fruits are the main sources of danger, which arises from the tendency of some glaze ingredients, especially lead, to separate and dissolve into the liquid forming a poison.

Adherence to the *Seger formula* principles in earthenware will minimize the risk (e.g. a *lead glaze* formula 1:0.3:3.0) but the use of leadless glaze for cooking ware may be made compulsory. Industrial sanitary ware, acid-holders and so on are generally of a *vitrified* ware and are sometimes *salt-glazed*, one of the most resistant of all glazes. Needless to say, the glazes should not be crazed.

(See also *lead solubility*, *metal release* and *Thorpe's ratio*.)

## ADOBE

A sun-dried clay-mud, with additions of straw or chaff, used in hot, dry climates for building. Very substantial buildings—a majority of the older, traditional houses of Cyprus for instance—demonstrate the high dry strength of some clays and clay-sand mixtures.

The adobe bricks or blocks, usually 12-18 in. (30-45 mm.) square and 4 in. (100 mm.) thick, are not, of course, subjected to sufficient heat to turn them into ceramic material, and they would disintegrate in persistent rain. Adobe is an excellent heat *insulator*. G. Woodman describes an adobe kiln for firings up to $1100°C.$ (PQ 23).

## ADSORPTION

The taking up of a liquid, vapor or gas on a solid surface. Adsorption may cause expansion of a body (even a fired one) and is one of the causes of delayed *crazing* after a period of exposure to the atmosphere. It is, of course, more likely on low-fired porous ware.

Water adsorbed on clay particles is resistant to evaporation and requires a temperature of at least $120°C.$ (figures as high even as $200°C.$ have been mentioned) to remove it. The volume of liquid is small but nevertheless expands very quickly and can break a pot. Clay cannot therefore be considered to be completely dry at room temperatures. Ware which has been heated at 120°C. and allowed to cool again will readsorb moisture and be more susceptible to damage than before.

## AEROGRAPHY

A method of applying color by means of a spray-gun powered by compressed air. (See also *spraying*.)

## AGATE

Cryptocrystalline silica. Used to burnish gold, or for small mortars and pestles.

## AGATE WARE

A pottery body resembling agate stone in its marbled appearance. Produced by layering different colored clays, which are pressed together and sliced through. Care must be taken that the relative shrinkage of the layers is nearly uniform; for this reason stains or oxides are often used to produce different colors from a single body. The technique is used by Lucie Rie in a very controlled manner.

*A porcelain pot by Lucie Rie, thrown from colored bodies in the style of agate ware.*

## AGGREGATE

The non-cement materials in a cement or concrete mixture. These comprise stones and sand in ordinary concrete; sand and crushed firebrick, grog or other refractories in a kiln mortar or brick mixture. Normally about five times the volume of the cementing material.

## AGING OF CLAY

Also known as *'souring'*. Authorities differ on the period necessary for the attainment of full plasticity and workability in a clay: a generation in China; two years according to Leach and Billington; a week (Rhodes). Isaac Button's suggestion of two months in a damp atmosphere followed by re-pugging yielded excellent results. (See also *algae, weathering.*)

## AIR

The gaseous envelope or atmosphere which surrounds the earth. Composed (on average) of 78% nitrogen, 21% oxygen, with very small amounts of other gases, water vapor and dust. The oxygen is 'free', that is, available to maintain life, or to form *oxides of elements. Oxidation* produces heat; when the reaction is very rapid (e.g. the oxidation of carbon) the heat can be used as a source of energy.

## AIR-SETTING MORTAR

Normal clay/grog mortar hardens on firing but fire resistant mortars or cements are available which harden at air temperatures. Useful for setting arches and unsupported parts of a kiln structure, but not essential. The makers of 'Sairset', a commercial air-setting cement, suggest its use as a protective coating on furnace linings, or mixed with crushed firebrick for patching kilns. (See also *kiln wash.*)

## ALBANY SLIP

A clay found near Albany, New York. Quoted analysis CaO 5.7, MgO 2.7, alkalis 3.1, $Al_2O_3$ 14.5, $Fe_2O_3$ 5.2, $SiO_2$ 57.6.

The high proportion of fluxes, combined with a very fine grain, cause it to melt at around 1240°C., and it is used as a *slip-glaze*. Recipes for its use may be found in R.CGP. Color—brown to black. Behrens in CM 20/4 gives two recipes using 90% Albany clay with 10% wollastonite or cryolite, the latter producing a 'patterned' glaze. (See also *temmoku.*)

## ALBITE

Soda *feldspar*. Ideal formula $Na_2O$, $Al_2O_3$, $6SiO_2$, 524. Most commercial feldspars are mixtures of soda and potash spar (orthoclase).

## ALGAE

In the *souring* and *aging* of clay, it was formerly believed that the activity of microscopic single-cell plants broke down the particles and increased plasticity. It now appears that the algae are a secondary but linking factor in the process of *ionic exchange*.

The $CO_2$ released will slowly alter the *pH* factor of the clay which, in turn, affects its plasticity.

## ALKALI

A sub-division of the chemical *bases*. Strictly speaking, the term refers to soda, potash and lithia, but it is also used to cover the alkaline earths. Alkalis are *glass-modifiers* and strong *fluxes*. Soda, especially, produces intense colors, e.g. *Egyptian body*. Unfortunately the alkalis have high *coefficients of expansion* with consequent *crazing*.

## ALKALINE EARTHS

The basic oxides of calcium, magnesium, barium and strontium. They act as *glass modifiers* (fluxes).

## ALLUVIAL CLAY

Deposits of clay left by rivers and by flood. In England, for instance, the valley clays of the Humber and Thames are alluvial. Composition very variable.

## ALPHA FORM

A term given to the crystalline form of quartz at temperatures below the *inversion* point.

## ALTERNATING CURRENT (or AC)

Mains electricity supply which alternates or changes direction of flow at a very rapid rate. The number of changes or cycles per second is called the frequency. In England the normal frequency is 50. Certain pieces of equipment, especially motors, are designed either for AC or for direct current (DC), and these must only be used on the supply specified. It is possible to pass AC through a rectifier to convert it into DC.

## ALUMINA

Oxide of aluminium, $Al_2O_3$. See under *aluminium*. Also supplied as alumina hydrate, $Al_2(OH)_6$, 156, which decomposes at around 300°C. to alumina.

## ALUMINIUM, oxide

A metallic element, A,127.
Oxide $Al_2O_3$, 102, m.p. 2050°C. Alumina.
  One of the essential ingredients of all clays and glazes. Chemically *amphoteric*, it has a balancing and unifying effect between bases and acids, and between glaze and body. Clay, china stone, feldspar and other minerals are used to introduce alumina into glazes. It occurs in a crystalline form as corundum and as the gems sapphire, ruby and topaz. Manufactured by calcining alum.
  As a separate oxide it is used mainly for placing pottery. Use calcined alumina for placing rather than alumina hydrate. It is also used as a heat insulator.
  The normal molecular equivalent in a glaze is 0.1-0.12 of the silica content. In excess it will produce a *matt* surface. It helps to prevent *crystallization* during cooling and increases the hardness and stability of a glaze. It also increases tensile strength and *crazing* resistance. High alumina clays (silliminite, fireclays etc.) are used for making kiln furniture. Alumina can act in a glaze as a *network modifier*.

## ALUMINOUS REFRACTORY

High in alumina and less subject to damage from *thermal shock* than silica refractories. The best grades of fireclays are aluminous. (See also *bat, kiln shelf brick, firebrick.*)

## AMBIENT TEMPERATURE

The temperature of the surrounding atmosphere.

## AMBLYGONITE

A *lithium* mineral of variable composition. Typical analysis: $Li_2O$ 7.8, $Al_2O_3$ 34.2, $SiO_2$ 2.8, $P_2O_5$ 47.5. Not common, but listed by Ferro.

## AMMETER

An instrument for measuring the current flow in *amperes*. Useful for checking the correct working, and the effects of aging, of kiln *elements*. A low reading will suggest that the elements are wearing thinner; a reading of no current on the ammeter indicates a broken circuit.

## AMMONIUM META-VANADATE

A less dangerous form of vanadium, $NH_4VO_3$, 117. 10% gives a rather weak yellow, improved by the use of an *opacifier*. Not greatly affected by stoneware temperatures (up to 1280°C.) or, according to the Fulham Pottery catalog, by reduction. (See also *vanadium.*)

## AMORPHOUS

Without shape. An amorphous mineral is one that does not build up into regular crystals. Diatomite is an amorphous silica. Flint was once considered to be amorphous but is now classed as micro-crystalline. *Glass* is an amorphous solid—or rather an amorphous 'frozen' liquid—and is without a definite melting point.

## AMPERE, amp

An electrical unit of current: the current that one *volt* can send through one *ohm* of resistance.
  Useful equations: amperes=*watts*÷volts
  amperes=volts÷ohms

## AMPHORA

A general name for pointed or very narrow-based pots, generally with two handles, typified by the Greek amphora.
  They are still thrown in a few places in the Mediterranean countries. The top half is thrown first, half dried, reversed onto a chuck, and the pointed base thrown onto it from a thick coil. The method is useful for any narrow-based form. (See also *two-piece throwing.*)

9

*A Cypriot potter throwing an amphora. A cylinder is pulled up (1) for shaping into the upper half of the amphora (2). This is left to stiffen and then inverted onto a clay chuck (3) (strips of paper were wound round the base of the chuck to prevent the pot sticking). A previously thrown thick collar is laid on the inverted form, the joint thrown together, and the collar thrown up (4) and inwards to form the almost pointed base (5).*

## AMPHOTERIC

Amphi—'two ways' or 'half'. An oxide which does not exhibit strong *acidic* or *basic* characteristics. The middle column of the *Seger formula*, $R_2O_3$. Alumina and ferric iron are amphoteric.

## ANALYSIS

The theoretical breakdown of a material into its constituent *elements, oxides* or *minerals*. A laboratory can produce an elemental or ultimate analysis listing the oxides as comparative or percentage weights. It is possible to re-group these into probable minerals—sometimes known as the rational analysis.

Example: Tony Benham's hop ash.

| | |
|---|---|
| Soda $Na_2O$ | 0.3 |
| Potash $K_2O$ | 10.8 |
| Lime $CaO$ | 12.9 |
| Magnesia $MgO$ | 1.5 |
| Alumina $Al_2O_3$ | 0.9 |
| Iron $Fe_2O_3$ | 9.6 |
| Silica $SiO_2$ | 35.3 |
| Phosphate $P_2O_5$ | 2.8 |
| Sulfate $SO_3$ | 9.0 |
| Chloride $Cl$ | 1.6 |
| Moisture $H_2O$ | 2.5 |
| Carbon $C$ | 2.8 |
| Undetermined | 2.1 |
| Carbonates $CO_2$ | 7.9 |

These oxides can be re-grouped as probable minerals:

| | | |
|---|---|---|
| Fine sand | 26 | The greater part of the silica |
| Chalk | 15 | Most of the lime and some carbonate |
| Calcium silicate mineral | 9 | The rest of the lime and some silica |
| Potassium sulfate | 20 | Potash and sulfate |
| Hematite | 10 | The ferric iron |

| Magnesium carbonate | 3 | Magnesium and the remaining carbonate |
| Granitic minerals | 4 | Bases, alumina, the remaining silica |
| Minor compounds carbon and moisture | 13 | |

Some reasonable inferences as to the behavior of this ash in a glaze are:

With 10% iron it will give a stained glaze.

Some of the 'fine sand' will fail to pass a 120 sieve.

Lack of alumina suggests instability and poor interface development if used alone.

The bases are adequate, over half consisting of lime.

The alkalis may be soluble and will be lost if the ash is washed.

With some feldspar and a little clay it should give an interesting iron glaze.

While analyses are useful in forming a general impression of a material, their value is limited, especially in assessing clays. Other factors, such as grain size, are important. Practical experiment is essential. An ultimate analysis can be re-formulated in terms of the *Seger formula* (see *analysis-into-formula*). C.PP, Appendix 10, gives details of a method for deriving the probable minerals from a list of oxides (calculated formula).

Potters' merchants will sometimes provide analyses, or there are firms of analytical chemists who will quote.

## ANALYSIS-INTO-FORMULA

The analyses of minerals have been listed in this book in the general order of the *Seger formula* (the *ROs* grouped together, and so on) but these represent parts by weight and must be converted to *molecular* parts for a true appraisal.

*Method:* Divide each of the figures by the molecular weight of that oxide. Group the RO and $R_2O$ oxides and total the parts. Divide each figure in the formula by this total.

*Example:* A mineral with the analysis by weight:

| | | | | | |
|---|---|---|---|---|---|
| 12.40 $K_2O$ | ÷ mol. wt. | 94 | = | 0.132 |
| 3.15 $Na_2O$ | ÷ mol. wt. | 62 | = | 0.05 |
| 18.60 $Al_2O_3$ | ÷ mol. wt. | 102 | = | 0.182 |
| 65.85 $SiO_2$ | ÷ mol. wt. | 60 | = | 1.096 |

Thus in the total RO group 0.132 + 0.05 = 0.182.

If we divide each of the results of the example above by this total we arrive at the formula:

| $Na_2O$ and $K_2O$ | 1 |
| $Al_2O_3$ | 1 |
| $SiO_2$ | 6 |

which is near the ideal formula for orthoclase feldspar.

A natural mineral will be more involved than the simple example above, but the method can still be applied.

$CO_2$, $H_2O$, and other *loss on ignition* oxides, if listed separately, can be ignored. If quoted as *carbonates*, the molecular weight of the carbonate will allow for the $CO_2$.

## ANDALUSITE

A mineral, $Al_2O_3.SiO_2$, 162. One of the *silliminite* group. Converts by firing into mullite $3Al_2O_3.2SiO_2$ plus silica (as cristobalite).

## ANHYDROUS, anhydrite

Without water of *crystallization*. A natural anhydrite is $CaSO_4$, often found in close conjunction with gypsum.

## ANISOTROPIC, anisometric

Different values in different directions, applied to *crystals*. The *lamellar* structure of clay can lead to uneven shrinkage if some plates are aligned and others random.

## ANNULAR

A disc with a hole in it—like a doughnut! Some potters consider it an easier shape to center on the wheel, especially with large masses of clay. A *bottle kiln* would have an annular *bag wall*. (See also *centering*.)

*Annular centering, especially useful for large pieces of clay. (See also photograph of Isaac Button centering.)*

## ANORTHITE

A calcium *feldspar*, $CaO.Al_2O_3.2SiO_2$, 278. There is a series of solid solutions known as the *plagioclase* feldspars between anorthite and albite, also called the Ab-An series.

## ANTIMONIATE OF LEAD

Approximately $3PbO$, $Sb_2O_3$, sometimes written $Pb_3 (SbO_4)_2$. A yellow pigment for earthenware, also known as Naples yellow. Toxic. Although unstable above 1150°C. it has a *refractory* nature and needs the addition of a soft lead fritt in the proportions of 1:1 when used as a pigment. It is not very satisfactory in or on a leadless glaze. Apply evenly and fairly thinly on *majolica*.

## ANTIMONY, oxides

A metallic element Sb (Stibum), 122.

Oxide $Sb_2O_3$, 291.5 m.p. 630°C., s.g. 5.5. A low-temperature *opacifier*. With lead oxide yields a yellow pigment (see *antimoniate of lead*). Also listed as a *glass-former* in the Seger formula. Toxic.

## APPLIED DECORATION

Three-dimensional decoration with a wide variety of character and method. It can be as simple and direct as the pressed or stroked-on pellets of clays found on English medieval jugs, or as mechanical and intricate as Wedgwood sprigs. The thumb pot illustrated shows how applied decoration can become part of the form.

The clay can be applied direct if the decorative element is small, but larger pieces must be slipped and carefully pressed on from the center outwards. (See further illustrated examples under *sprig, lug* and *knob.*)

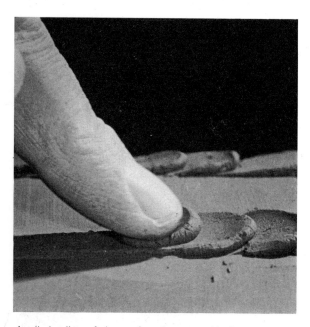

*Applied pellets of clay, as found on many Medieval jugs.*

*There is no real borderline between applied decoration and modelled form. The pinch pot illustrated has been transformed by additional material—strips and bosses. Pot by Alex Watson.*

## ARMATURE

A supporting core of wood or metal wire used in *modeling*. It must, of course, be removed if the piece is to be fired. Armatures or cores of tied newspaper which burn away during the firing (with much smoke!) have been used. Sculptors' techniques often trap air in the clay and also develop very uneven wall thicknesses, both of which can be disastrous in the kiln. Coiling or similar building methods are advised if the piece is intended for firing.

## ARMENIAN BOLE

An earthy compound of iron, used as a pigment. Now seldom listed by merchants.

## ASBESTOLUX

A trade name for steam-pressed sheet asbestos. Standard size 8 x 4 ft. (approx. 2.4 x 1.3 m.), thicknesses up to $\frac{1}{2}$ in. (approx. 12.5 mm.). Reasonably strong, but liable to crush at the corners. Can be cut with an ordinary saw. It does not easily warp and 'will not crack or shatter at furnace heat' say the makers. It is useful for the outer cases of kilns, where it will provide good thermal *insulation,* and also for working *bats* and for stiffening pots after throwing. If used for *throwing bats,* however, its high absorbency needs quenching with a coat of polyurethane varnish. Asbestos can cause lung disease and it is advisable to wear a mask (such as a handkerchief) when cutting it. (See also *wood asbestos, sindanyo.*)

*A piece of asbestos-bearing rock which is shown being teased with a penknife into the fluffy fibrous state with which we are familiar.*

## ASBESTOS

A fibrous natural mineral consisting of silicates of magnesia and calcium with iron. Resistant to heat and acids, with low conductivity. It loses water at 400°C. and rapidly weakens above 500°C. It can be woven into cloth or string, or pressed into sheets: *asbestos cement, Asbestolux, wood asbestos, sindanyo.* Its use as electric cable insulation for heat situations is being replaced by bertyl- and silicon-rubber, but these have much lower operating temperatures. Inhaling of asbestos fibres can cause disease and a mask should be worn when working with it, e.g. cutting asbestos sheets.

## ASBESTOS CEMENT

Cement and asbestos cast into thin sheets, one side smooth and the other textured. Strong but brittle, slightly absorbent, and liable to warp unless braced with timber. Will crack or shatter under heat and is not recommended for kiln casing.

## ASBOLITE

An impure *cobalt* ore, used by Chinese potters. Yields a pleasant quenched blue which we can approach only by adding red clay, ferric, manganese etc. to the pure oxide. Has been quoted as containing 2-20% $CoO$ with $MnO_2$, $Fe_2O_3$, etc.

## ASH

A powdery residue left after the combustion of any material. The ashes useful in ceramics are those from trees and plants (*bone ash* is dealt with separately) where the incombustible residue is composed of the *inorganic* substances, mainly metal oxides and silica, which they have taken up from the soil during their lifetime. The different parts of a plant will use or store certain groups of minerals: grass stems obtain much of their brittle strength from silica, and straw ash is therefore refractory. The trunk of a tree is likely to store lime in greater quantities than the bark, although the bark may become richer in silica as it ages. Box and apple wood, for instance, yield 5-10% of silica and 40% or more of lime; in reed ash the proportions are reversed. Cardew suggests that the first be considered an interesting alternative to limestone, the latter an impure silica. In general the harder and more woody the plant, the softer (more *fluxing*) the ash is likely to be. I have used a cedar ash which, alone, melts to a shiny liquid at 1260°C. This is a guide only: there are exceptions such as the Australian mahogany mentioned in C.PP. The younger, sappy wood on a large tree will be higher in CaO and *alkalis*.

Other factors influence the behavior of an ash; the type of soil and, possibly, the time of year the plant is cut. Few ashes are high in alumina, although those from fruits may contain more than others. The *alkalis* are often soluble and can be lost in washing. Magnesia and phosphorus can impart a milky lustre sometimes known as the *'Chun'* effect.

The very considerable variation, even in the narrowest field of study, makes the direct testing of every ash sample indispensable. A typical ash analysis is given under *analysis*. Several others are given in L.PB and C.PP.

Ash needs to be burnt well to a pale gray or white powder; black ash contains carbon. It can be reburnt, or calcined to about 700°C. in the kiln after washing.

Coal ash is fundamentally an aluminium silicate with iron and other impurities. It has low fluxing power and acts in a similar way to clay.

## ASH GLAZE

Glazes which contain large proportions of plant ash are not necessarily superior to more consciously formulated ones, though the subtlety of the natural ash compounds can give unique results. There is little value in using ash in glazes to be fired below stoneware temperatures. The particular qualities of ash glaze are better exploited in reduction than in oxidation, although interesting results can be achieved in electric kilns. Owing to *soluble* constituents, ash glazes are liable to give variable results even during the use of a single glaze batch. In partially burnt ash the carbon provides local *reducing* conditions during the firing of the glaze.

Few ashes will provide a satisfactory glaze used alone, and they tend to give a poor and powdery dip. Small test bowls will, however, give some idea of the *fusibility* or *refractoriness* of a sample. Normally an ash is used as an ingredient in a recipe. The 'classic' starting-point is 2 ash: 2 feldspar: 1 clay. Dolomite and nepheline are also useful additions, although the former may overload the lime content. One of the most interesting constituents of many ashes is the phosphorus (pentoxide $P_2O_5$) which can give a pearly or opalescent quality. (See also under *ash* for more discussion of ash behavior.)

An unusual coal-ash glaze suggested by Peter Smith is:

| | |
|---|---|
| Coal ash | 20.5 |
| S. Devon ball clay | 8.3 |
| Whiting | 21.5 |
| Feldspar | 31.8 |
| Red clay | 3.1 |
| Ochre | 1.6 |
| Quartz | 13.2 |

*A cedar-ash glaze, showing the very fusible nature of an ash from a hard wood. The tree was very old and had blown down. Illustration under slab pot shows a much more common refractory ash glaze; color plate 3, p. 129 a midway sycamore ash.*

## ASH-PREPARATION

To prepare plant ash for use, one must first ensure that it is well-burnt. Some potters go to great trouble to obtain a clean and perfect example, burning on a swept stone slab. Ash burned in a Baxi or other domestic fire with an efficient draft will give a good white ash. Cardew recommends calcining the washed ash in a kiln to about 900°C., packing it in a *saggar*. For practical work the ash must also be available in sufficient quantity—at least half a dustbinful, and preferably more. Ashes from various sources can be mixed, though this would be frowned upon by the dedicated ash-experimenter. Ash dust is *caustic* and care must be taken not to inhale it.

A careful initial sieving through a garden sieve will remove the rough stuff. It is then soaked in plenty of of water and passed through a 30 mesh. As the ash settles, the surface water will contain a considerable concentration of soluble alkalis and will be *caustic*. This liquid can be poured or scooped away and replaced with clean water. The ash is well-stirred and again left to settle. It is advisable to carry out these operations wearing rubber gloves. The 'washing' process can be repeated two or three times, during which *fluxes* will be removed and the ash will become progressively more *refractory*. Reasonable washing is essential for ash which is to be added to tableware glazes, but for purely decorative purposes a totally unwashed ash can give entertaining results.

After the final settling and decanting, the sludge is spread out to dry (beware of ash on plaster slabs—the alkalis will attack the surface). When dry it is stored and weighed like any other glaze ingredient, care being taken not to raise too much dust.

## ATOM

The unit particle of a chemical *element*. The smallest particle of matter which can partake in chemical action.

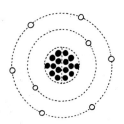

*A representation of the oxygen atom. The nucleus is composed of 8 protons and 8 neutrons and is surrounded by 2 'orbits' of electrons, the first of 2 electrons and the outer one of 6, a total of 8 to balance the positive charge of the protons. Oxygen occurs only as molecules of 2 atoms which share 2 electrons to make up the magic number of 8 in the outer shell.*

## ATOMIC NUMBER

The atomic number is derived from the number of protons (or electrons) in an atom. Thus hydrogen has a single proton and is number 1, helium has two protons and is number 2, and so on. (See *periodic table*.)

## ATOMIC RADIUS

The 'size' or radius of an atom will determine how it will act and which combinations it can form. Potassium and soda have large atoms which are close enough to be interchangeable in feldspar etc. Sodium and calcium are also very close and form the plagioclase series. Silicon is a small atom and can fit within a pyramid of four (large) oxygen atoms, forming the $SiO_4$ group on which all ceramics are founded. The radii are measured in ångström units, $10^{-8}$ cm., and vary between 0.20 (boron) to 1.43 (barium) in common pottery *elements*. (See C.PP for list.)

## ATOMIC THEORY

The 'classical' theory of the structure of matter is still broadly valid for potters. To quote H.IPC:
1 All elements are made up of small particles called atoms. Atoms are defined as the smallest particle of an element which can take part in chemical action.
2 Atoms cannot be created or destroyed.
3 Atoms are indivisible.
4 Atoms of the same *element* are alike in every way.
5 Atoms combine in whole numbers.

All these have been modified in the light of later research (we know to our cost that atoms can be 'split') but insofar as we are dealing with chemical change and *inorganic* materials, Dalton's postulates above are still useful in practice. The fourth is complicated by the discovery of 'isotopes', but constant isotopic mixtures occur so that, again for practical purposes, the application of this principle will be valid. The main effect of isotopes is to complicate *atomic weights*, which are no longer convenient whole numbers but are worked out as averages of the isotopes, and can therefore run into many places of decimals. In this book atomic weights are confined to one or two decimal places.

The application of simple atomic science to pottery is dealt with under *elements, molecules, valency*. Here we can discuss briefly the way in which the modern chemist views the structure of matter. For deeper insight into the theories see H.IPC, and CR 2-14.

The atom, once thought to be the ultimate particle, is now considered as having some parallel with a solar system and to be made up of a number of still smaller fundamental units. These are distinguished by their electrical characteristics: the neutrons, electrically neutral; the positive protons; and the much smaller negatively charged electrons, are the principal units. The first two make up the nucleus or core of the atom and account for most of its 'weight'. The electrons have 'orbits' round the nucleus and form from one to seven layers or 'shells' at various distances from it. The number of protons in the nucleus and, when the atom is electrically neutral, the number of electrons surrounding it, is called the *atomic number*. The chart of atomic numbers is called the *periodic table*.

The total weight of an atom consists of its total number of protons and neutrons as compared with hydrogen. Hydrogen is unity with one proton (no neutrons); oxygen has eight of each. Thus the atomic number of oxygen is 8 and its atomic weight 16. In the heavier atoms there are more neutrons than protons in the nucleus.

Isotopes are those atoms in which the proton number is constant but the number of neutrons varies. Since the atomic weight (a.w.) equals the sum of these particles, an element can have more than one atomic weight. Within the mass of an element, however, these variations occur in regular proportions, so that the atomic weight can be given as a mean weight. Thus chlorine has an a.w. of 35.5—most of the atoms weighing 35, but some 37.

The electrons directly affect chemical behavior. The shells lie at various distances from the nucleus, and each contains a fixed number of electrons. The outer shell is crucial to chemical action and to the formation of molecules or linked groups of atoms (lattices). It may hold from one to eight electrons. An outer shell of two or eight electrons is the stable state to which all atoms aspire, and the atoms will borrow or share one another's electrons to make up eight or to lose all so that the next innermost shell becomes the 'complete' one. Atoms behaving in this way are joined one to another in groups or chains or networks which make up the involved, infinitely various, and apparently distinct compounds which constitute the world as we experience it.

When an atom 'loses' an electron it ceases to be electrically balanced and has a spare positive 'charge' from a proton. The element symbol is altered from R to $R^+$. If, on the other hand, two electrons are 'gained' it is written $R^{--}$, and so on. Unbalanced atoms are known as ions. In many cases a number of elements enter into combination, and the sharing becomes complicated and on several planes, leading to the build-up of crystal structures. The bonds formed between ions are 'electrovalent'; where sharing which does not disturb the balance takes place 'covalent' bonds are formed and molecules result. (See also *valency, electron, electrovalent, covalent.*)

## ATOMIC WEIGHTS

The 'weight' of an atom is derived from the total of the *protons* and *neutrons* in the nucleus. It is a comparative number based on hydrogen at one or oxygen at sixteen. Used by potters as a means of translating *molecular* parts into tangible *recipes*. The 1961 International Atomic Weights Table is taken to seven decimal places, but we can be content with approximation to a single decimal place (it would not greatly affect the result to use the nearest whole number). Atoms in fact occur only as whole numbers as is obvious from the above definition, but the presence of *isotopes* complicates the weight of elements.

The principal elements of practical interest are:—

| Element | Symbol | Weight |
|---|---|---|
| Aluminium | Al | 27.0 |
| Antimony | Sb | 121.8 |
| Barium | Ba | 137.3 |
| Bismuth | Bi | 209.0 |
| Boron | B | 11.8 |
| Cadmium | Cd | 112.4 |
| Calcium | Ca | 40.0 |
| Carbon | C | 12.0 |
| Chlorine | Cl | 35.5 |
| Chromium | Cr | 52.0 |
| Cobalt | Co | 59.0 |
| Copper | Cu | 63.5 |
| Fluorine | F | 19.0 |
| Germanium | Ge | 72.6 |
| Hydrogen | H | 1.0 |
| Iron | Fe | 55.8 |
| Lead | Pb | 207.0 |
| Lithium | Li | 7.0 |
| Magnesium | Mg | 24.3 |
| Manganese | Mn | 55.0 |
| Nickel | Ni | 58.7 |
| Oxygen | O | 16.0 |
| Phosphorus | P | 31.0 |
| Potassium | K | 39.0 |
| Praseodymium | Pr | 59.0 |
| Selenium | Se | 79.0 |
| Silicon | Si | 28.1 |
| Silver | Ag | 107.9 |
| Sodium | Na | 23.0 |
| Strontium | Sr | 87.6 |
| Sulfur | S | 32.0 |
| Tin | Sn | 118.7 |
| Titanium | Ti | 48.0 |
| Vanadium | V | 51.0 |
| Zinc | Zn | 65.3 |
| Zirconium | Zr | 91.2 |

## AUTOCLAVE

An airtight chamber which can be used to test the liability of a glaze to *crazing* by heating it under steam pressure. The method is not entirely satisfactory as it confuses the effects of moisture expansion *(adsorption)* with *thermal shock.*

## AVENTURINE GLAZE

A decorative effect produced by the formation of *crystals (devitrification)* in a glaze, often brightly colored. The crystals are usually of hematite, $Fe_2O_3$.

Zinc favours crystallization (around 0.3 equivalents in the glaze formula), as do rutile and titania. Low alumina content combined with slow cooling, especially in the 900-700°C. range, are essential. A recipe quoted in D.DC is:

| White lead | 198.4 |
|---|---|
| Feldspar | 83.4 |
| Whiting | 8.0 |
| Ferric iron | 11.2 |
| Flint | 41.4 |

These glazes are only suitable for purely decorative pottery, and their aesthetic quality is sometimes questionable. B.TP 152 gives a recipe for a lead/borax aventurine glaze with copper and chromate of iron, together with the usual advice for the type—'apply thickly, fire slowly'.

| Lead/borax fritt | 75 |
|---|---|
| Cornwall stone | 15 |
| Oxide of iron | 6 |
| Oxide of copper | 1 |
| Chromate of iron | 3 |

# B

## BACTERIA IN CLAY

It is thought that the growth of bacteria in damp clay promotes acid gels which have a beneficial effect on *plasticity*. Rhodes recommends mixing a little well-matured clay with new batches. The bacterial action will assist vegetable decomposition which is a link in the chain leading to ionic exchange, a factor in plasticity. (See *algae*.)

## BAG WALL

A wall of brickwork built between the firebox and setting-space of a kiln. It deflects the heat upwards and also serves to prevent the flame from impinging directly onto the ware or the *saggars* (although it is possible to build a bag wall of saggars). Cardew recommends the use of a thin brick, 9 x 4½ x 1-1½ in. (approx. 220 x 110 x 30 mm.), with 3 in. (70 mm.) between the bag wall and the kiln wall, and terminating 5 in. (about 120 mm.) or so below the springers of the dome. Lightweight or *insulating* bricks have, obviously, no advantage for bag walls.

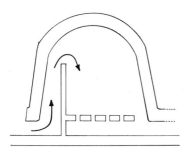

*Bag wall section through a down-draft (or cross-draft) kiln.*

## BALANCE

Finely suspended scales used in chemistry. Essential for weighing quantities under 10 gm. Normally only cobalt is likely to be used in such small amounts in working glaze batches.

## BALL CLAY

A secondary or transported *(sedimentary)* clay which is very plastic and fires to a pale color. Its name derives from the 30-35 lb. balls in which form it was originally made up for transport. As dug it often contains carbons which stain it blue or gray. In England the main beds are at Wareham (Dorset) and in Devon; in the USA, in Kentucky and Tennessee.

'Free' silica is often a feature of ball clays, which are then known as siliceous ball clays. They are all too sticky and fine-grained to use alone but are an essential ingredient of most pottery bodies, increasing *plasticity* and *dry strength*, and assisting *vitrification* upon firing.

A typical analysis by weight:

| | | | |
|---|---|---|---|
| $K_2O$ | 1.8 | $Al_2O_3$ | 33.0 |
| $Na_2O$ | 0.2 | $Fe_2O_3$ | 1.0 |
| CaO | 0.3 | $SiO_2$ | 49.0 |
| MgO | 0.3 | $TiO_2$ | 0.9 |

A *body* recipe for a 1290°C. firing might read:

| | |
|---|---|
| Fireclay or stoneware clay | 50 |
| Ball clay | 25 |
| Flint | 10 |
| China stone or feldspar | 5 |
| Fine grog | 10 |

(See also *clays, throwing, body*.)

## BALL MILL

A machine for grinding rocks and minerals, consisting of a horizontal cylinder made from, or lined with, an abrasion-resistant material (e.g. stoneware or porcelain), and of some mechanical means of making it revolve.

The materials to be ground are put into the cylinder together with flint or porcelain balls and water. As it rotates, the balls, rolling continuously to the bottom of the curve, grind very efficiently. In the industry dry milling may be practised, with a current of air taking away the finer material (elutriation). There is also a wet system where the mill is vertical and vibrates rather than rotates. The craftsman who buys commercial materials will rarely require a mill—the materials will be sufficiently ground (often too finely)—but a mill is useful for experimental and special purposes. For the pioneer potter it is indispensable. The smaller ball mills are called *jar mills* and are discussed under that entry.

Various critical factors must be taken into account when constructing a ball or jar mill.

*Speed* varies with the size. Slightly differing equations have been put forward: the simplest is:

$$\text{Revs. per minute} = 58.18 \div \sqrt{r}$$

where r is the radius of the interior of the mill in feet. Thus for a 6 in. (approx. 150 mm.) diameter mill the r.p.m. would be $58.18 \div \sqrt{0.25}$, i.e. $58.18 \div 0.5 = 116.36$. This is the maximum working speed, and one would grind at about 75% of this, i.e. 80 r.p.m. Other mill sizes work out at: 100 r.p.m. for a 4 in. (approx. 100 mm.) mill; 70 r.p.m. for 8 in. (approx. 200 mm.); 50 r.p.m. for 12 in. (approx. 300 mm.).

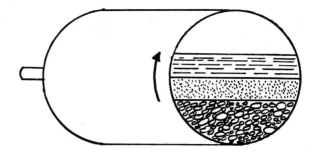

*Diagrammatic section of a ball mill showing pebbles, charge, and water in their approximate proportions. These will, of course, be intimately mingled when the mill is turning.*

*Balls.* Flint pebbles or porcelain, called the 'grinding medium' in merchants' catalogs. Size ½-2 in. (10-50 mm.) in diameter, and filling about 50% of the mill's capacity. ('Capacity' meaning two-thirds of the total space in the mill.) Some authorities recommend no more than one-half full.

*Water and charge* are each 15-25% of capacity. The charge must already have been ground to 'sand' size.

*Time* varies with hardness and grain size required, from two to eight hours. The mill will become warm if the charge is grinding correctly.

C.PP has an appendix on ball mills and also an ingenious system of finding the square roots of numbers below unity, useful in the speed equation above. (See *jar mill* for some details of construction.)

## BALLOON

The use of a rubber balloon as a former or support has been mentioned in CM 20/6 and elsewhere. A rounded shoulder on a slab pot, for instance, can be formed from a soft slab worked over a balloon which has been sufficiently inflated just to fill the top of the pot.

## BANDING

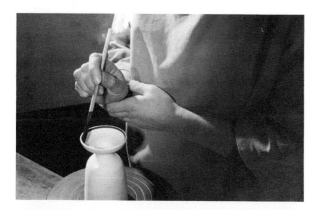

*Two methods of supporting and steadying the hand for banding. The left hand holds the right wrist, the potter standing to the work (1). When seated the elbow can be used as a pivot, resting it on the bench (2).*

The spinning of pigment lines onto a pot. The brush should hold sufficient liquid to complete the band without a refill, and the hand must be held perfectly still once the brush is in contact with the pot surface. Some support which will incline the hand towards the pot, such as an elbow set on a firm surface, is useful. Needless to say, the pot must be centered on the wheel or whirler, and sufficient smooth turning momentum obtained. A heavy *whirler* is essential for technically efficient banding. Banding is somewhat mechanical in appearance but is useful as a frame and foil for more *calligraphic* work—and to do it well is very satisfying!

## BANDING WHEEL

Although the term is used for any free-spinning circular turntable it is, strictly, a floor-standing wheel often with a cork inset surface. Also called a lining wheel. The term 'whirler' or 'bench whirler' is now more general for the table wheel normally used by potters. (See *whirler.*)

## BANK KILN

A kiln constructed against a hill or bank, the slope, usually about 30°, providing the draft. Though crude in conception, bank kilns were probably responsible for some fine pottery. Small bank kilns are sometimes constructed by potters today and they can be excellent teaching aids. The body of the kiln can be actually cut into the slope which will then supply efficient insulation. See R.K 18-20. The oriental, many-chambered *climbing kilns* are based on a similar principle.

## BARBOTINE

A French word for *'slip'* occasionally used in older books on pottery.

## BARITE

See *barytes.*

## BARIUM, compounds

A metallic element Ba, 137.3.
Oxide BaO, 153.3, Baria.
Carbonate $BaCO_3$, 197.3.
Sulfate $BaSO_4$, 233, *Barytes.*

An alkaline earth. Carbonate poisonous. Decomposes to oxide at 900°C.;s.g. 3.5. Acts as a *base* in glazes, its action similar in some respects to lime (calcium). A high proportion (20% plus) may dull the surface of a glaze and cause pinholes, unless the recipe also contains boron. Baria will give a hardness and brilliance to a glaze at 1150°C. and over. Behrens in CM 19/8 mentions additions as high as 50% and gives recipes:

| | | |
|---|---|---|
| Baria | 30.4 | 21.5 |
| Feldspar | 46.4 | — |
| Nepheline | — | 24.7 |
| Zinc | 7.5 | — |
| Flint | 15.7 | 31.5 |

| | | |
|---|---|---|
| Strontium | — | 12.4 |
| Whiting | — | 2.8 |
| China clay | — | 7.1 |
| | 1190°C. | 1225°C. |

Barium also occurs in a surprising number of Japanese recipes (see S.WJC). It will affect pigments, sometimes in a startling way, as with copper. Proportions are critical and considerable experiment is necessary. Behrens mentions a red with nickel in CM 19/8.

It is used industrially to prevent scum on bricks: the addition of 2-3% of the carbonate will do the same for red-clay biscuit ware (terracotta) which is liable to white discoloration. Wedge the carbonate into the body. The scum is caused by soluble salts, especially calcium chloride. To quote Billington: 'The barium effects a substitution: $CaCl_2 + BaCO_3 = BaCl_2 + CaCo_3$, both of which are insoluble. The sulfate will have a similar effect.

## BARYTES, barite, heavyspar

The natural rock of barium sulfate $BaSO_4$. It can be used to introduce barium oxide into a glaze so long as the sulfur can be efficiently dispersed. Usually fritted with carbon into barium carbonate. (See also *witherite*.)

## BASALT

The characteristic volcanic *basic* rock, smooth and black. Ground and fired it can form a glaze, but is high in iron. Ivan England's analyses and discussion of basalts and basalt glazes appear in PQ 31. A basalt dust is listed by Ferro and Podmores.

## BASALT WARE

*A thrown pot by Colin Pearson. Black body of basalt ware type.*

Originated by Wedgwood as a name for a black, vitreous body resembling *basalt*. A recipe quoted is:

| | |
|---|---|
| Ball clay | 47.0 |
| China clay | 3.0 |
| Ironstone | 40.0 |
| Manganese | 10.0 |

In effect basalt ware is a black slip body fired to vitrification. The recipes for *black slip* using iron, manganese and cobalt in various proportions can be adapted. A 'basalt' body is now supplied commercially. Among modern potters, Colin Pearson has used it effectively in winged cylinders, as illustrated.

A basalt body recipe given in CM 17/3 is:

| | |
|---|---|
| Red clay | 40 |
| China clay | 18 |
| Ball clay | 15 |
| Ferric | 16 |
| Manganese | 6 |
| Nepheline | 2 |
| Bentonite | 3 |

## BASE, basic

One of the main chemical groupings. Inorganic materials may be classed as bases or acids. In general the bases cause ceramic mixtures to become *fusible*: they are *glass-modifiers*. Bases and acids combine to form 'salts'. The bases are listed under the general term RO in the *Seger formula*; they also include the $R_2O$ oxides, usually of metals.

The principal bases in pottery are the oxides of lead, sodium, potassium, magnesium, zinc, lithium, calcium, strontium and barium. Also the pigment oxides of manganese, copper and cobalt.

The bases include the alkalis and the alkaline earths. (See also *flux*.)

## BASE CRACKS

During throwing the base of a pot undergoes less pressure, and is worked on less, than the walls. It is thus less aligned in particle structure and liable to greater shrinkage. Deliberate working of the base, or its compression from the outside later in the throwing, can help to prevent base cracks. (See also *cracking*.)

## BASIC ROCKS

Igneous rocks comparatively high in basic minerals. *Basalt* is the main type. Generally volcanic in origin. Can decompose into clay material but, to quote Cardew, 'tends to produce montmorillinite rather than *kaolinite*'. Its high iron content limits its use as a glaze material.

## BASIC SLAG

A byproduct of the steel industry, rich in phosphorus and iron, with some silica and calcium. Obtainable as fertilizer. Occasionally occurs in glaze recipes. Mentioned in G.EP 68, and C.PP 137. Can be used in stoneware glazes where it will introduce an interesting, if not always predictable, well-combined batch of ingredients. *Opalescence* can result from the phosphorus. It can be used with red clay for *temmoku* type glazes.

## BAT, batt

Applied to various types of sheet material:
1 Kiln shelves or cranks of refractory clays.
2 A slab of plaster or low fired biscuit for drying clay.
3 Sheet material used for supporting, transporting or drying pottery. Should be slightly porous so that it releases the clay as it dries. It is easy to slide a wet pot onto a glazed surface but almost impossible to remove it when leather-hard.
4 Removable wooden, plaster, or asbestos disc used on the wheel head for repetition throwing or for large pieces. (See *wheel bats, ejector head*.)
5 A bat-shaped piece of wood (e.g. a butter pat) for beating pots or stirring glaze.
6 A short brick. In USA a broken brick—hence brick-bat.
(See also under *kiln shelves*.)

## BATCH, batch weight

A proportioned .mixture of materials. Batch weights are in fixed proportions to one another but have random totals. For easier comparison and calculation, bring batch weights to percentages.

*Method:* Multiply each number in the recipe by 100 and then divide by the total, i.e. $\frac{BW}{T} \times 100$.

An example of the same recipe as batch weight and percentages:

| Batch weight | Percentage weight |
|---|---|
| 143 | 44 |
| 65 | 20 |
| 13 | 4 |
| 103 | 32 |
| —— | —— |
| 325 | 100 |

The answer in line 1 is worked out thus: 143 x 100 ÷ 325=44.

## BAT WASH

A *refractory* material applied to *bats, saggars* etc., to prevent ware sticking to them during firing. Flint or calcined alumina and a little clay mixed with water may be brushed on. The disadvantage of coated shelves is that they cannot be reversed. A thin dust of dry alumina is usually sufficient – this can be brushed off. Kyanite has been mentioned as a bat wash. Glaze rarely sticks to *silicon carbide* kiln shelves.

## BAUXITE

The ore of aluminium. The name derives from an early source at Beaux in France. A sedimentary rock of hydrated alumina with clay and iron. For detailed discussion of 'bauxitization' see C.PP 58-9. (See also *diaspore*.)

## BEAD

1 Special ceramic beads are used as electrical insulators threaded onto wires which are subject to heat. Can be used for sheathing outside connections on electric, kilns, although asbestos is more common.
2 Jewelry beads are often made in ceramic. The work is somewhat tedious, especially the glazing. Biscuit beads in colored or variegated bodies can be fired in bowls or on tiles. Beads need not be spherical, but may be square, cylindrical, conical, or of a flattened shape, with carved, rolled, painted, or molten glass decoration. Rolling a bead across a textured surface will transfer the pattern to the bead. The true bead will have a hole through it. This needs to be clear and without excessively sharp edges which may cut the string.

*A bead can be glazed by impaling it on a cocktail stick or toothpick. The other end of the hole is sealed with a blob of wax and the bead then dipped into the glaze.*

Glazed beads must either have a hole large enough to allow them to be threaded over a heat resisting *(nichrome)* wire, or be designed with one flat, unglazed surface on which they can rest. The wire can be supported at each end on a 'cradle' which you can make yourself. Partial or spot glazing is easier than full glaze covering, although even majolica painting is possible if you are prepared for the rather tiresome work of ensuring that the hole in the bead and a small circle around it are free from glaze. One can apply a spot of wax to one end, impale the other on a toothpick, and then dip the bead into the glaze. Threading the beads onto a fine drinking straw has also been suggested, the nichrome wire being inserted through the straw. The straw burns away during firing. The use of *Egyptian paste* will obviate much of this work.

The conception of a necklace has widened beyond the traditional string of beads, and the elements may be joined together in different ways—perhaps in combination with metals.

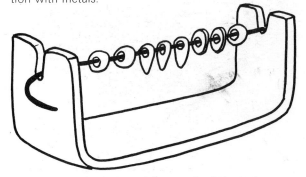

*A bead firing 'cradle', formed from a strip of clay and a length of nichrome wire. If the wire is too long—over about 6 in. (150 mm.)—or overloaded, it will sag during firing.*

## BEAKER

A drinking vessel with or without a handle and usually without a saucer. A very wide range of shapes is possible—the stumpy barrel being the least attractive.

## BEATEN DECORATION

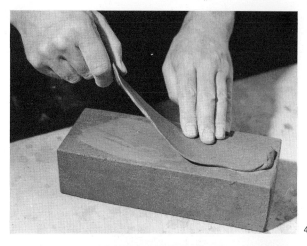

*Beaten decoration. The surface of a pot may be simply ridged with a sharp-edged bat (1). A circular 'sun' pattern is beaten into a slab of clay which is then applied to the slipped surface of a pot (2 and 3). Or an irregular slab of plastic clay can be luted on and the decoration then beaten in (4 and 5).*

Similar to impressed decoration, but more spontaneous and direct. The edge of a stick, or a textured surface such as a butter pat or string wound round a bat, can be used with wide-ranging effects from subtle indented marks to deep three-dimensional impressions. The beater can be ragged or irregular although too obvious a repeat in the pattern can become rather mechanical. The edges can be left sharp, or softened with a sponge.

Beaten patterns retain more of their characteristic quality under thin, spare glazes—dry ash glazes are very suitable—than with full thick coatings.

The actual surface of a pot can be decorated, or an applied slab of softer (perhaps differently colored) clay can be luted on. Large decorative 'sun' forms can be beaten from circular slabs of clay. These are attractive in themselves, and the exercise can be useful in releasing pent-up tensions in the potter!

## BEATEN FORMS

Thrown or hand-built pottery can be gently beaten to alter form, profile or emphasis, or to provide panels for decoration. It is a favorite technique among modern potters, offering a subtle contrast between curved and plane surfaces. The beating can be done as soon as the surface loses its stickiness or at any subsequent stage up to stiff leather-hard; the different clay states yield different styles and qualities of form. The bat should be wide enough to avoid edge marks; slightly chamfered or rounded corners will help. The clay undergoes considerable strain and the blows should be just hard enough to ease it into a change of shape without forcing it. Alternatively the pot can be flattened or rocked on the bench surface.

*A thrown pot by Geoffrey Whiting which has been beaten into a square plan. Combed glaze-over-glaze decoration.*

## BEATERS

For light work, butter pats make excellent beaters for knocking pots into, or out of, shape. Old pats can be found in junk shops and new ones are now available. For work requiring a heavier tool a cricket bat shape can easily be cut from a piece of 3 x ¾ in. (approx. 75 x 20 mm.) timber. Wood is the best material for beaters; non-porous surfaces such as plastic tend to stick to the clay. Edges should be rounded and faces sanded smooth.

Beaters or 'paddles' can be carved to give simple overall patterns and many Japanese potters keep a stock of decorated paddles. Plain beaters can double up as glaze-stirrers. (See illus. under *paddle*.)

*A slab pot by Ian Auld decorated with a mixture of scoring and beating.*

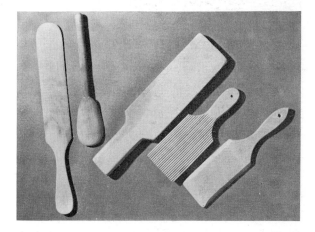

*A variety of bats and beaters. Two butter pats, a paddle, a flat-backed wooden spoon, and a cooking spatula.*

## BEDDING

See *placing*.

## BEIDELLITE

A clay mineral of the montmorillinite group from Beidell, Colorado. Rich in alumina.

## BELLY

The widest part (where this is not the *shoulder*) of a full-bodied pot form.

## BENTONITE

A very fine-grained *(colloidal)* clay of the *montmorillinite* type containing bases and iron. The name originated from a source at Fort Benton, USA. The particle size is probably under 0.03% of the average kaolinite grain. It is a very sticky clay with a high shrinkage (the bonding between the unit layers allows the ingress of more water than does *kaolinite*) and a tendency to crack during firing and cooling. It is therefore unworkable alone or in any large quantity in a body, but its super-plasticity (at least as far as *thixotropy* is concerned) can help short bodies such as porcelains. It also assists the *suspension* of a glaze.

Calcium bentonite is the most useful type. Sodium bentonite will swell as it takes up water. The iron content always colors bentonite but there is a so-called white bentonite with an analysis by weight:

$K_2O$    0.5
$Na_2O$   2.0    with $Al_2O_3$ 12.0, $SiO_2$ 64.2
$CaO$    2.0
$MgO$   2.3     $Fe_2O_3$   2.0

This will give a better color in reduction than in oxidation, if used in a porcelain body. Bentonites vary widely in plasticity and purity. A few, such as fuller's earth, are not plastic at all.

Bentonite is difficult to mix into a glaze batch. Work it into a thick slurry with a little water first and add further water only very gradually. If it is tipped dry into a glaze it will merely float in small globules. Pass the bentonite slip several times through a 120 mesh or small 200 color lawn. 3% is the normal maximum for addition to a body or glaze.

## BERKELY CLAY

A plastic refractory clay from South Carolina.

## BETA FORM

Generally applied to the crystal form of quartz at temperatures above the *inversion* point.

## BIN TROLLEY

A variation on the old 'sack truck'. A two-wheeled trolley with a flat base ledge, on which bins or sacks of material can be supported and moved. Wengers also list a 'stair-climbing' bin trolley. A bin 'dolly' is a flat, wheeled platform for moving bins.

## BIOTITE MICA

See *mica*.

## BISCUIT, bisque

Unglazed, ware, usually porous. In the USA and in the pottery industry the French form 'bisque' is preferred. The biscuit firing is for convenience, to render the pots less fragile and glazing easier. It is also reputed to produce a tougher glazed fabric. This is certainly the case in the industry, where the biscuit fire may be 150°C. higher than the glaze fire. *Earthenware glazes* are less likely to craze on a high-fired biscuit (see *cristobalite*) but it is difficult to apply the raw glaze onto a body which has *vitrified* to any great degree. Clay turns into ceramic at 500-600°C. so this is the minimum for a biscuit fire. Primitive firings (*bonfire, sawdust* etc.) do not always attain this temperature.

For stoneware the biscuit need not exceed 850-900°C. Ground-up biscuit is called *grog*. The term *terracotta* is often applied to biscuit modeling.

## BISCUIT FIRE

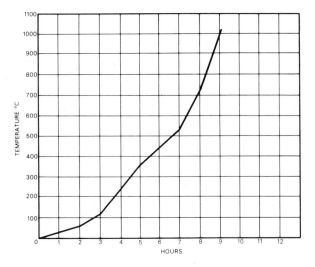

*A biscuit graph. It shows three hours' drying (including 'water smoke'), a slight slowing down between 400-600°C. (a by no means essential refinement), with a faster rise to 1020°C. A stoneware biscuit can be terminated at 960°C. or thereabouts, but biscuit intended for earthenware glazes will benefit from 1060-1090°C. if this can be done without vitrification.*

The firing of clay into ceramic at a minimum temperature of 500-600°C., usually as a preliminary to a second (glost) firing. A number of alterations and stresses occur during the firing:

| | |
|---|---|
| Up to 100°C. | 'Mixed' or water of plasticity is driven off as vapor. |
| 100-200°C. | The adsorbed water is lost and organic materials begin to burn out. |
| 573°C. | *Quartz inversion.* |
| 500-600°C. | *Chemically combined water* is lost and a new (ceramic) material is formed. |
| 600°C. upwards | Carbons, sulfur, etc. continue to |

burn out. There is a certain expansion in volume up to 800-850°C. *Vitrification* begins (different temperatures for different clays), the particles pack more closely, and shrinkage occurs.

The greatest risk of breakage or explosion is in the 90-150°C. range. Thick pieces are obviously more at risk than thin-walled ware. From 200°C. fairly quick firing is possible, indeed the clay-ceramic conversion may be virtually instantaneous (Peter Smith). One can quote the twenty-minute African brushwood firings, while the industry has experimented with even shorter periods. My own biscuit, fired (after thorough drying) in four hours, has a good ring at 980°C. However clays and kilns are so variable that no one can be dogmatic on their requirements. An average and conservative biscuit graph is shown.

### BISCUIT STOPPING
See *stopping.*

### BISMUTH, oxide
A metallic element Bi, 209.0.
Oxide $Bi_2O_3$, 466, m.p. 825°C.

Can be used to produce a mother-of-pearl lustre. Listed as a base in glazes, although its oxide suggests that it is *amphoteric.* Parmelee describes the preparation of a bismuth lustre in P.CG 292 using the resinate of bismuth, and suggests its addition to yellow and gray-brown lustres. Mentioned by Billington B.TP 154. (See also *lustres.*)

### BISQUE
See *biscuit.*

### BIT
See *crank.*

### BIVALENT
A valency of two, e.g. the valency of oxygen in water ($H_2O$) is two. Thus the calcium in CaO is bivalent. (See diagram under *valency.*)

### BLACK BODY
See *black slip,* and *basalt ware.*

### BLACK CORE

*A shard of Hertfordshire slipware showing the black core in the thickest part of the section.*

Bricks, shards of primitive pottery, and even seventeenth-century slipware often show a section which is red for a few millimeters from each face, but black in the centre. Caused by an inadequately oxidized or too rapid firing of a carbonaceous and generally high-iron clay.

In sawdust firing the black core is inevitable, but it can be a great decorative asset where it breaks through to the surface.

### BLACK GLAZES
The standard black earthenware glaze has been quoted as 4% each of iron, cobalt and manganese. Many black glaze and pigment recipes approximate to this combination. Rhodes recommends 2% of each: Billington 6% manganese, 4% iron in a lead and soda glaze, or 7% manganese, 1% cobalt and 2% iron in a lead glaze.

The high pigment content necessary to produce a near-black will affect glaze fusibility. The manganese is also liable to cause bubbling. Copper blacks are possible but rather tricky: 3-5% will produce a *matt* surface at earthenware temperatures (see also 'gunmetal' black mentioned under *black pigments*). Copper can be combined with iron to produce a 'mirror black' (Rhodes). Manganese/copper combinations have a very low *eutectic* and can cause running in glazes or pigments. Also beware of manganese with zinc.

In stoneware, especially in reduction, some 5-12% of iron oxide in a *siliceous* glaze, and preferably on a siliceous body, should give black, although in some glazes the higher proportions may oxidize on the surface to produce *kaki* reds. A different quality of color can be developed with 6-8% iron and 1-2% cobalt. A high concentration of manganese in an oxidized fire can give a metallic pewter-like surface up to about 1270°C. The finest quality black wares were produced in Sung China. Leach quotes the addition of 10% of medium wood ash to Hamada's 'building stone' glaze for temmoku. Potclays' 'black feldspar' could be the basis for a similar experiment. The so-called 'oil spot' or 'hare's fur' glaze markings may have derived from settled-down bubble craters. Some authorities, however, consider that they are more likely to be glass-in-glass melts. Rhodes is convinced that these are natural slip glazes, similar to Albany clay glazes. Manganese earthenware glazes, which also bubble, occasionally exhibit similar patterns. As well as Albany clay, ochre, burnt sienna, and spodumene have been suggested. (See R.CGP 187.)

### BLACK PIGMENTS
A true black pigment is difficult to mix from raw materials. The standard cobalt/manganese/iron mixture will tend to separate out, though often in a pleasant way. It will also run. In ready-made industrial colors the oxides are *sintered* together, with opacifiers and *refractories,* and are blended to maintain the hue and to minimize running and blurring. Black prepared pigments (underglaze or stains) will almost certainly contain chrome, so beware of chrome-tin reactions.

'Standard black' quoted by Dodd consists of 30 cobaltic oxide, 56 ferric iron, 48 chromic oxide, 8 nickel oxide, 31 alumina. Other black mixtures quoted in W.CNS are: for *underglaze*—ferric 36, chrome 7, manganese 12, cobalt 32, nickel 13; and for *stains*—iron chromate 51, nickel 9, cobalt 21, chrome 4, ferric 15.

There are also iridium blacks. A gunmetal black results from equal parts of copper, manganese and cobalt. Copper and manganese can give black with a gold sheen (on biscuit).

## BLACK SLIPS

The traditional black slip for lead glazed slipware is red clay with up to 10% dry weight of manganese dioxide. The biscuit fire must be kept low (ca. 1000°C.) to avoid vitrification which inhibits the glaze take-up.

Some of the manganese can be replaced with either iron and cobalt or both, but the distinctive quality of the simple slip will be lost. Manganese slip under a tin glaze will produce warm grays and even, on occasion, a gentle salmon blush. The *fusible* nature of manganese is ideally suited to staining through a normally opaque glaze. Any trace of cobalt will cool the color. Black slip applied thinly (flooded over or brushed on) on a buff body will fade unevenly under a lead glaze to browns and yellowish colors. Difficult to control but very attractive at its best.

The high shrinkage of red clay based black slip necessitates its use on clay which is slightly softer than leather-hard. Black slip, with perhaps a more sophisticated body base (see *engobes*) will be self-glazing (vitrified) at stoneware temperatures.

## BLEB, blebbing

An American term for small blisters on pottery caused by air pockets just below the surface. A minor form of *bloating*. Avoided by careful *wedging* and clean clay.

## BLISTERING

Bubbles of escaping gas are an inevitable feature of glazes at some point in their firing. Raw material glazes are more liable to blister than *fritts*. Most of the bubbles settle down as the glaze melts, but if the firing is terminated too early, or is carried on to a point where further reactions begin (often thought of as 'boiling') then unhealed craters will be left in the cooled glaze.

Blistering may be aggravated by too thick a coating of glaze; by the slight reduction of a lead glaze; by too rapid an end-fire (1240-1280°C. in stoneware); by sulfur compounds, perhaps in the body; by the use of *fluorine* minerals in the glaze; and, probably the commonest cause of all in earthenware, by the setting of newly glazed and inadequately dried pots in the kiln. Even a preliminary warming-up does not always help in an electric kiln and it is advisable to dry the pots thoroughly before packing.

## BLOATING

The development of gas pockets in a body after it has started to vitrify and is *pyroplastic*, causing it to develop local swelling. Bad mixing or wedging, or sulfides in the clay can be causes. Gas may also be generated by carbon obtaining oxygen from the body and forming carbon dioxide, or by minute pockets of water in closed pores deep in the fabric.

Care must be taken, when firing the biscuit, to avoid *vitrification* by sudden or local temperature rise (see also *flashing*), especially in bodies high in carbonates. In the stoneware fire Cardew recommends that oxidizing conditions be maintained to 1150°C. My own firing schedule is a rapid one and I find that, using comparatively high iron bodies in an oxidizing fire, there is a critical temperature—about 1275°C.— where bloating may occur.

As bloating normally occurs only when the clay is sufficiently 'molten' to swell without breaking, it is thus a feature of high-fired pottery. Most bodies will bloat if they are overfired or if they have a premature glass phase e.g. an excess of feldspathic material. Needless to say, any tiny pellets of body ingredients or 'foreign' materials will increase the risk. David Leach suggests an oxidized *soaking* at 1000°C. to burn out carbon.

Good preparation, clean clay, avoidance of over-firing, the addition of some opening material such as grog or calcined china clay will all help to avoid bloating. Potters have been known to bloat pots deliberately as a decorative feature.

## BLUE PIGMENTS, glazes, stains

There is a bewildering variety of blue colors listed in suppliers' catalogs. Most of them derive from cobalt, which can be mixed and fritted with other materials to give various shades of blue. Some of the shades quoted are:

Willow blue: quoted recipe (D.DC) cobalt oxide 40: feldspar 40: flint 20—a diluted blue.

Manzarine or royal blue from cobalt with various fluxes.

Matt blue, a cobalt aluminate. Recipe (D.DC) cobalt 20: alumina 60: zinc 20.

Peacock blue, with china stone, *standard black* (see *black pigments*) and flint.

Early blue fritts were zaffre and smalt. Most fritted blues are for use on earthenware. At high temperatures it is difficult to prevent the formation of rather strident cobalt silicates. Even with the use of cobalt aluminates, a eutectic is formed with the silica of the glaze at around 1200°C.

Many potters find modern cobalt oxides used as pigments too pure and stark and make additions of other materials to modify their stridency. Various combinations (up to 80% of the total pigment batch) of manganese, iron, red clay, nickel, or rutile have been suggested in an attempt to approximate to the impure *asbolite*. A simple dilution for use on earthenware is one part of cobalt to four parts of china stone. Unless specking is required, cobalt colors need careful sieving through a 200 mesh lawn, or levigating in the way described by Cardew (C.PP 29), who considers it a mistake to sieve any pigments.

Some prepared blues will contain chrome, particularly the dark blues and slate colors. Blue is also prepared from vanadium and zircon for temperatures up to 1280°C. i.e. 3-5% vanadium oxide; 60-70% zircon; with some silica. An involved formula for producing steel blue crystals from nickel at 1280°C. is described in W.CNS 20. Reduced rutile is reputed to produce a blue glaze, as is reduced vanadium. For a discussion of *turquoise* blue see under that heading. (See also *cobalt.*)

## BLUE SLIP

The addition of 0.5-2.5% of cobalt oxide to a pale-firing clay body will produce light to dark blue slip. The higher concentrations are useful under a *tin glaze*. The color can be rather hard and characterless, but may be softened by using a little red clay or any of the modifiers mentioned under *blue pigments*. Grind and sieve the colors through a 200 lawn.

## BLUNGER

A machine for stirring and mixing ceramic materials, usually the ingredients of a clay body, with water. The slip is then used as such, or dried to a plastic body. The machine consists of paddles revolving horizontally in a vat, usually hexagonal or octagonal in plan, the angles exerting some resistance to the circulation of the mix. A 15 gallon electric blunger may cost around £100, but the mechanism is simple and a potter who wished to prepare his own clays could build one. The paddles are driven from above the vat at between 100-200 r.p.m.

Smaller electric high-speed mixers are available for up to four gallons, and are suitable for clay which has already been broken into small pieces. Rhodes suggests an old washing machine. For small quantities clay need merely be steeped in water. The major problem in 'temperate' climes is not the mixing but the drying of the slip. The use of *dough mixers* bypasses the liquid stage. (See also *clay preparation.*)

## BLUSH

A pink area on a glaze caused by a reaction with a *volatilized* coloring oxide, usually either chrome or copper. Chrome can react with lead, lime and tin in an earthenware fire (see chrome-tin pink), or even in stoneware if a high-dolomite glaze with zinc is used. In reduction, copper can also stain adjacent pots. Prepared colors, especially dark hues, often contain chrome and may give rise to *blushing* on tin glazes.

## BODY

Any clay, mixture of clays, or admixture with other ceramic materials. Few natural clays are used alone but are blended together to produce a mixture with specific qualities. For instance, a plastic and *fusible* ball clay may be combined with a *refractory* fireclay, a little red clay and some grog to produce an easily workable, buff-colored, open textured stoneware body. Non-clay minerals—flint, china stone, sand, etc. may also be included. These will lessen plasticity.

There are as many body recipes as there are potters. Industrial earthenware bodies are still based on Wedgwood's eighteenth century experiments. The simplest recipe is equal parts of ball clay, china clay, stone, and flint. This is fired to about 1200°C. when it becomes a tough but still porous biscuit. At 1300°C. it vitrifies into a near-porcelain, but still opaque, material.

A potter can modify a prepared plastic body to suit his particular purposes. I use five parts of a buff stoneware body with one of a Staffordshire red clay, wedged together for a 1260°C. oxidized firing. It rings well, is reasonably vitrified, and of a warm color. Simple additions include sand or grog to give 'bite' and to open texture; ball clay to improve fusibility and plasticity (in very short bodies, e.g. porcelain, up to 3% bentonite); quartz or flint or a siliceous *fireclay* to increase refractoriness and to decrease *shrinkage*; red clay for fusibility and to warm the color; china clay for whiteness and to vary particle size; feldspar or stone for increased fusibility. Silica, in some form, added to earthenware bodies will assist *craze* resistance. The effectiveness or otherwise of body mixtures or additions must always be tried and proved in the kiln. The correction of vices in clays—*warping, shattering, cracking* etc.—can be a complicated process. *Porcelain* poses special problems which are discussed under that heading. Ready-blended plastic clays are often too smooth and refined and need further adjustments.

The preparation of bodies can be by simple layering and *wedging*. This is hard work but quite effective if done thoroughly. Cardew, however, gives a surprising warning concerning the wedging of unplastic materials (e.g. china clay) into plastic clay. The mixture, he states, will approximate to the *least* plastic of the ingredients! He recommends that china clay be added as a *slip*.

If a high proportion of powder or dried materials is used it is necessary to mix them together on a clean floor, work them into a slurry with water, dry to a plastic state, and wedge thoroughly. Alternatively one becomes mechanized and uses a *blunger* (or a large ball mill), followed by sieving, drying (see *dewatering*), and *pugging*. In all cases at least a week's 'rest' is necessary for the clay to mature before use. Other body-mixing equipment includes batch mixers with rotating runners, and *dough mixers,* which have had quite a vogue among studio potters.

A special addition to a red body is barium carbonate to prevent scumming. (See also *ovenware, glaze-body fit, shrinkage* etc.) Many body recipes can be found in L.PB, C.PP, R.CGP, and other books.

## BODY STAIN

Most of the pigment oxides and prepared stains can be used to produce colored bodies (see also *slips,* and under individual colors—*blue, green,* etc.). It is advisable, however, to limit body color to a few simple mixtures of iron, copper, manganese, or cobalt. Stoneware and porcelain glazes over stained bodies can be interesting. The swirling bands of subtle color in some of Lucie Rie's bowls and bottles are derived from 'marbled' stained bodies, generally manganese bodies, in an oxidized fire.

Unless speckling is required it is advisable to sieve all body stains through a 200 mesh lawn.

## BOLE

A friable earthy clay, stained with iron oxide. It was the type used in Turkey for underglaze red, known as Armenian bole.

## BOND, atomic

*Molecules* and *networks* owe their structure to bonds or linkages between *atoms*. These can be of several kinds: *electrovalent*, where electrons are transferred from one atom to another, producing *ions; covalent*, where electrons are shared; and weaker bonds involving electrically neutral particles known as Van der Waals forces. Also various combinations of these types: (See also *atomic theory, valency*.)

## BONE ASH

Calcium phosphate, $3CaO.P_2O_5$ [sometimes written $Ca_3(PO_4)_2$], 310 (equivalent weight 103).

A typical analysis by weight (Wengers):

| | | | | | |
|---|---|---|---|---|---|
| MgO | 1.27 | $Al_2O_3$ | 0.36 | $P_2O_5$ | 40.9 |
| CaO | 53.9 | $Fe_2O_3$ | 0.11 | $TiO_2$ | 0.01 |

Made by calcining bone, mainly cattle bone. Principal use in *bone china* body, which may contain 50% ash. Occasionally used as a glaze flux, giving a milky quality. Phosphorus is one of the glass-forming oxides.

## BONE CHINA

An English hybrid between soft-paste and true porcelain. The refractory and unplastic nature of English china clay inhibited the successful manufacture of porcelain. Bone china was developed during the eighteenth century and its ingredients fixed by Spode in 1800. It is a very translucent ware with great toughness, resembling *porcelain* though not in 'coldness' or structure at a fracture. The calcined bone forms about half the body. Billington gives a recipe: bone ash 40: china clay 32: china stone 28. This is obviously unplastic and must be thrown very thickly and *turned* to a thin wall, or, as is more usual, *slip cast*. Additions of ball clay, bentonite etc. are liable to spoil color and *translucency*. Shrinkage is around 10% up to 1250°C. Industrially it is *biscuit* fired at 1250°C. and lead glazed at ca. 1080°C. but it is possible to reverse this schedule.

## BONFIRE FIRING

The primitive method of bedding pots in brushwood, heaping wood and grass on top of them, and setting the heap alight. The method can still be a valuable educational exercise and may yield pots of a highly decorative character.

In other than tropical climes, the main danger is the *dunting* of the pots through sudden and uneven cooling. Pots must be resistant to *thermal shock*. This can be achieved by the addition of grog (preferable to sand), though the grog makes burnishing more difficult. Well rounded forms, thin-walled but with sturdy rims, are most likely to survive. Make all joins secure and keep the pots, during building, as evenly damp as possible. *Pinching, coiling* and *throwing* are suitable techniques; slab pots are not recommended. Pots can be prefired to a low biscuit and the bonfire used as decorative treatment.

For raw clay firing the pots should be pre-heated to expel *adsorbed* water. The African potter inverts her large pots over a small heap of glowing embers. The pots in the bonfire are protected by shards which also probably conserve some heat.

*Method.* Build your bonfire on dry ground or on a brick bed. Pre-heat the pots in a kiln or over a small fire, perhaps on a grill or grate, and immediately bed them in dry grass and brushwood. Lay radiating rings of sticks or brushwood against the pots, topping with grass or straw. Light at several points simultaneously. The firing can be maintained for a time with fresh fuel. Protect against wind if possible. Cover with leaves and soil as the fire dies down, to minimize dunting. The use of a pit and a grill or grate (of metal, or fired pottery cylinders) will increase heat and can also be used for the initial warming.

Experiments carried out by Southampton University confirm that good results are possible only on a fairly still, warm day. Their best pots were fired in a pit dug into a pile of used stable straw, layering the pots with dry leaves and burning from the top as in *sawdust firing*. 780°C. was reached.

## BORAX

Sodium diborate, $Na_2O.2B_2O_3.10H_2O$, 381.5. *Calcined* (anhydrous) borax, $Na_2O, 2B_2O_3$, 202 m.p. 600°C.

All forms of borax are soluble to a greater or lesser degree and are normally used in a fritted form. Borax provides the *base*, soda, and a very fusible *acid*, boric oxide. It is therefore very efficient at lowering the maturing temperature of any glaze. Soft glazes must contain either lead oxide or borax—often both.

A typical borax fritt, melting at 1000-1020°C:

Molecular parts—

| | | | |
|---|---|---|---|
| CaO | 0.632 | $Al_2O_3$ | 1.15 |
| $Na_2O$ | 0.336 | $SiO$ | 2.6 |
| $K_2O$ | 0.032 | $B_2O_3$ | 0.644 |

Very soft borax fritts (850°C.) can be used, with the addition of 3% of bentonite, for *raku*. Borax can also be added to salt to assist *salt-glazing*, although it will destroy the characteristic aesthetic virtues of salt glaze. (See also *boron*.)

## BORIC ACID

$H_2BO_2$. See *boron*.

## BORO-CALCITE

$CaO.2B_2O_3.6H_2O$, 304, also given as $2CaO.3B_2O_3$

$5H_2O$ (Wengers), 412.

The natural mineral, with a slightly different molecular formula, is *colemanite*. Can be used in small amounts (up to 3%) to lower the maturing point of a stoneware glaze without materially affecting its character.

## BORON, boric oxide

An element B, 10.9.
Boric oxide $B_2O_3$, 69.6.
Boracic acid $B_2O_3.3H_2O$, 123.7.
Also occurs as borax, and, in an insoluble form, as colemanite.

Boric oxide occupies an ambiguous position in the *Seger formula*. It is an acidic oxide and a *glass-former*, and as such is normally listed with the silica. Its apparent effect, however, is to soften (flux) a glaze and it replaces lead oxide in earthenware. Its formula suggests a third place, with alumina, as an *amphoteric*.

It has the great advantage over lead in that it is non-toxic—boracic acid is, of course, a mild disinfectant. However, little of the rich quality of a lead glaze is apparent in a borax glaze. With the increasingly stringent controls over lead compounds boron is becoming more generally used by craft potters, although it is still possible for lead glazes to pass all the tests. Earthenware leadless glazes are all boron glazes. They are confusingly marked L in catalogs, as distinct from LS, or low-solubility lead glazes. A typical soft L *fritt* is given under *borax*.

Soft borax fritts (boric oxide is usually added in the form of borax) can be used as a fusible foundation for subsequent additions by the potter. The fritt *formulas* now more frequently supplied by merchants are invaluable when modifying them with raw materials. Some clay in the batch will help the physical behavior of a boron fritt, improving its suspension in water. Boric oxide tends to brighten colors in a rather unsubtle way. Copper may tend towards turquoise, and manganese towards purple.

The usual molecular proportion of boric oxide to silica in a glaze formula is around 1 boric oxide: 4 silica. In larger amounts it develops milkiness and surface peculiarities such as glitter and shiny patches in a duller glaze.

For the use of boron in the form of colemanite, see under *colemanite*. A curious property of boric oxide, which makes it very useful in earthenware glazes, is that, in amounts less than 10%, it has a 'negative' *coefficient of expansion* which helps craze resistance.

## BORON PHOSPHATE

Compound $BPO_4$. 'Has been used as a constituent of a ceramic body which fires to a translucent porcelain at 1000°C.' (D.DC).

## BOTTLE FORM

Any pot form with a narrow neck tends to be called a bottle. It allows the maximum exploitation of contour and is favored by potters who wish to show glaze quality or other decoration to the full, the upper curve or shoulder being the most positive and eye-catching area of any pot. The neck is often too small to allow of any 'useful' function.

*A typical salt glazed bottle for water, cider, etc.*

Genuine bottles such as cider jars, bellarmines and the like include some of the most noble shapes in ceramics. It is not, however, easy to attain the generous sweep of shoulder when throwing a large bottle; it poses considerable problems of clay control. When throwing the initial cylinder, concentrate on the lower half and do not overwork the top; it will need all the strength and freshness it can be given. After opening out the belly throw the shoulder inwards rather than simply compressing it, and increase the wheel speed as the circumference decreases. Avoid soaking in water. Hold a finger inside when *collaring* to avoid buckling. Isaac Button, the Yorkshire potter, threw large bottles with very little collaring, but eased the shoulder over with the same movement as the rest of the throwing, using a steel rib outside. He may be seen working 28 lb. of clay in the film *Isaac Button, country potter*.

Another method is to throw an open ovoid onto which, when it has stiffened a little, a thrown ring is luted and the neck is then thrown from this. (See also *two-piece throwing.*)

Bottles can be made by coiling, with multiple *pinch-pots*, or with slabs. Bernard Leach has made some very handsome large rectangular *press-molded* bottles with thrown necks. Bottles with more than one neck, or with tube necks as in pre-Columbian American pottery, are entertaining variations.

*An evening class student's coiled bottle form. See also examples under press mold, slab pot, salt glaze.*

## BOTTLED GAS

Liquified petroleum gas supplied in cylinders or delivered to special storage tanks. It is an efficient but fairly expensive alternative to town or natural gas, and needs slightly different types of burners.

Bottled gas involves very little in the way of a chimney and can be useful for the occasional reduction-firing. It is clean enough for earthenware glazes.

The cost of a cylinder (England 1972) is about £5. Nearly a whole cylinder will be used in a single stoneware firing of a 6 cu. ft. (0.2 cu. m.) kiln. Pressure drops as the gas is used, and a standby cylinder to boost the end of the firing is essential. Supply can revert to the partly empty cylinder at the beginning of the next firing. A changeover valve can be fitted, or two or three cylinders can be connected to a manifold and a pressure gauge. Other hazards are pressure fall in cold weather through freezing caused by the rapid evaporation of the gas liquid, and the collection of any escaping gas at ground level (gas is heavier than air).

With tank installations pressure is more easily maintained, but a guarantee of a large yearly consumption must be given to the installing company.

Bottled gas may be supplied as Butane, Propane, Calorgas, etc. Butane has been quoted at 3200 Btu per cu. ft., propane at 93,000 Btu per gallon (20,700 Kjoules per liter). These figures compare very favorably with natural gas. (See also *gas fuel.*)

## BOTTLE OVEN

As late as the nineteen-fifties every street in Stoke-on-Trent, England, seemed to have its cluster of kilns. The kiln or oven itself was surrounded by a bottle-shaped casing or 'hovel'. They were coal-fired. The splendid skyline disappeared in a few years (together, it must be admitted, with a lot of smoke and grime) with the rapid introduction of *continuous* kilns. (See photograph under *kiln*.)

## BOULDER CLAY

Clay which together with an assortment of stones and rocks has been transported by glacial action and then dumped as the glacier has melted. Common to large areas of North America and Europe. Used for brick-making in the north of England.

## BOW

A single cutting wire held taut by a curved strip of cane, bamboo, or metal.

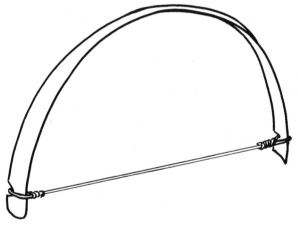

*A bow made from a strip of cane or bamboo. The cutting wire can be of metal or nylon.*

## BOWL FORM

At once the easiest shape to throw and the most difficult fully to succeed with. The subtleties of a really lively bowl are not easy to analyse. To some potters a bowl should have a sense of enclosure, of cupped hands, but this excludes a great family of flaring forms. If the bowl has a well-defined practical purpose its shape must, of course, be suited to its use, as seen in the Peter Dick mixing bowl illustrated. A sense of growth and spring from the base is essential and this involves a careful proportioning of the foot ring. The rim needs consideration, as its style will fundamentally affect the character of the bowl. A sturdy rim is more likely to maintain a circular plan but this is not always aesthetically desirable.

When throwing a bowl perhaps the commonest fault is caused by the sudden lessening of support as the inner hand leaves the base clay and begins to exert pressure on the walls. Unless a finger or a knuckle of the outer hand is tucked tight against the base to take the pressure, the all too common ridge and valley is formed. This becomes weaker as throwing proceeds and may finally collapse. In the earlier stages of throwing keep the wall more upright and with less curve than will be finally required, even to the extent of reversing the form—i.e. slightly convex instead of concave. The full curve is the last operation of all. The rim will benefit from being kept slightly thicker than the walls both throughout the throwing and in the finished piece. A generous rim can be an important feature and will help to maintain the bowl's circular plan.

*Throwing a bowl, showing the danger point when the inside pressure meets the base of the wall (1). The bowl has been cut in section to make the position clear, the outer finger tucked well in to the junction of clay and wheel head ready to take the pressure from the inside hand (2).*

For all sizes of bowl the wheel speed should be progressively lessened as work proceeds, in order to balance the centrifugal force exerted on the ever-widening wall. Do not over-wet the clay, and complete the throwing with as few movements as possible. Large bowls are more easily controlled on a kickwheel. The centering and initial throwing can be done on a power wheel, and then the wheel head transferred.

One can complete the bowl on the wheel, trimming the base with a bamboo or metal tool. The flat base must be reflected inside the bowl if a thick wedge is not to be left at the outer edge of the foot. Most bowls, however, will need turning, and sufficient clay must be left to form the *foot ring*. Cardew, some Japanese potters, and others throw a foot ring onto a reversed leather-hard bowl.

A number of bowls can be thrown from a large block of clay. This method is useful for test bowls. The mass of clay is roughly centered, the top part fully centered and the bowl thrown from this. Cutting off can be done Japanese-fashion with a loose thread which is allowed to wind itself into the clay and is then whipped sharply out, or a fine needle awl can be held sloping slightly upwards and cut in towards the center of the base.

Bowls may be *beaten* or cut (see *facet*). Other illustrations may be found under *foot ring*. Handbuilt bowls are less common, but for details see under *handbuilding*.

*A basic bowl form by Peter Dick.*

## BOXES

Pottery boxes rarely have a definite functional purpose, but are often very attractive objects and present the potter with interesting technical and aesthetic problems. The lids, especially of flattened forms, beg for decoration, even if this is simply the turning spiral of some of Richard Batterham's best boxes, or the speckled salt glaze of Gwyn Hanssen. A smooth curve will burnish well for *sawdust firing*. There are also unexploited possibilities for modeled knobs on lids. Many of Bernard Leach's earlier boxes had attractive, lively modeled knobs.

The method of holding the lid in place (the style and placing of the flange or slope) is open to many interpretations. The proportions between base and lid can be a recurring challenge and delight.

Boxes can be made by any technique. Rosemary Wren has shown how lively little boxes with excellently fitting lids can be made from *pinch-pots*. Boxes may be thrown as two shallow bowls or short cylinders. Slab boxes pose their own problems: the flange can look heavy, and the sides are liable to warp inwards. They should be fairly flat in profile and put together from quite stiff clay, the joints pressed home with a wooden tool.

A good fit between lid and base will be best maintained during firing if they are fired in place. This necessitates care and thought when glazing. Sticking is less likely if the rims are waxed where they are to be left unglazed. A very thin wash of china clay and flint or alumina can be spun onto the rim before waxing.

3

1

2

*Three very different types of boxes. A thrown porcelain box by David Leach (1); a slab box by Tony Gant, decorated with cog wheel impressions (2); and a pinched box by Rosemary Wren with melted glass in the lid (3). Also see color plate 2, p. 129.*

## BOXING

The packing of pots, especially bowls and cups, rim to rim and foot to foot. They must be of similar size, with level rims, and, of course, unglazed. The method is rather wasteful of space but helps to eliminate warping in the biscuit fire.

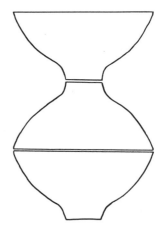

*Boxing bowls in a biscuit fire. The pile or 'bung' can be continued to a height of six to eight bowls depending on their sturdiness. It is also possible to fire glazed pieces in this way if they have biscuit rims and there is no chance of the glaze running.*

## BRAZIER KILN

A very simple type of coke kiln used for *raku*. First developed in England by David Ballantyne. It can be built in half an hour from common bricks—Flettons or any open-textured house brick. Fifty to eighty are needed. Also a saggar of approximately 12 in. (say 300 mm.) diameter, which can be purchased, or coiled from a well grogged body. Diagram A shows the plan, including the three half bricks on which the *saggar* stands: diagram B is a section through a completed kiln. A dry site is needed, or a foundation of bricks laid down. The interior diameter will depend on the size of the saggar which should preferably be about 9 in. (230 mm.) high. Allow 3 in. (75 mm.) between saggar and walls all round. The space between the three supporting half bricks is filled with coke or a smokeless fuel before the saggar is positioned, and paper or firelighters placed near the bottom gaps between the bricks so that they can be lit from the outside. A layer of sticks is laid on top.

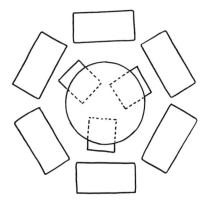

A

*Plan of a brazier kiln. (See text.)*

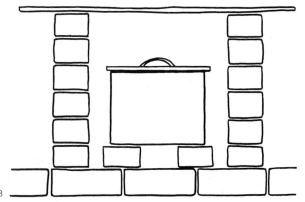

B

*Section through a brazier kiln. (See text.) For brazier kiln in action see color plate 4, p. 129.*

Walls are built up dry to a height of 6 in. (about 150 mm.) or so above the saggar, leaving 1-1½ in. (30 mm.) gaps between the bricks. The top row may be placed close together. A saggar lid must be provided, together with some means of removing it when hot. If your *tongs* will open wide, then the lid can be a simple kiln bat, otherwise a handle should be built onto it. The space between saggar and bricks is now filled with coke, or smokeless fuel if coke is unobtainable. The fire is lit at the base holes.

See *raku* for details of firing. The film 'Raku, English style' shows the building and firing of a brazier kiln; also the book R.RAT contains useful information.

**BRICK**

A clay or ceramic unit of building construction, the commonest shape being a rectangle of around 9 x 4½ x 2¾ in. (228 x 115 x 70 mm.). Bricks have changed little over the centuries, though they are now made in an ever-widening range of materials from red surface clays to bauxite and chrome ore.

The three main types of brick used by potters are easily distinguishable. They are:

1 Open-textured red clay building bricks, the cheapest being called Flettons in England.
2 Hard, heavy, close-grained refractory bricks.
3 Lightweight *insulating* bricks.

Group 1    Apart from their obvious building purposes, they can be used for the outer skins of kilns where they will provide better insulation than heavy bricks. Also for low temperature and 'primitive' kilns such as the brazier type.

Group 2    Includes all grades of *firebricks* from Super-duty, *PCE.33*, for working temperatures up to 1550°C., to Low Heat Duty, PCE 15, which soften at 1400°C. and must be used at well below that. Grading in England is by alumina content—45% downwards.

Group 3    These are easily abraded, very porous, light in weight, and superb *insulators*. They are made in many qualities and degrees of heat resistance. Those made from *diatomaceous earth* are either quarried and cut to shape or fired into blocks with a little clay. These are weak in structure and are comparatively fusible. The more *refractory* types are made from very pure and iron-free ceramic materials and have an open, sponge-like appearance achieved by physical means (mixing the raw material with sawdust, for instance) or chemical processes. These are graded by a K factor, the number denoting the degrees Fahrenheit which they will endure without failing, e.g. K26=2600°F. or 1430°C. The higher numbers are stronger but marginally less effective as insulators. They are all more expensive than firebricks.

The choice of bricks will depend on a balance being struck between the extra initial cost of high insulation qualities and the extra fuel costs due to the *heat storage* and *heat loss* of hard firebrick. (See *insulation, heat storage, conduction of heat*.) The care needed to avoid abrading or breaking the softer bricks may also weigh in your decision. For electric kilns group 3 is the obvious choice.

The standard insulating brick size is 9 x 4½ x 3 in. (228 x 115 x 76 mm.) but there is a wide range of special shapes and sizes designed for arches, bevels, domes etc. Insulating-brick is also available in blocks up to 18 x 9 x 4½ in. (460 x 230 x 115 mm.). Kiln bricks can be molded by the potter either as fireclay and grog mixtures (see details in C.PP Appendix 3), or cast from special bodies made from calcium/alumina cement with an aggregate of crushed firebrick or insulating brick, *grog* or expanded *perlite*. Use one part cement to four or five aggregate.

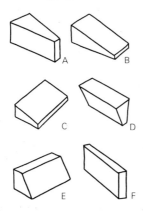

*Some of the special shapes of bricks available. A: End Arch brick; B: a Feather End; C: a Feather Side; D: a Side Arch; E: a Side Scew; and F: a Split. All may be useful in arch building and a Split is a shape almost impossible to cut from a whole brick.*

## BRICK CLAYS

A general name for a variety of clays, mostly red-firing and *fusible*, and containing lime and other impurities. Fired at 900-1100°C. Bricks can be made from many surface or near-surface clays so long as their shrinkage is not too great and they are not contaminated with lime nodules. Some 'brick earths' such as those of the Thames valley in England, are of recent origin, geologically speaking (Pleistocene, two to six million years ago), but others are from much older carboniferous times. Their quality depends partly on the underlying rock.

The addition of sawdust, chopped grass, or brick-dust can be added to brick clays to lessen the wet-dry shrinkage. Refractory bricks are made from the purer *fireclays*. (See also *marls.*)

## BRICKLAYING

Most of the potter's work in this field will be in the building of kilns. Here bricks are laid almost in contact with one another—merely a 'buttering' of mortar between them. The mortar is used as wet as possible, and the bricks either soaked or at least wetted on the surface. Some constructions, electric kilns in particular, can be dry-built.

Long horizontal joints in brickwork are inevitable, but vertical joints are avoided by overlapping. There are several systems, but the principle is similar in each case: that each brick should, as often as possible, span the join between the two below it. In 9 in. (230 mm.) walls, courses can be laid across the width (called 'header' courses because the head or end of the brick shows on the face), as well as along its length ('stretcher' courses). Bricks will often be needed in half-lengths

and can be cut with a brick hammer which has a chisel end, or with a 'cold' chisel or bolster. The brick may be chipped or scored along the line of the break and then tapped sharply across a hard edge.

Accurate bricklaying depends on a level and firm foundation and the frequent use of a good spirit level at least 18 in. (500 mm.) long. Stretched lines or board can guide straight walls; wooden templates are often constructed over which to build arches and domes. Rhodes gives advice on bricklaying in Chapter 4 R.K.; see also C.PP.

A brick structure will expand on heating: open (unmortared) joints about $\frac{1}{4}$ in. (6 mm.) wide should be left every four bricks.

*Simple bricklaying bonds. A: The English bond, which may consist of alternate header and stretcher courses or one header to two or three stretchers. B: The Flemish bond, bricks laid in alternate directions within each course.*

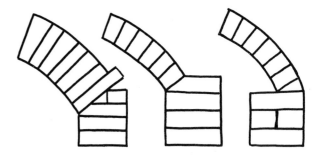

*Bricklaying: three ways of 'springing' an arch of bricks.*

## BRIGHT GOLD

See *gold*.

## BRISTOL GLAZE

A medium temperature glaze containing zinc oxide, originally developed in an attempt to avoid the use of lead. It is a difficult glaze to control and is subject to crawling and pinholes. The zinc-alumina-silica eutectic is fairly high—1360°C.—but can be brought down to below 1200°C. by the addition of feldspar and whiting. The use of clay in the recipe makes it suitable for use on green (unbiscuited) ware. Zinc glazes are not suitable for reduction.

Typical recipes:

| | | |
|---|---|---|
| Feldspar | 56.5 | |
| Whiting | 9.5 | |
| Nepheline | | 40.0 |
| Lithia | | 5.0 |
| Zinc oxide | 6.5 | 12.0 |
| Clay | 13.0 | 8.0 |
| Flint | 14.5 | 35.0 |

And from PQ 13 (Merritt):

| | | |
|---|---|---|
| Calcined zinc | 24.3 | |
| Feldspar | 113.2 | |
| Colemanite | 51.5 | |
| Barium carbonate | 19.7 | Firing |
| Talc | 18.9 | 1140°C. |
| Flint | 66.0 | |
| Calcium nitrate | 2.9 | |

The zinc is sometimes used in a calcined form to lessen drying shrinkage. (See *zinc*.) The zinc will affect colors (not often to their advantage), though copper is reputed to produce turquoise (Rhodes) and uranium a bright yellow. The firing of Bristol glazes is around 1180°C.

## BRITISH THERMAL UNITS, Btu

A measure of heat quantity. The heat required to raise 1 lb. of water through 1° Fahrenheit. Equal to 252 calories. 100,000 Btu = 1 *therm*. The heat value of various fuels can be stated in Btu for comparison.

The Unit *joule* is now superseding the Btu. One Btu is equivalent to 1050J or 1.05kJ (kilojoule).

## BROKES

Term used for a type of English ball clay which will not cut into balls. Generally of low plasticity. Fires grayish.

## BRONGIART'S FORMULA

A method of determining the weight, on a pint basis, of suspended solids in a slip or glaze.

*Method:* First weigh the container empty, then with one pint of the slip to be tested. The liquid weight is arrived at by subtraction. We then use the formula $P - 20 \times \dfrac{s.g.}{s.g. - 1}$ in which s.g. stands for *specific gravity* of the solid material and P for the pint weight arrived at as above. The 1 stands for the s.g. of water.

*Example:* The average s.g. of plastic clay is 2.6. If the pint weight was 27 oz. then:

$$(27 \text{ [oz.]} - 20) \times \frac{2.6}{2.6 - 1} = 7 \times 1.62 \text{ oz.}$$

i.e. 11.34 oz. of dry clay.

The calculation is complicated for glazes by the fact that materials with different specific gravities are mixed together. However, most common glaze minerals are in the range 2.5-3.0. Where the s.g. is much above this figure it has generally been noted in this book (e.g. lead oxide). A good approximation to the pint weight can therefore be arrived at.

## BROWN PIGMENTS, glazes

Iron oxide is the commonest brown pigment: 4-8% in most glazes. Small amounts of zinc (0.5-1.5%) will develop browns from chrome. Manganese gives browns often tending towards purple-brown. Nickel can be brownish in a barium glaze. Rutile gives broken browns. A recipe for a brown pigment given by Miss Pleydell-Bouverie is: 1 measure of cobalt oxide, 10 iron, 5 manganese, 10 china clay. Grind together in a mortar. Unglazed iron and copper will give blacks and browns.

## BRUSHED SLIP

If slip is used like a pigment it must be applied very liberally if it is not to vanish in the glaze fire. This is especially true with earthenware lead glazes which use a layer of the surface clay to fulfil their glass-forming function. Slips heavily loaded with pigment oxides can be used for painting on or under stonewares. Henry Hammond uses a series of slips for painting: 50% each of iron and local London red clay; a local red clay alone; ball clay alone; 98 parts of ball clay to one of cobalt and one of iron chromate; ochre and cobalt—all laid on fairly generously. (See also *hakame, engobe*.)

## BRUSHES

The painting brush traditionally used in the industry is the 'liner', very long-haired and square-ended. The high absorption of pigment by biscuit or glaze makes it essential that any brush should hold a great deal of it. It is a wonder that no-one has come up with a 'fountain-brush' for pottery.

For the more calligraphic style of painting, liners have limited value. The *cut liners* are more lively. Goat-hair *mops* are useful for background washes, e.g. in preparation for *sgraffito* or *wax resist*. Japanese brushes are more responsive but, being designed for inks, are, in general, rather soft, a quality which can, however, give great sensitivity to a stroke. There is an attractive hand-made flat brush on the market which Wengers call a 'hake' brush (from *hakame*?) available both 44mm. and 76 mm. (approx. $1\frac{3}{4}$ in. and 3 in.) wide. Cardew mentions a resilient type called Sen Pen Banka, from Muruzen Co., P.O. Box 605, Tokyo Central.

'Majolica pencils' are of sable, are slightly wider than paintbrushes and give a good point. Three basic brushes will fulfil most requirements: a large sable watercolor brush, a square shader (about $\frac{3}{4}$ in. (15 mm.) wide), and a liner, or medium Japanese brush. Experimental potters can try any sort of brush-like object with which to apply their slip or color: shaving brushes, cheap paste brushes (which give a useful dry, striated line), even fine twigs etc., dabbing and working the surface to provide fresh textures. The 'throw-away' plastic sponge brushes may also have possibilities for backgrounds. Brushes for *wax* need to be resilient and to have a good body.

*Lawn* brushes should be easily cleanable or they

will contaminate the next batch of glaze. It is advisable to keep a brush, clearly labelled, for each group of glazes and slips that you use, e.g. one for clear glaze, one for dark colors, and so on. The large bristle brushes often listed in merchants' catalogs are not easy to clean and they retain a lot of sludge during sieving. I consider the round nylon kitchen-brushes to be more suitable. Unfortunately they do not have very strong handles.

Brushes must be cared for. Wash and stroke to a point after use; store preferably hanging hair-down-wards. If kept heads-up in a jar, dry well or the hairs may rot at the base. Do *not* use brushes to mix colors. One cannot easily clean wax brushes unless water-soluble emulsions are used. Smooth the hairs to a point and leave them to set. A brush will be destroyed if dipped into hot wax when wet.

## BRUSHWORK

A serious gap in the potter's library is an expert and wideranging discussion of brushwork. Once the most widely practised technique for decorating ceramics, it has been overshadowed by textural and glaze surfaces and by the less consciously designed applications of slips and colors. Few potters today have the training or the desire to develop fresh ideas in brushwork. The reputation of Eastern calligraphy which, at its best, is as taut as a spring and as individual as hand-writing, has suffered through the careless and flabby copying of historical work. A few potters continue with majolica and lustre in skillful Moresque-type patterns, but little genuine modern work is done. Kenneth Clark and others made an impact with brush decoration in the nineteen-fifties, but he has little to say in his book (C.PC) except to try using brushes other than the traditional ones (see *brushes*) to achieve fresh and exciting marks.

A few do's and dont's become obvious with a little practice. The body of the brush should be used as a reservoir and kept full of pigment; the temptation to drain it on the side of the color container should be

*Harry Davis wax resist plate with brushwork of the liveliest and most expert kind.*

resisted—shape the point of the brush only. Use as large a brush as the design will allow. Keep the hand floating and free, and let the brush itself do as much of the work as possible by varying the pressure upon the hairs.

It is important to practise with any one particular brush to find out what it will do, and to adapt your design to the particular marks it makes most naturally and easily.

*Wax resist* has attracted more significant work than brushed pigment. It lends itself to strong blocks of color and to *glaze-over-glaze* techniques. It cannot be fussed over but must be completed quickly and firmly and has those elements of 'accidentals and incidentals', to quote Leach, which still find great favor. (See also *calligraphy* and *decoration*.)

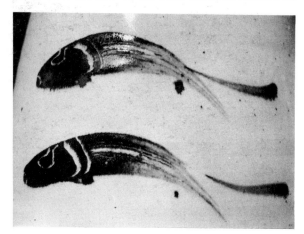

*A detail of brushwork by Bernard Leach, on a stoneware bottle.*

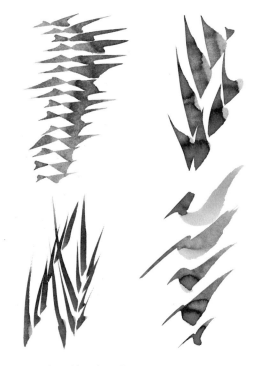

*Four examples of brushwork.*

## BRUSSELS NOMENCLATURE

An attempt made in 1955 to agree on an International Tariff Nomenclature of terms and meanings. Chapter 69 includes ceramics, listing china, earthenware etc. The definitions are occasionally mentioned in this dictionary, but are more accurately applicable to industrial work.

## Btu

See *British thermal units.*

## BUBBLES IN GLAZE

Most glazes go through a bubbling (gas releasing) stage. It is very marked in lead glazes. The bubbles must be given time to break and to settle down. If a glaze is fired beyond its optimum melting temperature, decomposition is likely to take place with the emission of further gases. The firing should therefore be terminated between these two phases.

Craters, pinholes, blisters, and milkiness in a clear glaze are evidences of bubbles. (See under *pinholes* and *blistering* for discussion of cause and cure.) Precautions that can be taken are the full *oxidation* of earthenware glazes and the careful drying of glazed pots *before* they are packed in the kiln. An even and adequate glaze coating followed by accurate firing and some *soaking*, especially of earthenwares, will minimize bubbling.

High manganese glazes are liable to gas release: $3MnO_2 = Mn_3O_4 + O_2$. Bubbles trapped in a stoneware glaze but not evident on the surface are often an attractive characteristic; they are less welcome in a too thickly applied earthenware glaze. Deliberate 'cratering' of the surface is used as a decorative finish—barium sulfate has been mentioned.

## BUFF CLAY

Few plastic clays fire white. Those containing 2-4% of iron fire cream—buff or grayish at higher temperatures, and the term 'buff body' is often applied. The clay may be much darker in the raw state, due to carbon stained ball clay or fireclay in the recipe. Many buff bodies have a long firing-range: that from Potclays (England) is adequate from 1000-1280°C.

Some local river clays will fire to a deep buff, but local surface clays which may be yellow-buff in the raw state are most likely to fire to a red-brown. Buff clays are very suitable for slips, taking some of the brashness from cobalt and giving a slight grayness to green slips.

## BULLDOG

An impure iron silicate, giving browns and blacks. Used in reduction to produce 'blue' bricks. It has now disappeared, at least under this name, from the catalogs.

## BULLER'S RINGS

*Annular* rings, like large washers, $2\frac{1}{2}$ in. (65 mm.) in diameter and made from ceramic materials. They are placed in a kiln near a spyhole or at a point where they can be hooked out during firing. Their contraction in diameter is measured in a special triangular gauge, a reading indicating the heat it has reached. Introduced about 1900.

They are normally used only in fairly large kilns but could be a post-firing guide to the temperature in various parts of any kiln. Their advantage over cones is that they do not melt and stick. They are made in four temperature ranges covering 960-1400°C.

## BULL'S HEAD WEDGING

See *wedging.*

## BUNG

1   The spyhole stopper of a kiln. Generally of a truncated cone shape and either cut from a refractory brick or thrown from grogged clay.
2   A vertical setting in a kiln, either of saggars, ware supported by special kiln furniture, or pots simply sitting one upon the other. (See *boxing.*)

*A bung of mixing bowls in the Soil Hill Pottery kiln. The rims are glazed to the edge and they rest on three flanges (just visible at the top left) which project from the very sturdy curved supports or 'cranks'. The bowls are about 16 in. (400 mm.) across.*

## BURNISH GOLD

See *gold*.

## BURNISHING

The polishing of the surface of clay by rubbing. A burnished pot can give considerable visual and tactile pleasure. It is developed from the clay itself, with a consequent sense of unity between body and surface. A burnished pot will not, however, be watertight.

Most bodies, even grogged ones, will burnish; the finer grained smooth secondary clays are the easiest to work on. Some micaceous material probably helps (see *mica*). The technique involves some restriction on form. Concavities, as well as lugs or other applied decoration, make work difficult. An unbroken rounded profile is the most satisfactory. Thrown boxes burnish well and show off the color variations of *sawdust firings*. The main polishing is done at the firm leather-hard stage of drying. The clay's response to burnishing can be tested at intervals during drying until the best results are obtained. Thrown pieces can be polished on the wheel immediately after turning, although this gives a somewhat more mechanical appearance. A final rub with the hands (so long as these are not calloused or rough) is given at the near-dry stage. Cardew mentions beating the surface in order to consolidate it: this may be useful with rougher clays.

Burnishing with a wooden tool (1) and with the flat of the palm (2). Red clay, hand-built pot. See color plate 5, p. 129.

Although hematite is the classic surface coating, I have found that pigments, such as ferric iron, or high iron slips, can be disappointing both as to surface and color. John Ablett has developed quite a palette of subdued colors for burnishing. A fine levigated slip, as is reputed to have been used for Samian ware, will certainly help.

The burnishing tool can be any conveniently shaped smooth object: a water-worn pebble, bone, plastic, metal, or hard wood are all possible materials. The only essential is a firm, perfectly smooth surface, preferably slightly convex and without sharp corners or edges. Work with a steady, even pressure in small circular movements. Glass burnishers are supplied for gold burnishing, and these may be used too.

The shine will diminish as the pot dries and should be further treated; often it suffices to work it in the hands or on a piece of cloth. The leg of one's trousers can often be used! Burnish may be lost if the firing is too high—850°C. is sufficient. Loss of shine can be remedied by re-rubbing with the hands or a soft cloth. The carbon saturation associated with sawdust firing assists the polish. A high burnish can be achieved even with a porcelain body. (See also *polishing clay, sawdust firing*.)

## BURNT SIENNA

Calcined *ochre* or ochrous earth. A reddish-brown pigment. (See also *sienna*.)

## BUTANE

$CH_3(CH_2) CH_3$ or $C_4H_{10}$.
See *bottled gas, gas fuel*.

## BUTTER PATS

See *beater*.

## BUTTON TEST

A test of the behavior of ceramic materials in the kiln. Many materials and minerals can be formed in a

A tile with six depressions in each of which a ball or button test of pottery materials—minerals, fritts, etc. have been placed. The materials are moistened and rolled. This is then fired, the hollows retaining any very fusible melt, and the results studied.

damp state into small balls or buttons. If these are fired on a biscuit tile one can obtain some idea of their fusibility and other qualities from the state of collapse or flow at a given temperature. An excellent educational exercise. The results of this test, however, can be slightly misleading. It is the reaction of one material with another which is of prime interest when compounding bodies or glazes. (See *chemistry of glazes*.)

# C

## CADMIUM, compounds

A metallic element Cd, 112.4. Used as cadmium sulfide CdS in low temperature pigments (enamels). Produces yellow and orange. Often combined with selenium which will withstand higher temperatures. *Volatile*. Obtainable only as a prepared pigment. May blacken in the presence of lead.

Cadmium released into food acids is a health hazard and it should not be used in jugs or storage vessels. (See *metal release*.)

## CALCEROUS CLAYS

Clays containing lime and thus liable to 'blowing'. (See *marls, lime blowing*.)

## CALCINE, calcination

To disintegrate by heat: the strong heating of a material resulting in physical or chemical alteration.

Flints, very hard in the raw state, become a friable white powder at around 900°C. but retain the same chemical composition. Bone, when calcined, loses its carbon and only the *inorganic* residue of calcium and phosphorus remain. Some metal oxides can be calcined: manganese will give a more powerful pigment; cobalt oxides are prepared by calcining, the gray oxide CoO to 1050°C., the black oxide to 750°C. The gray oxide is thus slightly more concentrated in use, and will not change its form or lose oxygen in firing. Calcining is also practised to eliminate the water of *hydration* e.g. calcined borax.

*A flint pebble and the calcined flint powder. The chemical make-up is not altered but the physical state is very different.*

## CALCITE, calcspar

A natural crystalline calcium carbonate, $CaCO_3$. It is the mineral constituent of limestone, chalk and marble. Many natural rocks are almost pure calcite, as also are oyster and some other shells. A method of determining the purity of a calcite rock sample is described in C.PP 51-2.

## CALCIUM, oxide, compounds

A metallic element Ca, 40.8.
Oxide CaO.57 (quicklime), m.p. 2570°C. Calcia.
Carbonate $CaCO_3$, 100, (lime).

The carbonate decomposes into the oxide at about 850°C. Although the melting point is very high, reaction with other ceramic materials forms material with a lower melting point. A eutectic is: CaO 1.0 $Al_2O_3$ 0.35 $SiO_2$ 2.48 as represented by 33.66% calcite, 30.39% china clay, 35.95% quartz.

$CaCO_3$ is almost pure in limestone and chalk, which are prepared as *whiting*. Because it is a pure material its proportions in a glaze must be carefully calculated. Its effect in glazes can be to shorten the solid to liquid phase. Either too much or too little can reduce the brightness of a glaze.

Lime is usually placed low in the table listing the *fusible* properties of bases. This is true for soft glazes, but somewhat misleading when considering stonewares, where it can be a major flux rendering the glazes more 'watery' or less *viscous*. In a series of experiments carried out some years ago it was found that 40% could be added to a stoneware glaze (at 1285°C.) before scum began to form. In some glazes, however, the maximum fluidity may be developed at around 15%.

The *coefficient of expansion* of calcium is only half that of the alkalis. It is reputed to assist iron reduction for celadons. It gives hardness and durability, and is responsible for the great strength of *bone china*. It tends to bleach color from red clays at lower temperatures. Lime in red clays will therefore yield yellowish colors as in some bricks which are fired at 1000°C. or less. In the Netherlands, up to 25% of a limey clay (marl) or lime was added to the body of majolica (Delft) tiles. According to B.TGH this helped to stick the glaze to the clay and to prevent crazing, although it also lowered its resistance to chipping.

Other calcium minerals are:

| | |
|---|---|
| Wollastonite | $CaSiO_3$ |
| Fluorspar | $CaF_2$ |
| Dolomite | $CaCO_3.MgCO_3$ (approx.) |
| Calcium chloride | $CaCl_2$ |
| Bone ash | $3CaO.P_2O_5$ |
| Colemanite | $2CaO.3B_2O_3$ |
| Wood ashes | Variable |
| Plaster of Paris | $CaSO_4.\frac{1}{2}H_2O$ |
| (Gypsum) | $CaSO_4.2H_2O$ |
| Anorthite | $CaO.Al_2O_3.2SiO_2$ |

## CALCIUM CHLORIDE

$CaCl_2$, 111. Occasionally used for the *flocculation*

of glazes—0.05%. Also accelerates the setting of Portland cement.

## CALCIUM PHOSPHATE

$3CaO.P_2O_5$. See *bone ash, bone china.*

## CALCSPAR

An old name for calcite, which is in fact listed under calcspar in the Ferro catalog.

## CALCULATORS

The standard sliderule is useful in glaze computation, but the most ingenious specialist calculator is the 'Rapid Glaze Calculator' which speeds up the arithmetic involved in converting recipes to formulas, shrinkage percentages, and the like. It would be better if a little larger and correspondingly more accurate, but even so it is very useful. Available from Ceramic Calculations, Marston Magna, Yeovil, Somerset, England. The 'Dial a glaze' calculator, available in the USA (CM 18/9) was not very enthusiastically reviewed in PQ 38.

## CALIPERS, callipers

A compass of metal, wood or plastic, with curved arms, or curved at the ends. It is used for measuring the inner or outer circumference of pots on the wheel. Metal calipers are the most accurate but may corrode under pottery conditions. 8-9 in. (about 210 mm.) is a useful size—one does not often need to repeat pots above 14 in. (350 mm.) wide! Tiranti's of London make excellent calipers. Their most frequent use is for the fitting of lids.

3

*Using calipers. The inside measurements of the flange of a pot are taken with the points curving outwards (1). The lid can be similarly measured or the calipers can be reversed (on a rule or from one set to another as shown (2)). Inward curved points being more convenient for making outside measurements (3).*

## CALLIGRAPHIC

In pottery the term is used rather loosely to indicate a free style of brushwork which uses the movement and shape of the brush itself from which to derive the design. It comes more from Oriental brush-script than from Western broad-nib writing, though there are some parallels here too.

## CALORIE

A unit of heat: that required to raise 1 gm. of water through 1 °C. The 'large' or food calorie substitutes a kilogram for a gram, and is sometimes written Kc. The *British thermal unit,* equal to 252 calories, is a more useful scale for potters. See also *joule.*

## CALORITE

A cylindrical pyrometric cone.

## CANDLE

Household candles vary in composition—wax, tallow, spermaceti etc.—but most are suitable for wax resist work if melted with an equal volume of thin machine oil.

## CANE HANDLE

A semi-circular hoop of cane or bamboo used for teapot handles, or occasionally for storage jars. Each end is split, one section cut away, and the remaining strip looped back round a lug on the pot.

1

2

The cane must be soaked or steamed, the ends slowly drawn together until they form rather more than a semi-circle (the curve will always spring out a little). (See *lugs* for fitting to teapot.) Cane handles are available from the Craftsmen Potters' Shop and several suppliers.

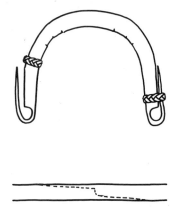

*The diagram shows how the attaching tag of a cane handle is cut and bent. Cane is difficult to cut and needs sharp tools and a good vice.*

*A cane-handled teapot by David Leach. Engraved porcelain with a Ying Ch'ing glaze.*

## CARBON, oxides, compounds

A non-metallic element C, 12.
Monoxide CO, 28
Dioxide $CO_2$, 44

Carbon occurs in all organic compounds and also in a pure state as graphite, charcoal and diamond. In pottery materials it is represented by the carbonates, where a *basic element* is in combination with carbon and oxygen as $CO_2$. In the carbonate form the bases are stable and often in a convenient physical form for use in bodies and glazes e.g. lime (calcium carbonate). The $CO_2$ is released as a gas during firing, leaving the oxide, RO. Carbonates are therefore always $RO + CO_2$ or $RCO_3$, where R is the basic element.

Carbon has a melting point of 3500°C. and is therefore one of the most refractory materials known: but this is true only in the absence of oxygen. The gas $CO_2$ is produced in great quantities when burning fuels in kilns. Insufficient air (oxygen) will cause this to be 'reduced' to CO, carbon monoxide, an unstable and very poisonous gas. This, in turn, will extract oxygen from the glaze pigments in order to regain its stable $CO_2$ form. Carbon itself, as smoke, is a reducing agent. (See also *reduction*.)

Carbon can be dissolved to a small extent in a melting glaze. A speck of carbon falling onto a glaze will reduce it locally.

The commonest carbon compound in pottery is *silicon carbide*, SiC, a highly conductive refractory.

Some coloring metals can be used as carbonates: copper carbonate is green which helps to distinguish it from other oxides when painting; similarly cobalt carbonate is a purplish blue. Unfortunately some of the carbonates are toxic.

### CARBON DIOXIDE

$CO_2$. The stable oxide of *carbon*. The product of *combustion*.

### CARBON MONOXIDE

CO. A poisonous oxide of carbon. A *reducing* agent. Unstable in atmosphere.

### CARBONIZATION

In raku and sawdust firing the body may be partly reduced, but is more likely to be saturated with unburnt carbon which will blacken it.

### CARBORUNDUM

A trade name, now become a household word, for *silicon carbide*. Used for grinding-stones. Biscuit which has been rubbed with carborundum must be well cleaned or glaze may scum. (See also *abrasive*.)

### CARD MEASURE

A piece of card cut in such a way that it can indicate 'vital statistics' of a pot for repetition throwing and for future reference. Other details such as clay weight and a diagram of the shape with handle position etc. can be recorded on it.

The card can be sprayed with varnish to prevent water saturation and to retain the information written on it. Linoleum or thin plywood are also excellent materials.

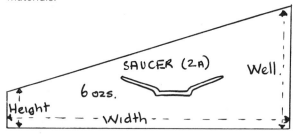

*A card measure for a saucer. It gives the shape, code number, weight (of clay), width, height at the rim, and width of well.*

## CAROLINA STONE

An American *china stone*.

## CASSEROLE

A deep lidded bowl for cooking in the oven. It should be of generous form with a well-fitting lid and an adequate knob. Usually has two *lug* handles or a short thrown one. The height of the average oven should be considered when designing pot and lid. (See also *ovenware* for discussion of body, glaze etc.)

*A fine, full-bodied casserole. Early Leach Pottery. Stoneware biscuit outside.*

## CAST

Made in a *mold*. The method of molding, e.g. slip-cast. As a noun, the molded object itself.

## CASTING

If a hollow plaster shape is filled with slip, water will be absorbed and a coating of clay will be deposited on the inner surface of the plaster. The level of the slip is kept topped-up as it is absorbed, and when the coating has become thick enough the remaining slip is poured out. The clay shape will slowly shrink away from the plaster mold and can be removed.

Casting is an industrial technique intended to produce a large number of identical objects, the initial shape often having been carved in plaster. It has little relevance to the work of the individual potter. It has its own skills and cannot be done in a professional way without experience and practice. (See also *molds*.)

There are many points at which slip casting can go awry. The molds will, of course, become saturated after several casts have been taken and need careful drying. (See *plaster of paris, casting-slip*.)

## CASTING-SLIP

A normal potter's slip has too high a proportion of water to solid material to be effective as a casting-slip. A slip which is too thick to pour can be made fluid by the addition of a defloculant (electrolyte) which weakens the bonds between particles. Sodium silicate and soda ash are deflocculants. The slip itself can be made less *viscous* by using only small amounts of

## FAULTS IN CASTING

| FAULT | DESCRIPTION | CAUSE | REMEDY |
|---|---|---|---|
| Pinholing | Small holes just beneath the surface on the mold side of the article | Fluidity too low | Increase water addition |
| Wreathing | Small uneven ridges on the slip side of the article | *Thixotropy* too low | Decrease alkali content |
| Brittleness | Difficult to fettle or cut | | |
| Casting-spot | Discolored patch appearing on the mold side after firing | | |
| Cracking | Small cracks where handles join the body of the article | | |
| Flabbiness | Soft casts difficult to handle without distortion | Thixotropy too high | Increase *alkali* addition |
| Slow casting | Casting time too long | Fluidity too high or thixotropy too low | Decrease water or decrease alkali addition |
| Bad draining | Slip failing to drain from narrow sections | Fluidity too low or thixotropy too high | Increase water or increase alkali addition |

By kind permission of the British Ceramic Research Association

plastic clay. The normal industrial slip is composed of ball clay, china clay, feldspar or stone, and flint. (See *body*.)

The percentage of deflocculant will vary with the type of slip from 0.5-1.5% of the dry weight. Most merchants list casting-slips and recipes. Some clays will not deflocculate. As a batch of casting-slip is used and re-used, plaster from the molds will reverse the action so that more alkali will be needed to maintain fluidity. Eventually the slip must be discarded. Non-electrolyte deflocculants are being developed.

## CATENARY ARCH

*The natural fall of a necklace forms a catenary curve!*

If a length of chain or rope is allowed to hang free between two level points it assumes a catenary curve. This curve, reversed, can be used as the basis for a very stable arched kiln. Rhodes (R.K) recommends that the height and width be nearly equal—'it is a beautiful structure'.

## CAUSTIC, caustic soda

The burning or eroding effect of certain substances, notably the *alkalis*. Water in which plant ash has been steeped will be *caustic*. Caustic soda is sodium hydroxide, NaOH.

## CELADON, celedon

The general name given to a *solution color* range of subtle green to blue-gray stoneware and porcelain glazes, deriving from iron in reduction. The name is said to originate, somewhat inconsequentially, from a character in French classical drama who wore green clothes.

The Yueh wares of China, dating back to early Han, were the forebears of the later and very fine Sung celadons (960-1260 A.D.) where its quality was likened to jade. The color is shown to greatest advantage on porcelain or pale bodied stonewares, although it can also produce a rich olive on darker bodies.

From 0.5 to 2.0% of ferric iron is added to a transparent glaze, which should be applied fairly generously to obtain the depth and richness of color and to maintain the iron in the ferrous state during cooling. (See *reduction*.) A particular quality of slight opacity in a

41

celadon is due to minute bubbles in the glaze. Cardew suggests a viscous glaze with an RO of 0.25-0.45 kNaO and 0.55-0.75 CaO, with very little magnesia. This may eliminate some wood ashes from which the early celadons are thought to derive. Rhodes mentions a little bone ash to provide *opalescence*. A series of recipes is given in L.PB 166-7, which include ochre (up to 9%) as all or part of the iron content, also $Fe_3O_4$ (black iron) instead of ferric.

In PQ 17 A. Lewis-Evans quotes the (now obsolete) Seger cone 3 formula

$$K_2O \quad 0.3 \qquad Al_2O_3 \quad 0.45$$
$$CaO \quad 0.7 \qquad Fe_2O_3 \quad 0.05 \qquad SiO_2 \; 4.0$$

which he translates into:

| | |
|---|---|
| China clay | 7.5 |
| Potash feldspar | 45.0 |
| Whiting | 17.5 |
| Quartz | 27.5 |
| Ferric iron | 2.5 |

## CELSIUS

The internationally approved name for the Centigrade scale. Luckily the sign °C. can stand for either.

## CEMENT

Any adhesive material which hardens as it dries, and particularly the large family of heat-treated mixtures of limestone, clay, bauxite etc. These provide various grades of hydrated cements which set and gain strength when mixed with water. True refractory cements harden only as a result of ceramic alteration at high temperatures.

The ubiquitous Portland cement will explode or melt if strongly heated, but high-alumina cements such as Ciment Fondu, Lumnite etc., can be cast with suitable *aggregates* into kiln bricks, element wire holders, etc. for firing up to 1320°C. Morgans and Gibbons (England) make refractory jointing cements. Keene's Cement is a hard setting *gypsum* plaster. (See also *air-setting cement*, and *mortar*.)

## CENTIGRADE SCALE

A temperature recording scale in which the interval between the freezing and boiling points of water is divided into 100 degrees. The symbol °C. also refers to the Celsius scale which is now the approved international scale, though seldom referred to outside the laboratory. It is, for most practical purposes, similar to Centigrade. (See *temperature degrees*, and *temperature conversion*.)

## CENTERING

Pressure applied to a ball of clay on the wheel as it spins, to persuade the whole mass to run true. Potters develop their own methods, but a steady pressure in one horizontal direction, either thrusting or pulling, is the basis of the action, with a secondary downwards thrust to maintain a roughly semi-circular mass. *Coning* is an associated but separate action.

Pots are also centered on a throwing wheel or

*whirler* for turning, banding and other work. Wheel heads are usually marked with concentric rings to simplify centering, but it can also be accomplished by a series of rapid taps on one side of the pot as it spins, a knack requiring practice.

1

2

3

4

*Centering by sideways pressure with the left hand, the right hand holding the mass down (1). The mass is centered by a pull with the right hand towards the potter's body (2). (See also coning.) The last two photographs (3, 4) show Isaac Button at the commencement of throwing. Centering merges into throwing and it is difficult to decide where one finishes and the other begins. (See film 'Isaac Button, Country Potter'; also annular centering.)*

## CERAMIC

Derived from the Greek *keramos*, 'burnt stuff', or 'an earthen vessel'. This suggests pronunciation with a hard 'c', but the soft 's' is popularly used, especially in the USA.

The term has now so wide an application as to have lost much of its meaning. Not only is it applied to the silicate industries but also to 'articles or coatings from essentially inorganic and non-metallic materials made permanent by heat—at temperatures sufficient to cause sintering—or conversion wholly or partly to the glassy state' (from the US definition, 1963). The net is now cast even wider to include cements and enameling on metal.

## CERAMIC FIBERS, filament

*A piece of ceramic fiber 'blanket' suitable for the outer insulation of kilns.*

A mass of thread-like crystals, known also as 'filaments' or 'whiskers', derived from *fused silica* or potassium titanate. Used as lightweight insulating material resembling felt. Highly efficient but more expensive than traditional heat insulators. More refractory than glass-wool (fiberglass). Fibrax and Ceafibre are trade names.

## CERAMIC SCULPTURE

A term generally applied to those ceramics which are not used as pots, or where form, invention, and decoration are the sole consideration. It occupies the attention of an increasing number of potters today but detailed discussion is outside the scope of this dictionary.

## CERMETS

Material containing both ceramic and metals. Can replace silica for *thermocouple* sheaths.

## CHALK

A soft white earthy limestone, $CaCO_3$. Ground and levigated into *whiting*. Formed from the shells of minute marine organisms. Deposits in England up to 2000 ft. (about 660 m.) thick.

Blackboard chalk is made from calcium sulphate, $CaSO_4$. (See also *plaster of paris*.)

## CHAMBERED KILN

Generally applied to the climbing kilns of the Orient, e.g. Hamada's at Mashiko (see R.K). In the West, semi-continuous brick kilns have twelve or more chambers (see *reverbatory*). Two-chambered kilns are quite common in studio potters' workshops, the second sometimes used for biscuit, or for oxidation. (See also *climbing kilns*.)

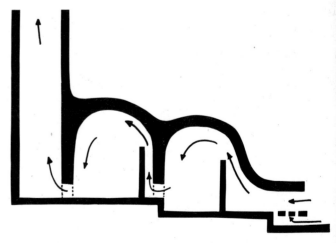

*A two-chambered kiln of a type often used by craft potters. Sometimes the bag walls are built of saggars at each setting. The second chamber may be used for biscuit or for oxidized firing. Occasionally the chimney may be used for biscuit.*

43

## CHAMOIS

A very soft and pliable leather, unrivalled for smoothing the rims of pots on the wheel. Unfortunately it soon becomes clay colored and not infrequently it is lost in the slurry to turn up later in a pot! An attached tab will help to avoid this.

## CHAMOTTE

A term found in Scandinavian and European books on pottery to denote a heavily grogged stoneware, often unglazed. It can also refer to the refractory *grog* itself. Also used in the USA. Watts, Blake list a chamotte body.

## CHARCOAL

Vegetable or animal substance heated with the exclusion of air. Impure carbons (See also *reduction*.)

## CHATTER

Corrugation of the surface of clay which can develop quite suddenly during turning. The turning-tool will begin to vibrate. A slack hold, clay which is too hard (or, occasionally, too soft), too sharp a tool, and uneven texture or hardness of clay, can all contribute to chatter.

To cure, continue turning with the long edge of the tool or a *steel palette*, held at an acute angle to the corrugations so that it rides across the tops and cannot fall into the dips. As soon as the surface is smooth again, revert to the normal position.

*Showing the position of the turning tool to cure chatter—see the corrugated surface.*

## CHEESE-HARD

Term sometimes used as a synonym for *leather-hard*.

## CHEMICALLY-COMBINED WATER

The water of hydration. Specifically, in clay, the $H_2O$ which is expelled at 500-600°C., altering the molecular pattern and forming a new material. The process cannot be reversed. Distinct from *absorbed* and *adsorbed* water. L.PB refers to it as 'hygroscopic' water.

## CHEMISTRY OF POTTERY

The early potters worked miracles of clay and glaze compounding and firing without true chemical knowledge, but their time scale was in generations while ours is in years. An ability to think in terms other than those of pure day-to-day experience has become essential. Simple chemistry and an outline of the current explanation of the behavior of atomic particles can short-cut many a tedious trial series and will help to explain and control results. On the other hand it is always what happens to your glaze in your kiln that matters.

One problem in presenting the subject of chemistry is that extreme simplicity can be misleading, the actual changes and reactions being complex. However, since the whole story is not known even to the specialist scientist, a general framework will be valid for most practical purposes. 'A complete chart of information . . . would probably be out of date before we had learned to read it' (Cardew). Chemistry should be seen as one of many valuable sources of information.

The raw materials of our world are legion. Their names tell us little about their make-up or properties. This endless diversity can be greatly simplified in chemical terms. All physical materials are combinations of a mere one hundred or so unique and separate parts called the *elements*. Potters use some twenty of these regularly, and another twenty occasionally. The field is thus dramatically reduced. The elements sometimes exist alone e.g. as the metal 'iron' or the element carbon as 'charcoal', but more often in combinations of two or more. These compounds are more than mere mixtures: they will rarely resemble in appearance or in general behavior any of the constituent elements. To take an extreme instance: the dangerously unstable metal sodium, in combination with chlorine, a poisonous gas, forms the harmless and useful sodium chloride—table salt.

It is possible, therefore, to describe materials by listing the elements which make them up. These can be written out in full but are generally noted as abbreviations or symbols. A list of the elements relevant to ceramics will be found under *elements* and *atomic weights*. The element symbols are international.

The commonest simple compound in *inorganic* chemistry is between an element and oxygen (another element. The result is called the *oxide* of the element e.g. iron oxide, silica (oxide of silicon). Elements form oxides under the influence of heat: the science of ceramics is, therefore, the study of reactions between oxides at high temperatures. Once compounds have formed they can be separated only by other chemical reactions or by the application of energy such as heat. Firing is essentially the rearranging of existing compounds e.g. clay, and the formation of new compounds from mixed materials e.g. glaze.

Oxides can be listed in three groups: the *bases*, the *acids*, and the *amphoterics*. In ceramics, the first group has a fluxing action i.e. it lowers melting points; the second comprises the *glass-formers* and is usually considered as refractory—it raises melting points; the third group has an intermediate balancing and uniting role. This rather crude view of the three groups is open to criticism, but will be found generally valid in practice. To decide the proportional amounts which enter into combination to produce a desired result e.g. an earthenware glaze or a porcelain body, we must enter at least the fringe of atomic and molecular science. (See also *atomic theory*.)

Atoms combine into compounds in certain fixed proportions. This proportion is indicated in the symbol by a number written after and below the element. For example: in silica the silicon, symbol Si, and the oxygen, symbol O, combine in the proportion of one to two. This is written $SiO_2$. The reverse is true when sodium, Na, combines with oxygen giving $Na_2O$. Ferric iron combines 2:3 i.e. $Fe_2O_3$. These proportions can be taken to apply to the atoms (the smallest particle of an element), the actual material being a repeat pattern of connected atoms in infinite extension. (See also *molecule, network, crystal, valency.*)

A mineral will often contain several oxides. Its chemical symbol will always be made up of the constituent elements and their atomic parts, but these can be arranged in several ways. The most obvious is to note each element and its proportion: for instance, potash feldspar, $K_2Al_2Si_6O_{16}$. This is, however, of little practical use for obtaining a general picture of the mineral or guessing at its probable behavior in the kiln. A more practical grouping, and that normally used by potters, would be $K_2O.Al_2O_3.6SiO_2$. It will be seen that, instead of writing $SiO_2$ six times, the number 6 has been placed before it. This grouping corresponds to the *Seger formula* and the base, amphoteric, acid divisions mentioned above. The mineral has six times as many molecules of acid oxide as it has of basic: we can therefore guess that it would make a glaze but only at stoneware temperatures—1250°C. and above, and this in fact is the case. (See *Seger formula, base, acid* etc. for further discussion.)

The letter R does not occur in the list of element symbols. It can be used to indicate any element in combination with oxygen. Thus $R_2O_3$ includes any compound which unites in a 2:3 ratio. The whole of the bases in a glaze formula may be denoted by RO in order to compare them with the amount of acid. All these symbols denote molecular parts and must be multiplied by their molecular weight to translate them into weighable materials. (See *formula-into-recipe.*)

For convenience, *minerals* are symbolized by their 'ideal' formula, i.e. as if they were quite pure, un-adulterated materials. This seldom occurs in nature but rocks are selected to have the nearest approximation. The perfect mineral may be given a separate name. For instance, pure clay material—$Al_2O_3.2SiO_2.2H_2O$ —is 'kaolinite'. For practical computation, china clay may be considered as kaolinite although it has some 2% of impurities. Similarly potash feldspar has the ideal formula as listed above, but the base is nearly always a mixture of potash and soda with very small

amounts of other materials, and is sometimes denoted as NaKO. Luckily the two alkalis act in a fairly similar way. An *analysis* will show how far the sample strays from the pure mineral.

## CHIMNEY

A vertical shaft of brick, metal or asbestos. A warm, rising column of air exerts a 'pull', drawing air and gases in from the base of the shaft. Different types of kiln require widely differing sizes of chimney. An electric kiln needs none at all; gas kilns often require only minimal chimneys; oil, wood, and coal need increasing size and height. An up-draft kiln forms its own chimney, and little if any extension is required at the top. The down-draft type obviously needs sufficient pull to force the hot gases to travel downwards through the chamber against their natural inclinations. As a rough guide, for solid fuel kilns, every 30 cm. (1 ft.) of downward draft and every 120 cm. (4 ft.) of horizontal movement needs one metre (say 3 ft.) of chimney height.

A long narrow chimney will exert more pull than a short wide one, but the expansion rate of gases must be taken into account. However the movement of gases through the kiln can be maintained by forced draft at the firemouth or a fan in the chimney, thereby cutting the chimney height to a minimum.

## CHINA

In England the term officially refers to *bone china*. Its wider use in the USA, and common usage elsewhere, covers any domestic vitreous whiteware. The Brussels Nomenclature equates it with *porcelain*.

## CHINA CLAY, kaolin

A general name for an almost pure clay material containing, on average, 98% kaolinite, $Al_2O_3.2SiO_2.2H_2O$, 258. A *primary clay*. Found in comparatively few areas: in great quantities in Cornwall, England; in the USA (Florida, Carolina); and elsewhere. Usually very white, though iron-stained kaolins are found. Of the millions of tons annually only about one-fifth is absorbed by ceramics. It is usually 'won' by washing from the rock face with high-pressure hoses, the resultant slurry carried along channels to settling troughs. The *micaceous* matter is separated out—this eventually forms the 'white mountains' of the St. Austell district of England.

Because of its large particle size its plasticity is poor. Some samples are more workable than others: Chinese kaolin being probably the most plastic and the Cornish clay the least. China clay is used in many bodies to increase whiteness and *refractoriness* and to vary the particle size of secondary clays. Industrial bodies may contain 30% or more; porcelains, 50%. In glazes it represents pure *kaolinite*. The term kaolin is often used as a synonym for china clay, but this is deprecated by some authorities. Calcined china clay is used as an 'opener' in bodies and to minimize wet-dry shrinkage. (See also *kaolinite, clay.*)

## CHINA STONE

A feldspathic mineral with the general formula of $NaK_2O.Al_2O_3.8SiO_2$, 644, but variable with an RO which may also include 0.30 equivalents of lime. Also known as pegmatite, Cornwall stone, Cornish stone, or, simply, stone. Godfrey spar from the USA is a similar material, as is *Manx stone*.

An analysis (Wengers): by weight

| | | | |
|---|---|---|---|
| $Na_2O$ 4.0 | $Al_2O_3$ 14.93 | $SiO_2$ 72.9 |
| $K_2O$ 3.81 | $Fe_2O_3$ 0.13 | $TiO_2$ 0.02 |
| CaO 2.06 | | |
| MgO 0.09 | | |

This is an analysis of a 'de-florinated' china stone. Raw stone often contains fluorine and is purple colored. There are 'hard' and 'soft' white grades (referring to *fusibility*) in which the alteration to kaolin and secondary mica is more advanced (D.DC).

Stone will form a glaze between 1300-1400°C. It is used in bodies and glazes to provide some soda. Also used as a dilutant for cobalt.

## CHITTERING

Glaze flaking, especially on rims. (See *shivering*.)

## CHROMATE OF IRON

See *iron chromate*.

## CHROME

Chromic oxide $Cr_2O_3$, 152. See *chromium*.

## CHROME-TIN PINK

An earthenware pottery pigment used for *underglaze* painting and as a *stain*. Used in the eighteenth century and originally called English pink. A reaction between tin, chrome and lime. 'The precipitation of fine particles of chromic oxide on the surface of tin oxide in an opaque glaze' (Dodd). The color does not often blend happily with craft pottery. It can be developed by accident in a firing in which the necessary ingredients are present, usually with lead glazes but also possible in stoneware.

## CHROMIUM, oxide, compounds

A metallic element Cr, 52.
Chromic oxide $Cr_2O_3$, 152, m.p. 2270°C.
Chromate of potash $K_2Cr_2O_7$, 294.

The green oxide of chrome is the form most used by potters. Although refractory it is also *volatile* over 1000°C. and can cause pink reactions. 'The potassium form is used in glazes and fritts' (B.TP).

The oxide is a very versatile coloring agent, especially at low temperatures. In a high-lead, low-alumina glaze, 1-2% can give red or orange at 900°C.; with lead and soda, a bright yellow. At more practical temperatures chrome yields dullish greens in a lead glaze and browns with zinc oxide. Colors are apt to be rather heavy and flat, and are always opaque. Cardew suggests the addition of *fluorspar* for a clearer color in

reduction up to 1320°C. The green may be spoiled by the presence of tin oxide. A brighter, lighter green can result from a high lime glaze (S.SCP). Lithium carbonate (6-8%), in a soft lead glaze with chrome, has also been mentioned. A small quantity (0.25-1.0%) with cobalt is reputed to give good colors in reduction.

Chrome, with tin and calcium, and especially in *lead glazes,* can develop pinks and browns which are not always attractive. This reaction is the basis for many prepared pinks—known as chrome-tin pinks. Chrome is a favorite addition to many prepared stains and colors, especially dark ones; its opacity, refractoriness and low solubility make it valuable as a stabilizer. Chrome-magnesium ores are made into specialist refractories.

## CHUCK

As applied to throwing, a chuck is a ring or block of clay for supporting a pot or bowl on the wheel head while turning, or for secondary throwing (see *amphora*).

A chuck of stiff clay inside an inverted bowl or pot is preferable to dabs of clay round the outside. The piece can be removed to check thickness etc., and is held true during the work. A chuck can be cut for the largest piece to be turned and pared down progressively smaller for the rest, or a stock of leather-hard chucks can be made and kept in condition in polythene.

*Method.* Stiff clay is beaten out to a flat block on a dampened wheel head and the piece to be turned pressed gently onto it, making a mark which will indicate its width. The block is then cut to fit with a pointed *turning tool*. Billington (B.TP illus. 71) shows bowls supported above the wheel head, but it is easier to maintain the same plane between rim and foot ring if the former is hard down, though this necessitates a precisely fitting chuck. (See also *turning*.)

A hollow chuck for supporting tall pots is usually in the form of a diabolo. It may be thrown and wrapped in polythene when leather-hard, or else biscuited prior to use. Biscuit chucks should be soaked in water before use. Cup heads can also be utilized.

*A beaten out slab chuck on a wheel head has been cut to receive the bowl for turning.*

## CHUN GLAZES

A type *of opalescent* Chinese glaze which has fascinated many craft potters. It has a milky bluish tinge but does not contain pigment oxides, the color arising from suspended globules of 'glass in glass' (Cardew) known as 'optical' color. (See *color*.) Phosphorus, usually derived from wood-ashes, is probably a necessary ingredient. The glaze is unaffected by kiln atmosphere except that the body color will show through to a degree and will influence that of the glaze. C.PP (pp. 142-3) deals at some length with Chun glazes. He recommends a thick application over a darkish body or even a temmoku. Talc is a useful addition. The 'Chun' effect can also result from suspended particles e.g. of dicalcium silicate which may precipitate in the molten glaze, or from minute bubbles of gas.

## CIRCUIT, electrical

The complete path travelled by an electric current (U.DS). An unbroken length of *conductor* between two terminals.

The wiring in a kiln will usually be split into several circuits, each one carrying a certain current (in amperes) and exerting a certain resistance (in *ohms*).

If a circuit does not embody apparatus which exerts resistance, unlimited current will flow—it will be short-circuited or 'shorted'. A weak link of easily melted wire—a 'fuse'—is put into all circuits to guard against this eventuality.

*A single circuit, the current flowing from live to neutral through a length of resistance wire which is connected as a series of elements as in an electric kiln. Other circuits can be taken from the mains connections at full voltage (see diagram under single phase and parallel wiring).*

## CLAMMING

The sealing of a kiln door and, after firing, the hearths, with coarse *slurry*.

## CLAMP

A heap of bricks or, in primitive firings, pots, either covered with brushwood or other fuel, or built to allow fires within the clamp. In a simple brick clamp only about 50% of the bricks are adequately fired. (See C.PP, Appendix 3.)

## CLAMP KILN

A firing method similar to *bonfire*. A shallow pit is dug and lined with wood or brushwood which is set alight. On to the glowing embers bone dry pots are set and more fuel is laid over them. Turves are finally laid over the whole area and the 'kiln' is left for 24 hours before being unpacked. Pre-heating of the pots to the *water-smoking* stage is advisable.

## CLAY

The 'ideal' clay material is *kaolinite*, $Al_2O_3.2SiO_2.2H_2O$, 258. This never occurs pure in nature. China clay averages 98% kaolinite.

Clay is the result of the decomposition of granite and igneous rocks. The alkalis are leached out; quartz, mica and clay remain. 'Primary' clay is found on the site of its formation and is therefore purer, whiter, but less weathered and plastic than are 'secondary' clays. The latter have been moved by glacial and rock-folding action (boulder clays), by water (alluvial, *estuarine*, fluvine, *lacustrine*), or by wind. The weathering and general battering they have received, together with natural *levigation*, have reduced the particle size with a corresponding increase in plasticity. Secondary clays have also picked up 'impurities' which lower their melting point, increase drying and firing shrinkage, and darken color. They occur very widely and are infinitely variable, but can be grouped, broadly, in order of refractoriness:

1  *Fireclays:* up to 1500°C.
   Associated with coal seams. Often black and compressed (see *shale*). Some free silica. Often high in alumina and low in alkalis. Fire cream to gray. Often excellent plasticity.
2  *'Stoneware' clays:* to 1350°C.
   Any plastic and reasonably refractory pale firing clay.
3  *Siliceous ball clay:* to 1300°C. *Ball clay:* to 1250°C.
   *Sedimentary clays* of very fine grain, which is an important factor in their *fusibility*, high plasticity, and comparatively high shrinkage. They fire ivory. Used in association with other clays.
4  *Red clays:* to 1100°C. (1250°C.)
   Plastic, very fusible, fire brown. Earthenware, slip-ware, *terracotta*, bricks, etc. A few stand the lower stoneware temperatures. Very variable. High in iron. Some so fusible that they will form a glaze at 1280°C. e.g. *Albany clay*.
5  *Other*
   Various minor deposits such as *pipeclay*. Also the widely distributed *marls* and 'loams'. Very contaminated surface clays have too high a shrinkage to be useful, though they can sometimes serve as an iron pigment.

Between the types listed there are many graduations. There are untypical examples within the categories, such as the Yorkshire potter Isaac Button's red clay, the melting point of which was reputed to be above 1400°C.

While most clays are derived from granite, similar minerals have formed from diorite, *volcanic ash*, basalt and other rocks. These include the *montmorillinite (bentonite)* group which is so fine and sticky (colloidal) as to be useless as a workable clay except in small additions to kaolinite bodies. There are also *illite* minerals.

*A clay seam.*

The structure of clay is lamellar (flat scales). In simplified terms, the electrical cohesion between the 'sheets' is sufficient to maintain the mass of a clay in any given shape, but can be momentarily disturbed by pressure. The scales, in effect, can slide over one another, lubricated by the molecular-thin layer of water between them. On the release of pressure the form-holding qualities are restored. The lamellar hypothesis assumes that other rock minerals, no matter how finely ground, will have no plasticity and this is true in practice. This unique quality is known as thixotropy. Other virtues we look for in a good potters' clay are a low water absorption, and standing strength. In montmorillinites the link or bond between plates is weaker and up to four 'thicknesses' of water molecules can penetrate. (See C.PP 18-32.) Substitution can also take place: iron and alkalis for alumina, for instance (base exchange), lowering refractoriness, darkening the color, and resulting in very variable compositions. Some bentonites swell when wetted.

In important recent research into montmorillinites and illite, some experts are beginning to think of plastic clays as mixtures of these minerals with *kaolinite*.

## CLAY TESTING

Any new clay, whether purchased or 'found' (see *clay winning*) will have its own distinctive qualities and vices. 'You cannot know too much about your subtle and elusive raw material . . . any clay must be deemed guilty until it is proved innocent' (Cardew).

Some simple tests can be made which will build up to an overall picture of the clay you are dealing with:

1 Free lime. A pellet of clay dropped into dilute hydrochloric acid will effervesce if lime is present.

2 Soluble alkalis, or lime, will cause staining or a whitish scumming on the surface of a dried or fired example.

3 Plasticity. A $\frac{1}{2}$ in. (12 mm.) coil rolled out and bent round a 1 in. (25 mm.) rod (a broomstick) should not crack unduly. A pinchpot is a fairly stern test. Try throwing. Newly prepared clay should be given at least a week's rest in a damp atmosphere (wrapped in polythene) before plasticity tests are made.

4 Shrinkage. Roll out and cut a strip of plastic clay to 10 in. (or 250 mm.) long. An engraved ruler can be pressed into the clay to leave an accurate mark of length. Measure again when dry (keep the strip flat). If it has shrunk to less than 9 in. (or 225 mm.) the clay is not likely to be very useful. Test also for dry strength at this stage.

5 Inspect dried samples for cracks or other faults.

6 Fire samples of pots and measured strips, preferably, at first, to about 900°C. If this biscuit is free from faults, try again at higher temperatures until it shows signs of *vitrification* and/or collapse. If a strip is supported at the ends only, the sag during firing will be an indication of pyroplastic *deformation* and *refractoriness*. Check the measured strip for firing shrinkage and compare with a known clay at the same temperature.

7 If you now have a biscuit sample of 'won' clay which is neither too dark nor faulted (cracks, bloats etc.) at 1000°C. then you are lucky and can go on to try the clay on the wheel for standing-strength and water-absorption.

8 Finally, try the clay with slip and glaze.

More elaborate trials establishing particles size etc. are described in C.PP 255-8. (See also *shrinkage, porosity, water of plasticity*.)

A clay may fail on its own but still be a useful addition to other bodies, or its vices may be minimized by additions of flint, china clay, sand or grog. (See also *body*.) 2% of barium carbonate will cure lime scumming.

## CLAY WINNING

Or clay getting. The practical work of finding and extracting clays. Books on geology are generally disappointing in their references to clay. Details of the younger sedimentary rocks, where useful material may be found, are sparse. Layers and deposits of clay may be revealed by deep cut river-beds or roads; records of old potteries are valuable, as is local soil knowledge and 'folk memory'. In some regions geological surveys have been made which are available on application to the appropriate authority. White clays found outside the recognized areas are usually in small pockets, are often unplastic and sandy, and may be contaminated with lime ('pipeclays' etc.). Surface clay topped by soil will be stained with organic matter to a depth of one to two feet. Hill clays which may once have been buried much deeper may be more rewarding. Soil Hill Pottery, on the Yorkshire moors, had a fine red clay topped by a buff slip clay further up the hill, and a refractory clay at the top—all on a single slope of about 400 yards. What you are least likely to find is a workable pale stoneware clay, and that is what most of us want.

Commercially, clay is dug from a pit, mined, or washed from the surface with high-pressure hoses. Seams and deposits are under continuous scrutiny and analysis.

Clay getting is exciting, if not always rewarding. Sticky garden clay is usually too contaminated for practical use other than as a pigment where it can be considered as an impure iron oxide. Local brickworks may guide you to clay. Few 'local' clays will take a glaze and many will *slag* above 1000°C., but for educational purposes (your own education as well as the children's) the work is of value and the material can be used in sawdust or other simple firings.

*Method.* Dig a pound or two of clay from various parts of your 'seam'. Immerse it in buckets of water and leave to soak. The way that it breaks in the water will give some idea as to whether it is sandy and *short,* or sticky and cohesive. Stir and skim off any floating matter. Heavy, coarse materials will sink and the clay slip can then be poured off. Pass through a cooking sieve and then a 60 lawn. One can see how much is left in the sieves and whether enough slip has gone through to make worthwhile the work of extracting it. Dry the slip to a plastic state. The sample can then be subjected to the tests listed under *clay tests.* A very pure-looking sample can be tried in the dug state. Try the slip also for slipware, and as a pigment especially on stoneware.

## CLIMBING KILNS

Many-chambered Oriental semi-down-draft kilns built on a hillside or on an artificial slope. The heat is drawn from one chamber to the next which is, in turn, side-stoked with wood until the required temperature is reached. Rhodes calls it a 'near perfect design'. Kilns may be 200 ft. long (60 m.) and 10 ft. (3 m.) high. (See also *chambered kilns* and *bank kilns.*) R.K. contains many illustrations.

## COAL

Ancient underground carbon deposits formed by the decomposition of vegetable matter over many millions of years. Peat, lignite, household bituminous coal and anthracite are the main types. Most of the *bottle kilns* in Stoke-on-Trent, England, were fired with coal up to the late nineteen-fifties. High quality coal was required and was available nearby. A 9 x 9 ft. (3 x 3 m.) setting space would take about 4 tons (4000 kg.).

Coal is not very suitable for small kilns. It needs a generous grate and a high chimney. Nevertheless Geoffrey Whiting (England) fired a coal kiln until 1970. It had two chambers. The final temperature of around 1300°C. was achieved with wood. (See the film *Geoffrey Whiting, craftsman potter.*) Coal lies between oil and wood for optimum efficiency per lb. of fuel at around 12,000 Btu or 12.600 kJ.

## COAL ASH

See *ash.*

## COAL GAS

See *gas.*

## COBALT, oxides

A metallic element Co, 59.
Black oxide $Co_3O_4$, 241. Equivalent weight 80.3.
Gray prepared oxide CoO, 75.
Carbonate $CoCO_3$, 119.

All oxide forms give stable blues at all pottery temperatures. The hue can be modified by the alumina/silica balance of the glaze and by other additions. (See also *blue pigments* and *stains.*) A cobalt aluminate is also quoted by Dodd as a stable color. Cobalt reactions are very complicated.

The blue from cobalt is strong and insistent. 'A few of the blues were overdone and the cobalt, in its horrible purple intensity, had triumphed over the iron' (Leach L.PB). This intensity can be subdued by using red clay, iron oxides and manganese as dilutants. This dilution is especially important for painting on stoneware. Leach uses 98 raw ochre to 2 cobalt. Boiled green tea is used as a vehicle for cobalt in Japan; the tannin is reputed to prevent spread under the glaze.

Its stability has made cobalt a favorite pigment on majolica where it was often used to outline more fugitive colors, and on porcelain—the ubiquitous 'blue and white'. It can be diluted with china stone when used thinly as a wash. Talc will also diminish its stridency. Excess cobalt will separate out during firing, causing 'ironing', a rusty surface which is, however, not always unpleasant on stoneware. In soft glazes cobalt can be *fritted* with alumina etc. to produce various tones (see *blue*), but in stoneware it tends to revert to the purplish-blue silicate.

Owing to its high melting point cobalt is difficult to 'fix' on biscuit. China stone, a fritt, or a little clay can be mixed with the pigment. In zinc glazes cobalt can produce a purple-blue or a green; with magnesia, pink. In a glaze it acts as a weak *base.* (See also the ore of cobalt, *asbolite,* and *smalt.*)

## COEFFICIENTS OF EXPANSION

Materials expand upon heating at a steady and progressive rate. There is a similar contraction on cooling. The rate varies between materials, and the various degrees of expansion have been worked out as a coefficient based upon expansion per unit length per degree Centigrade and, conversely, its contraction during cooling. It is the latter which is of primary interest to potters because it affects glaze-fit. Knowledge of the coefficients is also essential in preparing bodies for ovenware and fireproof ware.

There is some disagreement in the figures usually quoted for reversible linear thermal expansions of the various oxides and compounds. Also, since the expansion is a continuing process, it is usually given as a figure for a certain range e.g. 100-1000°C. This is a

| (All figures to power of $10^{-6}$) | Oxide | English and Turner | Winkelmann and Scott | Whole number average |
|---|---|---|---|---|
| Highest expansion and contraction | Soda | 41.6 | 33.3 | 37 |
| | Potash | 39.0 | 28.3 | 33 |
| Medium | Calcia (lime) | 16.3 | 16.6 | 16 |
| | Baria | 14.0 | 10.0 | 12 |
| | Titania | — | — | — |
| | Lead oxide | 10.6 | 10.0 | 10 |
| | Antimony | — | — | — |
| | Alumina | 1.4 | 17.0 | 9 |
| Lowest | Lithia | — | — | — |
| | Magnesia | 4.5 | 0.4 | 2 |
| | Zirconia | 2.3 | — | 2 |
| | Tin oxide | — | — | — |
| | Silica | 0.5 | 2.7 | 1 |
| (Negative expansion up to 10% of glaze material only) | Boric oxide | −6.5 | 0.33 | −3 |

useful range for glazes which all harden on cooling between 800-500°C. As mentioned above, there is need for more expert research on the coefficients. The tables generally available are those of English and Turner, and Winkelmann and Scott. The marked disagreements are for the values of alumina, silica, and boric oxide. We can strike a balance, but the figures should be considered as qualitative rather than literal. The progression from high to low values is borne out in practice and can be considered reliable.

It will be seen that *body* constituents have lower coefficients than have the glaze *bases*. Hence one of the causes of crazing, as the glaze contracts more than the clay. The negative expansion (i.e. expansion on cooling) of boric oxide is one reason for its wide use on earthenware. The physical meaning of the figures above is that they indicate the percentage expansion to the power of $10^{-6}$, i.e. to six places of decimals. Potash thus expands 0.000033% each degree Centigrade of heat rise.

The final computation is always complicated by *quartz 'inversion'* which, in effect, puts silica higher in the list and so eases matters for the potter. Also the reversible expansions we have been considering should not be confused with the changes in size which occur in ceramic materials, clay especially, due to *sintering* and *vitrification,* and which are non-reversible. (See *shrinkage.*) These do not greatly effect glaze-fit.

Coefficients are additive and one can get an overall value of a glaze by the following computation:
1   Multiply the analysis figure of each oxide by the coefficient.
2   Total the answers.
3   Divide the total by 100.

(For expansion of gases see *absolute temperature* scale.)

## COILING

An age-old technique of building pots by laying coils or ropes of clay one upon another and working them together. Until recently pots in which three or four people could stand were coiled in Cyprus. Built to hold wine they were also affectionately known as 'honeymoon pots'.

Pots can be coiled, after a little practice, to a size which it would take many years to learn to throw. Coiled pots have their own character and should not be looked upon as a stage on the way to throwing. Large models and asymmetric forms can be made only by coiling.

Rolling the coil is perhaps the most difficult part of the operation. I have found the following advice useful in teaching:
1   Use reasonably soft clay.
2   Give yourself plenty of room to work in.
3   Cut your clay from a block with wire and work it into a rough thick coil before starting to roll.
4   Use long, even movements from the shoulders. Hold the hands flat and the fingers together.
5   Use the whole length of your hand.
6   Start with the hands close together and move them apart as the coil lengthens. Inspect the ends of the coil occasionally to see that you are not forming macaroni!
7   Needless to say, the working surface must be clean, smooth and dry.

Rosemary Wren uses a special coil for her large models. It resembles a stubby inverted T in section and speeds up the building, while the wide base gives plenty of clay to work downwards, maintaining a wall of even thickness. The coil is first rolled and then worked into shape with the finger and thumb.

The lazier potter will extrude coils from a wad mill. In most countries where coiling is a traditional craft coils are rolled vertically between the two palms. (See film LK.)

*Method.* There is no point in coiling the base of a pot. This can be a flat, beaten-out, circular slab of clay. Cut a piece of paper to stick underneath so that the base will not stick to the working surface. When building the coils, make a complete ring for each layer:

it is much more difficult to control the form if the coils are spiralled. Cut or nip the ends to a wedge shape so that they can be overlapped. Do not wet or slip the surfaces. Coiling is the one exception to the rule that joins must be moistened. The first few coils will take all the weight, so make them fairly sturdy and work the base coil well into the base slab. Always join downwards from the latest coil to the wall already built, using the ball of the thumb to drag a little of the coil clay downwards, inside and out. If the form is widened too soon or too suddenly the whole thing is likely to heel over or collapse.

Coiling can be treated as a preliminary to pinching, stroking, or even throwing, and can be added to molded dishes. One must always take care, however, not to produce a characterless hybrid. Various illustrations in this book show coiling as an auxiliary technique. *Saggars* can be coiled. (See *formers, hand building*.)

A Cypriot potter rolling coils vertically. Note also the large cone of clay beside her from which she scoops the clay for each coil.

Fine coiled pots just unpacked from an up-draft wood kiln at one of the few surviving traditional potteries at Kornos in Cyprus.

Starting a coiled pot. The cut-out base and the first coil in process of being rubbed in (1). The wall is built up by stroking each coil into the wall beneath it (2).

Mass produced coiled pots! A corner of the storeroom attached to the Kornos (Cyprus) pottery. Each of the jugs is about 12 in. (300 mm.) diameter.

*A powerful coiled form by Ruth Duckworth.*

## COKE

A by-product of the process of burning coal for gas, now becoming scarce, in England at any rate. As a fuel it gives a glowing radiant heat rather than a long flame, and is therefore more efficient as a contact fuel. (See *brazier kiln*.) Less air is needed for combustion than with coal or wood. Producer-gas kilns have been designed which drip water onto hot coke.

## COLEMANITE

A naturally occurring calcium borate, $2CaO.3B_2O_3.5H_2O$, 412. Convenient formula weight 206, giving $1CaO:1.5B_2O_3$ in the melt. Found in Nevada and California. *Gerstley borate* is a colemanite. Only slightly soluble.

A powerful flux for most glazes. In earthenware it can be used to introduce some boric oxide in a relatively insoluble form (though it can cause a glaze to thicken or flocculate). More than 10% is likely to cause crawling. The boron content can develop opalescence in a glaze and, according to Rhodes, a broken mottled color, especially with rutile.

## COLLARING

Reducing the size of the neck of a pot on the wheel by encircling it with the thumb, index finger, and crooked second finger of each hand spread out, and exerting an inward and upward pressure. Another position, which helps to prevent buckling, is to hold the index finger of one hand inside the rim. Increase the wheel speed as the circumference gets shorter.

*Collaring a large cider jar.*

## COLLOIDS

Ultra-fine particles. The colloidal content of *secondary clays* is often as high as 25-30% and is thought to be associated with their plasticity. The word derives from 'Kolla'—glue. Colloidal particles dispersed in a liquid will remain in suspension for a long time but, once settled, are difficult to remix. Red copper glaze gets its color from colloidal particles.

## COLOR

The physicists' explanation of color—the absorption, reflection, and refraction of different light wavelengths—may seem largely irrelevant when we are mixing oxides or reducing iron glaze, but it is useful to know the various ways in which color can develop.

The simplest and commonest is the solution color. All wavelengths other than those we see are absorbed. The hue is similar by transmitted (seen through) or by reflected light. Many of our pottery colors are in this category. 'The color is influenced by the abundance or scarcity of oxygen in the atomic environment' (John Dunn PQ 17), which is a way of saying that the type and condition (i.e. reduced or not) of the glaze will affect the color derived from any one *pigment oxide*.

More difficult to comprehend is the effect of particles or fine films of matter so tenuous as to approximate to the light wavelengths. Examples are the iridescence of oil on water or the devitrifying surfaces of ancient lead glazes. Here there are no coloring pigments, but what might be called an optical effect, the cause of the color being in itself colorless. The blues of Chun glazes and the very subtle Imperial wares, Kuan and Ju from Sung China, are said to derive from ultra-fine particles in suspension. There is also an elusive opalescence on the surface of some white raku glazes. Cardew refers to optical colors as glass suspended in glass. In practice, a thick coating of glaze is necessary and probably a fairly dark slip or body. Billington mentions oxide of bismuth to produce a mother-of-pearl lustre. Slightly larger particles—the colloids—are responsible for many red-purple colors, e.g. reduced copper in which comparatively few particles of sub-wavelength copper will produce red.

Lastly, there are the very thin films of metal, usually copper or silver, sometimes so fine as to show iridescence, which we call 'lustres'.

Color terminology is imprecise and somewhat chaotic. Various attempts, such as in the British Standard Colors, and the *Dictionary of Color* by Maertz and Rea Paul, have been made to standardize names.

## COLORED BODIES

A colored slip can be dried to the plastic state and used as a body. A cruder alternative is to damp a finely ground oxide to a thick sludge, spread it onto thin layers of plastic clay and then to wedge them all together. This is something of a hit or miss method as regards final hue, but one can consider the plastic clay as two-thirds (0.66) solid material and weigh the oxide accordingly. Coarser pigment oxides—ilmenite etc.—or colored grog can be added to a body to give mottled and textural effects. *Red clay* is, in effect, a colored body.

Colored bodies are used industrially for colored tableware, sometimes with a skin of white clay inside cups. For the craft potter they can be useful in modeling, giving a decorative result without resorting to colored glazes. Also for *agate* and *basalt wares*.

## COLORED GLAZE

Color can be added to an otherwise clear glaze in the form of pigment oxides (the metal oxides) or prepared stains (*fritted* mixtures of oxides). If iron is required, it is available in various subtle forms as red clay, ochre, etc. Many of the coloring oxides are dissolved and therefore transparent in a clear glaze, forming 'stained glass'. The hue will be stronger where the glaze is thicker, an effect which can be exploited by engraving the clay. *Celadon* glazes are often used in this way. The body color will have a direct influence as it is visible through the glaze. Optical color and iridescent glazes are not stained. (See *color.*)

A completely different effect is obtained by the use of *opacifiers*, most of the light then being reflected back at or near the surface. The body still has some influence, but it is not so marked. Majolica painting is the local staining of an *opaque* glaze. Color will also diffuse upwards through an opaque glaze, but the effect will be more subdued and outlines less sharp. (See *underglaze, tin over slip.*)

The ingredients of a glaze will control the particular hue derived from any pigment. A glaze will have its own saturation point which varies with each oxide; an excess will render it opaque or be precipitated onto the surface. Remarkable effects will arise from the saturation of glazes, especially in stoneware, but beware *metal release* in kitchen or cooking ware. *Temmoku* and tessha are iron saturated. (See also *glaze trials*—colored illustration)—and under *black, red glazes* and so on. Also *line blends, color trials,* etc.)

## COLOR TRIALS

The color of a glaze does not necessarily proceed by simple stages from light to dark as *pigment oxides* are added to it. Nor can one very accurately guess the effect of a certain proportion of *oxide* in a glaze. The variables—type of *bases*, base-*acid* relationship, *opacity* etc.—all contribute to an infinite variety. Statements such as 'copper gives green colors', while broadly true, must always be tested in your particular glaze in your kiln.

Random tests can be made and are sometimes successful, but the most attractive combination is likely to be missed or a whole range condemned on insufficient evidence. More methodical trials, though by no means infallible, are more likely to be useful. The obvious method is to weigh and add progressively larger amounts of an oxide to a glaze, testing at each addition. This has its disadvantages: it involves a great deal of work weighing and sieving each time; cumulative error is likely; and one cannot easily return to a promising range.

An alternative is known as *line-blending*. First determine the limits between which you wish to explore. A simple example would be a clear glaze as one limit and the accepted maximum proportion of the oxide in a similar glaze as the other. Make up these two samples in equal quantities and, as far as you can judge, of equal consistencies. They are then combined in certain proportions, a test-piece being glazed at each stage. The series can consist of as many steps as you consider useful or practicable. Ten combinations will tell you quite a lot. The measures are by volume, using any spoon or small container as a standard unit.

A line blend is usually given as:

| Glaze | Percentage mixtures | | | | | | | | | | |
|---|---|---|---|---|---|---|---|---|---|---|---|
| A | 100 | 90 | 80 | 70 | 60 | 50 | 40 | 30 | 20 | 10 | 0 |
| B | 0 | 10 | 20 | 30 | 40 | 50 | 60 | 70 | 80 | 90 | 100 |

This does not represent ideally equal steps, however, and it is not immediately obvious how to use it in practice. I suggest the following method which fulfils the same function. We will call the glazes to be blended C and D—clear and dark, if you like.

| Test | | | | Total additions |
|---|---|---|---|---|
| 1 | To 10 measures of C | add | 1 measure D | 1 |
| 2 | To above mixture | add | 1 measure D | 2 |
| 3 | To above mixture | add | 2 measures D | 4 |
| 4 | To above mixture | add | 2 measures D | 6 |
| 5 | To above mixture | add | 4 measures D | 10 |

In Test 5 you have equal parts. It is extravagant in glaze to go on from here: we would need to add 50 measures of C to achieve a ratio of 1D-5C. We therefore start again from D, adding C in similar proportions:

| Test | | | | |
|---|---|---|---|---|
| 6 | To 10 measures of D | add | 1 measure C | 1 |
| 7 | To above mixture | add | 1 measure C | 2 |
| 8 | To above mixture | add | 2 measures C | 4 |
| 9 | To above mixture | add | 2 measures C | 6 |
| 10 | To above mixture | add | 4 measures C | 10 |

This brings us again to equal parts. You will in fact find that Test 5 is not identical to 10, due to slight differences in the consistencies of the glazes.

The series can be translated into percentages of oxide: if glaze C has no pigment oxide and glaze D has 4%, then in Test 1 the proportion of D in the batch is 1 part in 11 and the percentage of oxide is $\frac{1}{11} \times \frac{4}{1} = 0.36\%$. Test 2 is 2 parts in 12 and the percentage of oxide $\frac{2}{12} \times \frac{4}{1} = 0.66\%$ and so on through the series. When we reach the changeover point the proportion of D becomes 10 in 11 in Test 6; 10 in 12 in Test 7 and so on.

The whole range works out as follows:
Test 1: 0.36%; 2: 0.66%; 3: 1.14%; 4: 1.5%; 5: 2.0%. Test 6: 3.64%; 7: 3.33%; 8: 2.86%; 9: 2.5%; 10: 2.0%.

Dual blending can be practised with any two glazes, with two pigments, or with glaze ingredients. One can make a diagram for three variables (see *triaxial diagrams*), but not for more than three.

All this work is useless if the actual firing tests are not fully valid. Brushing a large number of test glazes onto a single tile or shard may be just adequate for pigment trials, but it gives little or no indication of a glaze potential. Make *test-pieces* of each of the bodies you are likely to use; dip the glaze carefully and try different thicknesses of glaze coating. Keep an accurate record. (See also *glaze trials, records.*)

### COMB, combing

Decoration by scoring with a toothed or pronged instrument. The technique has a long history. In its wider sense, the term also applies to sgraffito-like decoration through slip or glaze. The simplest 'combs' are always with us—our fingers. Finger combing must be done very rapidly with the slip or glaze in an almost liquid condition. Old English Devonshire slipware was sometimes finger-combed; Leach, Cardew and Whiting have used it extensively.

The more traditional combs may be of wood, metal, stiff leather, rubber, felt etc., each of which will give its own character to the line. Broken saw blades, hacksaw blades and Surform tools are useful. Simple pieces of broken wood or twigs can be utilized for irregular textural patterns.

The teeth of pottery combs are usually quite broad and well spaced. Hair combs often have too sharp a point and plow up a rather unpleasant furrow. The illustration shows a few types of comb and the marks they cut through pigment. Flexible or convex combs are needed for the insides of bowls etc.

Rough edges to the cuts can be removed with a stiff brush when quite dry. This work must be carried out with discretion, or the sharp quality of the decoration will be smudged.

*Showing the marks made by various tools used for combing through pigment to leather-hard clay. From left to right: a broken piece of Surform blade, a hacksaw blade fragment, and two metal sculptors' tools.*

### COMBINED WATER

See *chemically combined water.*

### COMBUSTION

The *oxidation* of *organic* materials, producing $CO_2$ and heat. Combustion takes place in all kilns except those fired with electricity. It needs a free air supply in a continuous draft, and hence a chimney. Fuels vary in their readiness to oxidize (burn). Gas is instantaneous; wood has a low ignition point; but oil must be vaporized by a jet of air, or evaporated by dripping onto a red-hot metal plate. Coal and coke need 'starters'— wood, firelighters, etc.—to bring them to a temperature at which they will ignite. All fuels burn more readily the hotter the kiln becomes: heated secondary air therefore increases efficiency. Kilns are designed to provide a steady supply of oxygen (air) to carbonaceous fuels; to convert them into carbon dioxide; and then to trap and utilize as much as possible of the heat-energy which is released in the process.

When combustion takes place one molecule of water is produced for every molecule of $CO_2$: a pint of paraffin, for instance, will liberate $1\frac{1}{2}$ pints of water. The formation of water vapor helps *reduction.*

### COMPOUND

A material of uniform composition containing two or more *elements* in a state of chemical combination. A compound possesses characteristics different from either of the elements which compose it. Iron (a blue-gray metal) plus oxygen (an invisible gas) produce the compound iron oxide (a red powder). All pottery materials are *oxides* and, therefore, compounds.

Elements combine in fixed whole-number proportions. These are indicated by numbers following and slightly below the symbols for the elements. The compound mentioned above combines as two parts of iron to three of oxygen and it is written $Fe_2O_3$, Fe being the symbol for iron. Chemical combinations are now interpreted in electrical terms (see *atomic theory*), but for practical purposes a simplified view is generally sufficient.

Two elements may combine in a variety of proportions, although one is generally the more stable (inert). More than two elements can enter into a compound. Carbonates are made up of the oxide plus carbon dioxide, e.g. $CaO + CO_2$ gives $CaCO_3$— calcium carbonate. The formula for complex minerals may include the compound symbol with a prefix figure. This is a convenient way of indicating the comparative number of whole molecules of an oxide in the make-up of the mineral. Clay, for instance, contains the oxides of aluminium (alumina), silicon (silica), and hydrogen (water) in the proportions 1.2.2 and is written $Al_2O_3.2SiO_3.2H_2O$. (See also *chemical background, valency.*)

### COMPRESSION

Squeezing. Glazes should be in slight compression. (See also *crazing, shivering, shattering.*)

## CONDUCTION OF ELECTRICITY

Electricity will 'travel' through some materials more readily than others. Metals are usually good conductors. Most dry-clay materials are non-conductors; although they contain a metal, aluminium, this does not conduct in its oxide form. Silicon carbide is a conductor and should not be used as kiln shelves or furniture in an electric kiln. Wet materials are better conductors than dry ones. A person standing on a wet concrete floor will conduct current (to earth) if he is in contact with 'live' or faulty equipment.

Copper metal is an almost perfect conductor and is used to carry current. Other materials may conduct, but at the same time put up some resistance to the flow of current, developing heat in the process. Electric kiln elements are especially designed to control conduction/resistance ratios.

| Conductors | Poor or non-conductors |
|---|---|
| Metals, especially copper iron aluminium tin | Dry or fired clay, hence bricks etc., and most clay minerals |
| Impure water and wet materials in general | Rubber Plastic |
| Silicon carbide | Distilled water |

## CONDUCTION OF HEAT

The rate at which heat is transferred through a material. An important consideration in kilns (and the walls of your pottery on a cold day). In general, the denser the material the more quickly it will conduct heat. In metal this is very rapid; *silicon carbide* is also a good conductor of heat. A porous brick has more resistance to the passage of heat than a non-porous one. The inner parts of a kiln—the shelves, saggars, kiln furniture etc.—should be reasonably good conductors, the walls poor conductors. (See also *insulation, heat loss, heat storage.*)

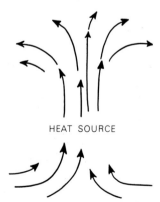

HEAT SOURCE

*Conduction of heat. The hot air becomes expanded and lighter than the surrounding air and so rises, drawing cold air in from below. As the warm air rises it cools again and movement ceases or else a circular movement is set up as in a room with a radiator.*

## CONE

More accurately 'pyrometric cone'. Made from mixtures of ceramic materials formed into triangular elongated pyramids, and designed to melt and bend over or 'squat' at a given temperature. The standard size is $2\frac{5}{8}$ in. (about 65 mm.) high; miniatures 1 in. (about 25 mm.) high. They are numbered to indicate the temperature at which the point will have dropped level with the base if placed in the kiln at a slight angle (8° for Orton). Because cones are composed of similar materials to the ware in the kiln, they are considered by many potters to be better indications of *heat-work* than *pyrometers*, which measure temperature only. The speed of firing will affect the behavior of a cone, a fast firing needing a slightly higher temperature to bend the cone. Quoted firing rates for optimum cone performance vary widely: Rhodes' 20°C. an hour is impractically slow; *Orton* cones are quoted for 60 and 150°C. per hour. In practice one can accept the nominal temperature equivalent and work from there according to practical experience of one's own kiln and glazes. It is often recommended that three cones of successive numbers be used, the first as a warning, the second being of the temperature required. The third should remain standing at the end of the firing. A personal system of one-cone firing may be of interest. I place the cone and socket on a piece of flat shelf so that the moment can be ascertained when the point of the cone just touches down onto the shelf as it melts. This is the point of reference, and the firing is continued for a certain number of minutes after this according to the pack and contents of the kiln. One need stock only one cone number for a 20-30° range of firing. A kitchen timer is invaluable.

At high temperatures, cones may be difficult to see in a kiln. They can be brought momentarily into relief by blowing gently into the spyhole. Beware singed hair!

There are several makes of cones. Numbers begin at about 022, diminish to 01, and then increase again to 42. Staffordshire and German Seger cones have a close similarity in temperature equivalents, but the American Orton cones do not often correspond with them. This leads to confusion when glaze maturing points are quoted as cone numbers, e.g. a cone 6 glaze which would indicate 1200°C. for a Staffordshire cone but nearer 1225°C. at the same firing speed for Orton.

The squatting temperature is sometimes called the 'end point'. Always leave enough room in the kiln setting to place the cone accurately and visibly. An error in reading the cone can ruin all the rest. (See also *P.C.E., Holdcroft bars, Orton cones.*)

*Numbers and equivalent temperatures for Seger, Staffordshire, and standard Orton cones. (See also under Orton cones.*

| No. | Seger | Staffs | Orton |
|---|---|---|---|
| 022 | 600 | 600 | 600 |
| 020 | 670 | 670 | 635 |
| 018 | 710 | 710 | 717 |

| No. | Seger | Staffs | Orton |
|---|---|---|---|
| 017 | 730 | 730 | 747 |
| 016 | 750 | 750 | 792 |
| 015 | | 790 | 804 |
| 015a | 790 | | |
| 014 | | 815 | 838 |
| 014a | 815 | | |
| 012 | | 855 | 884 |
| 012a | 855 | | |
| | | 900 | 894 |
| 010a | 900 | | |
| 09 | | 920 | 923 |
| 09a | 920 | | |
| 08 | | 940 | 955 |
| 08a | 940 | 950 | |
| 07 | | 960 | 984 |
| 07a | 960 | 970 | |
| 06 | | 980 | 999 |
| 06a | 980 | 990 | |
| 05 | | 1000 | 1046 |
| 05a | 1000 | 1010 | |
| 04 | | 1020 | 1060 |
| 04a | 1020 | 1030 | |
| 03 | | 1040 | 1101 |
| 03a | 1040 | 1050 | |
| 02 | | 1060 | 1120 |
| 02a | 1060 | 1070 | |
| 01 | | 1080 | 1137 |
| 01a | 1080 | 1090 | |
| 1 | | 1100 | 1154 |
| 1a | 1100 | 1100 | |
| 2 | | 1120 | 1162 |
| 2a | 1120 | 1130 | |
| 3 | | 1140 | 1168 |
| 3a | 1140 | 1150 | |
| 4 | | 1160 | 1186 |
| 4a | 1160 | 1170 | |
| 5 | | 1180 | 1196 |
| 5a | 1180 | 1190 | |
| 6 | | 1200 | 1222 |
| 6a | 1200 | 1215 | |
| 7 | 1230 | 1230 | 1240 |
| 7a | | 1240 | |
| 8 | 1250 | 1250 | 1263 |
| 8a | | 1260 | |
| 8b | | 1270 | |
| 9 | 1280 | 1280 | 1280 |
| 9a | | 1290 | |
| 10 | 1300 | 1300 | 1305 |
| 10a | | 1310 | |
| 11 | 1320 | 1320 | 1315 |
| 12 | 1350 | 1350 | 1326 |
| 13 | 1380 | 1380 | 1346 |
| 14 | 1410 | 1410 | 1366 |
| 15 | 1435 | 1435 | 1431 |

## CONE SOCKETS, plaques

These can be purchased as singles or in groups of three or four. Considering the fact that they can often be used only once, they are dear and it is easy enough to press a cone into a small block of grogged clay.

## CONE WHEEL

See *power wheel*.

## CONGRUENT MELTING

See *melting point*.

## CONING

A movement preliminary to throwing and associated with centering. The clay is allowed to rise into a column on the rotating wheel under horizontal pressure between the palms of the hands. The hands rise with the column, which is then forced down again with the right hand while the left controls the spread of clay. At the end of the movement the hands will regain the centering position.

*Coning by evenly-maintained side pressure from both palms, rising with the cone of clay (1). The position of the hands for depressing the cone to a centering position (2).*

## CONSISTENCY OF GLAZES AND SLIPS

The assessment and control of the relative consistencies, or thickness, of glazes and slips is a continuing problem for the potter. Industrial potteries, even with their great experience, still use a number of scientific checks while most craft potters rely on guesswork.

Dipping a finger into glaze and assessing the coverage is a crude check. The relative amounts of water and solid matter are an important guide, and this can be established, approximately, by a *hydrometer*. Other factors to be taken into account are:

1 *Flocculation* and *thixotropy*. Ash glazes and those containing colemanite are liable to thicken as they stand.
2 *Fritt* glazes should be used thinner than raw ones. They are more concentrated and their glassy nature renders them transparent when wet.
3 A clear soft glaze needs to be applied more thinly than an opaque one.
4 When trying a new glaze, check its hydrometer reading. After inspection of the fired result you will then know which way to alter the reading.
5 Glazes and slips will not maintain their consistency unless closely covered. Evaporation at room temperature is considerable.
6 Consistency is only one factor: biscuit porosity and speed of glazing are others. The more porous the biscuit or, for slips, the drier the clay, the thinner the mixture needs to be.

One cannot over-stress the necessity of repeated stirring before testing or during the use of a glaze or slip, especially lead or fritt glazes. (See also *glazing, slip, casting slip, porosity, Brongiart's formula.*)

## CONTINUOUS KILNS, firing

*An early circular continuous kiln for enamel firing. The trucks do not cease movement but this is so slow that the trucks can be packed and unpacked as they emerge.*

*The principle of the continuous or tunnel kiln. The loaded trucks are kept in continuous movement through a tunnel built of refractory materials, the center of which is kept at the maximum required firing temperature. The ware cools as it travels through the second half of the tunnel and is ready for unloading at the exit. The tunnel may be up to 250 ft. (75 m.) long. See under packing kilns for picture of loaded truck.*

Most industrial ware is now fired in long tunnels, the center of the tunnel being maintained at the peak temperature. Pottery travels through on special trucks, heating and cooling in a slow continuous motion. The craft potter normally fires in an *intermittent* kiln.

## CONTROLLING PYROMETER

A *pyrometer* equipped with mechanism which can partially or completely control the firing according to a prearranged, schedule worked out by the potter. The simplest type merely switches off the current at a given temperature; others will supply intermittent current to maintain top temperature (soaking). Unfortunately the normal model will not do both, so that the potter must be on hand to switch off after a period of soaking. To do both involves an additional time control. In the more elaborate pyrometers a plotted firing cycle is cut in card and inserted into the mechanism, the controls following the schedule without further attention.

In schools especially, these controllers can be of great benefit—if they work. But we have all heard of burnt-out kilns which have been left on 'control' over a weekend. If they are to be used in this way a 'fail-safe' device such as a *heat-fuse* must be fitted.

## CONVECTION OF HEAT

All fuel burning kilns are built on convection principles. Hot air or gas, being lighter (more expanded), will rise (e.g. in a chimney) so long as there is a supply of cooler air to take its place. Effective convection is negligible in an electric kiln, however, where the top is often the coolest spot. If top and bottom bungs are removed at the same time, however, then convection will take place into the outside atmosphere, so beware of this when peering at the cone if you value your eyebrows. Heat is transmitted by convection, *conduction* and *radiation*.

## CONVERSION FACTOR

A figure used to convert one scale or type of measurement into its equivalent in another scale with which it has a regular co-relationship. For instance: the factor turning inches into centimeters (both regular scales of linear measurement) is 2.54. Any number of inches multiplied by 2.54 will equal the same length in centimeters.

The conversion factor may alter with the particular case under consideration, e.g. any list of figures if multiplied by 100 and divided individually by the conversion factor of the sum of the figures will give percentages in the same proportions as the original numbers.

A useful list of conversion factors is given in *Ceramists' Handbook* (P.CH). Full conversion tables are, of course, even more useful. Conversion can be

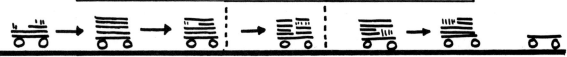

HOT ZONE

carried out on *calculators*. (See *temperature conversion*.)

Some useful conversion factors:

| To change | into | multiply by | to obtain converse multiply by |
|---|---|---|---|
| inches | cm. | 2.54 | 0.394 |
| feet | meters | 0.305 | 1.094 |
| gallons | liters | 4.546 | 0.22 |
| Imperial gallons | US gallons | 1.205 | 0.83 |
| pints | liters | 0.568 | 1.760 |
| ounces | grams | 28.35 | 0.035 |
| pounds | kilograms | 0.454 | 2.205 |
| cwt. | kilograms | 50.8 | 0.02 |
| oz./pt. | Gms. cu.cm. | 0.05 | 20.0 |
| Btu | Watt/hours | 0.29 | 3.41 |
| Btu | joules | 1050 | |

## COOLING OF GLAZES AND CLAYS

The effort and expense of firing go into the heating up of pots, but changes important to the finished article occur also on cooling.

For the majority of glazes, cooling to 1000°C. can be quite rapid. This inhibits the growth of crystals and keeps the glaze surface 'bright'. David Leach cools rapidly to 750°C. in a two-chamber kiln: the second chamber is brought up to temperature while the first is cooled all the time by the incoming draft. Slow cooling while the glaze is still fluid will develop *matt* qualities in certain glazes and is essential for *aventurine* glazes. Below 900°C. the glaze becomes increasingly rigid, but subsequent changes occur which put either the glaze or the body into a state of *stress*. If this is excessive *crazing*, *shivering*, or *shattering* can occur.

The main factors at work are:
1 The comparative *coefficients of expansion*.
2 *Inversions* of quartz and cristobalite, at 573 and 220°C. respectively.

The ideal is, therefore, reasonably slow cooling from red-heat almost to touch-heat. For most potters the cooling rate is built into the kiln design. Hearths and all vents in a fuel burning kiln must be *clammed*. An electric kiln could be covered with asbestos sheet or ceramic fiber blanket. The particular qualities and vices of a glaze or body will be affected by the heating and cooling behavior of the kiln—no two of which are identical. This fact lessens the value of *test kilns*. (See also *dunting*.)

## COPPER, oxides, compounds

A metallic element Cu, 63.5.
Black cupric oxide CuO, 79.5, m.p. 1149°C.
Red cuprous oxide $Cu_2O$, 143.0.
Carbonate $CuCO_3$, 123.5 [strictly $CuCO_3.Cu(OH)_2$].

The cuprous oxide is in the 'reduced' or lower oxide state and will revert to CuO in a glaze unless the reduction is maintained. (See *copper red*.) The green carbonate will decompose in hot water and is more toxic than the oxide.

A *basic*, versatile pigment, slightly *fluxing* in a glaze. Liable to *volatilize*. A great variety of transparent green colors derive from 1-3% of copper oxide; apple green in lead glazes; turquoise in low alumina alkaline glazes; and various shades in leadless glazes. Produces a rather watery color in slip and is usually combined with chrome.

In oxidized stonewares copper will usually give a rather characterless green-brown, but will sometimes surprise with buff to black in a high base matt, or rich blues with barium.

Copper is reputed to increase *lead solubility* to a significant extent, and care must be taken when using this combination for use on tableware. An excess of copper—3% and upwards—in any glaze will generally produce a rather cindery black. With careful experiment and control this can be made quite attractive in an earthenware glaze.

As a pigment, copper is used for green colors on glazes, or for browns and blacks on unglazed biscuit. It will tend to separate out if mixed with other pigments. Copper/manganese mixtures can give a definite gold color on biscuit at any temperature, but the low eutectic can cause running if thickly applied. Copper chloride is used in *lustres*.

An interesting method of preparing your own copper oxide for painting is given in S.WJC. Copper filings are soaked in salt water for a week, stirred and washed. Wash with water and finally with strong tea. Dry, and remove the top layer which will contain the tannin. Carefully separate the middle from the bottom layer (which will be metallic), and use this as a pigment. (See also *copper red*.)

## COPPERAS

A ferrous sulfate $FeSO_4$. Calcined for enamels, giving nasturtium reds at 600°C. and violet at 1000°C. (S.SCP).

## COPPER RED

Copper oxide, in reduction, will yield colloidal particles of cuprous oxide to produce red glazes. This can be achieved at any temperature from 800-1400°C. but is fugitive and difficult to retain in the cooling glaze. The color can range from blood red through purple to a rather muddy khaki. Billington recommends a little borax, and even lead, at slightly sub-stoneware temperatures (1150-1200°C.). At any temperature the glaze needs to be fairly fluid. Small amounts of tin oxide or zinc in glazes low in alumina and magnesia have been recommended. Finely ground silicon carbide in the same proportion as the copper carbonate can give a streaked red.

One can buy red cuprous oxide which some potters believe should be used for reduced copper glazes. It will quickly revert to cupric green in *oxidation*.

Use 0.5-1.0% of the oxide or carbonate. Maintain at least a non-oxidizing atmosphere during cooling i.e. keep the kiln as airtight as possible. The typical *sang de boeuf* Chinese reds occur on a blue Chun glaze. (See *color*.) A small amount of iron is reputed to help the red hue. It is difficult to duplicate copper red effects in detail. The colors, even at their best, are rather strident and need handling with discretion if they are to be anything more than technical achievements.

## CORDIERITE

Magnesium-aluminium-silicate, $2MgO.2Al_2O_3.5SiO_2$.

It exists as a mineral—there are deposits in Wyoming, USA—but is usually synthesized at a very high temperature from clay, talc and alumina. It has a low and uniform thermal expansion (*coefficient* 1-2.5) and attempts have been made to incorporate it in fireproof bodies. Serious difficulties, however, arise when it is combined with plastic clays. (See C.PP 75-6.)

## CORNWALL STONE

See *china stone*.

## CORUNDUM

A natural crystalline alumina, nearly as hard as diamond. Used as an *abrasive*. Also derived from high-fired bauxite.

## COSTING AND PRICING

It is said that an object is worth whatever someone will pay for it. Up to a point, this is true of pottery. Pots, even of the highest order, do not in the West command the prices paid for even second-rate paintings, very rarely approaching three figures.

The pricing of an individual piece is not, however, the main problem, which is how to arrive at a fair price for the run of tableware and 'useful' pieces which constitute the average professional potter's bread and butter. A balance must be struck between the estimated production costs and the average price range for similar wares. A comparative beginner will use more time and materials than an experienced potter, but cost cannot be expected to cover lack of skill!

One system is to keep a kiln log of the number and description of pieces produced. Over several months an average figure will emerge. If an approximate whole-sale price, based on those prevailing in the shops, is given to each piece, an estimate of one's likely gross income per week or per month can be arrived at. The wholesale price should be the shop price less 40%. This figure should be used even if you sell a lot of pots retail—remember it may take ten minutes to sell £1 worth of pots (longer if the customer is an interesting one!). Halve the gross figure. If the final sum is not sufficient as a private income you must either work harder, or more efficiently, or persuade customers that the pots are worth more.

*Example.* Over ten kilns and six months you have averaged per month eight coffee sets, 100 beakers, 60 bowls, ten lamps, ten individual pots and 100 various small items. Pricing these respectively at £10, £1, 75p, £8, £5, and 50p each, we arrive at an overall total of £405 gross, £240 wholesale, or £120 personal income per month (labour cost and profit). These are hypothetical figures, although fairly realistic in England

in 1973. The method is rough and ready but better than none. A more logical system, though often as arbitrary, is to try to estimate the actual cost of production. To arrive at the precise cost of each article is impossible, but again averages can be struck. A good deal of recording and office work can be involved.

Cost is made up of materials, time and 'overheads', plus a sum to cover future development, taxes, travel and 'profit'.

1 *Materials*  Assess all materials used over a given period (not less than six months). Clay, glaze, minor materials such as cones, sponges, wax, fuel for kiln etc. which are 'consumed' or used up.

2 *Time*  Your wages and those of any assistants. Make an assessment of hours worked and an hourly rate which would be acceptable.

3 *Overheads*  The proportion of rent, mortgage, telephone, building repairs, lighting, heating, which are attributable to the pottery. Exhibition and professional society charges.

4 *Equipment*  Wear and tear, and depreciation. See below for a method of calculating this.

5 *Development*  You should build up some capital for the future. The equipment figure is a guide to possible requirements.

6 *Taxes*  Value Added Tax if applicable, or its equivalent outside the European Economic Community. National Insurance, other insurances, other taxes, bank loan or overdraft charges.

7 *Other*  Traveling: allow mileage costs as estimated by motoring organizations. Cost of post and carriage. Boxes and packing, office materials, and sundries (laundry etc.).

Items 1, 2 and 3 must be calculated on the basis of six months' or a year's total cost.

No 4 is more difficult. The following example may help: if your kiln and kiln furniture cost £250 with an estimated £30 per year for replacements and repairs, and are expected to last five years, then the charge to be added to a year's costs will be:

$$\frac{£250 + (£30 \times 5)}{5} = \frac{£400}{5} \quad £80.$$

Double the figure arrived at in No 4 to cover No 5; i.e. for the above example £160 for equipment and development. This does not take inflation into account.

The calculations for 6 and 7 are based on one year's expenses.

The figure for each category can be reduced to a monthly rate by simple division. Add 10% for 'profit'. This final figure is the sum you should be getting for a month's gross output, as arrived at by the first system mentioned above.

This need not be a continuing process. One calculation can serve as a basis for several years, balancing prices against inflation.

## COVALENT BOND

The sharing by two atoms of a pair of *electrons*, one provided by each atom. (See *atomic theory, valency*.)

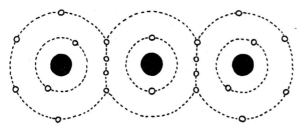

*Covalent bonds between atoms of oxygen which has 6 electrons and carbon with 4. Two electrons from each atom are shared, making up 8 in each orbit and forming the carbon dioxide molecule.*

## CRACKING

Cracks often result from the mishandling of clay at the leather-hard stage e.g. careless correcting of deformed pot or bowl rims. The strain may not show until the pot is bone dry or biscuit. Cooling too quickly through the *inversions* of quartz and cristobalite may cause cracks or *dunting*. This would be aggravated by an excess of silica in the body. A cooling crack is usually curved and sharp. Other possible causes of cracking:

1 Over-wetting parts of a pot, e.g. water left in the base during throwing.
2 Stretching the clay when making.
3 Uneven or forced drying—the last part to dry may crack.
4 Applying slip to a dish which is either too dry, or, conversely, has only just been pressed into a mold.
5 Very uneven wall thickness, especially the bases of pots.
6 Wet clay joined to drier clay.
7 High shrinkage-rate of clay.
8 Pieces of lime or stones.
9 Excessive weight on a pot or 'bung' of pots in the kiln, including piles of six or more tiles in plastic clay.
10 Slabs bent when too stiff, e.g. pots made around cylinders.
11 Over-*wedging*, giving a very short body.
12 Thick glaze on one side of a dish only.
13 The working of clay after it has dried beyond the plastic stage.

This is a formidable list, but in fact clean, well-prepared clay made into reasonably even-walled pots which are allowed to dry naturally will not suffer. (See *base cracks*.)

The filling (stopping) of biscuit cracks is not recommended, although preparations are sold for this purpose.

## CRACKLE

A term applied to the intentional *crazing* of stoneware or porcelain glazes. *Vitrification* of the body prevents excessive absorption of moisture.

On porcelain, crackle is used decoratively and can be stained with manganese or other color while still hot from the kiln. Nitrates of the pigment oxides are suggested by Behrens (CM). If pottery color is used it can be 'fixed' in a second fire. A second and wider

crackle may form long after firing. Crackle should be avoided on tableware.

Thick glaze with a high *coefficient of expansion* is needed for the development of crackle. Behrens (CM 17/8) suggests a body of 58 ball clay, 39 talc, 3 bentonite, with a glaze of volcanic ash, china clay, and fritt, fired to 1220°C. The formula of a talc crackle glaze by Victor Margrie, given in CR 2, reads:

$$K_2O \quad 0.20$$
$$CaO \quad 0.29 \qquad Al_2O_3 \; 0.20 \quad SiO_2 \; 2.0$$
$$MgO \quad 0.51$$

firing to 1260°C. on David Leach porcelain body. (See also *crazing*.)

*A celadon porcelain bottle by Annette Hoy, made at Buller's electrical porcelain factory, showing well-defined and stained crackle.*

## CRANK, bit

A thin refractory kiln shelf up to about 12 in. (300 mm.) long. May be rectangular or triangular, and have bent-over tabs for spacing. Used mainly for tiles. Small blocks to hold the cranks apart are called 'bits' or 'dots'.

A crank can also be a vertical structure with a series of 'pins' to hold plates or tiles of identical size. Maximum kiln temperature 1200°C.

Thirdly, the term may be used to cover all *kiln shelves*.

## CRANK MIXTURE

A coarse, *grogged* body of refractory clays used for making 'cranks' or kiln shelves. Used as a trade name for a somewhat variable mixture by Potclays, Stoke-on-Trent.

Useful for mixing with other clays to impart a more open texture, allowing thicker walls in models, coiled pots, etc. Very little shrinkage if used alone. Can be made into *saggars* for *raku*.

## CRAQUELE

An alternative term for *crackle*.

## CRATER GLAZE

A rather tricky decorative finish derived from burst *bubbles* in a glaze. The use of sulfates such as barium sulfate has been suggested. The 'craters' should be sufficiently melted to lose their dangerous sharpness. A recipe in CM 17/3 (Behrens) is given as:

| | |
|---|---|
| Talc | 43.5 |
| Lepidolite | 54.4 |
| Bentonite | 2.0 |

## CRAWLING

A glaze fault, the glaze bunching up in places leaving other parts bare. Some likely causes are:

1 In general, glazes with a high surface tension.
2 Too thick a coat of glaze, or repeated coatings. If the glaze shows signs of cracking as it dries then it will almost certainly crawl.
3 Glaze which has *flocculated* in the batch, due to soluble alkalis (e.g. ash) or colemanite.
4 Greasy or dusty biscuit.
5 Overloading with opacifying materials, or with feldspar, making the glaze too *viscous*.
6 Underfiring.
7 Glaze materials too finely ground.
8 An exceptionally smooth body can aggravate crawling.
9 Thick underglaze pigments, especially barely *sintered* oxides which have the same effect as dust.
10 Double glazing with the first glaze too dry.
11 Very 'hard' water used in throwing or sponging has been given as a cause.

Crawling on the rim of a pot is very difficult to cure. I have had to abandon otherwise excellent glazes because of this fault. Cardew suggests a higher biscuit fire, or altering the body by the addition of quartz or a hard, fine grog.

*Crawling used as a decorative effect on a stoneware dish by John Chalke.*

Crawling has been exploited as a decorative finish —for instance Hamada's white crawled glaze on the necks of pots, Sheila Fournier's hand built bowls where the crawling is made to 'heal over' in a second fire, Lucie Rie's very controlled all-over crawling, etc.

## CRAZING

A network of fractures in a glaze caused by differences in contraction between body and glaze during cooling, or by subsequent expansion of the body. Term generally applied to earthenware; a similar effect on high-fired ware is often called *crackle*. It should be avoided on all pottery made for table or kitchen use. If a glaze regularly crazes despite efforts to cure it, dispense with it. One may also have to abandon a body on which crazing regularly occurs.

Crazing is most apparent in clear glazes; it can be difficult to detect in *tin* or opaque glazes—until you wash up after that delicious bowl of raspberries. *Slip* can craze.

In general, the whiter, prepared bodies may be most liable to crazing under craft conditions since they are designed for a much higher biscuit fire. Industrial fritts are often applied too thickly by the student potter. Too thick a coating of any glaze will increase its susceptibility to crazing.

The perfect glaze is in slight compression after firing: it has contracted a little less than the body during the final 600°C. of cooling. The main factor working against this ideal state is the high *coefficient of expansion* of many of the *bases* used to *flux* a glaze. Soda and potash are the worst offenders, while silica and alumina have comparatively low coefficients. This means, in practice, using less feldspar or stone and a little more flint or clay, or a little boric oxide (as borax fritt). (See *negative expansion*.) Lead is reputed to have more elasticity than the other bases; some bi-silicate or a low-solubility fritt may therefore be advantageous.

A more fundamental approach is to tackle the body, increasing its contraction to put the glaze into *compression*. Silica, in a glaze, does not *crystallize* on cooling, and so contracts evenly throughout the temperature range. Crystals of silica in the body, however, undergo a very sudden change in molecular shape at 573°C. *(inversion)* accompanied by a contraction of around 1%. This helps to balance the glaze contraction and we get the apparently anomalous situation where the addition of silica to either glaze or body will help to minimize crazing. If the silica in the body is fired high enough to form *cristobalite* then another and proportionally greater contraction occurs at 250°-220°C., further aiding glaze compression, and at a critical temperature when the glaze is quite rigid. Cristobalite forms only very slowly at 1060°C. and above. A 1080-1100°C. firing, with soaking, is therefore necessary to achieve significant results. Very finely ground flint or quartz will form cristobalite more rapidly. Prepared cristobalite can be purchased and added to a body.

Remedies for crazing must be used with discretion.

Free silica in the body must be kept below 20%. To go too far in the alteration of glaze and body can build up too great a compression with subsequent *shattering*. Also a fired body with expansions in the cooking temperature range will suffer thermal shock, which may also cause the crazing, during normal household use, of a glaze which came whole from the kiln.

Ordinary precautions include careful temperature control, neither under- nor *over-firing*; the *soaking* of soft glazes for 20 minutes or so; refraining from opening the kiln too early (above 100°C.); avoidance of sudden drafts of cold air at dull red heat and cooler.

An indication of glaze-body fit can be obtained from the degree of deformation of a thin bar of clay coated fairly thickly with glaze on one face only, and fired on its side on a bed of alumina. Ideally it should curve slightly with the glaze side convex. (See also *Seger's rules, Harkort test.*)

Slips can craze due to excess shrinkage. It becomes apparent during glazing when the cracks show up as thicker deposits. To cure, apply slip on slightly damper clay or stiffen the slip with a refractory material such as china clay or fireclay. Slip-cracking is most often due to shrinkage rather than firing reactions.

A quite distinct cause of crazing is water *adsorption*, which slightly increases the volume of the body. This may show weeks or months after firing. A pot which is fully covered with a good glaze will not be at great risk.

## CRISTOBALITE

A crystalline form of silica with an *inversion* which is greater than that of quartz (3% linear expansion as compared with around 1%), and taking place at a lower temperature, 220°C. Beta quartz will slowly convert to cristobalite from 1050°C. Conversion continues to 1550°C. and is therefore never complete in a pottery body. Lime is said to accelerate its formation. Even small amounts, however, can be valuable in the prevention of crazing, known by some potters as the 'cristobalite squeeze'. *Soaking* during the biscuit fire at around 1070°C. will help earthenware. It can be obtained in a synthesized form.

## CROCUS MARTIS

A natural ferric oxide, $Fe_2O_3$, 'with some nitrate' (Billington). May give darker browns than red ferric, and black with cobalt.

## CROSS-DRAFT KILN

A semi-down-draft kiln usually with a single fire-mouth. (See figs. under *bag wall* and *chambered kiln.*)

## CRUSHING ROCKS

Small experimental quantities of rock can be crushed with a 2 lb. (1 kilo) hammer on a steel slab and then ground in a mortar and pestle, a teaspoonful at a time, or in a jar mill. Larger quantities require a jaw crusher and plate mill, normally beyond the resources of the

craft potter. A rare exception was Harry Davies who crushed and compounded local Cornwall rocks into glazes. (See also C.PP Plate 52.) Rocks will vary greatly in hardness (see *Moh's scale.*)

## CRYOLITE

A sodium-aluminium fluoride $Na_3AlF_6$, 210 (convenient formula weight 420). Fires to $3Na_2O.Al_2O_3$. m.p. 1020°C.

Can be used as a source of insoluble soda, but the accompanying fluorine will bubble through the glaze on escaping during the firing, and will leave pinholes unless the glaze is very fluid. The alumina is likely to give a matt surface.

## CRYSTAL, crystallization

*Molecules* or *lattices* which have built up into a three-dimensional repeat pattern. The solid substance assumes an individual and geometric form with plane faces. Most pure materials can be found in crystalline form, the larger crystals often used as gemstones, e.g. crystallized carbon as diamond, or aluminium silicate as topaz. Crystals can be very large or micro-crystalline and invisible to the naked eye, as in clay or flint. They form either in the melted, fluid state, or in solution. Their study is a wide-ranging and fundamental science. Perfect crystals may be transparent, hence the use of terms crystal-clear, or crystal-glass (the latter very much a misnomer). Non-crystalline materials are *amorphous*.

Crystals need time in which to form from a fluid compound. Glaze is normally cooled too quickly and remains largely *amorphous*, though some crystals can form to show as a matt surface if very small, or to sparkling or *aventurine* glazes if larger. A bright, clear glaze is wholly non-crystalline: it is a super-cooled liquid—a sort of ice.

High alumina or calcium glazes are apt to form crystalline matt glazes 'thought to be anorthite' (C.PP). Zinc and titanium promote crystallization (See also *devitrification.*) Soluble material and very

*The regular shapes built up by crystal formation in a tin-lead alloy.*

soft fritts will re-crystallize from a solution, e.g. a fritt raku glaze.

## CULL
US equivalent of a 'waster', a kiln-spoiled pot.

## CULLET
Pieces of colored glass used in pottery decoration. Also supplied, finely ground, as a cheap but variable glaze flux.

## CUP
A drinking vessel, generally with a handle. Its design should be considered in relation to the saucer on which it is set. There should be room under the handle to accommodate a spoon and to allow the cup to be lifted without tipping it. The handle itself should be easily gripped without the fingers contacting the hot cup surface. The lip should not turn inwards nor flare excessively. A heavy handle will deform a thin rim in the firing, if not before.

## CUP HEAD
A hollow *wheel head*. Can be used for supporting circular molds, e.g. for *jigger and jolley,* or for turning narrow-necked pots. (See also *molds, turning.*)

## CUP LAWN
A small conical or cup-shaped sieve, usually of metal, and 2-3 in. (50-75 mm.) wide.

## CUPRUM, cupric, cuprous
Copper Cu. The cupric is the higher oxide $CuO$, cuprous the lower or reduced oxide $Cu_2O$. (See *copper.*)

## CURRENT, electric
The flow of electricity as measured in *amperes.* (See *electricity.*)

## CUT-CORNER DISHES
A slab technique for making dishes. Allows variations in size and shape which the mold denies. It has its limitations, and some practice is necessary. The dishes look their best in a fairly chunky style. They can be stoneware fired.

The photographs show the principal stages. The template, cut in stiff paper, is laid on a slab of fairly soft plastic clay, and the clay cut to shape. The corners must be cut at a slant so that they can be overlapped to give a strong joint. The surfaces are slipped, the sides raised up until the corner can be luted together. Overlap the faces by about $\frac{1}{8}$ in. (2 mm.) to avoid any thinness when the joint is worked together. Supports must be prepared. The inside face can be smoothed with a *kidney rubber* and, later on, with a *steel palette.* The top edge will need trimming flat and the back must be scraped or planed when stiff. Any style of decoration can be used on these dishes. A fairly fine grog in the clay helps, especially for stoneware.

## CUTTING OFF

After throwing, pots are normally cut from the wheel with a twisted wire or thread. This may be drawn through the base, holding the stretched wire hard down on the wheel head with the index fingers and cutting away from the body. The Japanese method is to hold a thread at one end only; allowing the free end to wind round the base of the pot, then to give it a sharp horizontal pull. This involves throwing the pot on a mound of clay an inch or two above the wheel head.

The two-handed technique will give various patterns beneath your pot according to whether you pull the wire through straight, allow it to curve as you cut, or cut as the wheel is coming to a halt.

*Stages in making a cut-corner dish. A template is cut from a sheet of paper folded in four (1), and a clay slab cut to the template shape (2). The corner segment is cut at a definite angle (3), the segment removed, the faces slipped and brought up together (4). Clay supports as shown hold the dish in shape while it dries (5). The joins must be worked gently together and the inside of the dish shaped by stroking with a rubber kidney (6). At leather-hard the inside can be further finished and the outside finished with a steel palette or plane.*

*Cutting off, holding the wire hard down onto the wheel head with the forefingers while drawing it under the base of a thrown pot.*

### CUT LINER

Also called a 'sword liner'. A soft squirrel brush cut at an angle and pointed at the end.

### CUTTING CLAY

The choice of tools for cutting clay will depend on its state of dryness. For plastic clay a wire can be used or, for molded dishes and the like, a wooden spatula tool or a very fine metal tool such as a needle awl. If wide metal tools are used on soft clay they will tend to stick and tear. For leather-hard clay, use a slender *knife* with a good handle. When cutting clay for slab pots take care to hold the knife vertical and always draw it towards you. For a new cut turn the clay; do not turn the knife to an awkward angle.

*The typical shell pattern from a twisted cutting wire used just before the wheel head comes to a halt.*

## CUTTING-WIRE

A wire for cutting pots from the wheel should be strong, fine and flexible. It is difficult to find one material which combines these qualities and which will also twist into the stranded form which acts like the 'set' of a saw, thus making the cutting both easier and more efficient. Steel wire is too springy for comfort; copper is too weak. A brass wire with a steel strand, as sold for picture hanging, is a compromise. Nylon is strong but will not remain twisted. A fine nylon can be plaited.

The degree of twist is important. It should not be too tight; the normal twisted steel wire is too finely wound. The gauge of wire used should be heavier for wedging and cutting blocks of clay. Coarse nylon can be useful here. Treat cutting wires with care and avoid twisting a loop which may result in an ineradicable kink. Bends can be smoothed out by pulling the wire tightly back and forth across a piece of wood or table-edge. Wires for *harps* and multiple cutters can be of steel, sometimes known as 'piano wire'.

Handles are essential (it is painful to use a wire loop). They can be of wood dowelling, or made from clay and fired. Wires of varying lengths are required; a long wire shortened by twisting it round the fingers will not last long—neither will the fingers.

# D

## DAMP-CUPBOARD, damp-room

A cool, airtight cupboard with non-absorbent walls. A saturated atmosphere is built up which ceases to absorb further moisture from the pots. There has often been some confusion, especially on the part of school architects, on the subject of damp-cupboards. Various measures, such as trays of wet plaster—even felt walls in one new building—have been tried. But every time the door is opened (in a school read 'left open') the built-up humidity is dispersed. Happily it is now virtually obsolete, having been replaced by the widespread use of polythene. A cool cupboard with well-fitting doors by all means, but polythene as well!

A clay cellar or damp-room as described by Cardew (C.PP 216) is a major construction and suitable only for the large-scale professional potter.

## DAMPER

A sliding plate which can close or decrease the chimney opening and thus the draft through the kiln. Must be of stout iron or of refractory ceramic. The removal of a chimney brick will have a similar effect, by-passing the pull through the kiln chamber.

## DARNING HEAD

A wooden mushroom shape used normally for darning, but useful to potters for pressing clay into molds and *formers*.

## DE-AIRING CLAY

The removal of air from clay by passing it through a partial vacuum, usually in a special *pug mill*. The clay must be shredded prior to de-airing. De-aired clay is denser and reputedly more plastic. For the enthusiastic do-it-yourself potter, plans have been issued by Harry Davis for a splendid de-airing pug.

## DECALCOMANIA, decals

Lithographic *transfers* (USA). Term has been traced to the craze or mania for paper transfers which occurred at the end of the nineteenth century in America.

## DECOMPOSITION

The breaking up of chemical compounds. During firing carbonates decompose into the oxide and $CO_2$ which is given off as a gas; red lead breaks down $(2Pb_3O_4) - 6PbO + O_2$; and so on. Glazes can decompose *(devitrify)* with age.

## DECORATION

To quote Billington (B.TP) 'Design freely, do what and only what pleases you, and only apply principles as an aid to criticism if something goes wrong', and Leach 'Subordinate to form but intimately connected with it is the problem of decoration and whether the increased orchestration adds to the total effect or not' (L.PB).

*Large thrown and decorated pot by Staite Murray.*

It is difficult to disassociate decoration from the discredited nineteenth century idea of 'applied art'. Most potters today follow the rule 'if in doubt—don't'. Some recent, gayer ceramics, using bright *enamels*, may break the spell which 'texture' and 'glaze quality' have exercised for two decades. While we do not want to follow the extremists in the use of house paint, a glance at the pottery of the past, from Suza to Spanish lustre, will indicate what we are missing.

Dora Billington goes on 'diffidently' to give advice on the fundamental basis of design and discusses scale, balance, variety, contrast and tension; the last conspicuously absent from much modern work. Her remarks are based on a lifetime of experience and are well worth assimilating (B.TP 171-2). The potter Kenneth Clark also gives advice from a painter's point of view. His 'range of visual contrasts' is useful (C.PC 33).

The techniques of pottery decoration are discussed under *sgraffito, slip trailing, brushwork, wax resist, applied decoration, beaten decoration* and *paper resist.*

## DEFLOCCULATION

The dispersion of particles especially in a clay slip leading to increased *fluidity*. Its prime use is in *casting slip*. It assists particle *suspension* and reduces comparative shrinkage (less water is needed) in a body mixture. It is achieved by the use of an *electrolyte* (usually sodium) in silicate or carbonate (soda ash) form. The electrolyte alters charges on the molecules, causing them to hold away from one another (disassociate). Sodium tannate, pyrophosphate and other compounds are used in special cases. If a clay already contains *free alkali* it will not deflocculate. Excess defloculant will reverse the effect, the slip thickening again.

Recipes and instructions for using electrolytes appear in most suppliers' catalogs (see also R.CGP 29-32). For maximum effect the balance should be a delicate one and should vary from body to body. Add the electrolyte drop by drop if you are working with liquid slip, or weigh dry against dry powdered body according to the advice of the suppliers of the body. 'One half per cent dry weight will turn soft plastic clay into slip' (Billington).

## DEFLUORINATED STONE

China stone from which fluorine has been extracted, now often listed by merchants. May help to prevent *pinholes* in glaze.

## DEFORMATION

*Pyroplastic* deformation occurs at the temperature at which a ceramic body can no longer hold its shape due to the formation of molten compounds within the fabric. It is normally a slow and continuing process, but can be quite sudden in high-calcium bodies and artificial low-temperature porcelains. Deformation usually leads to slumping. *Warping* may have other causes (see *plastic memory*.)

Kiln shelves are tested for 'deformation under load'. The softening effect occurs at each firing so that a curved or sagged shelf can be reversed in the next firing. (See *kiln shelves.*)

## DELIQUESCENT

A material which will absorb moisture from the air to such a degree that it will itself become liquid. The commonest deliquescent pottery materials are soda ash and potassium carbonate.

## DELTA WIRING

See *star and delta, three phase.*

## DEVITRIFICATION

The change from a glassy to a *crystalline* state. Glaze may partially devitrify during a slow cooling (see *matt, aventurine*) giving a frosty look. 'Common in high clay or silica glazes' (Rhodes). Soft glazes will devitrify with great age: the iridescence on ancient Near Eastern pots is an example, especially those high in soda; see color plate 7, p. 132.

*A much magnified view of the remarkable crystalline pattern, resembling frost, developed by glass which has been melted at stoneware temperature in a pot but has started to devitrify during cooling. To the naked eye it appears as a whitish rough patch about $\frac{1}{3}$ in. (8 mm.) across.*

## DEWATERING CLAY

The drying of *slip* to plastic clay. It is the practice in the pottery industry to render all bodies to slips, which are then *filter-pressed* to a plastic state. A craft potter can easily rig up a blunger but, in temperate climes at any rate, the dewatering of the slip is a major problem. The slip will settle and the surplus water can be poured, scooped, or siphoned off but we are still left with a runny slurry. If space is available this can be poured into cloth bags (a fine one inside a stronger coarser one) which can be hung up to drip and stiffen, like cheeses, for three or four days. Plaster molds are useful for small quantities but soon saturate. Shallow troughs such as those used at St. Ives need roofing over if they are not to flood in winter, and they entail space and time. In hot weather the simplest method is that practised by Harry Davis: the slip is poured into a large sheet spread in a depression in the ground, the corners of the sheet being brought together and knotted. The knot acts as a wick, the water is drawn up and evaporates in the sun. Davis has also designed a piece of home-made dewatering equipment which is an ingenious reversal of the industrial filter-press. In it the water is extracted by suction in a semi-vacuum. At Soil Hill Pottery the hot gases from the kiln were drawn under a long brick trough before they reached the chimney. Cardew shows plans for brick dewatering-troughs in C.PP 85.

Most potters bypass the problem by buying plastic clay or by mixing clay powder and water in a dough mixer.

*The dewatering and drying of blunged clay slip in a brick trough under which the hot kiln gases are drawn prior to entering the chimney (Soil Hill Pottery).*

## DIASPORE CLAY
A high-alumina clay used for *refractories*.

## DIATOMITE
Sometimes called 'infusorial earth' or 'Kieselguhr'. Formed from the accumulation of the siliceous remains of minute aquatic vegetable organisms (diatoms). It has very high porosity and heat resistance up to about 800°C., making it a useful kiln insulation material. It can be used as loose granules, fired into bricks, or as a concrete aggregate. *Ceramic fibers* and other synthetic insulators with greater refractoriness are tending to replace diatomite.

## DIE
A *pug* or *wad box* attachment which fastens over the mouth. The clay is forced through holes to form coils and other shapes. Bricks and pipes are made industrially by means of dies. A 'die-press' is a damp-clay tile press.

## DIELECTRIC
Capable of withstanding electrical stresses, e.g. porcelain insulators. An iron-free *vitrified* body is essential.

## DILATANCY
The opposite of *thixotropy*, i.e. becoming less fluid when stirred or under pressure. Wet sand 'dilates'. Dodd mentions ceramic bodies which are deficient in fine particles.

## DIOPSIDE
A calcium mineral, free of alumina. $CaO.MgO.2SiO_2$. Occurs as a crystal, and in *basalt*.

## DIPPING GLAZES
See *glazing*.

## DIRECT CURRENT
Or DC. Electric current flowing in one direction only. Batteries and most home generators will develop direct current. The normal mains supply is alternating current.

## DIRECT FIRING
Given by Dodd as synonymous with open firing i.e. firing without saggars.

## DISAPPEARING FILAMENT PYROMETER
See *optical pyrometer*.

## DISH
A shallow container which may be thrown, molded or built. *The Concise Oxford Dictionary* defines it as a 'flat-bottomed, usually oval or oblong vessel'. Both of these shapes can be developed from thrown dishes by cutting the base (see *oval shapes*) or by *beating*. Molded dishes benefit from good craftsmanship and a tidy finish. It is because the technique seems simple that those made by students and in schools are often scamped and poor.

The method for non-circular molded dishes is shown in the figures under *pressed dishes*. A wire *bow* is sometimes used for cutting the rim; this is difficult to control and can easily slice down into the body of the dish. Molded dishes do not develop that structure in the clay fabric which gives strength and stability to thrown pieces, and they are liable to warp if not well supported in the firing. Molded dishes, with the possible exception of flat based pie-dishes, are not suitable for stoneware.

For cutting circular molded dishes a wheel is needed. The mold is dropped into a *cup head*, or centered and fixed to a wheel head. The clay slab is eased into or over it *(hollow* or *hump mold)* and roughly trimmed. It is then sponged close to the form with the wheel turning. The final cutting of the rim is done on the spinning wheel with a wooden spatula tool. Hold the tool with both hands and find a firm resting-place for both elbows, approach the surface of the clay slowly and hold the tool firmly as it cuts into the clay.

The method of making a *cut-corner dish* is described under that heading. Slab and coiled dishes are possible but neither method is very suitable for kitchen use.

## DISINTEGRATION OF GLAZES

Glazes are very resistant to atmosphere but may start to disintegrate or *devitrify* over a long period, or, more quickly, in chemically active conditions e.g. in the presence of strong acids or alkalis. *Earthenware glazes* are more at risk than feldspathic *stoneware* or porcelain glazes, although much depends upon the inherent stability of the glaze. Disintegration is evident as a 'patina' on some Han and early Persian wares. (See also *metal release, soluble lead.*)

## DISSOCIATION

The reversible decomposition of the *molecules* of a compound. In pottery the dissociation is usually brought about by heat. Dolomite, for instance, breaks down into the carbonates of calcium and magnesium quite early in the firing. (See also *decomposition, volatile.*)

## DISTORTION

Going out of shape. (See *deformation, warping, plastic memory, pyroplastic.*)

## DOD BOX

See *wad mill.*

## DOG'S TEETH, dragon's teeth

Irregular tears in an extruded length of clay from the *pug*. Caused by friction against the mouth of the pug or the edge of a die. Clay which is too dry, *short*, or unevenly mixed is liable to this fault, but a badly cleaned pug mill is most often to blame.

## DOLOMITE

A mineral $CaCO_3.MgCO_3$, 184. The double carbonate of calcium and magnesium. Typical analysis: CaO 31%, MgO 20%, Loss ($CO_2$) 43%, minor impurities (silica 1.5, with other bases and alumina 4.5%.

Used mainly in stoneware glazes. Although of world-wide occurrence it has only lately been generally available to the craft potter and in 1973 is enjoying a considerable vogue. There are other suitable sources of calcia, but insoluble magnesia is less common (see *talc*).

Dolomite acts as a *flux* but, if used to replace whiting, it will raise the maturing temperature of a glaze. (See *magnesium.*) Average proportion in a glaze is 3-6% but up to 20% can be used for special effects. 2% or so may be added to a porcelain body. The typical magnesia effect derived from the use of dolomite is a smooth buttery surface.

## DOUBLE GLAZING

See *glaze-over-glaze.*

## DOUGH MIXERS

These machines, until recently used by small bakers, have found a new lease of life in craft potteries for

*A large dough mixer. The simple up and down scooping action of the pronged arm mixes the clay and water by continually turning it over and mashing it down. The great value of the equipment is proved by its popularity—it cuts out a good deal of laborious work. The process, however, needs some attention in this type of mixer; see also text. About 3 cwt. (170 kg.) can be mixed in thirty minutes ready for pugging, or wedging.*

mixing powdered clay and bodies with water into a plastic state, thus bypassing the blunger, drier etc.

Large mixers can deal with 150 kg. (330 lb.) of dry powder and water in 30 minutes; smaller ones 100 kg. (220 lb.) an hour. There are two types: the one illustrated in which the arm moves forward, down and up, turning and mashing the mixture; and the revolving arm type. The former needs some attention but the latter can be quite automatic in its action.

## DOWN-DRAFT KILN

A kiln in which the hot gases from the fireboxes rise first to the roof and are then drawn down through the setting and out into the chimney through flues in the kiln floor. The heat is better distributed and more efficiently used than in an *up-draft* kiln. The hot gases can be subsequently channelled under a brick floor for drying clay or pots. Rhodes (R.K 48-53) shows several types of down-draft kilns, while Cardew (C.PP 184) discusses the general principles. A good chimney is needed to exert the necessary 'pull' which forces the heat downwards against its inclination. A starting-fan or small chimney fire may be used to create the initial draft.

*Climbing kilns* and the Western two or three *chambered kilns* utilize a *diagonal down-draft.*

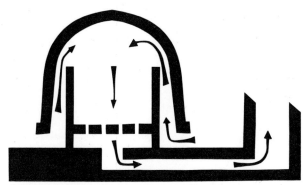

*A down-draft kiln with more than one fire mouth.*

## DRAPE MOLD

A mold or former over which clay is spread or 'draped'. (See *hump molds, formers.*)

## DRAFT

The upward movement of hot gases as a result of their expansion, and their replacement by further air from the atmosphere. This process is controlled in a fuel-burning kiln by the concentrated rising column in the chimney, the replacement air being drawn through the firebox or through secondary air vents. A slide or check put across the chimney, or a vent in the chimney (withdrawal of a brick) will both decrease draft.

Forced-draft may be introduced either by the use of a fan to speed the exit of gas in the chimney, or by pumping compressed air or gas into the kiln at the firemouth.

Draft is dependent on the diameter and height of the chimney and on the sizes of inlet and outlet apertures relative to the *expansion of gas.* (See also Cardew C. PP 180-6.)

## DRAWING A KILN

Unpacking a kiln.

## DRAW TRIALS

Test pieces withdrawn during the firing. Only possible with a large kiln spy-hole or when a brick can easily be withdrawn. *Buller's rings,* glazed rings or small pots can be quickly cooled and inspected. They will show shrinkage and the degree to which the glaze has melted, but color and other characteristics will be falsified to some extent by the rapid cooling.

## DRIP-FEED, oil

A simple type of burner in which the oil is dripped onto a heated metal plate or plates. The heat *volatilizes* the oil, which will then ignite. An ingenious horizontal box burner is illustrated in R.K 69-70.

There must be some method of supplying initial heat to the pan to start the process. This could be by the use of a more volatile material such as paraffin (kerosene), or with a gas jet (perhaps *bottled gas*). Cotton waste to soak up oil and act as a wick has also been suggested. An oil and water mixture, dripped simultaneously from separate jets, has been found to be more efficient than oil alone. The plate must be protected from too direct an inrush of cold air. It has a relatively short life, but the whole burner is so simple that this is no great drawback. An attractive looking design using a small coke fire to heat the drip pan, and utilizing a reverbatory design, was published in PQ 7 by John Dan.

It has been found that drip-feed systems are very smoky, especially early in the firing, and an open site is required. They have other limitations and are not suitable for large kilns. On the other hand crude or sump oil can be used.

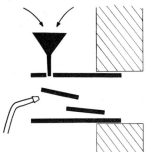

*Oil-drip pan based on a design in R.K. Oil and water are dripped in from above. A removable gas jet is shown which can heat the plates in order to start the process without too much smoke.*

## DRYING OF CLAYS AND GLAZES

Drying from slip to plastic state is dealt with under *dewatering.*

When plastic clay dries, water evaporates from the surface which becomes porous, further moisture being drawn by capillary attraction from the body of the clay. This action is sufficient to bring a thin-walled piece of pottery into balance with the humidity of the surrounding air. Further evaporation requires artificial heat or a drier atmosphere. This explains why clay dries more quickly on a cold night when most of the water in the air has been precipitated, than on a humid day in summer. For this reason too a pot appears to stay *leather-hard* for quite a time and then change color quickly.

Drying is accompanied by shrinkage. A thick wall of close-textured clay will tend to enclose a core of moisture which will have difficulty in getting away. The inclusion of grog or other coarse-grained material is necessary to maintain open pores in thick pots or models. Shrinkage is caused by the particles of clay packing closer together as the layers of water between them disappear; the greatest shrinkage is therefore from plastic to leather-hard. At leather-hard the lubrication between particles is poor and they can be moved relative to one another only by careful beating. When dry this lubrication is nil. Rapid drying is not dangerous in itself, but any unevenness in the drying will cause one part of a pot to shrink, putting the fabric into tension which can be relieved only by warping or cracking.

The precise state of dryness is not easy to establish. As mentioned above, *ambient* air humidity will control natural drying. A pot, even though thoroughly dried over heat, will reabsorb moisture if left long before firing. There are various ways of testing for dryness: David Leach places the rim or other surface of a warm pot against a pane of glass; any steam will soon be precipitated onto the glass. A thick-walled piece may be too hot to touch and yet still show steam if a piece of glass or plastic is held over the mouth of the pot.

Apart from the water mixed with the clay, which is driven off at 100°C., there remains the more stubborn adsorbed water which may need 200°C. to disperse fully. (See *adsorbed water, water-smoke*.)

The technique of *wet-firing* (described in CR 1) seems to contradict these statements, but other factors are at work here (e.g. the cooling effect of very rapid evaporation) and the system is hedged about with special provisions.

Glazes, especially soft glazes, must be fully dried before firing and, preferably, before packing in the kiln.

## DRYING SHRINKAGE

The shrinkage of a clay or body from plastic to dry is usually expressed as a linear percentage. Dodd (D.DC) quotes 6-10% for china clay; 9-12% for ball clay. Most of this occurs up to the leather-hard stage. Drying shrinkage is one indication of the usefulness of a clay sample (see *clay tests*). It is useful to work out the factor for your particular clay body; it will allow you to calculate the size of a lid, for instance, which is needed for a dried pot. The equation is $\frac{X}{Y} \times \frac{100}{1}$, where X is the percentage shrinkage of your test-piece and Y is the dry length of the test-piece. Example:

$$\frac{15 \text{ (\% shrinkage)}}{85 \text{ (dry length)}} \times 100 = 17\%.$$

The lid needs to be 17% larger than the pot. (See also *shrinkage*.)

## DRY STRENGTH

Clays vary greatly in their dry strength. A porcelain body will be very weak, *a secondary clay* may be nearly as hard as *biscuit*. Dry strength is probably increased by a well-graded particle size from medium to very fine, allowing a close 'pack'. It is associated with plasticity. Ball clays have a high dry strength, partly due to their fine grain, but also to the lignin humus (organic wood tissue) content of 'black' ball clays (W.C). Coarse-grained bodies such as poreclain will be easily shattered.

The form of a pot and the technique used in making it will have some effect on its dry strength. A bottle or other well-rounded thrown shape has greater resistance to blows and stresses than, for instance, a slab trough or a molded dish.

Resinous and fibrous bodies have been developed to give sufficient dry strength to obviate the firing of clay models in schools. They are not, of course, recommended for pots. (See *Newclay*.)

## DUNTING

The cracking of pottery in the kiln due to drafts of cold air striking it when firing or cooling, causing one area to contract more than the rest. *Free quartz* will increase the risk of dunting at dull red heat, and *cristobalite* at lower temperatures. Biscuit is more likely to dunt than glazed ware. A dense body is more susceptible than an open one. Rapid all-over cooling will not necessarily cause dunting—if it did, there would be no raku. *Sawdust firing* is very prone to severe dunting if not protected from draft. Ray Finch once-fires his large plates to minimize dunting, while others set large flat plates on clay wads so that they will not be affected by the different cooling rate of the kiln shelf. (See also *cracking, shattering*.)

## DUSTER

Flat duster, or a soft flat brush, $\frac{1}{4}$-1 in. (5-25 mm.) wide for laying on background color.

# E

## EARTHENWARE

The dictionary definition is 'vessels of baked clay'; in general usage it indicates pottery ware with a porous body which may or may not be covered with glaze. The Brussels Nomenclature agrees with this definition but excludes 'pottery made from common clay'—we are not told what this is to be called. The bulk of all ceramics is *earthenware*, which may range from the 1200°C. biscuit fired, fine-grained 'Queen's Ware' of Wedgwood to the soft red 'earthen platter' from Portugal.

The same clay body can often be used for *stoneware* or earthenware, according to whether it has been taken to its *vitrification* point or not. The normal dividing line is around 1200°C. but the craft potter's earthenware is rarely taken above 1150°C.

## EARTHENWARE GLAZES

Also known as 'soft' glazes. Broadly speaking, they are those glazes which mature below 1150°C. and are used to cover a porous body. The typical earthenware glaze is shiny and smooth. It can provide a very white background if required, on which colors are bright and clear. These qualities have been exploited to the full in past times, giving us the splendid *slipwares*, painted *tin glazes, lustres, turquoise, rakus*, and *underglaze* decoration from all parts of the world.

The formulas for earthenware glazes differ from those of stoneware and porcelain mainly in their choice of *bases*, and in the ratio of base to silica. A soft glaze can be prepared with soda as the only *flux* (the basis of Egyptian turquoise), but these are unstable, difficult to handle, and they always craze. More commonly, lead oxide has been used as the sole or major base. This type is now being called into question (see *soluble lead*), but a well-balanced and adequately fired lead glaze will be safe for the majority of tableware purposes. Lead gives a richness of quality which other fluxes cannot imitate. If a soft glaze does not contain lead oxide in significant amounts (at least 0.5 equivalents in the *RO group*) then it will need to contain boric oxide. This is generally added in the form of borax which is a soluble material and requires *fritting*. (See also *colemanite*.)

Soda, potash and lime are the usual secondary fluxes, with zinc oxide, lithia, strontia and magnesia sometimes playing a minor role. Boric oxide, though technically an acid and a *glass-former*, nevertheless lowers the melting point of a glaze and to this extent can be thought of as a fluxing agent. Lead and boron are used as silica fritts, the first because of its toxic nature, the second because it is soluble in water.

Recipes are legion and we cannot explore them in detail. Several are quoted in R.CGP, B.TP, P.CG and in most how-to-do-it books. It is more important to have some understanding of the principles, using the *Seger formula*.

The $RO/RO_2$ ratio of the majority of soft glazes is between 1:2 and 1:3. The $R_2O_3/RO_2$ ratio is between 1:8 and 1:12. (R stands for any appropriate element.) A typical formula might therefore read:

1 $RO:0.25. Al_2O_3:2.5 SiO_2$ where the RO group includes at least 0.5 PbO. If lead is absent, then boric oxide must comprise about 0.2 of the total $RO_2$ group. (See also *glaze, formula-into-recipe, base,* and under all the glaze *oxides*.) A variety of bases will help to give a more transparent and fully matured glaze.

The choice of bases will also influence the color reaction of any *pigment oxides*. An increase in the alumina content will take the shine from the surface. Opacifying agents will tend to harden, so raise the firing temperature; manganese will act as a flux. *Oxides, minerals* and *fritts* can be combined on one batch—a mixture is, in fact, advisable. It makes the physical process of glazing easier. Earthenware glazes are generally applied as a somewhat thinner coating than are stoneware glazes. A *soaking* fire of about 20 minutes will improve the quality of soft glazes and the *glaze-body* fit. (See *crazing, glazing,* and other entries.)

## EASY-FIRE

Firing terminated below the maturing temperature of a body. Soft biscuit.

## EFFLORESCENCE ON CLAY

A white surface scum which forms during firing, or occurs later, usually on red clays. It cannot be easily removed, even with abrasives. It is caused by soluble salts, mainly calcium, but occasionally other bases, sulphur, or chlorine, migrating to the surface during drying. Modeling, or any pottery subjected to a lot of handling, is especially prone. The addition of 1-2% barium or barytes to the body will help. Billington (B.TP) mentions a teaspoonful to a pint of red clay slip. (See also *Egyptian paste*.)

## EGOTE

Japanese name for a *throwing stick*.

*Three Japanese egote or throwing sticks. They are of wood with one rounded or bevelled edge.*

## EGYPTIAN PASTE

The body of the original Egyptian turquoise ceramics is reputed to be about 90% quartz with some soda. The glaze has been given as 75% silica, 20% alkalis and calcium, 1.8% copper oxide, by analysis. A. Lucas (L.GE) suggests common salt added to the body to give some dry strength, and to give soda flux.

An approximation in modern materials may be made as a paste or body from which soluble glaze materials will 'migrate' or effloresce onto the surface during drying. It follows that the drying should be slow and that the piece should be handled as little as possible. Place it on stilts ready for the kiln as soon as it is completed. Firing temperature 950-990°C. The body is short and open. The usual coloring material is copper, which gives the characteristic turquoise, but other *carbonates* can be used, e.g. manganese. The material has little plasticity when moist, and is friable when dry. It is generally restricted to jewelry and other small pieces.

Typical recipes:

A 'measure' recipe (Behrens CM):

| | |
|---|---|
| Flint or quartz | 16 spoons |
| Bentonite | 4 spoons |
| Sodium bicarbonate | 2 spoons |
| Copper carbonate | ½ spoon |

By percentage weights:

| | |
|---|---|
| Feldspar | 35 |
| Flint | 35 |
| China clay | 12 |
| Bentonite | 2 |
| Sodium bicarbonate | 6 |
| Sodium carbonate | 6 |
| Copper carbonate | 2–3 |

A more plastic version given in CM 16/2:

| | |
|---|---|
| Ball clay | 25 |
| Nepheline syenite | 25 |
| Fritt ferro 3134 | 15 |
| Flint | 20 |
| Fine sand | 5 |
| Anhydrous (calcined) borax | 3 |
| Soda ash | 4 |
| Bentonite | 3 |
| Copper carbonate | 2–3 |

Dextrin or other *siccative* can be added for dry strength. Also note that copper carbonate is toxic. Variations may be made in the feldspar/flint ratio between 20 and 40%; some ball clay can replace china clay. Up to 5% of whiting is sometimes recommended, while borax can be used to supply soda. Soluble varieties of the color oxide, e.g. copper chloride, may help. (See color plate 8, p. 132.)

## EJECTOR HEAD

A wheel head in the form of a shallow dish, the base of which can be raised to eject a plaster or wooden throwing-bat. Useful for large pots or for *repetition throwing*. (See also *wheel bats*.) When casting plaster bats in ejector heads (e.g. those from Potter's Equipment, London) the inner surface must be lightly greased with Vaseline.

*A pot on a plaster bat is lifted from an ejector head by upward pressure on a metal ring underneath.*

## ELASTICITY

The resumption by a material of its original shape and size when forces acting on it are removed. It is a valuable quality in bodies and glazes. It is said that *lead glazes* are more elastic than others.

## ELECTRICAL INSULATION

See *insulation, electric.*

## ELECTRICAL PORCELAIN

A very hard *'proto'-porcelain* with high *dielectric* strength but little or no *translucency*, from which electrical insulators, switches etc. are made. A recipe quoted is similar to that for industrial earthenware, but fired to *vitrification*: ball clay 28: china clay 22: quartz 25: feldspar 25. (See also *porcelain.*)

*Enormous power-station insulators in glazed electrical porcelain at Buller's factory. These fine shapes are built up, section by section, and generally fired whole. Trolleys are used, or 'top hat' kilns which are lowered over them. The testing area with continuous sparks from thousands of volts is quite an experience and the 'ozone' is marvellous!*

## ELECTRICITY

Electricity is a form of energy generated by the movements of electrons. The concept of electrical charge is the basis of *atomic science,* and enters into all chemical changes.

The term is commonly applied to the energy supplied as electric current either through metal cables from a generating-station or across the terminals of a battery. If a conducting material is placed across the terminals of an electric supply between the live (L) and neutral (N), current will flow. It will flow to an excessive and dangerous degree if there is nothing to stop it, a state known as a short circuit. However all materials exhibit a greater or lesser *resistance* to this flow, and it is in overcoming resistance that electrical energy is converted into heat. This heat is used to produce light, heat for kilns, and so on.

The heat produced is equal to the square of the current flowing. Where resistance is total no current flows, and the material is known as an insulator; where current flows with negligible resistance the material is a conductor. Many materials, especially in the presence of water, fall between these extremes. Even the best conductors will get hot and eventually melt if too much current is passed through them. A conducting wire must therefore be stout enough to withstand the current it is expected to pass. As explained below, the thicker the wire the less resistance it will exert. *Kiln element* wire has a controlled resistance in-built to produce heat according to certain equations.

Electricity is supplied at a given 'pressure' (to use an understandable but not quite accurate term) called the *voltage;* the amount of current is measured in *amperes;* the total power in *watts.* The resistance mentioned above is calculated in units called *ohms.* These four units—volts, symbol E (electromotive force); amperes, symbol A; watts, symbol W; and ohms, symbol R (resistance) are all interdependent. It is not necessary to understand the exact natures of these units to use them for simple electrical calculations.

Basic arithmetic:

If you have figures for any two unit values it is easy to arrive at the third by the equations:

1 $\dfrac{W \text{ (power)}}{E \text{ (volts)}} = A$ (current)

or the same equation another way round

$A \times E = W$

2 $\dfrac{E \text{ (volts)}}{A \text{ (current)}} = R$ (resistance in ohms)

(In books on electricity the physical quantity of current will be denoted by an italic *I.* For our purposes, however, it will simplify matters for us to retain A throughout. The sign $\Omega$ is used for resistance).

To turn the equations into a specific example: If our supply is at 240 volts and we want to design a 10,000 watt (10 kilowatts or kW) kiln then we need to pass $\dfrac{10,000}{240} = 41.6$ amperes of current.

If the kiln is wired in a single *circuit,* the resistance of the total wire (all the elements in *series*) must be: $\dfrac{240}{41.6} = 5.76$ ohms.

If it is to be wired in two circuits then each must pass $\dfrac{41.6}{2} = 20.8$ amperes, and the resistance in each circuit would need to be $\dfrac{240}{20.8} = 11.53$ ohms.

There are two laws concerning resistance in a wire which has, in fact, some parallel with the way water flows through a pipe. The first is that the thicker the wire (the greater the cross-sectional area) the less resistance it will offer and the greater amount of current can flow; and the second law states that the longer the wire the more resistance it will offer, and this will reduce the current which will flow. Thus a long thin wire will pass less current than a short thick one of the same type. These considerations must be borne in mind when conducting current to a kiln as well as in the kiln itself. (See under *electric kiln elements, electric wiring to kiln.*)

The third connection which you will find on all appliances is the E (earth) terminal. This is a safety measure. Normally the flow of current will be through the apparatus connected between L (live) and N (neutral) and will be under control. If, however, a live conductor accidentally comes into contact with another conductor not in the circuit, current will start to flow through it and it will become 'live'. A direct line to the ground, especially under damp conditions, will conduct a very high current, heating up rapidly in the process. This sudden surge can cause electric shock (burning) in human beings, or fire in a building. The earth terminal is literally what it says it is—a connection direct to the ground which will help to siphon off current which has strayed out of the circuit, and out of control. A long continuation of the flow is prevented by the insertion of a weak link in every circuit which will melt before much damage is done, and break the line. This is called a 'fuse'.

## ELECTRIC KILN

A pottery kiln heated by *resistance wire* or rods. It is, fundamentally, a simple piece of equipment. No provision need be made for the disposal of gases (chimney), for ash waste, or for vast supplies of air. All that has been done at the power-station, and energy is derived at 'second hand'. Like other 'canned' products it lacks 'incidentals', and variety must be attained through the ingenuity of the potter.

A box, constructed of insulating materials and housing a length of resistance wire, constitutes a kiln. The box can have an opening in the front or in the top. The heat is 'radiant', and this limits its size to about 24 cu. ft. (slightly less than 1 cu. m.). The proportions of the box will affect its efficiency (see *heat loss*). *Insulation* is of prime importance. A comparatively high initial outlay will soon be repaid in lower fuel bills. (See *insulation of heat.*) The inner brickwork must be very refractory and the element slots must be of an iron-free ceramic. The slots can be cut from H.T. insulating bricks such as those supplied by Gibbons or Molers in England, or they can be cast as larger units from *alumina cements.* The outer insulation may be of lower heat resistance bricks or slabs (around 850°C. for stoneware firing), or of ceramic fiber, *micropore,* Moler's 'Kipsulate' etc. The casing should be of asbestos sheet (not *asbestos cement*) or metal sheet. The skeleton structure is of angle iron or a similar material (Dexion etc.).

The fact that an electric kiln has no chimney means that sulfurous and other gases liberated by some clays pollute the atmosphere of the kiln room or pottery. Ventilation is essential but experiments in venting the actual kiln atmosphere through an outside wall have seriously retarded the temperature rise rate. The weight of a kiln should also be considered when planning an installation: on average the weight is one cwt. (50 kg.) for every kilowatt.

## ELECTRIC KILN ELEMENTS

This entry should be read in conjunction with that entitled *electricity.*

The power input to a kiln should be 3-3.5 kW per cu. ft. (0.03 cu. m.) of setting space up to 5 cu. ft. (0.15 cu. m.); 2-3 kW for 5-10 cu. ft. (0.15-0.3 cu. m.) with an additional kW per cubic foot above that. The lower figures are for earthenware, the higher ones for stoneware. (See also *heat loss.*)

The wiring for a kiln is first broken down into suitable circuits. A convenient maximum load is around 5 kW per circuit. Each circuit is then considered separately in calculating the length of wire needed. There are factors limiting the rating (wattage) of a circuit. If too much current is passed through too short or too thin a wire, the wire will be unable to disperse the heat produced and will burn out.

*Nichrome* wire is suitable only for low temperature kilns. *Kanthal* or a similar wire is needed for regular firings above 1000°C. Each gauge or thickness of wire is given a rating of so many ohms of resistance per foot or meter length. It is a simple matter to divide the total ohms required by this figure to arrive at the length of a circuit. The gauge recommended for stoneware is 13 s.w.g. or thicker. (See *Kanthal.*) The ohm rating (for *Kanthal* A1) is roughly 0.1 per foot or 0.33 per meter. The wire needed for a 5 kW circuit on a 240 volt supply is therefore:

$$\frac{5000}{240} = 20.8 \text{ amperes}$$

$$\frac{240}{20.8} = 11.5 \text{ ohms}$$

$$\frac{11.5}{0.1} = 115 \text{ feet of 13 s.w.g. A1 Kanthal.}$$

or $$\frac{11.5}{0.332} = 34.6 \text{ meters.}$$

Replacing the above with symbols so that the equations become general:

$$\frac{W}{E} = A$$

$$\frac{E}{A} = R$$

$$\frac{R}{R \text{ per foot}} = \text{circuit length of wire.}$$

standard wire gauge.

It is possible to use one gauge thinner for stoneware [14 s.w.g. (2.03 mm.)], and down to 18 s.w.g. (1.219 mm.), for earthenware. It is difficult for a potter to wind wire thicker than 13 s.w.g. (See *element winding.*)

As mentioned above there is a minimum practical length for a circuit. As a very rough guide, reject any computation arrived at by means of the above equations which results in less than 100 ft. (30 m.) of wire to produce $4\frac{1}{2}$ kW.

Another limitation on possible wiring schedules is the length of wire which can be physically accommodated in a kiln. As a guide: 17 ft. (5 m.) of 13 s.w.g. wound on a $\frac{3}{8}$ in. (10 mm.) mandrel will give 30 in. (760 mm.) of stretched element. The arrangement of elements is important. They should be housed in the floor, rear wall and two side walls of a front-opening kiln; in the floor and all four walls of a top-opener. There is always loss of heat through the roof especially in *top-loaders*, which can be minimized by placing the upper elements closer together. The floor needs about one-fifth of the total circuitry.

Connections: the length of the element 'tails' must be the width of your kiln wall plus an extra inch (25 mm.). It is a good idea to allow twice this length so that the tail can be doubled back on itself and twisted together. This effectively doubles its cross-sectional area, lowering its resistance and preventing heat being generated where it will do no good. The connectors known as *line taps* are the best type for securing the element to the asbestos-covered connecting wires. These wires join the elements of a single circuit into a continuous run, the ends of which are connected to a live and neutral of the electrical supply. (See also *circuit*). All connections must, of course, be shielded from any possibility of being accidentally touched. (See also *silicon carbide elements.*)

Resistance wire tends to be more brittle in cold weather even before being fired. After a few firings it becomes almost as brittle as glass and it is difficult to extract a fired element whole.

## ELECTRIC WIRING TO KILN

Apart from the computations involved in the *resistance* wiring of a kiln, the current must be conducted to it. The wire used for this purpose must be able to take the full load for long periods without getting hot. The same rules hold as for resistance wire: less resistance in thicker, shorter wires; more in longer or thinner ones. Short runs between supply and kiln are therefore preferable where possible.

*A switchboard for a three phase electric kiln.*
*The mains cables (three phase in this case) enter at the top, pass through the meter (top center) and then through the contactor (bottom right) which is controlled by the clock at top left. Finally the wires enter the fused switch box in the center (shown opened). The other two boxes are bottom left, a second switch which isolates the contactor if anything goes wrong with it, but this is not strictly essential; and the smaller switch top right is an earth trip which again cuts off the whole system if a 'short' occurs. This switch is compulsory in some regions. There would be fewer wires in a single phase system but similar equipment would be needed.*

A composite cable holding the live, neutral and earth can be used to conduct *single-phase* current, but *three phases* and neutral are each given a separate wire which is then housed in a protective metal or plastic tube, or 'conduit'.

Switchgear etc. must all be rated at or above the load your kiln will need. *Three-phase* switches are rated at *amperes* per phase, e.g. a 30 amp fused switch will carry a total of 30 x 3=90 amps.

The following is a guide to the wire gauges for conducting various loads. The wire is stranded. The first figure denotes the number of strands, the second the diameter of each strand in millimeters. The table is for p.v.c. insulated cables.

| Size | Nominal cross-section area in mm³ | Current rating (amps) In conduit | On surface |
|------|------|------|------|
| 1/1.13 | 1.0 | 11 | 13 |
| 1/1.38 | 1.5 | 13 | 16 |
| 1/1.78 | 2.5 | 18 | 23 |
| 7/0.85 | 4.0 | 24 | 30 |
| 7/1.04 | 6.0 | 31 | 38 |
| 7/1.35 | 10.0 | 42 | 51 |
| 7/1.70 | 16.0 | 56 | 68 |

An isolator (a fused switch-box), and possibly a contactor if you are using off-peak current, will be required by the Electricity Authority.

## ELECTROLYTE

'A compound which, when dissolved in water, partially *dissociates* into *ions* (electrically charged atoms and molecules). Added to clay slips . . . to control flow properties' (D.DC). Electroyltes in common use in ceramics are sodium silicate, soda ash and sodium tannate. (See *deflocculation*.)

## ELECTRON

An elementary particle or basic unit constituent of an *atom*. Electrons make up the outer 'shells' and determine *valency*. An electron bears a 'negative' electrical charge. They can be freed from their atomic orbits and taken up by other atoms which then become electrically unbalanced—a negative *ion*. The atom which 'loses' an electron becomes positively charged.

Atoms are most stable when their outer shells contain two or eight electrons. To achieve this state, sharing and transfers occur between atoms of elements forming 'bonds' and building up molecules and networks—i.e. *crystals* and all the materials of the physical world. (See also *atomic theory, valency, ion, lattice* etc.)

The number of *electrons* in the successive orbits of 'shells' of atoms in the commonly used pottery elements:

| ELEMENT | | 1st | 2nd | 3rd | 4th | 5th | 6th | 7th |
|---------|----|-----|-----|-----|-----|-----|-----|-----|
| Hydrogen | H | 1 | | | | | | |
| Lithium | Li | 2 | 1 | | | | | |
| Boron | B | 2 | 3 | | | | | |
| Carbon | C | 2 | 4 | | | | | |
| Oxygen | O | 2 | 6 | | | | | |
| Fluorine | F | 2 | 7 | | | | | |
| Sodium | Na | 2 | 8 | 1 | | | | |
| Magnesium | Mg | 2 | 8 | 2 | | | | |
| Alumina | Al | 2 | 8 | 3 | | | | |
| Silica | Si | 2 | 8 | 4 | | | | |
| Phosphorus | P | 2 | 8 | 5 | | | | |
| Potassium | K | 2 | 8 | 8 | 1 | | | |
| Calcium | Ca | 2 | 8 | 8 | 2 | | | |
| Titanium | Ti | 2 | 8 | 10 | 2 | | | |
| Chromium | Cr | 2 | 8 | 13 | 1 | | | |
| Manganese | Mn | 2 | 8 | 13 | 2 | | | |
| Iron | Fe | 2 | 8 | 14 | 2 | | | |
| Cobalt | Co | 2 | 8 | 15 | 2 | | | |
| Nickel | Ni | 2 | 8 | 16 | 2 | | | |
| Copper | Cu | 2 | 8 | 18 | 1 | | | |
| Zinc | Zn | 2 | 8 | 18 | 2 | | | |
| Selenium | Se | 2 | 8 | 18 | 6 | | | |
| Zirconium | Zr | 2 | 8 | 18 | 10 | 2 | | |
| Cadmium | Cd | 2 | 8 | 18 | 18 | 2 | | |
| Tin | Sn | 2 | 8 | 18 | 18 | 4 | | |
| Barium | Ba | 2 | 8 | 18 | 18 | 8 | 2 | |
| Praseodymium | Pr | 2 | 8 | 18 | 21 | 8 | 2 | |
| Lead | Pb | 2 | 8 | 18 | 32 | 18 | 4 | |
| Uranium | U | 2 | 8 | 18 | 32 | 21 | 9 | 2 |

## ELECTROVALENT

Bonds formed between atoms through the transfer of *electrons*, forming positive and negative *ions*. (See also *atomic theory, bond, valency*.)

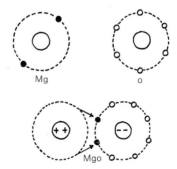

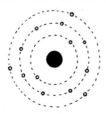

*An aluminium atom, showing 'orbits' of 2.8.3 electrons round a nucleus which consists of 13 protons and 13 neutrons.*

*Electrovalent bonding of magnesia, between magnesium with 2 electrons in its outer shell and oxygen with 6. The oxygen makes up an orbit of 8 by annexing the 2 magnesium electrons thus becoming a negatively charged ion—an O⁻⁻ ion. The magnesium loses the whole of its outer (third) shell leaving a complete second shell of 8 electrons. The loss leaves 2 unbalanced positive protons and it becomes a Mg** ion.*

## ELEMENT, chemical

'A substance which, so far as we know, contains only one kind of matter' (Mellor). There are about one hundred elements and all creation is built up from these simple materials.

Elements are denoted by internationally agreed symbols. These may correspond to the English name or may be derived from the Latin e.g. tin from *stannum*. Elements seldom exist alone in nature, but are found as compounds of two or more. Those elements of specific interest to potters are listed with their symbol and atomic weight under their English name in the entry for *atomic weight*. Here they are listed alphabetically according to their symbol. This will be a convenient reference when deciphering formulas.

| | | | |
|---|---|---|---|
| Al | Alumina | Mg | Magnesium |
| Ag | Silver (argentum) | Mn | Manganese |
| B | Boron | Na | Sodium (natrum) |
| Ba | Barium | Ni | Nickel |
| Bi | Bismuth | O | Oxygen |
| C | Carbon | P | Phosphorus |
| Ca | Calcium | Pr | Praseodymium |
| Cd | Cadmium | S | Sulfur |
| Cl | Chlorine | Se | Selenium |
| Co | Cobalt | Sn | Tin (stannum) |
| Cr | Chromium | Sr | Strontium |
| Cu | Copper (cuprum) | Ti | Titanium |
| F | Fluorine | U | Uranium |
| Fe | Iron (ferrum) | V | Vanadium |
| Ge | Germanium | Zn | Zinc |
| H | Hydrogen | Zr | Zirconium |
| K | Potassium (kalium) | | |
| Li | Lithium | | |

## ELEMENT, electric kiln

A convenient section of a *circuit* which can be housed in a single element slot or, as a 'hairpin' element, in two slots of an electric kiln. The elements which go to make up one circuit are connected one to the other outside the kiln by line taps and asbestos-covered wire, or by other means (solid brass connectors etc.). An element is, therefore, a suitable length of wire wound into a spiral, with a 'tail' or connecting length at each end long enough to go right through the kiln wall. Occasionally a thin wire circuit may be wound into a continuous element, but multi-length elements are difficult to manipulate with wire thicker than 15 s.w.g. (1.8 mm.).

The individual element length can be varied so long as the total wire length over the whole circuit is not altered. Elements can also be in the form of resistance tapes or rods (see *silicon carbide elements, electricity, kiln elements, Kanthal, element winding*).

## ELEMENT-WINDING

Electric kiln resistance-wire up to 13 s.w.g. (2.34 mm.) can easily be wound into elements by hand. The winder is simply a length of iron rod bent into a handle at one end and set in two bearings [holes in a piece of $\frac{3}{4}$ in. (20 mm.) timber are sufficient]. The length of the frame depends upon your element length when tightly wound (i.e. not the stretched length). The bearings will need to be about 6 in. (150 mm.) further apart than this. As a guide: 17 feet (5 m.) of 13 s.w.g. will wind into about 14 in. (350 mm.) of close coils. An element must always be pulled out to twice its wound length, so this example will span a 30 in. (750 mm.) kiln slot. 18-22 in. (460-560 mm.) is therefore a reasonable distance between bearings. Some means of gripping one end of the wire must be provided, and it must be possible to slide the completed coil from the rod. The illustrations show one system, but others will occur to you. A wallpaper-trimmer has been utilized by Tony Benham.

During the winding, the wire must be kept taut by feeding it through a V-slot in a wooden block which runs along a second shaft. Single and hairpin elements can be wound on this machine at the rate of a dozen or so an hour.

*Method.* Cut the wire to the appropriate length, leaving enough for twisted tails at each end. The tails can be twisted in a vice before you start winding. Always use wooden jaws in the vice, and take extreme care never to nip, score, or damage the wire with metal tools during any process—it will only be as strong as its weakest part. Wind at a regular speed and keep the coils touching one another. Perfect elements will come with a little practice. Remove the coil from the rod, grip one end in a vice and the other with pliers or both hands, and pull it steadily apart until it has reached the length of the slot in which it is to be housed. You should be able to slot a piece of the same wire between the stretched coils.

1

2

3

4

5

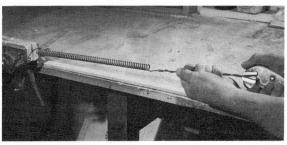

6

*Making and fitting kiln elements. After measuring the required element lengths plus the ends which go through the walls of the kiln—the 'tails'—the ends are folded back for 9 in. (230 mm.) and twisted together (1). Use hardwood jaws in the vice and take care not to twist the wire beyond the double section. The object of doubling the wire is to minimize the resistance at this point. A typical home-made winder and the start of a wind is shown (2). Wire is fed through a wooden block which acts as a guide and keeps the wire taut (fairly strong wrists are also required) (3). You may be able to invent a better way of removing the*

*wound element but in the winder illustrated the bar is removed from the frame (4) each time and the element slides over the handle (5). A hairpin element is shown, which has been wound from each end. The close winds must now be stretched out to the length of the element slot (at least twice the wound length). One end of the element is clamped in wooden vice jaws, the required length of the element marked on a batten or on the bench, and steadily pulled from the other end (6). It will always spring back a little when released.*

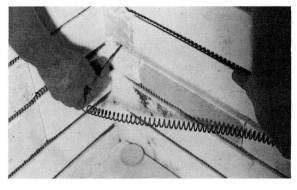

*Setting the element (a hairpin) into the slots in a top loading kiln.*

*A section through a kiln wall showing the shape of the element slots and the position of the coils. Silicon carbide elements need more clearance (see diagram under that heading).*

## ELUTRIATION

The separation of particles according to their *specific gravity* by a controlled jet of air or steam. Can also be used as a method of determining particle size.

## EMBOSSING

Decoration applied to clay. Strictly speaking, it should be in the form of a 'boss' or circular motif, but the term is also used in a more general way. Very free single or repeat patterns can be achieved with deft strokes of the finger on pellets of clay applied to a dampened surface, as on some splendid medieval jugs. A potter's *seal* can form a significant embossed break on a smooth surface. One can *comb* added clay or build up three-dimensional patterns. (See also *sprigging, applied decoration.*)

## EMPIRICAL FORMULA

The simplest type of formula, merely listing the proportions of the elements which make up the material. (See *rational formula.*)

## ENAMEL

Enamels, or enamel colors, are on-glaze pigments with a firing range of 690-850°C. They are applied to already fired glazed ware, which is then given a third firing to melt and fix the enamels. They are, in effect, very soft colored *fritts*. They may contain slightly toxic materials.

The term 'enamel' (like 'majolica' when applied to a glaze) is sometimes used, in a confusing way, to indicate opaque, stained earthenware glazes, but we will confine discussion here to the low firing pigments.

The color range is wide, with many strong reds which do not feature in the higher-fired pigments. The general tone is bright and clean. In the West enamels are traditionally handled in a rather genteel way. Japanese potters and, recently, a few in the West have a bolder approach with vivid sweeps of the brush, especially on *raku*; see color plate 9, p. 132.

Enamels are mixed rather like oil paints, working and grinding the pigment with a *palette knife* on a glazed tile or a glass *muller*. The traditional medium is *fat oil* of turpentine (not substitute turpentine). It can be prepared by leaving turpentine in a cup to evaporate for a few days until a gummy residue remains. Prepared medium can be bought with the colors. The industry has a method of applying an even coating called *ground lay. Silk screen* printing can give interesting and bold effects.

The kiln must be well-ventilated during the early burning-off stage of the firing, and accurate temperature control established. Frequently more than one firing is required, the higher temperature range of colors being painted and fixed first, with subsequent firings for the more fugitive reds and golds. Enamels can be combined with underglaze pigments and even used on stoneware, though they may be difficult to 'fix' and will require a fairly smooth glaze.

Enamels will eventually wear away in use. A special type is commonly used on metal.

## ENCAUSTIC

A somewhat misleading term for pottery *inlay*, especially tiles.

## ENDOTHERMIC

Heat absorbent. Clay has an endothermic peak during firing at 580°C., when it releases its combined water. Corollary of *exothermic*.

## END POINT

The squatting temperature of a cone.

## ENGINEERING BRICK

A highly vitrified brick which may be red or black according to kiln atmosphere. Of low *porosity* and great strength. A poor heat *insulator* and not suitable for kiln building. Used where high mechanical strength is the prime consideration. Made of etruria *marl* or clay with a fairly high flux content.

## ENGOBE

An American term for *slip*, but which also covers a wider field than traditional *slipware*.

Engobes may contain very little plastic clay, being largely composed of materials more usually associated with glazes—feldspars, flint, opacifiers and fluxes. As distinct from the earthy qualities of European slipware, engobes are sophisticated and often white or near-white, providing a base for coloring oxides. Engobe recipes appear involved and artificial to an English potter, but they are more adaptable to stonewares and can even be used on biscuit.

The six groups of materials listed by Rhodes (R.CGP 160) are:
1 The clays—with china clay for its whiteness and to control shrinkage.
2 *Fluxes*—the various base fluxes used in glazes.
3 Fillers—mainly flint.
4 Hardeners—borax and gums.
5 *Opacifiers*—zircon etc.
6 Colorants—the *pigment oxides*.

Rhodes also lists a number of recipes. It is possible to use a commercial white casting *body* on most conditions of clay or on biscuit (which should be dampened) (CM 20/4 Behrens).

Too great a shrinkage of the engobe will cause cracking or *crazing;* too little, scaling and *flaking*. Materials should not be too finely ground. A *vitreous* engobe can replace a glaze. (See also *slip*.) Parmelee also discusses engobes at length in P.CG Chapter 10.

## ENGRAVING

A design cut into clay, usually with a wooden or bamboo tool cut to an angle or to a rounded point. This is preferable to a sharp metal point, which will give a weak and furrowed line. Experiment on various conditions of clay, up to leather-hard; the drier the clay the tighter and sharper will be the cut line. The traditional glaze for engraving is a transparent colored stoneware such as *celadon* on a fairly pale body. The increased depth of glaze in the cut line deepens the color and delineates the design. (See David Leach teapot under *cane handle*.)

## EPSOM SALTS

Magnesium sulfate $MgSO_4.7H_2O$, 246.5. It has been mentioned as a glaze *suspender:* 3 parts of water to 1 part salts giving a concentrated solution of which 2 teaspoonsful to a pint is an average addition.

## EQUILIBRIUM DIAGRAM

See *phase diagram*.

## EQUIVALENT WEIGHT

A term used in connection with glaze formulas to indicate the amount, or unit, of an *oxide* which enters into a glaze. This is usually but not always the same as the molecular weight of the raw compound or mineral.

Red lead, for instance, is $Pb_3O_4$, while the unit entering into the glaze composition (that at the head of the column when translating *formula-into-recipe*) is PbO. If we include three parts of red lead this will give nine parts of lead oxide, PbO. To keep the arithmetic correct we divide the molecular weight of red lead by three: $\frac{685}{3}$ =an 'equivalent' weight of 228.3. Such modifications are noted against the compounds concerned in the appropriate entry in this book. Colemanite is the most common example in glaze computation.

## ESTUARINE CLAYS

Clays which have settled in a river estuary. 'One of the better clays' (Cardew). Often deposited in thin layers with considerable variation. The ball clays of Wareham, Dorset, are valuable estuarine clays.

## ETRURIA MARL

An ancient clay (carboniferous, three hundred million years ago) used for bricks, tiles and for *engineering bricks*. High iron-content. Occurs on sites other than those at Stoke-on-Trent, from which it derives its name.

## EUTECTIC POINT

That mixture of two or more substances which has the lowest melting point of the whole series. Some mixtures have more than one low or eutectic point.

A eutectic diagram looks like this:

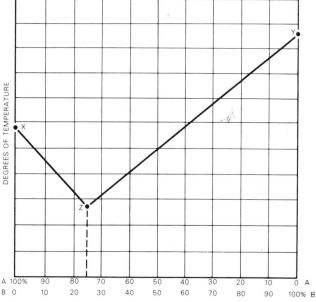

*A eutectic point (Z) between two materials with different melting points. X is the melting point of material A (if each division on the scale represented 200°C. this would be 1075°C); Y is the melting point of material B. For further explanation see text.*

In this case the eutectic would be 75% A and 25% B.

It will be seen from this diagram that even though one material may have a much lower melting point than the other, the eutectic is lower still. It follows that

an increase in the amount of either material—i.e. a movement to one side or the other of the low point—will raise the melting point of the mixture. This must be remembered when compounding glazes, an increase of the nominally *fluxing* material not necessarily continuing to 'soften' the glaze.

Glaze formulas for clear glazes aim at the eutectic. For expressing eutectics of three materials a *triaxial diagram* is needed; for more than three the problem becomes, mathematically speaking, very involved. Eutectic combinations form from materials within a pottery body, forming fluid glasses and lowering their *refractoriness* and *deformation point*. Glazes also go through liquid-in-solid phases.

The alumina-silica eutectic of 1595°C. occurs at 5.5 alumina: 94.5 silica.

Near equal mixtures of calcite, kaolinite and quartz have a low eutectic below 1200°C. This is equivalent to the formula 1.0 CaO. 0.35 $Al_2O_3$. 2.49 $SiO_2$. (Cardew). The eutectic of potash, at 770°C., is 1 $K_2O$. 0.5$Al_2O_3$. 5.5 $SiO_2$.

## EXOTHERMIC

Releasing or creating heat by chemical reaction. Occurs in the firing of most clays at 900-1000°C.

## EXPANDING PULLEY

A pulley wheel in which the flanges are separate. They are held together by a spring, but can be forced apart by the strong pull of an A-shaped belt. As the belt approaches the center of the pulley, the speed ratio will be altered. The system has been utilized for varying the speed of a *power wheel*. See PQ 34 for building details (Bill Read).

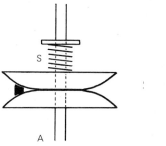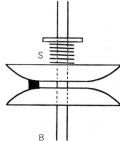

*The principle of the expanding pulley: A, shows the belt (black section) near the perimeter of the pulley when under minimum tension, the spring S. holding the faces of the pulley together. If the tension or pull on the belt is increased it forces the halves apart and the comparative turning speed of the pulley is increased—as in B.*

## EXPANSION

Expansion takes place when a material is heated. In pottery materials there are three types of thermal expansion:

1 The reversible expansion common to most materials, which occurs steadily and progressively upon

heating, with contraction upon cooling. Oxides have different rates of expansion which have been worked out as *coefficients*. An understanding of these is of great help in compounding glazes, especially with reference to crazing.

2  The expansion associated with quartz and cristobalite *inversion* which takes place very suddenly at 573°C. and 220°C. respectively. These are reversible.

3  The expansion which occurs in a clay body up to about 750°C. This is not reversed on cooling. A low-fired biscuit pot will be slightly larger than the dry clay pot. As soon as *vitrification* begins it involves a non-reversible shrinkage. At Crowan Pottery, Harry Davis fired very soft biscuit and then packed his glazed pots actually touching one another in the saggars, the shrinkage being sufficient to part them before the glaze melted.

A fourth, very slight, expansion can result from moisture *adsorption* by the fired pot. It will be enough to cause delayed *crazing* if the glaze is already in slight *tension*.

## EXTRUSION

Forcing clay through a *die* on a *pug* or *wad box*. Coils or more involved shapes can be extruded. In the industry handles, bricks, pipes etc. may be made in this way.

# F

## FACET

Thrown pots and bowls can be beaten or cut to produce facets or panels. Cut bowls are thrown thickly and cut with a wire while still soft, or may be roughly beaten prior to cutting; the resultant circle within a polygon is an attractive contrast. Beating may be done at the leather-hard stage. The blunt directness of John Reeve's work illustrates one extreme of the style.

*A cut-sided faceted bowl by John Reeve.*

## FACTOR

See *conversion factor*.

## FAIENCE

Applied to once-fired tin-glazed wares of eighteenth-century France, the name derived from Faenza where tin-glazed *majolica* was extensively made. Later used to denote any glazed earthenware. The French call the fine-bodied English earthenwares 'faience-fine'. In the USA it indicates a clear-glazed decorated pottery, a definition still further from its origins. Even more surprisingly it is applied to any large ceramics used on buildings.

## FAT CLAY

A highly plastic and workable fine-grained clay.

## FAT OIL

The thick varnish-like residue resulting from the exposure of turpentine to the air for a period of time. Fresh turpentine can be added periodically. The traditional vehicle for underglaze and on-glaze pigments. (See also *enamels*.)

## FEATHERING

A type of decoration in which *trailed* lines and dots of *slip* are drawn out by means of a thin and preferably pliable tool, such as the center rib of a feather. If the tool is drawn in alternate directions an overall pattern develops. The technique should be used with discretion—design values can be lost in an excess of random feathering. With skill, a number of variations can be developed—curved lines, or a quick flick at the end of a stroke, for instance. Often combined with design trailing, e.g. for delineating a bird's beak or fish scales.

Both the base slip and the trailed line must be wet and fluid. One should avoid cutting into the clay beneath. Use the feather fairly upright; if its length is dragged through the slip, a dead and muddy line will result. Turn the dish to reverse the line direction. Feathering on upright or convex surfaces, as done on seventeenth century beakers, for instance, needs considerable skill.

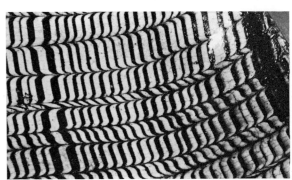

*A close-up of a nineteenth century trailed dish which has been feathered back and forth in parallel lines.*

*A John Shelley dish feathered radially.*

## FELDSPAR, felspar, minerals

Feldspar is now the internationally agreed spelling. A large group of minerals which have decomposed from granite and *igneous* rocks and are thus allied to clay. Of world-wide occurrence.

The main group consists of the alumino-silicates of potassium, sodium, calcium, and, more rarely, barium. The ideal formulas, never quite achieved in nature, are:

| Potash feldspar | Orthoclase Microline | $K_2O.Al_2O_3.6SiO_2$ | 556 |
| Soda spar | Albite | $Na_2O.Al_2O_3.6SiO_2$ | 524 |
| Lime spar | Anorthite | $CaO.Al_2O_3.2SiO_2$ | 278 |

Most feldspars are mixtures and are selected according to the predominance of one or other base. A typical analysis of an orthoclase spar by weight:

| | | | | | |
|---|---|---|---|---|---|
| $K_2O$ | 10.3 | $Al_2O_3$ | 17.5 | $SiO_2$ | 68.2 |
| $Na_2O$ | 2.5 | $Fe_2O_3$ | 0.2 | | |
| $CaO$ | 0.25 | | | | |
| $MgO$ | 0.12 | | | | |

There is a series of mixtures between soda and lime spars known as the *plagioclase*. There is no potash-lime series.

Feldspars are the most useful minerals in ceramics, apart from clays. Used as a primary *flux* above 1200°C. and as a secondary flux in earthenware. Also in *bodies* and *engobes*. Many spars begin to melt at 1180°C. and continue to form complex fluids up to 1500°C. They are natural *fritts*. Molten feldspar has a high *viscosity* which assists the standing-strength of porcelains and helps prevent glazes running during firing.

China stone is a slightly more refractory spar containing all three bases. *Nepheline syenite* is a fusible feldspathoid, high in alumina. (See also *feldspathic*, *spodumene, petalite etc.*)

## FELDSPAR CONVENTION

The normal *analysis* of clays will list the *oxides* present. A rational analysis, listing the assumed *minerals* present, is more useful as a guide to its behavior and in calculating its *Seger formula*.

Under the feldspar convention it was assumed that the minerals in clay were kaolinite, feldspar and quartz. Recent research suggests that *mica* rather than feldspar more accurately fulfils the theoretical grouping of oxides. Hence the *mica convention*. Both however are arbitrary, and the practical value of considering feldspar as a mineral in the rational formula is not greatly diminished.

Cardew points out that the mineral *illite* may have to be considered, and that some kaolinite may be replaceable by *montmorillinite*.

## FELDSPATHIC, glazes, minerals

Containing feldspar. Generally used in connection with stoneware or porcelain glaze where the mineral is used to provide the primary flux. Characteristically a smooth clean glaze if sufficiently thickly applied, but without a strong character.

The feldspathic minerals constitute a large family: as well as those discussed under *feldspar*, there is also leucite which, with nepheline, is sometimes called a feldspathoid.

## FELDSPATHOID

A term sometimes applied to the more distant members of the feldspar family: nepheline and leucite.

## FELSPAR

See *feldspar.*

## FERRIC CHROMATE

See *iron chromate.*

## FERRIC IRON

The stable, red oxide of iron $Fe_2O_3$, 160. The mineral is hematite. Ferric iron has a high melting point (1565°C.) and does not act as a flux. Ferrous iron, however, has very different effects.

All iron compounds revert to the ferric form in an oxidized fire. Many will be listed in merchants' catalogs, all with the formula $Fe_2O_3$. A 'synthetic' ferric is produced, very fine and pure, but I have not found that it noticeably improves color. Crocus martis is a natural ferric; ochre, sienna and umber are earthy oxides. Ferric is the coloring in red clay. Hematite produces the sparkle in *aventurine* glazes.

Ferric can be used as a pigment in all glazes with a normal maximum addition of 12%. The red quality is lost in most glazes where ferric produces yellow-brown to black. Iron precipitated onto the surface in *kaki* glaze holds nearest to the original color. (See *red glazes.*) Results are more interesting and variable if red clay is used to supply ferric. (See also *iron.*)

## FERROSO-FERRIC IRON, magnetite

$Fe_3O_4$ ($FeO.Fe_2O_3$). (See *iron.*)

## FERROUS IRON

The 'lower' oxide of iron FeO, 72, m.p. 1370°C. Will revert to ferric in an oxidized fire. Ferrous (reduced) iron in a body will act as a flux, causing it to melt, slump, or slag if present in quantity. In high-temperature glazes it may be ferrous iron which produces the typical reduced greens and blues. (See also *ferrous titanite, ilmenite.*)

## FERRUGINOUS

Iron (oxide)-bearing. Ochre, for instance, is a ferruginous earth.

## FETTLING

Term used more often in the industry than by craft potters. It signifies the trimming and smoothing of a leather-hard pot, especially the sharp edges left by molds. Cardew uses the term to cover the removal of glaze from foot rings, lids etc., but this is unusual. Fettling is best done with a fine-bladed knife (see Wengers 2071 W).

## FILLER

The silica addition to an *engobe* or body. Rhodes also mentions *pyrophyllite*.

## FILTER PRESS

Equipment for dewatering clay, consisting of a concertina-like set of canvas bags which are filled with body-slip. These are squeezed from either end, forcing out the water. Filter presses involve major engineering work and occupy a lot of space. They are of limited effectiveness with very plastic clays, which quickly coat the canvas and render it almost waterproof. For a more promising approach for studios see *vacuum filter.*

## FINGER-COMBING, finger sgraffito

Decoration in wet slip on the surface of a dish or pot. Two or three fingers are drawn steadily across the slip, either straight or in a wavy line. The work is done a few minutes after slipping. The slip coat should not be too thick. A similar effect can be achieved with glaze and *glaze-over-glaze.*

*Finger-combing a dish. A swift and sure movement is essential. The technique can also be used for glaze (see example under beaten form).*

## FIREBRICK

A *refractory* brick, generally made from *fireclay* and *grog.* Industrial firebricks are given *P.C.E.* ratings. In America these are:
1  Superduty—P.C.E. 33.
2  High-duty—31.5.
3  Medium heat duty—29.
4  Low heat duty—15.

Grade 2 is recommended for kilns. The P.C.E. refers to the deformation point. In England the grading is according to alumina content: those with more than 38% alumina are called aluminous fireclay refractories (1650-1750°C.).

The refractoriness of firebricks increases with their alumina content. They are strong and resist *spalling,* but their high density reduces *insulation* value. *Conduction* loss is five or six times that of the same thickness of a No. 23 grade insulating brick, with four times the *heat storage.* Against this, firebrick has greater strength and abrasion resistance than insulating brick. Firebricks are never used in electric kilns, but are usual in oil-fired kilns. See under *bricks* for some available shapes of firebricks.

Super-quality firebricks are made from 'soaked' refractory minerals producing *mullite* and silliminite in the body. (See also *silliminite.*)

## FIRECLAY

A general name for *sedimentary clays* usually associated with coal measures—they are very ancient deposits. Many are black and shaly, compressed to a coal-like consistency, and must be pulverized before use. The 'underclays' immediately beneath the coal seams break down more readily in water. In the best fireclays impurities, i.e. minerals or oxides other than kaolinite, alumina and silica, should not exceed 5%. Not all fireclays are especially *refractory,* however, and may contain carbonates of iron and calcium. Particle size averages 0.1-5.0 *microns.* Reasonable plasticity and dry strength. Fired color is buff to light-brown. Used by potters in refractory mixtures and as a *body* component.

Grading of the refractory clays is by alumina content. Those with 38% $Al_2O_3$ or more are called aluminous fireclays. The common fireclays have 35-37% alumina—the high-duty clays 45% or more.

Rich glaze quality and color in *celadons* and other reduced iron glazes is reputed to derive from the use of fireclay in bodies. Mr Noakes of Potclays calls it 'sweated color'. The *pyrites* in fireclays also add interest.

## FIRECORD

A Japanese pot decoration. Straw rope is soaked in salt water and wound round a pot; the whole is then fired, giving semi-glazed lines.

## FIRECRACK

May be due to the opening up of an incipient crack caused by mishandling in the leather-hard state, bad joins, uneven thicknesses in the pot wall (particularly the base), over-wetting, or joining soft clay to hard. In all these cases the crack will be rather ragged. If due to dunting the crack is likely to be curved and sharp. Dodd mentions too rapid a fire, but this is not confirmed in practice, although the termination of a biscuit fire at 500-600°C. (dull red heat) is likely to result in extensive cracking. (See also *shattering*.)

Bad packing in the kiln: too great a weight in a *bung* of pots or bowls; the sitting of one pot in the neck of another, etc., can lead to cracking during firing.

## FIRE-EXTINGUISHER

Few cases have been reported of fires started by kilns (a bag of weed-killer may prove a greater danger as Mick Casson discovered), but precautions should be taken. If you employ assistants a fire-extinguisher is a statutory necessity. The solid (powder) extinguishers are recommended for electrical fires.

## FIRING

The heat treatment of ceramic materials at least to the *sintering* stage, in practice to a minimum of red heat (600°C.). It is the indispensable factor in pottery. A kiln should therefore be the first consideration when setting up a pottery or school department. Neither sun heat nor a cooking-oven will 'fire' pottery. *Sawdust* kilns frequently fail to develop the minimum temperature.

Firing involves two cycles: heating and cooling. The following chart shows the principal changes and alterations.

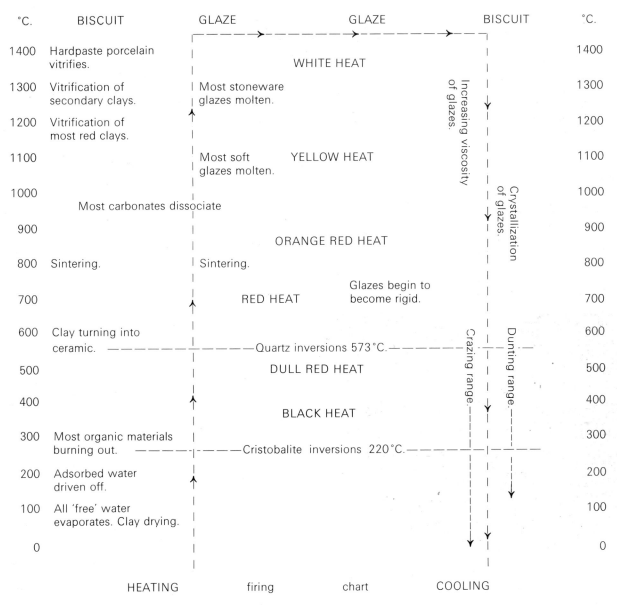

| °C. | BISCUIT | GLAZE | GLAZE | BISCUIT | °C. |
|---|---|---|---|---|---|
| 1400 | Hardpaste porcelain vitrifies. | | WHITE HEAT | | 1400 |
| 1300 | Vitrification of secondary clays. | Most stoneware glazes molten. | | | 1300 |
| 1200 | Vitrification of most red clays. | | | | 1200 |
| 1100 | | Most soft glazes molten. | YELLOW HEAT | | 1100 |
| 1000 | Most carbonates dissociate | | | | 1000 |
| 900 | | | ORANGE RED HEAT | | 900 |
| 800 | Sintering. | Sintering. | | | 800 |
| 700 | | | RED HEAT | Glazes begin to become rigid. | 700 |
| 600 | Clay turning into ceramic. | — — — Quartz inversions 573°C. — — — | | | 600 |
| 500 | | | DULL RED HEAT | | 500 |
| 400 | | | BLACK HEAT | | 400 |
| 300 | Most organic materials burning out. | — — Cristobalite inversions 220°C. — — | | | 300 |
| 200 | Adsorbed water driven off. | | | | 200 |
| 100 | All 'free' water evaporates. Clay drying. | | | | 100 |
| 0 | | | | | 0 |

Increasing viscosity of glazes.

Crystallization of glazes.

Crazing range.

Dunting range.

HEATING   firing   chart   COOLING

Involved chemical and physical changes take place during firing: firstly sintering, then a series of melts in the fabric as *eutectics* are reached. Clay expands slightly up to about 800°C., then begins to shrink as particles come closer together, either taking part in the glass-making activity of packing in a glassy matrix. When a certain proportion of glass is formed, the ceramic will begin to flow. This is the deformation point of a body. The normal reversible expansions and *inversions* also cause molecular changes in volume. (See *crazing, thermal shock, etc.*) The speed as well as the temperature reached will affect the result of a firing.

It will be seen that the most significant changes take place early in a biscuit fire and late in a glaze fire. Firing schedules should take this into consideration. While science and logic both suggest slow firing and cooling the tolerances are, in fact, very wide. The Japanese kilns at Tamba were raised from 700°C. to 1300°C. in two and a half hours, and cooled nearly as quickly. Biscuit, in a bonfire, develops almost instantaneously, while *raku* shows what stresses an open body will stand without serious damage. *Bone china* has been fired to 1250°C. in seven minutes!

In test kilns glazes are fired very quickly. All one can say for certain is that the quality of a glaze will vary considerably with the firing schedule, but only experience can show whether fast or slow firing gives the more desirable results.

### FIRING-GRAPHS

A kiln *graph* is the most economical and most easily

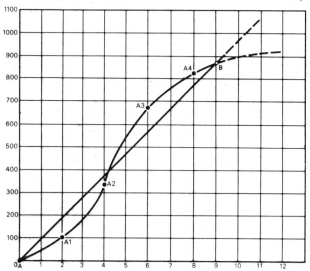

*A firing graph with a projection—dotted line—of the kiln's possible further performance had the firing continued at a steady rate. It will be seen that if only two points, A and B (the commencement and finish of the firing) had been marked in, the speed of temperature rise would have been falsified. A—a1—a4—B shows intermediate readings on a pyrometer and help us to plot a very different path which indicates that, in this case, the temperature rise will probably level out (the kiln failing to get any hotter) at below 1000°C.*

interpreted method of recording a firing, but it must be based on a minimum of three readings, either from *cones* or *a pyrometer*. The graphs show how a single end-point can be misleading.

The progressive heat loss which occurs as the gap between the *ambient* temperature and the temperature inside the kiln increases always produces a slowly flattening curve, and explains why the last few degrees are sometimes so difficult to attain. Graph lines can start at intervals along the base line for successive firings, to facilitate direct comparison. (See *graphs, kiln log.*)

### FLAKING

Usually applied to a fault in the *raw* rather than in the fired glaze. It is due to the surface coat shrinking less or much more than the body. *Flocculated* glazes (ash, colemanite) are prone to flaking. Flaking of fired ware is called shivering.

### FLAMBÉ

A glaze, generally on porcelain, streaked with reduced copper reds and purples, i.e. flame-like. Some crude modern copies are produced by an *on-glaze* method.

### FLAMEPROOF WARE

Flameproof pottery, as distinct from *ovenware*, is difficult to achieve. The very considerable thermal shock due to expansion and the inversion of *cristobalite* in a high-fired body, combined with the comparatively low conductivity of ceramics (relative to metal, for instance) present almost insoluble problems.

3

*Three views of a Portuguese flameproof dish. (1) Shows the curved base. The dish is glazed inside only (2). Obviously fired in heap or a crude bung as evidenced by the glazed ring beneath (3).*

The solution among primitive and less sophisticated communities is to use a body so soft and open that the shock can be accommodated within the structure. This involves a comparatively coarse body and presents glazing difficulties. A soft lead glaze is traditional, but this is frowned on today. The body needs to have a range of particle sizes and a minimum of 'free' silica. Porous red dishes up to 20 in. (500 mm.) diam. from Portugal and elsewhere are miraculously flameproof (and can be put onto a gas-ring) if soaked in water for twenty-four hours before being used for the first time. There is no obvious explanation. Perhaps *adsorbed* water helps to balance *thermal shock.*

Shape is a factor: For instance a shallow but continuously curved base which can expand without putting excessive strain on the wall. This may also be a reason for the predominance of rounded bases found in primitive pottery throughout the ages. There is no intermediate ceramic material between this type and a high-fired body of very low *thermal expansion,* e.g. true porcelain (1400°C.).

Cardew discusses the use of petalite and spodumene i.e. lithium bodies (C.PP 75-77). Zircon, also, has a *low coefficient of expansion.*

## FLANGE

A flat narrow projection, usually at right-angles, in the form of a collar or rim. Most commonly used by potters in connection with the seating of lids. (See under *lids* for several diagrams.)

*A lid flange being thrown on a casserole.*

## FLASHING

Accidental and partial reduction or over-firing, usually on biscuit. Also applied to the effect, on a part of a glaze surface, of a tongue of flame or hot gas which smoke-stains or alters the degree of *reduction.*

## FLASH WALL

See *bag wall.*

## FLAT LINER

A long, slender square-cut flat brush. (See *brush.*)

## FLATWARE

An industrial term for plates, saucers, etc. Flatware presents problems in throwing, drying and firing, especially when using highly plastic clay. This is evidenced by the dearth of hand-made plates. (See *plates.*)

## FLETTON

An English building-brick. Named after the original centre of manufacture near Peterborough, but now made in vast quantities from a deeper and harder clay seam which stretches from Yorkshire to Dorset, known as Oxford (Jurassic) clay. It is shaly and contains organic matter which assists firing. Flettons are made by a semi-dry method. Suitable for *raku* and similar firings and for the outer skins of higher temperature kilns. Flettons are more *porous* and better *insulators* than firebricks.

## FLINT

A dark blue-gray boulder pebble found in chalk seams. It is *calcined* into a white powder. It is a form of micro- (or crypto-) crystalline silica, $SiO_2$, of considerable purity.

A typical analysis (Wengers) by weight:

| | | | | | |
|---|---|---|---|---|---|
| CaO | 0.68 | $Al_2O_3$ | 0.29 | $SiO_2$ | 97.9 |
| $Na_2O$ | 0.05 | $Fe_2O_3$ | 0.07 | $TiO_2$ | 0.01 |
| MgO | 0.01 | | | | |

It is used to provide silica in glazes and bodies, and to whiten the latter. It is less pure but finer-grained than quartz, and thus more readily converted into *cristobalite.* It can be a health hazard if inhaled, and its use as a setting material is giving way to *alumina.*

In America 'flint' refers to any form of ground silica, including quartz.

## FLOATATIVES

An American term for additions to slips and glazes which prevent them settling in water. The English equivalent is *suspender.*

## FLUID, fluidity

A substance that takes the shape of the containing vessel. A liquid (or a gas).

The degree to which a material (glaze, slip etc.) approaches a liquid is its fluidity. The reciprocal of *viscosity.* Glazes are less fluid than glass, which does not contain alumina. Alkalis increase the fluidity of glazes. The unit of fluidity is the *poise*.

### FLUORINE

A gaseous element, F, 19. Known as a halogen or salt-producer: it reacts with alkalis to form a lattice similar to that of common salt. It also reacts with other pottery oxides. Can cause blisters on release from a glaze—(see *fluorspar*). China stone is sometimes defluorinated. Cryolite, sodium fluoride and lepidolite will also provide fluorine. In CM 19/7 Behrens discusses fluorine and gives some simple recipes, e.g.

| | | |
|---|---|---|
| Lepidolite | 52.0 | |
| Sodium fluoride | 2.8 | Cone 4 |
| Fluorspar | 12.4 | |
| Flint | 32.8 | |

He mentions that the glazes may be smooth or 'cratered' (bubbled), but does not give further advice. 'Considerable color variation from the norm' may be expected from the pigment oxides.

### FLUORSPAR

'Derbyshire spar'. $CaF_2$, 78. Decomposes in the presence of silica, forming a gas $SiF_4$, leaving CaO in the glaze. 'It perhaps has a catalytic effect on the calcium and other elements in the batch' (Cardew). Not widely used in pottery glazes, where over 5% may cause blistering. Can help to give a more transparent green stoneware glaze from chrome. Acts as a powerful flux in a multi-base glaze. (See also *fluorine*.)

### FLOCCULANT, flocculation

A material *(an electrolyte)* which hastens the settling of clays etc. in water (e.g. common salt). The flocculation, or flocking together, of river-borne clays as they enter salt or brackish water is responsible for deposits in estuaries—estuarine clays.

The immediate effect of flocculation is a thickening of a slip or glaze so that it needs more water to render it fluid. A flocculated glaze will adhere more easily to a high-fired, low-porosity biscuit (Rhodes). Ash and colemanite will sometimes cause flocculation. If water is then added to 'thin' the glaze, its drying shrinkage will be increased, leading to cracking and flaking.

Flocculants include aluminium sulfate and Epsom salts. Use 0.5-1%.

### FLUTING

The cutting of grooves into the surface of a pot. Leach (L.PB) illustrates a fluting tool: a thin strip of metal with a short cross-cut about $\frac{1}{2}$ in. (12.5 mm.) from one end, beaten down to form a tooth which gives a controlled, curved cut (very like one of the individual cutting edges on a Surform tool). A fine wire-ended tool, perhaps with a 'stop' on it to prevent too deep a cut, is more easily available. Less 'accurate' but livelier cutting is done with a bamboo tool sharpened to a chisel edge towards the outer, harder skin of a large-diameter bamboo.

The state of dryness of the clay will affect the character of the cuts. Fluting on softer clay is more fluid—or 'fluky', to quote Cardew. David Leach works on leather-hard clay and cuts with a sweep of the arm from a supported elbow, 'locking' the wrist to a fixed position.

### FLUX, fluxing, fusible

In ceramics the term indicates an oxide, generally a *base*, which lowers the melting point of an *acidic* oxide, especially silica. Boric oxide has an ambiguous position. The fluxes are *network modifiers*.

Individual oxides may have a high or low melting point (e.g. $Sb_2O_3$ 656°C., CaO 2570°C.) but it is the reaction between the oxide and silica which is of interest to potters. Lime can be a very fluid flux at stoneware temperatures. From the *eutectic* it will be seen that a 'fluxing' oxide will be increasingly effective up to a certain proportion; beyond that it will begin to reverse the effect and lead to *crystallization* of the cooling glaze. *Basic matt* glazes can be achieved in this way, but care must be taken not to develop an unstable formula with resultant *metal release*.

Oxides vary in their effectiveness as fluxes—i.e. the temperature at which they become active. With certain exceptions, a variety of bases will be more efficient than a single one. The following list is a general guide, starting with the most active fluxes; the later ones are used in stonewares.

Lead oxide PbO
   *Soft glazes* only. Can be used as sole flux.
Boric oxide $B_2O_3$
   Essential in soft *leadless glazes*. The only *acidic* oxide in the list.
Potassium oxide $K_2O$
   Features in all glazes. Primary flux in stoneware and porcelain, secondary in earthenware.
Sodium oxide $Na_2O$
   All glazes. Can be a primary flux in soft glazes.
Lithium oxide $Li_2O$
   Efficient at low temperatures.
Strontium oxide SrO
   Some similarities to calcium but more effective at low temperatures.
Zinc oxide ZnO
   Up to 3% effective in earthenware. The major flux in *Bristol* glazes (1180°C.).
Calcium oxide CaO
   Secondary flux in small amounts in earthenware. Can be very fluid above 1250°C.
Magnesium oxide MgO
   Used in small amounts. Most effective from 1150°C. upwards.
Barium oxide BaO
   Fairly refractory. Stonewares.

Of the pigment oxides, manganese is very fusible; cobalt and copper are weak fluxes. Iron is fusible in a body in *reduction*. Fluxes in a body will also, of course, form glasses, leading to *vitrification*.

### FLY ASH

Ash carried by draft through a kiln. Can be responsible for 'kiln-gloss'.

## FOAMED CLAY

Insulating-bricks made by generating bubbles, physically or chemically, in thick *slip*. These are trapped as it dries.

## FOOT RING

Sometimes referred to as a 'foot rim'. Most bowls need a foot ring. It is, in effect, a low pedestal which can be thrown onto the turned, inverted bowl, or cut from the surplus clay left at the base when it was thrown. The bowl section should not vary to any great extent throughout its whole curve. The proportions of a foot ring—its height, width and splay—can make or mar a bowl form. It must be in tune with, and emphasize, the character of the bowl: its sturdiness, lightness, roundness etc. Physically it must support the curve: a small foot on a flat bowl can result in *slumping* or *warping*. The foot should be visible from an oblique viewpoint.

*A foot ring being turned on a bowl. For more detail see under turning.*

*A charming bowl on a high foot ring which is a major feature of the form, by Eric Mellon.*

The ring width will appear to be smaller (narrower) when you are turning it than it will when the bowl is set right way up. Cut a somewhat smaller ring, therefore, than you think the bowl will need or, better still, use an inside *chuck* so that it can be removed and checked during the turning. Cut your initial ring quite wide so that it can be corrected later. Most foot rings are vertical but variations are possible, even the slightest of which can alter the general character of a bowl. (See *turning*.)

## FORCED DRAFT

A mechanical augmentation of the normal chimney draft through a kiln. Air is either blown into the firing chamber, or movement in the chimney is speeded up with a fan. A fan can be used to blow air into the combustion chamber of a wood kiln which needs a great deal of ventilation. A forced draft kiln may need only a minimal chimney (see also *oil burners*).

## FORMALDEHYDE, formalin

Chemical formula HCHO. Suggested as an additive to prevent the decomposition of gums used in glazes. Formalin is the liquid form. (See *suspender*.)

## FORMER

A convenient term for a 'natural' *mold*, or one which is used as an adjunct to the process of shaping.

In Japan, small pots and bowls have for centuries been formed over the elbow, the knee or the hand. Many common objects—a pebble, a balloon, a bag of sand, a roll of paper—can be used as formers. Clay release is easier if the material is slightly absorbent. C.MPWW deals with many variations.

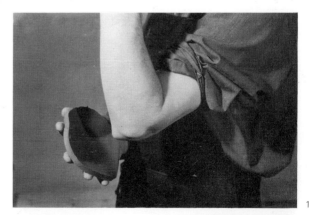

11

12

*Examples of formers. Making a dish over one's elbow (1, 2). Several dishes made over stones and joined together (3). Stages in pressing a large dish or unit of a construction in a biscuit former or mold. First the block of fairly soft, grogged clay is pressed out with the palm (4) and then worked into the shape with a darning head (5), scraping and smoothing the surface with a steel palette (6). Extensions of the form can be coiled onto the rim (7, 8). A simple former is made from four strips of leather-hard clay. A slab is eased into the former to make a shallow wide-rimmed dish (9, 10, 11); completed dish, raku fired, by Sheila Fournier (12).*

## FORMULA

A chemical or *molecular* description of a material. A glaze may be written as a formula or as a *recipe*. A formula is written as a list of the elements or *oxides* which enter into the fired glaze; a recipe is a propor-

tional list of the *minerals* and other materials which will most nearly achieve the formula.

The *element symbols* are used in the formula. A small figure following and slightly below the symbol (e.g. $Pb_2$) indicates the number of *atoms* in the *molecule*. A figure preceding an oxide formula indicates the number of molecules of the whole oxide. Thus $3Al_2O_3$ represents three molecules of alumina, which is itself made up of two atoms of aluminium to every three of oxygen.

The ultimate or empirical formula merely lists the relationship between the atoms of the material, e.g. $Al_2Si_2H_4O_9$, or it might read $Al_2Si_2O_5(OH)_4$. These tell a potter little about the material, except that the second formula suggests that it is a *hydrated* mineral. If the same elements are grouped into oxides as $Al_2O_3.2SiO_2.2H_2O$, we can recognise kaolinite. This is the *rational formula*.

The symbols are, of course, relative ones, and do not refer to any practical amounts of weights. They can, however, be translated into weighable minerals and oxides. (See *formula-into-recipe; analysis.*)

## FORMULA FROM PERCENTAGE WEIGHTS

To turn a weight percentage list of *oxides (analysis)* into a molecular *formula*, divide each number by its *molecular weight*.

Example:

46.5 $SiO_2$, 39.5 $Al_2O_3$, 14 $H_2O$.

$$\frac{46.5}{60} = 0.775$$

$$\frac{39.5}{102} = 0.387$$

$$\frac{14.0}{18} = 0.777$$

If each is divided by the smallest number a molecular ratio is arrived at—$2SiO_2.Al_2O_3.2H_2O$ or the formula for kaolinite.

The figures derived from an analysis can also be used in *Seger formula* terms by adding the bases together and dividing all the figures by the total.

## FORMULA-INTO-RECIPE

The fundamental equation is:

Molecular parts x molecular weight = parts by weight. 'Parts by weight' refers to physical comparative weights: gm. oz., or what you will. It is rarely possible, however, to use simple oxides in a recipe. They will more often be one constituent of more elaborate minerals. To simplify the arithmetic, various charts have been suggested. The molecular make-up or formula of a glaze or mineral is tabulated according to the *Seger formula*, i.e. in the proportions of the *bases, amphoterics* and *acids*, the sum of the bases being kept at unity. This can be transcribed into a list of physical materials with their proportional weights, as follows.

A simple lead glaze.

Formula: 1.0 PbO. 0.3 $Al_2O_3$. 3.0 $SiO_2$

A chart is made up of as many columns as there are

## FORMULA-INTO-RECIPE — Chart A

| PbO | $Al_2O_3$ | $SiO_2$ | Material | Molecular parts x weight | | Parts by weight | | % |
|-----|-----------|---------|----------|--------------------------|---|-----------------|---|---|
| 1.0 | | | Litharge | 1.0 x 223 | = | 223 | = | 50.2 |
| | 0.3 | 0.6 | China clay | 0.3 x 258 | = | 77.4 | = | 17.4 |
| | | 2.4 | Flint | 2.4 x 60 | = | 144 | = | 32.4 |
| 1.0 | 0.3 | 3.0 | TOTALS | | | 444.4 | = | 100.0 |

oxides in the formula, plus five more, and as many horizontal spaces as there will be raw materials in the recipe, plus two.

It will be seen that the 'molecular parts' figure is that represented by unity in the formula for the mineral. For instance, the clay is $Al_2O_3.2SiO_2.2H_2O$. The $H_2O$ is lost in the firing and is ignored (although allowed for in the total molecular weight of clay); of the rest, the alumina is at unity so the figure of 0.3 is used. The *molecular weight* for oxides and minerals is given under each entry. The bottom line gives the totals for the oxides, which must correspond with the formula.

The recipe is always approximate, as the minerals are considered to be in exact accordance with the *ideal formula*, which is rarely the case. It is possible to have each mineral analyzed into its actual oxide proportions, but for the average craft potter this is impractical. Results of these computations can be taken as a reference-point and guide. The proof is always in the firing.

Decisions as to which materials to use to translate the formula are a matter of trial and error. Start with materials which will satisfy the *RO (base)* requirements. These may be oxides or carbonates such as litharge or whiting, in which case the decision is a simple one. In many cases this will not be so. Lead oxide is forbidden in schools, and a fritt must be used. This will automatically introduce silica into the glaze batch. In the example shown in chart B below, sesquisilicate is listed; this has the formula PbO. $1.5SiO_2$. For every one molecule of lead, one and a half molecules of silica are introduced. We could use the monosilicate, proportions 1:1, or the bisilicate, 1:2, entering the

appropriate proportions of silica in its column. Working from left to right, alumina is the next oxide to be considered. It would be possible to use calcined alumina, but it is too coarse and, as a general rule, natural minerals are preferable to synthetic ones. We need a mineral which does not include unwanted oxides. China clay fulfils the requirements, introducing one alumina molecule to two silica. The 0.3 alumina is therefore entered in the appropriate column and the accompanying 0.6 of silica in its column.

In satisfying the lead and alumina requirements we have, willy-nilly, put 1.5 + 0.6 silica into the batch, a total of 2.1. This falls 0.9 short of the required 3.0 parts and, luckily, there are two minerals which are nearly pure $SiO_2$: flint and quartz. This completes the formula. If we had used bisilicate of lead, only 0.4 parts of flint would have been required.

One more example with a longer formula: a hypothetical stoneware glaze.

Example:

| | | | | |
|---|---|---|---|---|
| $K_2O$ | 0.3 | $Al_2O_3$ | 0.32 | $SiO_2$ 3.3 |
| CaO | 0.6 | | | $TiO_2$ 0.2 |
| MgO | 0.1 | | | |

Working from left to right as before: 1. $K_2O$. The most convenient material is potash feldspar which will also bring in, for one part of potash, one part of alumina, and six silica, e.g. for 0.3 $K_2O$, 0.3 alumina and 0.3 x 6=1.8 silica. See that these proportions are not more than are required. 2. CaO. This can be used as the carbonate, whiting, 0.6 parts. Nothing else is added in the process. 3. MgO. The most readily available source of magnesia is dolomite where it

## FORMULA-INTO-RECIPE — Chart B

| PbO | $Al_2O_3$ | $SiO_2$ | Material | Molecular parts x weight | | Parts by weight | | % |
|-----|-----------|---------|----------|--------------------------|---|-----------------|---|---|
| 1.0 | | 1.5 | Lead sesqui-silicate | 1.0 x 313 | = | 313 | = | 70.5 |
| | 0.3 | 0.6 | China clay | 0.3 x 258 | = | 77.4 | = | 17.4 |
| | | 0.9 | Flint | 0.9 x 60 | = | 54 | = | 12.1 |
| 1.0 | 0.3 | 3.0 | TOTALS | | | 444.4 | = | 100.0 |

| $K_2O$ | CaO | MgO | $Al_2O_3$ | $SiO_2$ | $TiO_2$ | Material | Molecular parts x weight | | Parts by weight | | % |
|---|---|---|---|---|---|---|---|---|---|---|---|
| 0.3 | | | 0.3 | 1.8 | | Feldspar | 0.3 x 556 | = | 166.8 | = | 48.47 |
| | 0.5 | | | | | Whiting | 0.5 x 100 | = | 50.0 | = | 14.53 |
| | 0.1 | 0.1 | | | | Dolomite | 0.1 x 184 | = | 18.4 | = | 5.34 |
| | | | 0.02 | 0.04 | | China clay | 0.02 x 258 | = | 5.2 | = | 1.50 |
| | | | | 1.46 | | Quartz | 1.46 x 60 | = | 87.6 | = | 25.52 |
| | | | | | 0.2 | Titania | 0.2 x 80 | = | 16.0 | = | 4.64 |
| 0.3 | 0.6 | 0.1 | 0.32 | 3.3 | 0.2 | TOTALS | | | 344.0 | = | 100.0 |

occurs in equal parts with calcium. If we use 0.1 parts of dolomite to provide magnesia we also add 0.1 parts of CaO. We must therefore reconsider the whiting and alter the 0.6 parts to 0.5, so that the total introduced by whiting plus dolomite does not exceed the formula requirements. 4. $Al_2O_3$. The feldspar has already provided 0.3 parts, leaving only 0.02 to be accounted for. Using clay we can add this amount, with the appropriate 0.04 entry under silica. 5. $SiO_2$. Feldspar has given 1.8 and clay 0.04. We require 3.3, or 1.46 more and can use flint or quartz. 6. $TiO_2$. Titanium oxide can be used, 0.2 parts. (See Chart C.)

In all three cases dealt with above it has been possible to satisfy the formula with common minerals. If, however, formula C had required 0.45 parts of potash, this would have given similar parts of alumina—more than required—and so feldspar could not have been used. In fact there is no common mineral which would have been suitable, and you would have had to resort to a *fritt*. Where this situation arises it may be better to reconsider your formula, especially where a stoneware glaze is being formulated.

## FORMULA WEIGHT

Also known as the *molecular weight*. The total of the atomic weights of all the elements which make up the formula. Example: clay, $Al_2O_3.2SiO_2.2H_2O =$ 2 x 27 (Al) + 2 x 28 (Si) + 4 x 1 (H) + 9 x 16 (O) = 258. The figure following the formula for each of the minerals in this book is the molecular or formula weight. (See also *equivalent weight*.)

## FREE SILICA

That proportion of silica in a raw or fired body which is not combined with other oxides, i.e. as crystals. Quartz or flint added to the body may remain 'free'. During heating and cooling the free silica undergoes *inversions,* with consequent strain on the body. At temperatures above 1070°C. it is slowly converted into another $SiO_2$ form—cristobalite. Siliceous *ball clay* contains quartz grains. (See also *crazing.*)

## FRENCH CHALK

A preparation from *steatite (talc).*

## FRITT, frit

A ground glass or glaze. The craft potter utilizes naturally occurring minerals as far as possible, but sometimes it is difficult to find an *insoluble* and non-toxic source for a required oxide. Borax, for instance, the main source of boric oxide, is soluble even after *calcining*. Litharge, white and red lead are all poisonous and are usually used as soft silicate glasses or fritts.

The potter can prepare his own fritts in small quantities, but they are normally made by the industry and sold in a finely powdered state. Glaze materials, soluble and otherwise, are mixed and melted together in a special oven, often in the form of a revolving cylinder. When quite fluid the molten glaze is let out in a stream into a tank of cold water. It will break into fragments under the thermal shock, resembling granulated sugar. The grain-size can be further reduced in a ball mill.

The craft potter has to melt his materials in a bowl in the kiln, break the bowl away and pulverize the fritt, or else heat them in a crucible and continue as above. If ground in a mortar and pestle, a teaspoonful must be dealt with at a time. A ball or jar mill is a virtual necessity. Nature has fritted materials together and these remain as spars, colemanite etc.

Fritts are always used on industrial pottery in order to ensure uniformity of color and other qualities, and to avoid uneven settling in the glaze batch. Fritts have lost any combined water, carbon dioxide, etc. which may have been present in the raw materials. They are therefore concentrated and must be applied more thinly. The transparency of the glaze immediately after dipping can be misleading—one feels the coating is too thin. Fritts settle rapidly in water. They are best used as a basis for further additions of raw minerals, i.e. treated as one item in a *recipe*. Common salt is reputed to assist *floatation*. To use fritts scientifically one must know their *formula*, which should be treated like any other multi-oxide material. The lead silicates and the softer borax and alkaline fritts are useful to the earthenware potter. With few exceptions (one being David Leach's stoneware glazes issued by Podmores) all prepared glazes are fritts. Fritting can alter and control colors.

## FUELS

Materials used to produce heat by rapid *oxidation*. (See *gas, oil, wood, coke, paraffin*.) *Electricity* is not, in this sense, a fuel: it is energy supplied at one remove. Fuels vary in their flame temperatures. The maximum attainable heat has been given as around 1370°C. for wood, 1500°C. for coal, 1650°C. for oil.

## FULLER'S EARTH

A non-plastic *montmorillinite* type mineral.

## FUSE, electric

A 'weak link' of easily melted wire put into a *circuit* to avoid the over-heating which would develop from the flow of more *current* than the *conducting* wires will take, i.e. from a *short-circuit*. Fuses are graded according to the current in amperes which they will conduct without failing, e.g. a 15 amp fuse will begin to melt at 16 amps and over (in practice probably at 20-25 amps.). Fuses may be either of wire or wire enclosed in a capsule. (See also *heat-fuse*.)

## FUSE, fusion, fusible

To melt together. Fusible materials are those which melt easily or lower the melting point of a mixture such as a glaze. Some oxides are *refractory* in themselves but act as fusible agents (see *flux*) in a glaze.

## FUSED SILICA

A translucent or transparent vitreous silica made by fusing quartz sand in an open furnace.

# G

## GALENA

A lead ore, lead sulfide PbS, 239, s.g. 7.5.

Widely distributed, and was thus available to early potters. Used on medieval pottery and seventeenth century slipware. Toxic but less so than litharge or white lead. Contains copper and other impurities (some silver is extracted) which enhance its value for slipware but not for more sophisticated glazes. Needs plenty of ventilation during firing to disperse the sulfur and to form PbO. Not, therefore, very suitable for electric kilns. Galena-glazed pots are often once-fired (as in the film *Isaac Button, country potter*). Other types of glaze in the same kiln may be spoiled. 'Up-draft kilns are best for galena glazes' (Leach).

Example of a raw-clay galena glaze recipe:

| | |
|---|---|
| Galena | 66 |
| Plastic clay | 16 |
| Flint | 18 |

Raw clay or once-fired glaze uses part of the body

surface to assist its maturity during firing; it will thus eat away thin *slip*.

## GANISTER

A fine-grain silica rock found in lower coal measures (e.g. in Yorkshire, England). It is ground, mixed with clay, and used in silica refractories.

## GARNET

A group of crystalline minerals used as abrasives and gemstones. The *RO* constituents vary, the general formula being $RO.R_2O_3.3SiO_2$.

## GAS

Any substance in the gaseous state, scientifically defined as 'occupying the whole of the space in which it is contained' (U.DS.). Its molecules are in a free state and not connected to one another in any pattern. Air is the most common gas. In everyday use 'gas' is usually taken to mean gas fuel.

## GAS BURNER

*Gas fuel* must be mixed with air for *combustion*. This is normally done at the point where the gas escapes from the pipe. The burners may be divided into three groups:

1 Atmospheric or inspiratory burners where the forward movement of gas under pressure draws in the air needed for combustion.
2 Burners in which a current of air draws in gas, itself under small or nil pressure.
3 Where gas and air are mixed in a chamber behind the burner.

The first of these is the simplest and the most commonly used. Gas is easily ignited and the burners are more simple in construction and principle than those used for oil. (See also R.K 76-81, for other useful information.)

## GAS EXPANSION

The expansion for a given temperature rise of any gas will be the ratio in *Kelvin* degrees. Example: air at 10°C. is at 283° K; at 1100°C. its equivalent in K is 1373°. The expansion will be $\frac{1373}{283}=4.68$. Thus at atmospheric pressure a cubic meter of air at 10°C. will have increased in volume to 4.68 cubic meters at 1100°C. Kilns must be designed to accommodate such volume differences between cold air inlets and hot air outlets.

## GAS FUEL

'Town' or coal gas has a high proportion of free hydrogen; 'natural' or well-gas is largely methane.

The Gas Board arrives at therms for costing purposes by multiplying the volume of gas (or the weight) by its calorific value and dividing the result by 100,000.
e.g. 7,500 cu. ft. of natural gas=

$\frac{7500 \times 1,000}{100,000}=75$ therms

| % volume of | Coal gas | Reformed gas | Natural gas | Propane | Butane |
|---|---|---|---|---|---|
| Methane $CH_4$ | 15 | 25 | 94.5 | | |
| Higher hydrocarbons | 5 | 2 | 4 | $C_3H_8$ | $C_4H_{10}$ |
| | | | | Known as L.P.G. | |
| Carbon monoxide CO | 14 | 2 | nil | Liquid petroleum gases | |
| Carbon dioxide $CO_2$ | 4 | 14 | nil | | |
| Hydrogen $H_2$ | 55 | 57 | nil | | |
| Nitrogen $N_2$ | 7 | nil | 1.5 | | |
| Calorific value (gross) | | | | | |
| Btu/cu. ft. | 500 | 500 | 1000 | 2500 | 3000 |
| Btu/lb. | | | | 21500 | 21200 |
| Specific gravity | 0.49 | 0.49 | 0.59 | 1.5 | 2.0 |
| Air required for combustion, given as cu. ft. per cu. ft. of gas | 4.5 | 4.5 | 9.5 | 24.0 | 31.0 |

(by kind permission of South-Western Gas Board (UK))

*or* 350 lb. of propane=

$$\frac{350 \times 21,500}{100,000} = 75 \text{ therms}$$

The proportions of ingredients will vary a little but it will be seen that N.G. has none of the very poisonous CO while its high methane content gives it greater efficiency and, reputedly, a 'cleaner' and better firing in the kiln.

Cylinder or *bottled gas* (L.P.G.) produces nearly three times as many Btu per cu. ft. as natural gas. Supply gas is lighter than air and will rise, whereas L.P.G. is heavier than air and will collect at a low level making it dangerous in enclosed spaces or basements.

## GAS KILNS

If gas supply is available in sufficient quantity (a 2 in. (50 mm.) mains is the minimum requirement), a gas kiln can provide clean, versatile, and comparatively trouble-free firing. Design can be of the open-chamber or *semi-muffle* type, and there are several ways of burning the gas. Most kilns mix the fuel and air at the primary air or burner point.

For smaller kilns, a pressure of around 8 oz. is required [somewhat higher for those of 15 cu. ft. (0.5 cu. m.)] or more. The Gas Board should be consulted.

The design of gas kilns, both for supply and *bottled gas*, allows of wide variations and can be very simple. 'Strict rules for (proportions of parts) should be viewed with some reserve' (Casson). There are normally several burners or jets.

Mick Casson has found that natural gas has a lazier flame and that the burners are easily extinguished when burning low. Ideally the burners should be within the kiln wall. Good *secondary air* control is essential—Natural gas takes much more air for combustion than does town gas. Similarly, large flues are needed. Great heat and strong reduction are possible, with some tendency for *spalling* and disintegration to occur in *refractories*.

*Gas kiln built by Michael Casson. A semi-muffle down-draft kiln using natural gas. The hot gases flow up the sides and are drawn over the half walls, downwards to a gap at the front of the floor, under the floor to the back of the kiln and so up the chimney.*

## GAULT CLAY

A brick clay with a high calcium content and consequent short *vitrification range*.

## GERMANIUM, oxide

A metallic element Ge, 72.5. Oxide $GeO_2$ 104.5. Sometimes listed as a *glass-former*, i.e. with silica.

## GERSTLEY BORATE

An impure colemanite or borate of sodium and calcium with some magnesium, from the Gerstley Mine, Death Valley, California. It has proved to be a particularly 'well-behaved' form of colemanite.

## GIBBSITE

An *hydrated* alumina mineral $Al(OH)_3$ or $Al_2O_3$. $3H_2O$. *Calcined* at a high temperature to eliminate its high shrinkage.

## GILDING

Dodd defines gilding as 'The painting of pottery with liquid gold to be fired-on at 700°C.' (See *gold*). As a general term 'gilding' indicates the application of gold leaf with an adhesive.

## GLACIAL CLAYS

Clays which have been transported by glaciers are deposited more or less as they are picked up; they are not separated into particles sizes as are river-borne clays. They are therefore often mixed with non-clay matter and with boulders—hence boulder-clay. Cardew cites the Fremington clay of North Devon in England as a possible glacial clay.

## GLASS

A 'melt' of *inorganic* materials cooled sufficiently quickly to prevent crystallization, and retaining its *amorphous* structure. A super-cooled liquid. It has a three-dimensional *network* structure, but without the symmetry of crystals. *Glaze* is a special form of glass, containing alumina, and with a comparatively low thermal expansion.

Foremost of the materials which can form glass is silica. It will 'fuse' alone at 1713°C. but in combination with larger atoms of lower valencies it will melt at lower temperatures. These elements, generally the *bases*, weaken the network bond. Glass can be so soft as actually to dissolve in water (sodium silicate), or hard enough to withstand great abrasion or chemical reaction (salt-glaze, which is also a soda-silicate but of different formation). Window glass will lie somewhere between these extremes and is produced with little or no alumina. (See also *glaze, glass-formers, network modifiers, Seger formula* etc.)

## GLASS CULLET

Pieces of transparent or colored glass. (See *cullet*.)

## GLASS DECORATION

See *melted glass decoration*.

## GLASS FORMER

Or network-former. Only a few materials, all *acidic* oxides, can form glass. The most useful to potters are silica and boric oxide, the former being the prime essential in all glazes and in the great majority of ceramic bodies. Antimony oxide and phosphorus pentoxide are of some interest. Germanium oxide and arsenous oxide are also listed. Under some conditions alumina can also assist in glass-forming.

The silica tetrahedrons form a random network of linked molecules in the liquid state which can be 'opened' or modified by *bases* to become fluid at a lower temperature. Quick cooling 'freezes' the random network, which cannot then arrange itself into crystals.

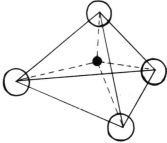

*The configuration of a small silicon atom (black) and four larger oxygen atoms set in a pyramid formation which is the basis of the silica glass forming network. It does not exist as a separate entity but is extended in every direction, another Si atom sharing each face with a further O atom. In the whole complex there are therefore twice as many oxygen as silicon atoms and it is written $SiO_2$ in glaze formulas, etc. The atoms are, in fact, probably packed more closely than shown.*

## GLASS MODIFIER

See *network modifier*.

## GLASS MULLER

A sort of flat-ended *pestle* for grinding and mixing color, especially *enamels*, with medium. Used on a glass slab or glazed tile.

## GLASS PHASE

A stage in the heating of ceramics when glass begins to form in the fabric. If excessive the piece may collapse or *deform*. (See *vitrification, phase diagrams, clay, porcelain* etc.)

## GLAZE

A ceramic glaze is a special sort of glass, differing from window-glass and glassware in its lower thermal expansion and higher alumina content, which increase its *viscosity* and help it to adhere to the clay body. The general principles are discussed under *glass, glass formers, network modifier, Seger formula* etc.

All glazes start as mixtures of a number of oxides and minerals with water. The craft potter may use these as *raw materials* even *once-firing* them on a clay pot, but an industrial pottery will use them as ground glass or frit. Prepared glazes will be fritts.

One can arrive at a glaze *recipe* either by the empirical trial-and-error method, or by the application of the principles of simple chemistry. Neither, alone, is sufficient. Science is one valuable aid among others, which include careful observation and intuition. Glazes are discussed in this book under *earthenware, stoneware, porcelain* etc., but the differences are not fundamental. They lie mainly in the choice of *bases*, some of which are not active at the lower temperatures (see *flux*).

The most useful guide to glaze computation, and the easiest to handle, is the *Seger formula*. This discusses glazes in terms of *molecular* equivalents rather than physical weights, but the translation from one to the other is not difficult to make (see *formula-into-recipe*).

The main factors governing the overall behavior of a glaze are:

1 The base:silica ratio. The normal practical limits of this ratio are 1:2 and 1:4.5. An average *soft glaze* will in the region of 1:2.8, a stoneware 1:3.8. Above 1300°C. the proportion of silica rises sharply and porcelain glazes may be as high as 1:10.
2 Choice of *bases*. They vary in their effectiveness as fluxes (see list under *flux*). Multi-base formulas are generally preferred to single-base ones.
3 The use of boric oxide. Although a *glass-former*, boron operates at a very low temperature and its visible effect is that of a flux. It must be used where lead is not present in a soft glaze. It is usually listed as part of the acidic oxide $RO_2$, and this can lead to some untypical formulas e.g. 1 RO: 4.8 $RO_2$—the acid made up of 4.0 of silica and 0.8 $B_2O_3$—for a soft fritt.
4 The alumina ratio. Alumina is essential for a stable, well-adhered glaze. The ratio for a clear, bright glaze is alumina:silica from 1:8 to 1:10. An excess is liable to produce a matt surface.
5 Pigment oxides. These will behave like other glaze ingredients, the acids rendering the glaze more refractory, the bases tending to soften the glaze.

Some materials such as iron oxide are influenced by the kiln atmosphere, and many stoneware glazes appear to achieve greater maturity in *reduction*.

For advice on the formulation of glazes see *chemistry of pottery, Seger formula*, and under special glaze headings such as *earthenware glazes, aventurine, Bristol, celadon*, etc. The influence of the various *minerals* is discussed under their entries.

## GLAZE-BODY FIT

Glazes and bodies undergo a number of expansions, contractions and shrinkages which affect the final state of the cooled ceramic. If the glaze has contracted more than the body after it has become rigid (700°C. and below) it will be in a state of *tension*, which can be relieved only by the glaze crazing. If the reverse is true and the glaze is in slight *compression*, then it will be stable and can also accommodate some thermal shock and expansion through *adsorption*. Excessive compression of the glaze will have a similar effect on the body as that of tension in the glaze, *shattering* being the result in extreme cases, or the glaze may *shiver* away on rims etc. Large dishes which are glazed on one side only are very vulnerable.

Glaze-body fit is arrived at by sensible application of the principles of thermal expansion and inversions, and by the careful observation and evaluation of results from the kiln. (See especially *crazing, shattering, coefficients of expansion.*)

## GLAZE MIXING

The ingredients of a glaze can be tipped into a large bowl or bin of water as they are weighed. If they can then be left to soak, the sieving will be easier. The exceptions to this method are talc and bentonite. The first needs mixing with other ingredients and should then be worked into a paste with a little water before soaking—otherwise it will float on the surface and refuse to mix. Bentonite should be similarly treated, adding water very gradually to form first a thick paste and preferably put through a 200 sieve before being added to the batch.

The soaked ingredients can be brushed through a nylon sieve before the appropriate lawn is used—60 or 100 for stoneware, 100 or 120 for earthenware. Sieve twice if the glaze is to be used immediately, and stir very thoroughly.

## GLAZE OVER GLAZE

A technique of decoration where one glaze is poured over another in part, as a complete re-coating, or in conjunction with *wax resist or sgraffito*.

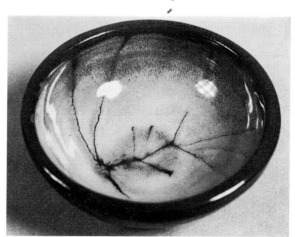

*Glaze over glaze. An earthenware bowl with a saturated manganese glaze which has been painted with a wax design and then covered with a tin glaze. The original waxed line has become finer and narrower with the running of the glaze.*

In earthenware attractive results can be obtained by covering a *saturated glaze*, on which a bold, simple wax design has been painted, with a clear glaze. This is most successful on tiles, bowls and dishes, i.e. on semi-horizontal surfaces. The second coating should be poured or dipped while the first is still damp but not shiny. Practice is required, as with all glaze over glaze techniques, to assess correctly the comparative consistencies of the glaze batches used, and to avoid too thick a final layer. There will always be a degree of flow from one glaze to another, softening and altering the shape of the resist line. Fire experiments on a bat with plenty of alumina in case of running. A thinner cop coat will give a crisper design but less contrast. It is advisable to wax the rim after the first coat. Stoneware glazes, being more viscous, run and merge less than *soft glazes*. Experiments can be carried out using a more *refractory* underglaze.

Panels can be dipped, or the pouring action itself can be used to provide a pattern. A number of modern potters pour glaze; sweeps of contrasting color from the center line outwards give a variety of patterns. Glazes may also be treated like slip and trailed one onto another. A *flocculant* can give some *viscosity* in the trailer, but a sure and rapid motion is called for.

Glazes can be *sprayed*, either in the open air or with an efficient extractor.

The comparative thicknesses of the glazes, the types of glaze (*refractory, matt, opaque,* etc.), the colors, the soaking time in the kiln and other factors will all influence and vary the results.

The second glaze can be poured over a fired glaze. This will give a less contrasting effect. *Crazing* will sometimes absorb glaze when dipped, or a *crawled* glaze can be filled with another color by sponging a thick glaze into the cracks.

*Decoration derived from varying the glaze thickness of an oxidized dolomite/copper glaze which goes black where it is thicker. The bowl was dipped first one side and then the other, the center swathe being the overlapped portion. This dark shape, together with that formed by the extra thickness where the glaze was poured off, gives a subtle and integral design. By Robert Fournier.*

## GLAZE STAINS

The term 'stain' is generally applied to the *fritted* colors in suppliers' catalogs, as distinct from the *pigment oxides* used raw. Variations in hue, apart from the combining of various oxides, are obtained by *sintering* with such non-coloring additions as alumina, soda, flint etc. which alter the hue. When redissolved in a glaze, the stain may revert to the typical oxide color, and care must be taken to use only the glaze recommended for the color. Stains are more dilute than oxides and are added in proportions of around 10%, or as directed by the makers.

## GLAZE THICKNESS

The thickness of a glaze coating is a critical factor in its behavior and fired appearance. Too thick, and it is liable to *peel, crawl* or *craze*; too thin, and it will fail to develop its true character. There is no one ideal consistency; each recipe has its optimum thickness which can be decided only by trial and experience. A reading with a *hydrometer* is useful, while tight-fitting bin lids will help to control the inevitable evaporation between firings.

Factors controlling glaze coating are:

1  *Biscuit porosity*. The glaze take-up depends on water being absorbed, leaving a solid coat of glaze material on the surface. Keep biscuit firings as standard as possible. The thickness of the pot wall is allied to porosity. A thin wall will saturate quickly and cease to develop further coatings—in fact the glaze already

solidified can be re-saturated from the water in the batch and may wash off again. If this happens the pot must be cleaned, dried over a strong heat, and another attempt made. A thick wall will absorb more moisture and thus retain a thicker coating. Good glazing therefore depends on even-walled throwing and making. An open, *grogged* body will obviously be more porous than a close one. The more porous the pot, the more water is required in the glaze batch in relation to solid matter. (See *tongue test*.)

2  The batch consistency. It follows from the previous remarks that a thicker mixture will result in a thicker coating. Test with a hydrometer, or more roughly by dipping in a dry finger or test-strip; note the reading for future occasions. A glaze may appear to thicken as it stands; this is a result of *flocculation* caused by soluble alkalis or colemanite. This glaze will have a jelly-like consistency. If further water is added, it may lead to excessive contraction of the glaze-coating followed by peeling. *Ash glazes* are liable to flocculation; more careful washing of the ash will help to minimize the trouble.

3  Speed of work. Quick dipping will give less time for absorption than a slow one, and thus cause a thinner coat to develop. Very slow dipping may saturate a pot wall so that the glaze will fail to dry. A steady but unhesitating action is called for. Do not shake violently after dipping; a short circular or twisting movement will cast off the drips.

4  Type of glazes. Glazes vary in their optimum thickness; and you may actually want to vary it for different effects. Raw glazes need a thicker coat than do frits, which have already lost their *volatile* com-

pounds. Fritts, being powdered glass, will look very thin when the pot is lifted from the glaze but the coating will become opaque as it dries. In general a transparent glaze will need a slightly thinner coating than an opaque or colored one.

5 Double-dipping needs careful preparation, the first coat acting as a very porous body if allowed to get too dry. (See *glaze over glaze*.)

To summarize, as a general guide:

A thinner glaze mixture for:
>Fritts
>Porous biscuit
>Thick-walled pots
>Slow glazing (difficult pots)
>Clear glazes (earthenware)

A thicker glaze mixture for:
>Higher-fired, low-porosity biscuit
>Thin-walled pots
>'Skimming' of tiles
>Opaque glazes (generally)

## GLAZE-TRAILING

Glazes as well as slips can be *trailed*. The decoration is necessarily fairly broad in style. Trailing can be done on the biscuit, or on a glaze coating. A certain spread and softening of the line are inevitable when two glazes are used, but trailing can be quite crisp on biscuit or on a refractory glaze.

2

1

3

*Glaze-trailed pots: (1, 2) by Shoji Hamada, probably dribbled through a hole in a spoon! A more representational approach on a large cooking dish by Ray Finch (3).*

## GLAZE TRIALS

One is always faced with the necessity to compromise in the making up of test glaze batches. Large quantities will be wasteful, but small samples are liable to error during weighing, in the relative dampness of the ingredients, and in preparation losses. 300 gm. (10½ oz.) must be considered a minimum batch. *Line blends* or *triaxial blending* allow larger initial batch weights.

The object of a series of glaze trials is to arrive at a

useful *recipe*. Haphazard, unrepeatable mixtures are merely tantalizing. It is necessary to record at least the weights, subsequent alterations and the firing temperature. Never rely on memory. (See also *records, glaze trial log.*) The recipe is, of course, only one factor: others include the size of the kiln, speed of firing and cooling, kiln atmosphere and glaze thickness.

Glaze trials merely brushed onto tiles or shards are insufficient. Small bowls can be thrown very rapidly from cones of clay, cylinders can be cut into sections, or curved tiles about $2\frac{1}{2} \times 1\frac{1}{2} \times \frac{1}{4}$ in. (60 x 30 x 5 mm.) can be stood on end, or formed over a rolling-pin. Circular discs with a hole may be glazed and filed, or hung on a board or on the actual glaze-bin. For the ultimate trials, full-sized production pieces are used.

The golden rule for glaze trials or any other trial is: alter only one ingredient at a time. If two variables are operating together, it is difficult to decide which of them is primarily responsible for the result. This is admittedly a counsel of perfection and is not followed in all the permutations of the second series discussed below.

It is useful to test materials on their own (see *button test*), but, unless they are natural or artificial *fritts* (e.g. feldspar or lead silicate) the essential reaction between the material or oxide and silica will not be shown. (See *calcium* for an extreme example.)

Trials with three simple materials such as a lead fritt, clay and flint can be of great educational value with students. A simple series may run as follows:

| Trial No | 1 | 2 | 3 | 4 | 5 | 6 | 7 |
|---|---|---|---|---|---|---|---|
| Fritt | 100 | | | 33 | 70 | 15 | 15 |
| Clay | | 100 | | 33 | 15 | 70 | 15 |
| Flint | | | 100 | 33 | 15 | 15 | 70 |

Nos 1, 2 and 3 are for testing the materials alone; No. 4 tests them in equal quantities; and 5, 6 and 7 are tests involving an excess of one ingredient over the other two. The use of red clay would further differentiate the results. For stonewares, almost any three minerals can be tried out in similar proportions. Plate 6, p. 132 shows the fired results of the series above.

Plate 10B, p. 133 illustrates an interesting series of glaze trials which were achieved by a mixture of line blending and more intuitive experiment. The series may be taken as one model (among many) for a trial sequence. It by no means covered the field but it did give a useful general picture. The variables were: five similar batches of glaze, each with the accepted maximum proportion of a coloring oxide (i.e. 'saturated glazes'); a similar opaque glaze with 10% tin oxide which was added in various quantities to dilute the colors; and a softer fritt which tested the effect of both dilution and a more fluid melt.

The series, which was repeated for each color and for eight permutations of two colors, was as follows:

Group A—single color

| | Colored glaze | Tin glaze | Soft fritt | |
|---|---|---|---|---|
| No 1 | 2 | 1 | | parts |
| No 2 | 2 | 1 | 1 | parts |
| No 3 | 1 | 4 | | parts |
| No 4 | 1 | 4 | 2 | parts |

Group B—two colors

| | Color (1) | Color (2) | Tin | Fritt | |
|---|---|---|---|---|---|
| No 5 | 1 | 1 | | | parts |
| No 6 | 1 | 1 | 1 | | parts |
| No 7 | 1 | 1 | 3 | 1 | parts |
| No 8 | 1 | 4 | | | parts |
| No 9 | 1 | 4 | 3 | | parts |
| No 10 | 1 | 4 | 5 | 2 | parts |
| No 11 | 4 | 1 | | | parts |
| No 12 | 4 | 1 | 3 | | parts |
| No 13 | 4 | 1 | 5 | 2 | parts |

The standard 'part' was a dessertspoonful. All tests were fired at the same temperature and on buff and red trial pieces.

To work back from any mixture to a recipe, multiply each of the ingredients of the constituent glazes in the mixture by the 'parts'; list them in a chart, find the totals and divide each figure by the total number of 'parts' as shown in the chart below:

| Glaze | Parts | Lead ses. | Clay | Whit-ing | Flint | MnO$_2$ | Tin | Fritt | CuO |
|---|---|---|---|---|---|---|---|---|---|
| C1 | 1 | 60 | 15 | 5 | 20 | | | | 2.5 |
| C2 | 4 | 240 | 60 | 20 | 80 | 40 | | | |
| T | 5 | 300 | 75 | 25 | 100 | | 50 | | |
| S | 2 | | | | | | | 200 | |
| Totals | 12 | 600 | 150 | 50 | 200 | 40 | 50 | 200 | 2.5 |
| Recipe | 1 | 50 | 12.5 | 4.1 | 16.5 | 3.3 | 4.1 | 16.7 | 0.2 |

The same type of chart can be used for any mixtures or blends.

*Example.* In the chart Test No 10 in the above series has been worked back to a recipe assuming that:

| C (1) was | Lead sesquisilicate | 60 |
| | China clay | 15 |
| | Whiting | 5 |
| | Flint | 20 |
| | Copper oxide | 2.5 |

and C (2) was a similar glaze with 10% manganese dioxide,

and T was a similar glaze with 10% tin oxide, S being a soft fritt.

## GLAZE TRIAL LOG

The records which a potter needs to keep will vary with particular kinds of work. The closer one gets to a final *recipe,* the more information one needs to keep. A possible log book is shown in the chart on p. 126. The information on the actual glaze trial can be tied in with *kiln logs* or records; this is especially important in reduction firings.

## GLAZING

It is probable that more pots are spoiled during glazing than at any other stage. That 'it will all smooth out in the firing' is a common delusion. Certainly some glazes are more accommodating than others. Opaque and colored glazes will show differences in thickness more clearly than transparent ones.

Bubbling, *crazing* and other ills can often be traced to faulty glaze-application. In all cases, the tidier a pot looks when it goes into the kiln the better it is likely to look when it comes out. Consistency of the batch is discussed under *glaze thickness.* Pots can be dipped, rolled, poured or sprayed. Speed and smoothness of movement are the keys to good glazing. Think carefully before starting each piece, and work out the best procedure for it.

Where there is plenty of glaze, the quickest and easiest method is immersing. Hold a pot by the rim and base, or a dish each side of the rim, using as few fingers as possible or, better still, a wire gripper (see *glazing gripper*). After a quick sweep through the glaze —with dishes, the far edge in relation to you enters the glaze first—hold the piece vertically to drain for a moment and stand down on a *stilt.* Pots, beakers etc. in a shallow glaze should be held with two fingers on the base and two on the rim 'walked' round the pot so that the piece revolves in the glaze. Tip it the right way up for an instant to ensure that the base is covered inside, and then invert to drain.

Tiles can be held across the back with fingers and thumb and skimmed across the glaze surface, the leading edge entering first. With practice, a neat glaze line along the edges can be achieved.

For stoneware and other pieces which are not to be glazed over the base there are three possibilities. They can be filled, emptied and dipped in quick succession. Large pots may need to have glaze poured over them. If it is possible to grip the base, turn the pot as far round in one direction as possible, so that a smooth and complete revolution can be made as the glaze is poured. Use a big enough jug and a large bowl to catch the surplus. If the pot is too heavy or awkward it can be supported on a central stick, across two supports on the bowl, or on a turntable.

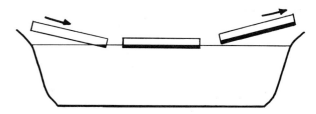

*Glazing tiles by skimming them across the surface of a well-stirred glaze. The tile can be held with the thumb and finger or with a glaze gripper.*

The 'water-spout' dip takes some practice (try it when washing-up!), but it is ideal for the rapid glazing of beakers, wide-mouthed pots, bowls, etc. particularly for stonewares. The piece is gripped by the foot or base, dipped to the desired level outside, then sharply lifted straight up until it barely leaves the glaze, the suction causing a 'water-spout' to rise. Very quickly the pot is pushed downwards onto the rising column of glaze which will coat the interior even of tall jugs. After trying it, you will probably add 'sometimes', but with practice it is a very reliable method.

Spraying. Blowing glaze through a spray is dangerous. A bulb or mechanical pump should be used, together with an extractor-fan. It takes a good deal of spraying to achieve a thick enough glaze coating, but for slip glazes, thin layers and special effects it can be useful, though it always results in a somewhat mechanical finish.

Some general notes:

1 Pour some of the clear water from the top of a glaze before stirring. Keep this water handy in a jug and add again if necessary.

Stir your glaze very thoroughly and keep it stirred during use.

2 Label permanent containers clearly. Beware changing containers when re-sieving a glaze, which will be necessary from time to time.

Use a container of a suitable size and shape for the piece to be glazed.

3 Touch up holding marks with finger or brush immediately after glazing. Smooth the repair over as it dries, and carefully scrape down blotches or runs with a sharp knife (e.g. a photographic re-touching knife).

Although for tableware and much other pottery a smooth, even coating of glaze is desirable, it is obviously possible to use different thicknesses of glaze in a free and exciting way on more decorative or sculptural pieces. Even on tableware, the marks left by the gripping fingers of a skilful potter can add to the attractions of the pot. Other glaze faults such as *crawling* or even *peeling* can be used positively.

4 It is easier to protect a surface from glaze than to scrape it off afterwards. This can be done by brushing on wax (see *wax*).

Teapots present problems, especially clogging of strainer holes. One can fill the teapot with glaze and pour it all out of the spout. This saturates the strainer and a sharp jerk will free the holes, or you can blow sharply down the spout (don't eat the glaze!) Alternatively a pad of clay can be pressed over the holes prior to glazing, or they can be thickly *waxed*.

*Glazing. Filling and dipping (1-4). The pot is filled to the brim with glaze, or partly filled and revolved as it is emptied. It is dipped immediately, lifted out and given a slight sideways twist to shake off drips. The whole process is a continuous movement. The tricky process of glazing a teapot is discussed in the text. Here a teapot made by Geoffrey Whiting is glazed, the process embodying some of his glazing methods. The flange and base are waxed (5, 6) in order to resist the glaze at these points, and the pot filled with glaze which is steadily poured from the spout (7, 8) (see text). The shoulder and the end of the spout are glazed by inverting and dipping (9, 10), the teapot turned right way up, gripped by the inside of the lid flange and again dipped (11) until the glaze levels overlap, but taking care that none runs down the spout (12). The resist on the base repels the glaze (13). The lid is dipped upside-down, just to the top edge of the rim. The completely glazed teapot (14). For pouring glaze over a tall pot, it is first held as far round towards the body as possible (15). The glaze is poured steadily from a large jug into a large bowl while the pot is given a complete revolution (16, 17).*

5

3

4

1

5

2

6

100

7

8

9

10

11

12

13

14

15

16

17

## GLAZING GRIPPER

Metal grippers are especially useful when glazing flatware or bowls. They can be cut from sheet alumina or brass, or made from thick galvanized wire. It is possible to work with a single strand on each arm, but two claws on one arm give a firmer hold. Two or three sizes will be necessary to cover the likely range of pottery: 3-6 in. (70-150 mm.), 6-10 in. (150-250 mm.), 10-14 in. (250-350 mm.) spans.

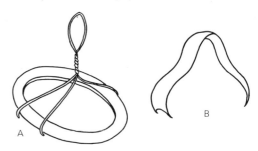

*Glazing grippers. (A) of galvanized or kiln element wire, (B) of sheet metal—aluminium or brass.*

## GLOBAR

A trade name for *silicon carbide* kiln elements.

## GLOST FIRE

Term used for the glaze-firing of ceramics, especially in the industry and in America. More rarely applied as 'glost ware'.

## GLOVES

Fireproof, heat-insulating gloves or mittens are essential for *raku* and occasionally useful for straight firing. If a pot burns your hand, however, it is still too hot to take from the kiln. The best gloves are woven *asbestos;* these are expensive, and leather gardening gloves or kitchen oven gloves are alternatives (though much less efficient).

## GOLD

Gold *enamel* is fired onto glazed pottery at about 700°C. It is used as a prepared liquid and painted on with a brush. Before firing it is brown and sticky. It is prepared as either a gold chloride (Billington), or as a gold sulphoresinate and a flux, perhaps bismuth (for 'bright' gold), or as gold powder in essential oils for 'burnish' or 'best' gold (Dodd).

Bright gold comes from the kiln shiny; burnish gold is dull from the firing and must be rubbed with a stone (traditionally a 'blood-stone' or agate) or with a glass burnisher to bring up the surface glint.

Leach mentions the admixture of gold dust with red enamel in Japan, which softens the crudity of the color. Experiment on these lines might be rewarding. Curious colors result from the use of gold in raku firing. Painting with prepared gold will reveal any hidden crazing. Gold and tin oxide give *purple of cassius.* Pinks and reds in enamels are also obtained from gold.

The firing must be very precise, especially if the painting is done in thin strokes. A few degrees over and a purple may develop. On some glazes, however, the gold cannot be subdued even at 1000°C.

*A pottery brooch by George Martin. It has been glazed in an earthenware tin glaze and brushed with a dryish line of manganese which has skated over the impressions in the body. On the fired glaze similar strokes of gold enamel have been applied, holding the brush flat so that the 'scales' have still remained white. The break-up of color and thin application has reduced the stridency of the gold and produced a more subtle result.*

## GRANITE

Most *intrusive* rocks are in the form of granite, which is classified as an *acidic* rock, i.e. with a high silica content. An analysis of a typical granite shows some 70% of silica; 14.5% alumina; various bases in percentages from 4.5 potash to 0.05 baria; 3% of iron compounds; together with phosphorus and titanium.

In decomposition, therefore, granite contains the ingredients of the pottery minerals—feldspar, stone, quartz etc.—and, at one remove, clay. The range of rocks of which granite is one is known as igneous (from fire).

## GRAPH

A graph is a pictorial or diagrammatic representation of the relationship between two variables. The information it contains would take many sentences to describe; it can estimate intermediates between known points and can sometimes be extended to indicate probabilities.

A graph consists of a vertical measured line and a horizontal one, joined at their lower left-hand terminations. Each line is divided into regular units appropriate to the data. A familiar example will explain how to set out a graph.

Graph for variable time and temperature during a firing.

The vertical numbers represent intervals of 100°C., the horizontal ones hours. At any point in your firing you can consult the pyrometer and draw a horizontal line from the temperature and a vertical one from the time which has elapsed since commencement. Readings every two hours are shown. The points of

conjunction can be joined by straight lines or drawn as an estimated curve. If the slowly increasing curve is continued beyond the last reading it will give a rough indication of the maximum temperature the kiln may reach, or at what time it would reach a given higher figure.

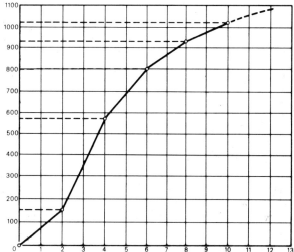

*A typical firing graph with readings taken every two hours (horizontal figures). The dotted lines connect the vertical (°C. figures) scale with the time divisions. The points of intersection are marked. The slowly flattening curve is typical of firing graphs (the increasing heat loss slowly balancing input). A possible 'projection' is shown as a dotted line.*

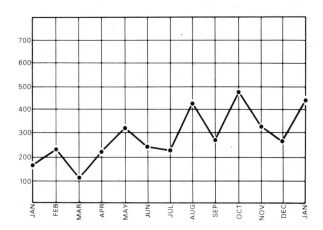

*Another typical graph. The numbers could represent monthly pot production and the sequence of months. This does not show a very even output but there is an overall improvement in production evident. The number of pots could be related to their value and a second graph superimposed.*

Graphs can be drawn for any two sets of variables. A particularly ingenious one is described in C.PP, Appendix 8, to produce approximations to square roots below unity. Graphs do not have to show a steady progression, but can show broken lines and sharp angles, frequently caricatured as profit and loss graphs. The principle remains the same.

A graph may be misleading if based on insufficient or inaccurate information.

The use of squared paper facilitates graph making. (See diagram under *firing graph*.)

## GRAPHITE

A natural form of carbon. Also called 'blacklead' and 'plumbago'. (See also *reduction*.)

## GRATE

The bars which support burning fuel and allow the passage of air through it. The development of the fire-grate (grating) marked a significant step forward from the flat surface with its heaped-up fuel and ash mixture. It made a hotter and more controllable flame possible, with the ash falling away and more easily disposed of. The modern type of grate was used by Bottger to achieve his remarkable 1300°C. plus for porcelain. The heat can either travel direct into the kiln from the fuel surface or, as suggested in R.K 60-1, be drawn through the bars (in a wood-fired kiln).

The development of refractory steels and casting has produced grates with a long life, but care must be taken that the ash never comes into contact with the under-side of the metal or the bars will twist and fail. Oil or gas burners, of course, do not require grates.

*A Roman hearth or grate for an up-draft kiln. The 'bars' are made from pottery cylinders.*

## GREEN GLAZES

There are two families of green colors in glazes: those derived directly from pigment oxides, usually copper or chrome; and those from reduced iron.

We will deal here mainly with the first group. Chrome is a hard, dense opaque coloring agent, and it is advisable to keep the proportions in a glaze to 1% or less. It will give green in a zinc-free multibase *lead glaze* at 1050-1150°C., and in stoneware glazes. At lower temperatures it may give very different colors. Combined with cobalt the color is brighter and some-what less dense, though still liable to give a rather lifeless surface. Although *refractory* it will *volatilize* and can be a danger in the presence of tin oxide. (See *chrome-tin pink*.)

Copper, in proportions of 1-3% in an oxidizing atmosphere, will give a variety of greens in soft glazes: apple green in a lead glaze, a brighter color in a lead-lime-potash or leadless glaze, progressing towards turquoise as the alkalis are increased and the alumina content diminished.

Greens from copper or chrome can be modified or assisted by additions of other oxides. Cobalt has been mentioned (use only about 0.2% in the batch). Iron, nickel, rutile, vanadium and antimony can be experi-mented with. Prepared stains have been derived from cobalt/uranium, zirconium/vanadium, and praseo-dymium phosphate. Iron and cobalt mixtures tend to give gray rather than green, but lead antimonate/cobalt may give better results used as a pigment. Nickel oxide can give gray-green in a lead-borax glaze. Some magnesium in the formula is said to improve the color. Most of these mixtures and stains are more suitable for soft glazes, but Fulham Pottery lists a zircon/vanadium/praseodymium green stain which will hold for temperatures up to 1280°C.

True turquoise in a soft glaze demands a soda-flint glass, which is unstable (see *turquoise*). In stoneware a range of blue-greens can result from the use of barium with dolomite, and feldspar, using up to 3% of copper. In fluid glazes copper will volatilize and is apt to be uncertain in its effect above 1200°C.

Kathleen Pleydell-Bouverie gives a sea-green or olive-green mixture for addition to *oxidized stone-wares*:

| | |
|---|---|
| Iron | 1% |
| Manganese | 0.3-0.5% |
| Copper | 0.3-0.5% |
| Cobalt | 0.5% |

For a discussion of reduced greens see *reduction*, and *celadon*.

## GREEN GLAZING

A term sometimes applied to once-fired ware, i.e. glazed on the raw or 'green' clay. (See *once-fired ware*.)

## GREEN PIGMENTS

Copper, either as the oxide or carbonate (slightly toxic), is commonly used on earthenware glazes to produce various hues of a rather watery kind. It is normally used as a wash or filler for a design, and needs applying with care, since any excess will fire black and cindery. Chrome is also difficult to use alone, being refractory and having a heavy opacity. Beware pink reactions from chrome. Prepared colors are generally mixtures of these oxides fritted with zinc, whiting, borax etc. to induce variety of hue. The coloring agent for Victoria green is stated to be $3CaO.Cr_2O_3.3SiO_2$. Cobalt can be added to chrome with advantage. Simple mixtures of cobalt and iron, or cobalt and antimoniate of lead (or yellow stain), can give subtle greenish colors on a *tin glaze*. Green pigment is seldom used on stoneware. Cobalt on a zinc glaze can produce a rather strident green. See also *green glazes* for some less familiar compounds which are also utilized in green pottery pigments.

## GREEN SLIPS

Chrome and copper in equal parts will provide a reasonably pleasant and stable green in slip. The first is too hard and opaque alone, the second too watery. 1.25% of each, in a pale buff slip, is adequate. Iron or a darker slip will gray the tone. Blue slip under a *honey* glaze will tend towards green.

## GREENWARE

Unfired pottery. Leach uses the term for leather-hard clay suitable for turning and cutting, but it is also used for dry clay. Green strength is an important virtue in a body (see *dry strength*.)

## GRINDING OF ROCKS

Most commercially supplied materials are in a finely-ground form—sometimes too fine. For breaking down experimental quantities of rock etc. a *mortar and pestle* can be used, or a *ball* or *jar mill*. A primitive but effective grinding pan used until recently at Soil Hill Pottery, Yorkshire was simply a circular metal container with a revolving central shaft which dragged flat stones round on chains.

## GRINDING-WHEEL

An abrasive disc which can be revolved on a central axis. The old, large wheels were turned quite slowly with a treadle; the modern wheel is spun at high speed by an electric motor. It needs to be true on the centre or considerable vibration will be set up.

The disc can be of bonded *silicon carbide* or *alumina*, the second is preferable for grinding biscuit (see *abrasive*). There are many grades and grain-sizes. A hard grade of medium grain and with a vitrified bond would be of general use, but finer wheels may be necessary for glaze grinding.

## GROG

Ground, fired biscuit (sometimes even ground up glazed ware, in porcelain factories). Incorporated into clay bodies to give texture, to impart 'bite' when throwing, to assist drying, or to increase firing strength.

It will reduce the rate of clay shrinkage during drying and in the firing, up to the temperature at which the grog itself was fired.

Standard grog is made from a refractory *fireclay* and is inert at potters' temperatures. It is graded according to the size of grain, e.g. 30 grog to dust would be the only grades to pass a 30-mesh *sieve;* 30-60 grog will pass a 30 mesh but be retained in a 60. Some suppliers (e.g. Wengers) grade still more carefully, e.g. all through 40, 25% retained in 60, 25% by 100, 50% through 100 mesh. This would be a very fine grog, almost too small even for throwing clay. A grog which is too fine may be a hazard, causing the clay to absorb water rapidly. For a normal body up to 10% of grog may be added, but much more for large pieces and special work.

Grog can be made in small quantities by crushing dry clay to a suitable size and firing it in an unglazed bowl. Colored grog can be tried for particular effects, e.g. red-clay grog beaten into the surface of stone-wares. Grog for raku can be crushed soft brick. (See also *ilmenite*.)

As a rough guide to grog size: that which passes a 50 sieve is no more than a calcined clay dust; through 30 would be a fine grog; through 14 a medium one; and through 8 mesh a coarse sample.

## GROUND-HOG KILN

Cross-draft kilns partially buried in a bank of earth, Rhodes quotes their use by country potters of the Southern Highlands of the USA. (See illus. in R.K.)

## GROUND-LAY

A method of applying an even layer of pottery color by first coating the biscuit or glaze with a tacky oil, onto which the pigment is then dusted. Mainly used in the industry on bone china, but the principle, in a more flexible form, could be adapted to craft ceramics and modeling.

## GROUT

To fill the joins between tiles or tessarae after they have been set in cement, glued, or otherwise fastened down. The grouting material should be of the same kind as the backing if set as described under *mosaic*. For tiles there are a number of proprietary grouting materials, but most are white and could well be stained to make the grouting less conspicuous. Portland cement can be used if dried very slowly under polythene (2-3 days).

## GUM ARABIC, tragacanth

Vegetable gum can be purchased as liquid or as powder. Powders are dissolved in water or denatured alcohol by soaking overnight, boiling for a few minutes and straining through a 40s mesh.

Sometimes added to glazes (e.g. raku) or colors to give a harder coating when dry, avoiding rubbing and smudging. All gums will decay in time and spoil the glaze. A little *formalin* has been suggested to counteract decomposition.

Gum arabic has some *deflocculant* effect. Tragacanth promotes *suspension* or *floatation*. Dextrin is an alternative. Cardew mentions a gum and quartz mixture for painting lid flanges etc. to prevent sticking during firing. Fine alumina might be preferable in place of the quartz.

## GUMBO

A very sticky surface clay (Rhodes).

## GYPSUM

A widely distributed evaporate rock (from evaporation of salt water). A hydrated calcium sulphate $CaSO_4$ $2H_2O$. Shells embedded in clay and attacked by sulfuric acids from metallic sulfides form transparent gypsum crystals. Most gypsum is derived from *anhydrite*. The pure micro-crystalline form is alabaster.

When crushed and heated in a revolving cylinder to 120°C., gypsum loses more than half of its water of crystallization and becomes an unstable demi-hydrate powder. Upon the addition of water it re-assumes something of its original hard state. This is *plaster of paris*. If the powder or plaster is heated above 120°C. it becomes 'dead-burnt' and will not reset. So do not dry *molds* on a hot kiln!

# H

## HAKAME

Decoration, using thick white slip and a coarse brush often as a ground for iron brushwork. Early examples can be found on the rough pots and bowls of the Korean Yi period. L.PB has a drawing of a hakame brush described as 'a miniature garden broom made of the grain ends of rice straw'. This technique is used by Bill Marshall of St. Ives, and Hamada. The slip, which must be very thick or it will vanish under the glaze, is normally spun onto the surface on a slow-turning wheel or banding-wheel. The effect is a very subtle contrast between the body and slip and the slip must therefore fire a little lighter in color than the body. Leach recommends Pikes siliceous ball clay G.F.S., perhaps with the addition of china clay and feldspar, though to go too far with additions to the natural clay will destroy the quality of the result which, to quote Honey 'implies a principle fundamental in all the arts— it speaks clearly of a process'.

*The application of brushed slip onto a fairly dry surface in the style of hakame (1). The strokes need not be spun on but can be freely applied as in this pot by Warren Mackenzie (2). (See also glaze trailing for hakame by Hamada.)*

## HAEMATITE

See *hematite*.

## HAKE

A soft, flat hand-made Japanese brush, $1\frac{1}{2}$-$3\frac{1}{2}$ in. ($3\frac{1}{2}$-9 cm.) wide. From 'hakame'?

## HALLOYSITE

A kaolinite (clay) mineral in which the plate-like structure is rolled into tubes, causing high and uneven shrinkage due to their sudden collapse on drying. The mineral may be present in various clays. Found in New Zealand, Japan, North Africa, and Mississippi, USA.

*The possible structure of halloysite showing curled 'plates' which collapse during firing leading to excessive and uneven shrinkage.*

## HAND-BUILDING

A convenient term for the forming of ceramics without a wheel. Can include *coiling, pinching, slab building, molding,* or combinations of these. Bowls and other rounded forms can be stroked and beaten out of a ball of clay as in many primitive and traditional techniques. The illustrations show a bowl made by a combination of pinching, stroking and coiling, using rubber and *steel palettes*. (See also *formers, cut-corner dishes* etc.)

*Stages in the hand-building of a bowl. A sufficiently large ball of fine-grogged clay is pinched into a hollow form, using both hands (1). This is further thinned and shaped by holding the curve in the palm and stroking the surface with the fingers of the other hand (2) and smoothing with a kidney rubber (3). It is then dropped into a biscuit bowl to stiffen (4). At the soft leather stage (5) the inside and outside are further smoothed and shaped with a steel palette. The bowl is reversed onto a whirler, an area brushed with slip (6), and a foot coiled on (7, 8). The base is carefully levelled with a needle awl (9), and finally worked over with a palette (10). The finished bowl (11).*

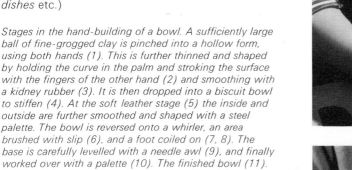

4

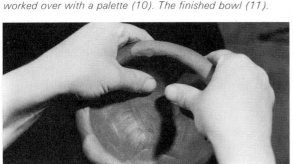

1

5

2

6

3

7

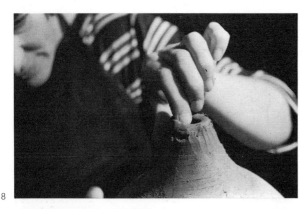

8

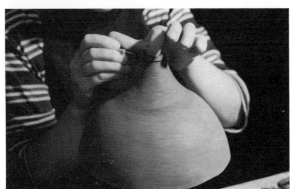

9

10

11

A hand-built pot by Ruth Duckworth: the top main form could have been made by joining two shallow bowls, as seen under formers. See also color plate 11, p. 136.

## HANDLE

A handle is fixed to a container so that it can be lifted. This is obvious but it means that where there is no need for a handle on a pot there should not be one: a handle is an integral part of the pot, cup, mug and not a decoration. The use therefore should dictate the type of handle. The forerunner of the handle was the pierced lug, one on either side of the pot. These can be found in the Shang Yin pots from Central China and in ceramics from the near tropical countries from Africa to Peru. They are still used by potters, sometimes decoratively, sometimes when the pot is designed to be suspended, which was their original use.

The inward curve of a jug and the spring of the handle merging into a related whole.

Michael Casson making a handle on a large jug. The fairly soft clay, after being well-wedged, is slapped into a tongue shape (1). The important movement of breaking the end away (2) with a flick of the thumb to leave a curved face which is then applied to a slip-coated area of the jug (3). It is well worked and fixed all round the joint (4), the whole jug tipped to a horizontal position and supported on one palm while the other hand begins to 'pull' the handle with a squeezing and stroking motion (5) forming the surface grooves in the same process (6). When the handle has reached the correct size and thickness, the jug is stood down and the handle curved over, supported at the top by the hand (7). With one hand inside, the lower junction is pressed home and 'wiped' off with firm strokes of the thumb (8). The finished handle (9).

4

1

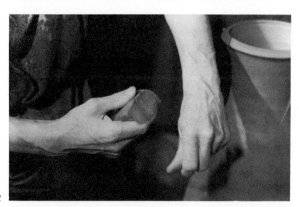

5

2

3

6

7

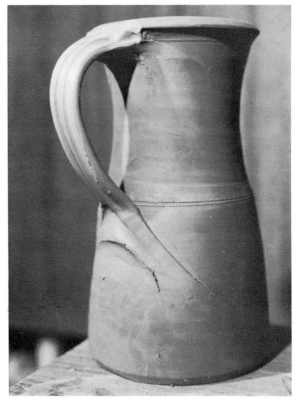

9

8

Contrasting types: The type of handle applied to commercial pottery is very different from that found on craftsman-potter's work. In industry the handle may be carefully considered in relation to the pot, but it is always made, in a press or slip-mold, as a separate entity. A distinct point of junction is thus apparent. A 'stop' or thumb-hold at the top may be worked into the design to prevent the hand from slipping. These handles need not have a smooth, arched flow of the pulled handle but may be angled or built up from broken curves. However, the clean articulation of parts is distinctive of the best industrial ceramics.

At the other end of the scale, an English Medieval jug handle springs like a branch from the main form, to which it is firmly secured by strokes of the thumb. This apparently natural growth gives satisfaction from all angles; not merely from a profile view. The strong 'pulling lines' and bold wipe of the clay each side of the juncture are delights in themselves. The thumb movement at once fastens the handle and decorates the pot.

Placing: The placing of a handle is governed by three main considerations: the curves of the main form; the number of fingers required to lift the vessel when full of liquid (the thickness and width of the handle must also be in direct relation to this weight); physical and formal balance.

Between the curve of the pot and that of the handle there is a space. Not only must this be sufficient to accommodate the finger or fingers comfortably, but the

110

shape of the space is of great aesthetic importance. On a more or less cylindrical jug or beaker it may be no more than the simple letter D—the one-finger handle is an example—but on the inward curve between the belly and neck of a well-designed jug it will be very subtle. These related curves should merge into a whole.

It is usually advisable to spring the handle across a concave section of the pot form. If it straddles a bulge a rather ugly crescent is formed and the handle may become awkwardly long, or difficult to hold, or both.

When dealing with the question of placing, one can say generally that a handle which springs higher than the rim of the pot will make it awkward to invert for draining, while one that is too near the base will not allow a firm grip when picking up or setting down.

Within these limits, however, a case can be made for both high and low positions. For instance, the centre of gravity of a beaker may be said to be below the half-way mark as it is rarely quite full of liquid. A low handle should, therefore, give a better balance. On the other hand, the leverage resulting from a low placing gives less control when drinking from the beaker. This is a matter for individual discretion.

*An attractive 'wishbone' handle on a three thousand-year-old Cypriot ladle.*

### HANDLE CUTTERS
Shaped wire rings, attached to a wire or wooden handle, illustrated in L.PB 90 and used for cutting clay for pot *handles*. An alternative to pulling or extruding, but like the latter of these methods it results in an even thickness and width from top to bottom of the handle.

### HARDENING-ON FIRE
A separate firing, usually up to about 800°C., which fixes *underglaze* pottery pigments onto the *biscuit* in order to prevent smudging or washing off during glazing. The process is common in the industry, but for craft potters it can be avoided by painting onto the raw clay, or by adding a little clay to the pigment if it is to be used on biscuit, as practised by Geoffrey Whiting. If neat oxides are used, some will still be loose on the surface at 1020°C. A little *flux* may be added—china stone will help with cobalt. *Gum* can be added but this will affect glaze take-up.

### HARD LEATHER
Used in this book to indicate clay on the dry side of leather-hard.

*Two stages in making a strap handle for a casserole. The lid, which can be flat as shown or in the form of a shallow inverted bowl, is thrown together with another, smaller, bowl with a flat rim, and both dried to leather-hard. The strap is cut in the lid as shown and the smaller bowl luted beneath it.*

### HARDNESS SCALE
Also known as Moh's scale. Based on a series of minerals in order of hardness: each mineral can be scratched by the one below it.

| | |
|---|---|
| 1 Talc | 6 Feldspar (orthoclase |
| 2 Gypsum | rock) |
| 3 Calcite | 7 Quartz |
| 4 Fluorspar | 8 Topaz |
| (fluorite) | 9 Corundum |
| 5 Apatite | 10 Diamond |

The scale is used as a convenient reference, e.g. a mineral or rock might be rated 5-6, between apatite and feldspar. *Hard paste* porcelain rates 6-7.

## HARD PASTE

The name given to 'true' porcelain of European type firing at 1350-1450°C. and composed of china clay (kaolin) with china stone or feldspar. Craft potters rarely fire to this range and it is difficult to find a pure clay which will also throw. The theoretical ideal composition of hard paste is 25% quartz, 25% feldspar, 50% kaolin. CR3 gives a recipe (Richard Parkinson) for a throwable 1320°C. porcelain. (See under *porcelain*.)

## HARE'S FUR GLAZE

A name given to a range of mottled or streaked dark brown Chinese glazes. Rhodes asserts that these are slip glazes. Fairly fluid, and subject to blistering—the healed over blisters causing the darker marks. I have found that manganese as well as iron, if heavily loaded into a glaze, will give something of the same effect. The temperature is critical and varies with the glaze. (See also *temmoku*.)

## HARKORT TEST

A method of testing a glaze for its liability to *craze*. The piece is heated repeatedly and at successively higher temperatures from 120°C. to 190°C., and plunged into cold water between each stage. A note is made of the temperature at which crazing becomes apparent. The higher the temperature stage, the longer its probable craze-free life (from 3 months to $2\frac{1}{2}$ years). There are other factors in crazing besides *thermal shock*, but a simple form of this test gives an indication of the strength of your glaze and of glaze-body fit. In professional equipment the pieces are heated under steam pressure.

## HARP, bow

A clay-cutter in the form of a semi-circular hoop of metal or bamboo with a wire or wires stretched across it. The harp can be used for trimming clay—e.g. rims on the wheel or the edges of *molded dishes*—or it can be dragged through a block of clay to cut slabs. In the latter case it needs to be sturdily constructed with the wire fixed at a given distance from the ends, so that, when the cut is made and the ends pressed tightly to the bench surface, an even thickness slab results. A number of notches can be provided to control the cut, or several wires used at once. For slab cutting, very strong steel 'piano wire' is used. There is a slight

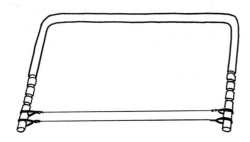

*A harp with two wires on a metal frame. For cutting multiple slabs.*

tendency for the wire to rise in the middle, and considerable power is needed to cut a large slab.

## HARRISON PYROMETRIC CONES

See *Seger cones*.

## HEAT

Heat is the result of the translation, rotation or vibration of molecules. It is energy which can be put to work by potters to rearrange the *molecular* structure of matter, e.g. forming ceramic from clay. In a fuel-burning kiln it is the result of the chemical combination of carbon with hydrogen and oxygen; in an electric kiln it is the result of *electronic* and molecular movement. It can be transmitted by *conduction, convection* and *radiation*. Heat is not gauged merely in terms of temperature. In the firing of pottery, time is also a factor. (See *heat work*.)

## HEAT-FUSE

Electric current can be conducted through a short length of metal inside the kiln which will melt at a given temperature, break the *circuit,* and cut off the supply to the kiln elements. Similar in appearance to a *pyrometer*. The fuse must be rated somewhat above the optimum firing temperature and its object is to prevent a total burn-out of the kiln. It is not an automatic cut-off for normal firing.

## HEAT INSULATION

See *insulation of heat*.

## HEAT LOSS

Heat can escape from a kiln in various ways. With combustible fuels the chimney takes away probably a third or more of the heat produced at the hearth. Hence the attempts by down-draft, multi-chamber kilns, and other designs, to utilize as much heat energy as possible before the chimney is reached. Simple up-draft kilns are the most spendthrift; the ancient Eastern climbing kiln or the modern electric kiln probably the most economical. In the industry, the tunnel kiln wastes very little heat.

Heat loss through the walls can be more easily controlled by the use of *insulating*-bricks. Unfortunately the most efficient of these are also the most easily abraded and broken. Heat loss increases as the difference between ambient and chamber temperature increases.

The loss is also proportional to wall area (rather than to the volume of the firing-chamber). A perfect cube is ideal in this respect, a long narrow rectangle the least efficient. The total area can easily be worked out and compared with volume. A 2 x 2 x 2 ft. (0.6 x 0.6 x 0.6 m.) chamber will have a volume of 8 cu. ft. (0.216 cu. m.); a 4 x 2 x 1 ft. (1.2 x 0.6 x 0.3 m.) chamber will also contain 8 cu. ft. (0.216 cu. m.). The first, however, has 24 sq. ft. (2.23 sq. m.) of wall area (four sides, floor and roof) while the latter has 28 sq. ft. (2.6 sq. m.) or 16% more. Wall loss will obviously vary with the type of bricks or other insulation used but it has been estimated at up to 20% at higher temperatures.

Bricks will also store heat, i.e. use up energy in getting hot themselves. This will vary dramatically between a close, heavy *firebrick* and an open, *insulating-brick*. (See *heat storage*.) If, for reasons of strength and heat resistance, the *hot-face* must be of firebrick, this should be as thin as possible and backed by more insulating material. (See *insulation*.) When other heat expanders such as the production of steam and poor combustion are taken into account, not much more than 20% of the actual hearth heat is available to fire the pots. (See also *thermal conductivity*.)

Too little attempt is made to utilize chimney and other heat losses in a kiln for space-heating, clay drying etc.

## HEATPROOF WARE

See *ovenware*, and *flameproof* ware.

## HEAT RESISTANCE

The power of resisting change (to the molten state) when heated. (See *refractories, eutectic* etc.)

## HEAT SHOCK

Taking pots from too hot a kiln can cause *crazing* which may not occur during slow cooling. (See *thermal shock*.)

## HEAT STORAGE

The amount of heat that kiln bricks, kiln furniture, saggars etc. will 'hold', i.e. that amount required to heat them to the point where they radiate as much energy as they take in. This storage represents wasted fuel; bricks should be chosen with as low a heat storage as is compatible with abrasion resistance etc. (See also *heat loss*.) The denser the brick, the more heat it will absorb. The average firebrick will store some 30,000 Btu (30.6 mJ) per square foot 9 in. (230 mm.) thick; a high quality insulating brick 6-8000 Btu (6-8 mJ). The familiar household storage heater utilizes the heat storing properties of heavy brick.

## HEAT-TREATMENT

The control of temperature during cooling to create special effects, especially crystal formation. The temperature may be held at various stages, or a degree of reheating may be practised. Changes can also be made in the glaze by means of subsequent refiring at sub-maturing temperatures. Many of the interesting glazes from Scandinavia and Germany are heat-treated.

## HEAT-WORK

In the firing of pottery there are two factors, temperature and time, which taken in conjunction will represent the energy input or heat-work. Thus *soaking* will alter glaze qualities although the temperature remains constant. *Pyrometric cones* respond to heat-work in a similar way to glazes, and this is their principal advantage over *pyrometers*.

## HEMATITE, haematite

The mineral of ferric iron $Fe_2O_3$. Described by Billington as 'an iron-earth . . . found in a stonelike form'. Has been recommended for coating pots prior to burnishing to give a good color, but the type of hematite generally offered by merchants is too pure and the burnish tends to fade.

## HOLDCROFT BARS

Holdcroft *Thermoscope*. Special ceramic bars $2\frac{1}{4}$ in. (57 mm.) long, supported at each end and used like *pyrometric cones*. A bar will sag at the temperature indicated by its number. Numbers are from 10-360. Temperatures are in °C.

| | | |
|---|---|---|
| No 40 — 700° | No 230 — 1100° | No 270 — 1250° |
| No 120 — 905° | No 250 — 1140° | No 280 — 1280° |
| No 190 — 1000° | No 260 — 1200° | No 290 — 1300° |
| No 210 — 1060° | No 265 — 1230° | No 360 — 1490° |

Supplied by Harrison-Meyer.

## HOLLOW DISH-MOLDS

A concave mold of plaster or biscuit in which a dish is formed. It is the easiest type of mold to make. Hump molds can be made from it.

Method. The illus. shows a block of clay which has been cut with a tool and finally shaped with a template to an inverted version of the required dish shape. Make sure that there is a sharp and clean angle between the clay and the board and ensure that this is not undercut at any point. A watertight wall of clay, corrugated card, metal or leather is built round the clay shape and about an inch from it. This is then filled with plaster of paris poured steadily onto the middle of the clay form until it rises to a level $\frac{1}{2}$ in. (12 mm.) above the highest point. This is left to set, the wall removed, the whole reversed, and the clay-former peeled out. The surfaces of the mold can be scraped smooth and clean and the top inner edge cut to a sharp corner. The outside corners are bevelled with a plane. (For use see *dishes*.)

*A hollow mold in use, of the type shown being made in the diagrams overleaf.*

H

*Making a hollow dish mold. (A) shows a block of clay which has been cut to the desired mold shape. Start with a flat-topped block, cut the plan shape with the aid of a card template, then steadily pare the curve away with a wooden spatula tool. Finish with a template of metal, stiff card, or wood as shown in the diagram. The template is scraped round the form until it touches at all points. Build up any area which has been cut too low. Ensure a sharp and clean angle between the clay and the board. The sides of the shape should not be too steep or it will be difficult to ease clay into the finished mold when making dishes. There should be a flat area on the top of the form so that the dishes made from it will sit firmly.*

*In (B) a wall of lino, corrugated card, or similar material is built round the completed former and made water tight, as shown in section. A smooth mixture of plaster of paris is prepared (see under plaster for mixing) and poured over the former allowing it to flow into the surrounding well until the level is about ½ in. (12 mm.) above the clay as in (C).*

*When the plaster is set the wall is removed, the clay former is peeled out and the outer corners of the mold bevelled. Keep the inner angle sharp. See also pressed dishes.*

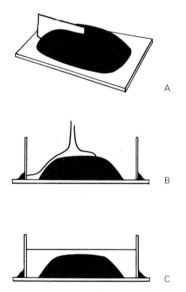

## HONEY GLAZE

A general name for a high-lead glaze with some iron oxide, generally introduced by the use of *red clay* in the recipe. The natural impurities in the old slipware glazes gave a slightly yellowish or 'honey' tinge which had a unifying effect on the design. A typical modern 'honey' glaze recipe is:

| | |
|---|---|
| Lead sesquisilicate | 70 |
| Feldspar | 10 |
| Red clay | 12 |
| China clay | 6 |
| Whiting | 2 |

fired at around 1070°C.

## HORNEBLENDE

An intermediate *igneous* rock. Complex silicates of calcium, magnesium, iron and sodium.

## HOT-FACE

The inner surface of a kiln wall.

## HOT-FACE BRICKS

Bricks capable of standing great heat and, in a solid fuel kiln, abrasion and *spalling*. The various qualities of high-alumina *firebrick* are generally used, except in electric kilns where the more efficient but softer insulating-brick composes the hot-face and often the entire wall. (See *insulation, heat loss,* etc.)

## HUMP-MOLD, mushroom-mold, drape-mold

Dish molds with a convex surface. Useful for *trailed* and *feathered* dishes. The disadvantage of the type is that the dish may crack across it when drying. A hump-mold without a foot can be used as a 'master' from which to reproduce hollow *molds*. If hump-molds are cast from a hollow one, the expansion of the plaster can cause trouble and it is advisable to line the hollow mold with a thin sheet of clay to accommodate this expansion. Hump-molds can also be made from metal pie-dishes (thinly greased before casting). If other concave shapes are used, always bear the expansion factor in mind—it is powerful enough to split glass or pottery.

The diagrams below show the methods of making a mold from a pie-dish.

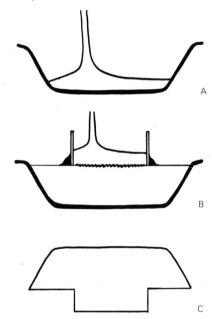

*A hump mold made in a metal piedish. The dish is lightly greased with warm Vaseline and filled with an even mix (see under plaster) of plaster of paris until the level is just below the point where the dish begins to turn out towards the rim (A).*

*(B) shows the central area of the surface of the plaster scored or roughened, a watertight oval or oblong wall of card, lino, or similar sheet material set on it, and filled to a depth of about 2 in. (50 mm.) with plaster. (C) shows the completed (reversed) mold extracted from the piedish former.*

## HYDRATE, hydration

A compound containing *chemically combined water*. Clay is a hydrated aluminium-silicate. Firing drives off the water leaving alumina silicate. In this case the operation is irreversible, but this is not always so. With *gypsum* it is partially reversible under certain conditions.

## HYDROCARBON GASES

Gases of carbon and hydrogen compounds, e.g. methane $CH_4$. The paraffin series are hydrocarbons, also *natural gas*. Mentioned in connection with *reducing atmospheres*.

## HYDROGEN

A gaseous element H, 1. Lightest substance known. Inflammable (see *gas fuel*); combines with oxygen to form water, $H_2O$. True *acids* will contain hydrogen in their formula but the acidic oxides used in pottery do not. Originally used (as unity) to calculate *atomic weights*, but now superseded by oxygen for this purpose. Hydrogen is the unit of *valency*.

## HYDROMETER

Or 'slip-gauge' (Leach). An instrument for determining the specific gravity of a liquid/solid mixture, i.e. the consistency or thickness of a slip or glaze. A hollow glass cylinder (a test-tube, for instance) or a wooden road about 1 in. (25 mm.) x 6 in. (150 mm.) is weighted at one end so that it floats upright. The more solid matter present in the mixture, the greater the length of hydrometer which will show above the surface. A scale can be marked on it, using its position in clear water as a base line. Its value lies in its ability to compare one glaze with another or to maintain a standard for any one glaze. Approximate readings for true weight and volume can be noted by testing the hydrometer in a batch of known dry weight and water content.

Pottery suppliers have not yet thought of supplying hydrometers, but they are not difficult to make. Wooden ones must be protected by paint or varnish from absorbing water.

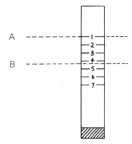

*A simple hydrometer. Crosshatching indicates the weighted end which holds it upright in the liquid. The dotted line A indicates its level in pure water. In a thick glaze it would float higher: in the diagram the level B indicates a possible position, reading at 4.3 on the scale engraved on the hydrometer. The divisions of the scale are arbitrary and for comparative reference only.*

## HYDROXYL, hydroxide

An *ionic* combination of one oxygen atom and one hydrogen atom forming part of a *compound*. Known as the OH- group and shown as $(OH)_n$ in formulas The alkalis, boron and phosphorus can form hydroxides.

## HYGROSCOPIC WATER, substance

Term occasionally used to indicate the *chemically combined water* in clay.

A hygroscopic material, however, is one capable of absorbing water from the surrounding air. Exceptionally hygroscopic substances are *deliquescent*, e.g. potassium carbonate.

## IDEAL FORMULA

The theoretical formula for a mineral, to which natural materials approximate: the simple ones, such as flint or whiting, very closely; more complex formulas such as the feldspars less so. The ideal formulas are used to represent natural minerals in simple glaze computations.

## IGNEOUS ROCK

From 'fire' (Greek). Rock which has been molten and has formed during the cooling of the earth, or by intrusions from a molten core into the earth's crust in more recent times. In some cases the cooling has been slow and the rocks have had time to crystallize into individual minerals. *Granite* is the prime example. These old rocks are generally acid, i.e. they have a high silica content of 70% or more.

The molten material which has been forced through the crust—volcanic or extrusive rock—has solidified rapidly as lava and has a very fine *crystalline* grain. This material tends to be basis, with 50% or less of silica. *Basalt* is the commonest. One might say that the granite systems represent the body and the volcanic rocks the glaze of a ceramic.

Feldspars and *kaolinite* clays have decomposed from granitic rocks; *montomorillinite* more probably from extrusive ones. In England many igneous rocks are often used as roadstones, and could be used as a foundation for a stoneware glaze. It is worth trying any hard rock dust that you can get. *Chemical Analyses of Igneous Rocks* was published in 1931 (South-West England) and 1956 (Northern England) by Her Majesty's Stationery Office.

## ILLITE

Described variously as a hydrous *mica* or a clay mineral. 'In London clay the mineral is thought to be 90% illite' (Cardew). W.C. doubts its separate existence: 'It seems likely that (illite, etc.) . . . are mixtures rather than pure minerals.'

Illite has less potash and more *OH* groupings than mica and may have been converted by seawater from kaolinite. Secondary clays may contain a proportion of illite. The name originates from Illinois, where it was first isolated.

## ILMENITE

An ore, ferrous titanate, $Fe_2O_3.TiO_2$, 152, m.p. 1365°C. s.g. 4.7. A similar combination to rutile, but with more iron. Found as beach-sand in Australia, South-West India, America and Scandinavia. Grinds to grog-like granules and can be used in bodies or glazes to provide speckle—'a peppery appearance' (Rhodes). The iron will dissolve at the perimeter of the granule to give an amber 'halo'. 1-3% is the normal addition. Can be bought in various grades.

## IMPERVIOUS, impermeable

Will not *absorb* water or allow water to pass through. In pottery the degree of vitrification controls permeability. There are strict industrial tests. (See also *porosity*.)

## IMPRESSING

Impressed decoration has been one of the most popular techniques of the mid-twentieth century. The ideal of a close integration between pot and decoration is combined with direct and spontaneous 'instant' action and an enhanced glaze interest.

The *roulette or stamp* are less favored than the chance patterns developed by 'found' objects: a broken edge of wood, a cog-wheel, rolled string etc. This can result in freedom and freshness, or incoherence and muddle, according to the degree of skill and sensitivity employed.

Order and design are more easily obtained by restricting one's impressing tools to two, or even to a single one, building up a pattern by repetition and variation of placing. If several sheets of clay are rolled out, experiments can be made before working on a pot. Impressing is very suitable for *slab pots* and can be done before the piece is assembled. *Beaten decoration* is a related technique.

## IMPURITIES

In a mineral, any oxide or material not included in the *formula*. 'Purity' is the prime object of the industrial potter, since it ensures uniformity. The careful extraction of iron traces from clay by electromagnets is an instance.

Commercial suppliers are industrially orientated and the craft potter has to accept a greater degree of purity than he wants. The alternative is to go and find materials for himself. The subtlety and quality of the older ceramics—early Chinese blues, slipware glazes etc.—arose partly from impurities which it was beyond the technology of the time to remove. There is no genuine way of returning to unrefined materials except by pioneering in the way that Cardew and Harry Davis have done.

We can still use some composite natural materials, e.g. red clay to introduce iron, colemanite instead of borax fritt etc. G.EP suggests trials with everyday materials such as scouring powder, fertilizers etc. Copper metal can be *oxidized* in a kiln or in salt water, iron oxide can be scraped and ground as rust, and so on. Leach tells of Hamada's 'building-stone' used neat as a glaze. Potclays list an interesting 'black feldspar'. But, in the West, we tend to put a premium on time and take out the quickest way out.

## INCONGRUENT MELTING

Pottery materials may dissociate during firing into compounds with varying melting points, i.e. into liquids within a solid. The whole structure melts incongruently. This is especially true of bodies, although it also occurs in glazes during the firing. (See *eutectic, melting point*.)

## INLAY

A technique of decoration used in medieval floor tiles, Korean Koryu wares etc. The clay is inlaid with another of a contrasting color to a depth of up to $\frac{1}{8}$ in. (3 mm.). The typical pattern is fairly bold and broad, although the Korean wares mentioned were often very fine in line.

*Impressed decoration. A wide variety of marks made in a slab of soft plastic clay by common objects.*

*Tile inlay. The design has been cut into a leather-hard tile and slip piped or trailed into it. When stiff, the surface can be cleaned level with a knife or scraper.*

## IRON, oxides, compounds

A metallic element Fe, 56.
Oxides:
Ferrous (reduced) $FeO$, 72
Ferric $Fe_2O_3$, 160, (hematite)
Magnetic, ferro-ferrosic $Fe_3O_4$, 232 (magnetite).

(For other iron compounds see under *crocus martis, ilmenite, rutile, ochre, sienna, red clay, copperas, iron chromate, synthetic iron oxide.* Also *Albany clay.*)

In earthenware, iron gives buffs and browns (1-8%) or more reddish colors in a high alkali, lime-free glaze (P.CG). It can be combined with other oxides for black, or to modify cobalt etc. Red clay is the most subtle source of iron for many colors and glazes; in *honey* glazes and in many stonewares where it also has a fluxing action, it can be used in amounts up to 50%. With manganese it can be used to approximate cobalt to *asbolite.* Crystalline glazes are produced from hematite. Avoid zinc with iron. In coarse particles, such as ilmenite, iron produces specking.

Chemically an amphoteric, it will have little effect in an oxidizing fire but will behave as a flux in reduction. The most stable iron form is the *spinel* $FeO.Fe_2O_3$, or $Fe_3O_4$.

Iron leads the field as a coloring agent in reduced glazes, with a range from brick-red to blue. (See *celadon, reduction, temmoku* etc.)

## IRON CHROMATE

Chromate of iron, ferric chromate, $FeCrO_4$. By analysis $Fe_2O_3$ 34.6, $Cr_2O_3$ 49.8. In a glaze 0.5-2.0% will produce grays. Also used in bodies as a stain. Brown with zinc. Used in *crystalline* glazes. May be used to modify other pigment oxides.

## IRON EARTHS

A series of impure, clayey, high-iron compounds, sometimes with manganese. They are generally more stable to 1400°C. than iron oxides, and are preferred by some potters for introducing iron into glazes, slips and pigments. (See *ochre, umber, sienna.*)

## IRONING OF COBALT

Reddish to black patches on cobalt caused by too high a concentration. Due to crystallization of cobalt silicate (Dodd). Generally considered a fault, but can sometimes be pleasant on a brushstroke. To avoid ironing, cobalt can be diluted with china stone or a fritt, or modified with other oxides, e.g. red clay or manganese.

## IRONSTONE, ironstone ware

A hard iron ore. Ironstone ware has a dark colored vitrified body.

## ISOTOPE

It has been found that, though *the proton* number of an element is constant, the number of *neutrons* varies. Since the *atomic weight* is the sum of these fundamental particles, an element can have more than one 'weight'. The deviations from the formerly accepted weight are called isotopes. Luckily the ratio of the number of isotopes is constant in a mass of material, so that an atomic weight can be worked out which is an average or mean number. Thus if two-thirds of an element has a weight of 14, and one-third a weight of 15, the atomic weight of a mass of that element would be 14.33 recurring (a hypothetical case). As a result, the convenient whole numbers have given way to several places of decimals. (See also *atomic theory, atomic weights, atomic numbers.*)

# J

## JAR MILL

A small *ball mill,* usually turned by friction on revolving horizontal rods about 2 in. (50 mm.) in diameter. The jars range from 2 pints (1 liter) to a gallon (5 liters). The advantage of the jar mill mechanism is that various sizes of jars can be used, and more than one jar at a time. The critical factors are those given under *ball mill.*

The jar can be of a hard ceramic. The lid must be quite watertight, and capable of firm closure. Size from 4 in. (100 mm.) internal diameter upwards. The mechanism is shown in the diagram. Only one roller is driven, the other(s) run free. One might compromise by constructing the drive and purchasing the jars from a merchant.

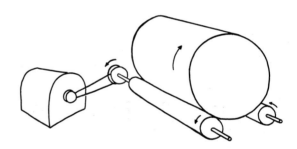

*A jar mill. The diagram shows a drive from the motor to one roller. The second roller runs free. In practice some gearing or speed reduction system would be needed between the motor and roller and a computation made for the roller and jar revolution speeds by comparison of their respective circumferences.*

## JASPER WARE

The name given by Wedgwood to a fine-grain, unglazed, *vitreous* stoneware, often stained with oxides. A quoted recipe:

| | |
|---|---|
| Ball clay | 26 |
| China clay | 18 |
| Barytes | 45 |
| Flint | 11 |

## JERSEY STONE

An American equivalent to china stone.

## JIGGER AND JOLLEY

A machine for molding hollow ware and flatware. The clay is squeezed between a profiled metal tool (the template or 'die') and a revolving plaster mold. The face of a plate or saucer is formed by throwing a slab of clay onto a revolving mold, while the shape of the back and the thickness are controlled by the die, which is brought down by means of a pivoted arm onto the spinning clay, squeezing and cutting away the surplus. For hollow shapes the outside is formed by the mold, and the inside by the die.

It is essentially an industrial operation for large-scale production of identical pieces. It needs some skill (although automated systems are now taking over) but is obviously a mechanical technique. To say that the method destroys the 'plastic feeling' is to ignore the fact that the bodies used have little plasticity anyhow. Plastic clays such as the craft potter uses are rather sticky to operate. 'Jiggering' usually refers to hollow ware, and 'jolleying' to flatware.

Hollow forms are limited to those which will lift directly from the mold—fundamentally cylinders or inverted cones. Foot rings are minimal on all shapes. Several hundred molds may be used for one service, each piece being left to stiffen before it can be removed from its mold.

Amateur jolleys can be rigged up for special purposes—cutting the clay former and the plaster foot of a circular dish mold, for example. Jolley arms can be purchased. The template or die can be sheet brass or wood; this will tend to cut rather than squeeze the clay, and the process is slower and less precise.

*Making a plate. The clay is roughly pressed into the revolving mold with the fingers (1), the final form and thickness being controlled by the metal template (2). In the industry the plate would normally be pressed out upside-down, the base and foot formed by the jolley arm. (Potter: Robin Welch; photographs: Eileen Lewenstein.)*

*A jigger and jolley used to form a cup (industrial). The spread of the clay in the plaster former is being assisted by the hand, the template pressing the final form and thickness. The process is now quite automatic in many factories.*

### JIKI
Given by Dodd (D.DC) as a Japanese name for porcelain.

### JOLLEY
See *jigger and jolley.*

### JORDON CLAY
A light-burning stoneware clay from New Jersey, USA.

### JOULE
The standard international unit of heat quantity (work or energy). Symbol J.

1 Btu  = 1050 J
      = 1.05 kJ
1 Therm = 100,000 Btu
      = 105,000,000 joules
      = 105,000 kJ
      = 105 MJ
kJ = one thousand Joules ($10^3$)
MJ = one million Joules ($10^6$)

## JUG SHAPE

A satisfactory jug shape combines a generous and well-defined form with utility. Cardew suggests a combination of beaker and sphere (C.PP 102) and gives advice on throwing this basic pottery form. The 'inverted beaker' shape has, however, been much favored. Medieval English pottery provides a pattern-book of splendid jugs in a wide variety of shape and finish. The *jug handle* is crucial to its form and should be balanced by the *lip*.

Points of utility to be remembered are that a jug must be easily cleanable, though with modern kitchen tools it is not essential to be able to get one's hand inside. It should withstand moderate thermal shock. When full, its weight will be more than doubled and the handle should be *seen* to have sufficient strength to lift it without danger. The handle should not rise above the rim of the jug.

*Stoneware jug by Bernard Leach.*

*An early Michael Cardew slipware jug, wood fired at Winchcombe.*

# K

### KAKI

Japanese for 'persimmon', applied to a series of red-brown, broken-color, *reduced*-iron glazes. In Mashiko the use of a local building-stone, crushed, gave kaki glaze without additions. Leach mentions glazes with a high *feldspathic* content, some limestone and about 5% iron oxide. Several recipes are given in L.PB 170-1. They have a higher iron content—up to 20-30% of ochre—and also suggest that the color can be obtained in *oxidation*. Rhodes includes kaki under *slip-glazes,* and there is some parallel here with the ochre recipes. Certainly the iron needs to be in sufficient quantity for some to be precipitated onto the surface where it will react with oxygen and crystallize on cooling. (See also *red glazes.*)

A translation (S.WJC) from Japanese to American materials of a kaki recipe gives:

| | |
|---|---|
| Nepheline syenite | 38.7 |
| Colemanite | 20.0 |
| Zinc | 8.1 |
| Barium | 9.85 |
| China clay | 25.8 |
| Flint | 33.3 |
| Iron | 2.0-6.0% addition |

### KALIUM

See *potassium*.

## SOME DATA ON KANTHAL A1 RESISTANCE WIRE
Maximum wire temperature 1350°C.

| Wire gauge | | Diameter | | Resistance in ohms per foot | ft./lb. |
|---|---|---|---|---|---|
| | | in. | mm. | | |
| s.w.g. | 18 | 0.048 | 1.219 | 0.3786 | 179.4 |
| B. and S. | 16 | 0.0508 | 1.290 | 0.3376 | 160.3 |
| s.w.g. | 17 | 0.056 | 1.422 | 0.2781 | 131.9 |
| B. and S. | 15 | 0.0571 | 1.450 | 0.2677 | 127.1 |
| s.w.g. | 16 | 0.064 | 1.626 | 0.2129 | 101.0 |
| s.w.g. | 15 ⎫ | 0.072 | 1.829 | 0.168 | 79.85 |
| B. and S. | 13 ⎭ | | | | |
| s.w.g. | 14 | 0.08 | 2.032 | 0.136 | 64.6 |
| B. and S. | 11 | 0.0907 | 2.304 | 0.1059 | 50.3 |
| s.w.g. | 13 | 0.092 | 2.337 | 0.1031 | 48.87 |

## KANTHAL

Suppliers of a wide range of electrical resistance materials for use in kilns and furnaces. Originating in Sweden, they are now made under licence in other countries: in England by Hall and Pickles of Sheffield; in the USA by Kanthal of Bethel, Connecticut. Alloys are made into wires, strips, rods, tubes, ribbons etc.

For potters' kilns the A1 quality wire is the most widely used element material. It will run at a maximum of 1350°C. but, since there is always lag between element temperature and that of the kiln, the working maximum firing is 1300°C. The wire will last longer at 1275°C. Kanthal 'Super' is a special molybdenum/silica alloy rated at 1700°C. Kanthal A is suitable for earthenwares.

The *Kanthal Handbook* is a very useful technical reference book for serious kiln-builders. Some of the information is reproduced below. Well-designed and carefully wound elements should last up to 200 stoneware firings in *oxidation*. They become thinner and slower with use, and the coils tend to collapse sideways. At their present price they are very economical if not abused.

Wires are supplied in 37 different diameters in two series or gauges called s.w.g. (standard wire gauge), and B. and S. (Brown and Sharp). Diameters between 1.6 mm. (approx. $\frac{1}{8}$ in.) and 2.35 mm. (approx. $\frac{3}{16}$ in.) are the most useful to potters. These are in the ranges 16-13 s.w.g. and 14-11 B. and S. The higher the gauge number, the thinner the wire. The thicker wires are recommended for stoneware firing. (See also *electricity, electric kilns, elements, electrical, winding elements* etc.)

## KAOLIN

The name derives from the Chinese *Kao*—high, and *Ling*—hill, a ridge or mountain where it was discovered. It is synonymous with *china clay*, the latter name being preferable to avoid confusion with *kaolinite*, the pure, theoretical clay substance or mineral.

## KAOLINITE

The 'ideal' clay mineral $Al_2O_3.2SiO_2.2H_2O$, 258, to which china clay approaches most closely. The true kaolinite crystal consists of alternate layers of $SiO_4$ groups and $Al(OH)_6$ groups, arranged in the *lamellar* structure which gives clay its quality of plasticity. In most natural clays this 'stacking' has been disorganised to some degree, allowing the intrusion of alkalis, iron etc.

The mineral is the result of the decomposition of alumina-silicate rocks, e.g. feldspar. Non-kaolinite clays include the *montmorillinites*. (See *also illite*.)

## KAOLINIZATION

The action of hot gases, mainly $CO_2$ and $H_2O$, have in geological time acted on *feldspathic* minerals to leach out the alkalis and to form kaolinite. A very simplified notation for the process is:
Feldspar + steam + carbon dioxide, rearranged as Potassium carbonate + quartz + clay
In chemical terms:
$K_2O.Al_2O_4.6SiO_2$ + $(2)H_2O$ + $CO_2 = K_2CO_3$ + $(4)SiO_2$ + $Al_2O_3.2SiO_2$.

There are doubts as to whether kaolinization, by weathering, is still proceeding.

## KELVIN

Symbol K. A temperature scale allied to Centigrade but beginning at absolute zero —273°C. (See *absolute temperature scale, sintering, gas expansion, conversion*.)

## KICKWHEEL

A foot-operated potter's wheel. There are two types:
1 The genuine 'kicked' wheel. The potter sits over a large stone flywheel which he rotates by direct friction with the sole of his foot. This is the traditional wheel of the Mediterranean and other countries, and is occasionally used by the modern craft potter. There is often no tray, so throwing must be fairly dry.

2   The crankshaft wheel, where the 'kick' is transmitted to the shaft via a bar or connector. The potter may stand on one leg and swing a frontally suspended bar with the other. This type is not recommended for serious potters; one's stance is unstable and the strain on the standing leg is considerable. It is however found in many schools and colleges. The seated type is better-designed, affording greater control with the minimum exertion. The direct drive to ·the shaft imposes a limited speed but recent refinements include a geared wheel giving a ratio of about 1:1.5 between kick-bar and wheel head speeds.

3

1

2

*Views of one type of kick wheel with tray removed. It was constructed in oak, in 1947, and has been in continuous use ever since. Timbers are $3\frac{1}{2}$ x $2\frac{1}{4}$ in. (90 x 55 mm.). Details of the crankshaft and kick-bar are shown in (3). The connecting rod is from an old car, the flywheel from a lathe. A thrust bearing is set at the base of the shaft and a ball bearing at the top, protected from water by a disc of ply and plastic. The bar support is taken back to the axis of the bar.*

The kickwheel is especially useful for turning. Many potters prefer its direct and instinctive control to the one-remove of the power wheel. A well-made seated kickwheel with a good flywheel, about 60 lb. or 25 kg., can be worked for hours without unduly tiring the potter.

There are many wheels on the market. Sturdy construction, good bearings, quietness and comfort are points to check. Wheels are not difficult to build if one has minimal carpentry and/or metalwork skill. Use a hard wood for the frame—beech is excellent. The frame is triangular in plan, each side about 36 in. (1 m.) long. Height depends on the stance you like to adopt when throwing, but the average is 30 in. (800 mm.). Joints should be short mortice and tenon, not glued but pulled in tight with studding (threaded $\frac{1}{2}$ in. or 25 mm. rods with a nut at either end. The bar is supported in some designs by a vertical chain and, as a result, swings in an arc. This is comfortable for the leg, but is a difficult movement to transmit to the crankshaft. A flexible leather connector may be used, but a better system mechanically is shown in fig. 1-3, where the support is taken back diagonally to the same pivot line as the kick-bar itself, ensuring a true horizontal drive. David Ballantyne has developed a geared wheel in which the arc and horizontal drive are ingeniously combined. The actual wheel shaft is normally made of 1 in. (25 mm.) steel, but an increase to $1\frac{1}{8}$ in. (28 mm.) will reduce 'whip' very considerably. The almost vertical kick movement of some commercial wheels gives an uncomfortable action, and these should be avoided.

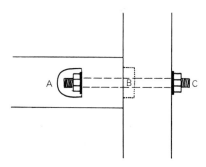

*The jointing system used in the kickwheel shown above. A short mortise and tenon is made between the bar and upright which should fit adequately but not be glued. A hole is drilled through the upright, the mortise, and the horizontal bar as shown, and a slot cut large enough to take a washer and nut at (A). A length of ½ in. (12 mm.) studding threaded metal rod) is inserted, screwed into a nut at (A) and the joint drawn up tight with a second washer and nut at (C). This is repeated for all joints. As the wood contracts or compresses the nut can be tightened. The whole structure can be easily dismantled (a touch of grease will prevent the nuts rusting on).*

## KIDNEY TOOLS

The kidney-shaped tool, embodying several curves, is a favorite one with potters. It may be of hard or soft rubber, or of thin, pliable sheet-steel. Sheet-steel kidney tools are called 'steel palettes'. The tools may be used for scraping, smoothing, turning and pressing. The hand potter will find them invaluable.

## KIESELGUHR

A German name for *diatomite*.

## KILN

Called an 'oven' in the industry. Essentially a box of refractory bricks, into or around which heat is introduced either by combustion or by radiant heat. A kiln must be capable of reaching at least 600°C. (1112°F.). A cooking-oven, therefore, cannot be used as a kiln. In small kilns the ware is packed straight into the box, in large ones it may be protected and supported by *saggars*.

Up to the nineteen-fifties the most striking aspect of Stoke-on-Trent was the skyline, broken by countless coal-fired 'bottle' ovens—a splendid sight. These have gone, replaced by the continuous kiln—a 6 ft. (nearly 2 m.) high tunnel, up to 250 ft. (76 m.) long.

The very primitive, but nevertheless often effective, brushwood bonfires cannot be said to have used a kiln at all. In some cases the pots were covered with a layer of shards as protection and to retain heat, and this represented the first step towards a kiln. Cultures which aimed at a finer type of pottery soon began to enclose their wares in brick or stone boxes which allowed a greater control and higher temperatures. In the simplest kilns, a fire is lit under the floor, the heat rises through the pots and out at the top. The whole kiln acts as a chimney. Though more economical and

reliable than a bonfire, its heat utilization is low. The final step was to direct the heat against its inclination across the kiln setting and, eventually, downwards through it. A strong draft or pull is essential; this is provided by a tall chimney (a straight-up kiln needs no separate chimney) as in most Western kilns, or by a stepped series of firing-chambers as in the East. All intermittent kilns are variations or improvements on these types. An electric kiln has no combustion or draught and is thus a simple fire-proof box. R.K gives an excellent account of the history, types and designs of kiln. (See also *insulation of heat, up-draft, down-draft, chambered kiln, brazier kiln, clamp kiln, sawdust firing, gas kilns, oil kiln, electric kiln, climbing kilns, ground-hog kiln.*)

*The skyline of bottle kilns at Stoke-on-Trent in 1960; now, alas, gone for ever.*

## KILN FURNITURE

Term applied to pieces of *refractory* material used to support pots during firing, including *shelves* and *props*. More particularly, the term refers to the small equipment designed to prevent glazed ware sticking to kiln shelves.

The commonest piece of kiln furniture is the *stilt* which has three radial arms ending in upright conical points. *Spurs* have one point up and three down; three or more can replace a stilt when supporting larger dishes or irregular shaped pieces. Triangular sectioned *saddles* will hold tiles or flat-based models. There are ingenious constructions called cranks, which hold similar sized plates or tiles apart from one another in a pile or bung. Tile bats may also be called cranks and can be built up on their own 'cranked' or turned-over edges, or with spacing cubes (bits).

It is important to bear in mind that all clays become *pyroplastic* during firing. When placing 'furniture', try to imagine that the piece of pottery (especially flat plates and dishes) is still plastic and can sag under its own weight. A plate will warp on a small out-of-center stilt or on spurs placed too far apart.

Kiln furniture, in the sense of stilts and similar articles, is intended for oxidized earthenware only.

It will fail at temperatures over 1200°C. Even shelf *props*, if *cast*, will collapse in stoneware reduction unless made specifically for this purpose. Stoneware, therefore, is normally left with an unglazed base. (See also *kiln shelves, bat, prop*, and under the individual items mentioned.)

## KILN LOG

A record of firings is always useful, especially with a new kiln or during the first year of work in a new pottery. A kiln log will materially assist *pricing and costing*.

The record can be a very full one, or merely a list of pieces with length of firing and top temperature noted. It is advisable to keep the same sort of record each time so that the data is comparable. Priorities

| TEST no | 1 | | 2 |
|---|---|---|---|
| RECIPE | Lead sesquisilicate    70<br>China clay    20<br>Flint    10<br>Tin oxide    12<br>(500 gms) | | |
| TEST PIECE | Curved tile | | |
| BODY | Red | | |
| TEST SURFACE | Impressed | | |
| GLAZE THICKNESS | Thin and medium | | |
| KILN and FIRING | 1080°C<br>Small kiln | Soaked<br>10 mins. | |
| POSITION IN KILN | Middle | | |
| NOTES | Biscuit low fired | | |
| TYPE | Opaque | | |
| COLOR | White | | |
| SURFACE | Shiny | | |
| NOTES | Breaking well to red-brown at sharp edges<br><br>Poor where thin | | |
| ASSESSMENT | Good | | |
| ALTERATIONS | None needed | | |
| NAME | Soft tin glaze | | |
| | | | |

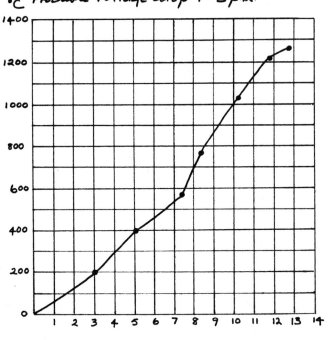

Firing no 22. Feb 3rd '73. Sunday.
Tight pack. Middle hot, floor cooler
12 hours 50 mins 1270°C    173 units
°C  Probable voltage drop 1 – 3 p.m.

| No | 1sts | Value | | |
|----|------|-------|---|---|
| 15 | Plates | 20 | | Cobalt too strong |
| 12 | Saucers | 3 | | |
| 16 | Cups | 6 | | |
| | Tall pot | 5 | | |
| | " | 3 | | Ash 1 glaze |
| | " | 7 | | Ash 2 glaze |
| 30 | Egg cups | 7 | | |
| 7 | Various small pots | 10 | | Blue slightly overfired on middle shelves |
| | 2nds | | | |
| 2 | Plates | 1 | | Underfired |
| 2 | Saucers | | 30 | Spinners |
| 1 | Tall pot | 2 | 50 | Crawled (Floor left) |
| | | 64 | 80 | |

will vary with type of kiln and work fired. If your kiln has a chimney it will be sensitive to weather. L.PB lists weather, oil pressure, temperature of kiln at various stages, time, atmosphere, and damper positions, for all of which he has developed a private notation. The number of pieces of pottery firsts, *seconds* (and *lump*), with their approximate value, may be noted for costing. C.PP 232-3 suggests recording the weight of clay used in the kiln setting, which will also give density of packing, an important factor affecting firing. A broader indication of density such as 'loosely packed', 'large pots', 'very full', or the number of shelves used, is more practicable. In electric firing the weather is not of direct consequence unless the kiln is in a very cold and drafty place, but *voltage drop* may occur in winter.

A firing-graph will replace many words and may be used as a basis of the kiln log. A possible layout is shown above.

A reduction graph will show 'steps' in the line. A deliberate stepped firing known as 'fire-change' is used in Japan. Geoffrey Whiting uses a stepped graph in an electric kiln to obtain special colors. (See also *heat treatment*.)

## KILN SHELVES, bats, batts

Kiln shelves are made of compacted high-alumina clay, *sillimanite* or *silicon carbide*. It is difficult to make one's own bats. The underlying science which controls the behavior of shelves under load is a complicated one. Some of the problems are discussed in C.PP. Silicon carbide shelves are strong, wear-resistant and more conductive than clay, but are expensive. They conduct electricity as well as heat, and are not recommended for electric kilns.

One of the major manufacturers in England, Acme Marls, has provided the following data on shelf performance in the kiln:

1   Cracks may be due to fast heating or cooling—the hot load cooling slowly while the shelf cools more rapidly. Also to gross overloading, usually because of a badly placed prop.

2   An overloaded bat will normally bend and will ultimately tear.

3   The life of a shelf is dependent on how much it bends in the firing; this is governed by the load, the unsupported span, the temperature and the thickness.

4   The bending rate will also depend on the time that any given temperature is maintained.

## SPECIMEN DEFORMATION DATA ON KILN BATS

| Temperature in °C. | 900–1050 | | | 1050–1200 | | | 1200–1250 | | | 1250–1280 | | |
|---|---|---|---|---|---|---|---|---|---|---|---|---|
| Thickness in cm. | 12.5 | 17.5 | 25 | 12.5 | 17.5 | 25 | 12.5 | 17.5 | 25 | 12.5 | 17.5 | 25 |
| Size of bat | | | | | | | | | | | | |
| 47.5 x 41.5 | 14 | 40 | 77 | 6.5 | 22 | 45 | 0 | 7 | 19 | 0 | 0 | 6 |
| 44.5 x 42 | 16 | 42.5 | 81 | 7.7 | 23.5 | 47 | 0.6 | 6.5 | 21 | 0 | 0 | 8 |
| 40.0 x 28 | 14 | 35 | 60 | 7.4 | 21 | 36 | 2.2 | 9 | 17 | 0.25 | 3.5 | 7.5 |
| 35.5 x 21 | 12 | 32 | 59 | 6.5 | 19.5 | 37 | 2.5 | 9.5 | 20 | 0.5 | 4.5 | 10 |

These figures represent the loads in lb. which the shelf will take without deformation. The load to be spread reasonably evenly over the surface. Calculations made for alumina shelves and reproduced by kind permission of Mr. H. Gautby of Acme Marls, Hanley, Stoke-on-Trent.

5   It is quite in order to turn shelves over to correct bending.
6   A bat bends more rapidly at the beginning of its life than at the end, roughly as follows:

| Percentage of life | Percentage of bend |
|---|---|
| 8% | 25% |
| 12% | 50% |
| 60% | 75% |
| 100% | 100% |

7   Concentrated loads will have the effect of reducing the life afterwards.
8   A good test for a cracked bat is to support it on a pad in the center, cover it with fine, dry *alumina*, and hit it sharply to make it resonate. The alumina parts where there is a crack.
9   The following table gives a rough idea of the normal distributed loads which bats will stand at different temperatures. There is no smooth graduation in the series of figures for different thicknesses. A bat must carry its own weight as well as the load and this must be subtracted from the gross loading.

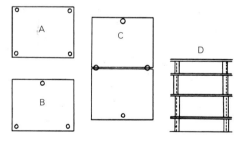

*The propping systems for kiln bats. (A) shows a logical but unsatisfactory position for supports: it is difficult to get a firm seating on four columns while the stresses are along edges or across the longest diagonals. In (B), the use of three columns gives an automatically firm seating and also shortens the diagonal spans. Two closely adjacent shelves should be supported as in (C). In the elevation (D) the props are not immediately above one another but the dotted lines show that the shelves are nowhere cantilevered, i.e. the weight is all taken by the props and not by the shelves.*

### KILN-WASH

A thin layer of *refractory* material spread over the *hotface* of the kiln. *Air-setting cements* have been suggested for this, washed over with a brush or sprayed on (see *Sairset*). 'Pebesil' is another commercial surface-cement which can be applied to soft *insulating*-brick to make it more abrasion resistant. It has high heat-retention. (See also *bat wash*.)

### KILOWATT

Symbol kW. 1000 *watts*.

### KIMMERIDGE CLAY

A Dorset brick clay, often contaminated with lime or bituminous substances.

### KNEADING CLAY

See *wedging*.

### KNIFE

A really sensitive knife which will also be strong enough for use on clay is very difficult to find. The ideal is a blade $\frac{1}{2}$ in. (12 mm.) wide and tapering, about $1\frac{1}{2}$ in. (38 mm.) long with a fairly fine back edge, and with a comfortable handle. 'Stanley' knives are too short and clumsy; scalpels with renewable blades are too delicate and too sharp for safety; penknives do not always have a good grip. Photographic touching-up knives are useful. A local cutler will generally grind a knife to your specification. Some merchants now offer more attractive knives than the usual *fettler*. Wengers 2071W is a pleasant example.

### KNOBS

The knob of a *lid* is no trivial object. A quick survey of ceramics will reveal not only rich variety but also show that the lid and its knob or handle can be the crowning glory of a pot. Modeled knobs of considerable size and intricacy, such as the splendid teams of stylized

1

2

3

*Three ways of forming a knob. Turning the shape from the stem of a thrown lid (see lids) (1); throwing a knob on a flat casserole-type lid (2); and throwing a hollow knob on a recessed lid (3).*

horses, are found on early Greek pots. Those from the Far East may be more subdued, but are carefully considered in relation to the overall form of the pot and sometimes have a touch of fantasy. Michael Casson's early knobs and Ian Godfrey's often crowded and dominant lids are modern examples. (See also under *lids* for a simpler form but one with a touch of genius.)

The principle underlying good design is to provide a stem of length adequate to accommodate finger and thumb, spreading out to a wider top. No matter how elegant or aesthetically suited to the main form, a knob which cannot be easily gripped and held must be accounted a failure. But within these limitations there is a multitude of possible forms. The knob should not be too high on ovenware.

The illustrations show various ways of making the knob. It can be modeled and luted on; turned from the thick base of a thrown lid; thrown onto the leatherhard turned lid; inset into a cut lid; or made in the form of a pulled handle or a simple thumbed-down coil.

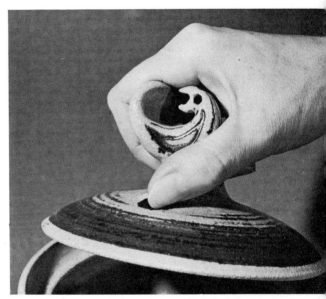

*A fine modelled knob by Michael Casson, showing the firm and satisfying grip it affords.*

### kW

The symbol for a kilowatt or 1000 watts. A kilowatt hour (kWh) is the electricity consumed by a one kW piece of apparatus in one hour. (See also *electricity, units of electricity.*)

### KYANITE

A mineral $Al_2O_3.2SiO_2$, similar to *silliminite* but with different physical properties. Considerable volume increase at 1300°C., when it breaks down into *mullite* and *cristobalite* (D.DC). Has been mentioned as a *bat wash*. Obtainable from Kyanite Mining Corporation, Dillwyn, Virginia, USA.

Plate 1. Above. Lead antimoniate used as a background wash on a tin glaze with free brushwork in manganese oxide. By a thirteen-year-old girl at Cheshaunt Grammar School.

Plate 2. Above. A slab-built box in porcelain by Sheila Fournier. Note method of retaining lid in place. The decoration by wax resist: the left-hand brushstrokes resisting the color, the right-hand strokes resisting the glaze.

Plate 3. Below. A splendid bracken-ash glaze by Waistel Cooper.

Plate 4. Below. A brazier kiln in use for raku.

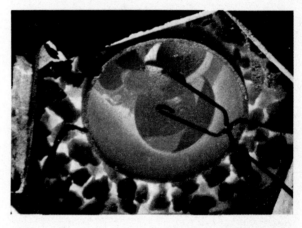

Plate 5. Below. A large burnished dish by John Ablett.

# L

## LACUSTRINE CLAYS

Clays which have been deposited, in geological time, on the bed of a lake. Similar to *estuarine clays*.

## LAMELLAR

In the form of sheets or scales. Clay is thought to be lamellar in structure and this is a possible explanation of its plastic qualities. (See *plasticity, clay*.)

## LATEX RESIST

A preparation which can be used cold in the manner of *wax resist*. It can be peeled off or fired away. Brushes can be cleaned in water.

## LATTICE

A regular three-dimensional pattern or network of linked atoms building up into a *crystalline* substance. Quartz, for instance, has a lattice unit of one silicon atom and four oxygen atoms in a pyramid or tetrahedron. Further Si atoms share half the electron charge with each of the O atoms, the pattern being repeated in every direction. This is known as the $SiO_4$ lattice. This crystalline lattice has a tight structure but it can be altered and weakened by the intrusion of other atoms (see *network modifiers*, and diagram of $SiO_4$ under *glass former*.)

## LAVA

Rocks of variable composition equivalent to around 50% feldspar and 50% ferro-magnesium minerals (Frazer, CR 17). The iron content is high and the rock yields dark-colored temmoku-type glazes.

## LAWN

A fine-meshed *sieve* originally of woven silk or fine linen (hence the name) but now usually of phosphor-bronze wire. The mesh (the tiny holes where the wires cross each other) is graded according to the wires per linear inch (25.5 mm.): 80 wires per inch for a number 80 lawn, etc. Some quoted apertures for comparison are: No 30 (USA 35)   0.50 mm.

|       |           |
|-------|-----------|
| 60    | 0.25 mm.  |
| 80    | 0.18 mm.  |
| 120   | 0.125 mm. |
| 200   | 0.075 mm. |

It will be seen that the aperture halves as the number doubles. Lawns are seldom made below 40 mesh, the coarser wire or nylon sieves taking over for wide apertures.

Lawns are mounted on ash-wood, plastic or metal rims. (See also *sieve*.) A phosphor-bronze lawn carefully used will last a lifetime. Useful rim sizes are 6 in. (150 mm.) for glaze trials, 10 in. (250 mm.) for slips, 8-12 in. (200-300 mm.) for glaze batches. Color sieves or 'cup' sieves about 3 in. (75 mm.) across are made for pigments. Lawn mesh sizes in general use are: 60-80 for slips and many stoneware glazes; 100-120 for earthenware glazes; 200 for pigments and stains.

## LAWN PROVER

A small glass magnifier, set above a one inch square aperture through which one can count the wires in a lawn to determine its gauge or number. Would rarely be of use to a studio potter unless he bought unmounted lawns.

## LAYERING CLAY

See *wedging*.

## LEAD, oxides, compounds

A metallic element Pb, 207.
Oxides:
Litharge PbO, 223.
Peroxide, red lead $Pb_2O_3$, 686 (useful equivalent weight 228.5)
White lead (basic) $2PbOCO_3:Pb(OH)_2$, 775 (equivalent wt. 258)
Galena (sulfide) PbS.239.

A *base*, and a powerful *flux* in the 750-1150°C. range. It is the principal or only base in most soft glazes which do not contain boric oxide. The rich quality of many early glazes owes much to the use of lead. Its *coefficient of expansion* is in the middle range and lead glazes are reputed to adapt to tension better than others.

Lead oxide is toxic both as a raw material and in an unbalanced or ill-fired glaze from which it may be dissolved by food acids (see *lead solubility*.)

Litharge is the traditional oxide for slipware glazes. Galena has been widely used in the past but needs a very well-ventilated kiln. Lead is now normally used as a fritt (see *lead fritts, lead glazes*).

## LEAD ANTIMONIATE

A compound of lead and antimony, quoted by Wengers as $Pb_2(SbO)_4$. Composition variable. Toxic. Used as a yellow pigment—'Naples' yellow. Dilute with a lead fritt for painting. Up to 8% can be added to a soft lead glaze. Not suitable for use in stoneware. Color plate 1, p. 129.

## LEAD FRITTS

The use of lead in the form of *silicates*, now compulsory in schools and factories though studios and some colleges may still use the oxides.

The commonest fritts in use are:
Lead monosilicate $PbO.SiO_2$, 283, m.p. 670-750°C.
Lead sesquisilicate $2PbO.3SiO_2$, 627, ($PbO. 1.5SiO_2$ 313) 690-850°C.
Lead bisilicate $PbO.2SiO_2$, 343, 710-800°C.

The actual fritt batch sometimes includes small amounts of alumina (up to 3%), or titania. Podmores also quote a 'coated' fritt, reputed to be less liable to *metal release*.

Sesquisilicate is perhaps the most useful for potters. Monosilicate does not comply with British regulations governing lead in glazes. The melting points given above are derived from those quoted by various suppliers.

Apart from the simple silicates, many lead fritts are available for temperatures up to 1150°C.

## LEAD GLAZES

Lead can be used as the only *flux* in an earthenware glaze. The formula limits are:

1 PbO. $0.23$-$0.35Al_2O_3$. $2.0$-$3.5SiO_2$ with an average $1:0.3:3.0$ firing at 1100°C. with a recipe:

| | |
|---|---|
| Lead sesquisilicate | 70.5 |
| China clay | 17.4 |
| Flint | 12.1 |

See also honey glaze for the use of red clay in the recipe. This is useful for *slipware,* especially slip-trailing.

Lead can be combined with other *bases* but must represent at least 0.5 of the *RO group,* e.g.

0.6 PbO
0.2 $K_2O$
0.2 CaO

If the lead equivalent is less than 0.5, boric acid must appear in the $RO_2$ column, unless it is a high soda glaze.

If there is any significant lead content in a glaze it is generally labelled as a 'lead glaze'. The mixed base glazes are more purely transparent and viscous than simple ones, and are therefore chosen for underglaze painting and for tin glazes (see *majolica*).

*Once-fired earthenware* generally utilizes lead oxide as the main or only base. Higher proportions of the oxide are used—although not the 100% litharge mentioned by Billington. Some typical recipes: 70% litharge, 12% plastic clay, 18% flint; or 75% lead bisilicate, 10% china stone, 15% plastic clay.

Most pigment oxides readily dissolve in lead glazes giving: yellow-brown from iron; apple-green from copper; blue from cobalt; purple-brown from manganese. Lead and soda glazes produce brighter colors and have been suggested for soft-glaze *black.* Lead oxide is toxic and if the formula is not a balanced one can consistute a health hazard even when fired in a glaze. (See discussion under *soluble lead*.)

Glazes recommended by Kenneth Clark in CR 9:

| | | | |
|---|---|---|---|
| Lead bisilicate | 72.8 | Lead sesquilicate | 52.8 |
| China clay | 12.1 | Feldspar | 31.1 |
| China stone | 13.5 | Whiting | 5.6 |
| Flint | 1.6 | China clay | 7.2 |
| 1060-1080°C. | | Flint | 3.3 |

Strontium is used in some countries as a substitute for lead oxide in glazes.

## LEADLESS GLAZES

A glaze with not more than 1% its dry weight of PbO (British regulations). Most leadless glazes (rather confusingly marked 'L' in suppliers' lists) have no lead content at all. It is replaced, in effect, by boric oxide, although this is listed with the $RO_2$ in the *Seger formula.* The bases can include soda, potash, strontium, lime, magnesia, and zinc oxide.

There is no form of insoluble boric oxide which can be used in a soft leadless glaze. Calcined borax is the nearest approach, but it will crystallize in a comparatively short time (as will very soft leadless fritts). Colemanite can help, but introduces lime. A leadless fritt which melts at 1000°C. or lower can be mixed with raw materials such as clay to aid suspension and strengthen the dry coating. Many suppliers quote the formulas for their *fritts:* these can be entered in the glaze formula computation (see *formula-into-recipe*).

High soda fritts, e.g. $Na_2O. \begin{matrix} 3.5\ SiO_2 \\ 2.0\ B_2O_3 \end{matrix}$

will produce a turquoise from copper, but the lack of alumina renders it unstable. A more regular L fritt might read:

$$\begin{matrix} 0.27\ Na_2O \\ 0.13\ K_2O \\ 0.59\ CaO \\ 0.01\ MgO \end{matrix} 0.42\ Al_2O_3 \begin{matrix} 4.7\ SiO_2 \\ 0.96\ B_2O_3 \end{matrix}$$

firing at 1040°C.

It will be seen that the silica and alumina ratio is much higher than one would expect from the normal Seger ratios. This is caused by the anomalous position of boron which, in practice, acts as a flux and could quite logically be listed with the bases. In the above formula this would bring the silica equivalent down to 2.5. Leadless earthenware glazes have been compounded from strontium and zinc additions. (See *Bristol glaze.*)

Leadless fritted glazes need to be applied more thinly than lead or raw glazes. Colors from manganese, copper and cobalt are apt to be unsubtle and strident. They should not be fired with high lead glazes which can coat them with a thin skin of lead oxide and make them dangerous in use.

The term has little meaning in connection with stoneware and porcelain glazes, which are outside the lead range.

## LEAD SOLUBILITY

See *soluble lead.*

## LEAN CLAY

A clay or body of low *plasticity. Aging* will help some lean clays.

## LEATHER-HARD

A stage in the drying of clay when it has become almost rigid but is still damp. One might elaborate by using the terms 'soft-leather' and 'hard-leather' to indicate stages either side of leather-hard, and these are occasionally used in discussions in this book. Work done at leather-hard includes: *turning, engraving, sgraffito, planing,* and techniques involving the use of metal tools.

At this stage most of the drying shrinkage will already have occurred—the particles are just touching one another. The size difference between leather-hard clay and soft biscuit is small. There is just enough plasticity in leather-hard clay to allow gentle beating

Plate 6. Above. Earthenware glaze trials as described under glaze trials — the lead fritt, clay, and flint series. Red clay was used in this case. It will be seen that the fritt alone is too melted and has run; the clay has merely biscuited while the flint is almost unaltered and is peeling away. Of the mixtures, text number five is a mature glaze; number four and six are interesting but matt surfaced, making a form of engobe.

Plate 8. Above. Devitrification on an eleventh century Persian bowl, the lead glaze showing iridescence.

Plate 7. Below. An Egyptian necklace (twelfth century B.C.) showing a variety of colors from copper, with alkaline fluxes in a glaze. See Egyptian paste.

Plate 9. Below. The broad and lively treatment of enamels on a small bowl of cheap, mass-produced porcelain.

A

Plate 10. Glaze trials as described in text. The top row (A) shows the basic glaze colors of which the series below (B) are mixtures together with a plain white tin glaze and a soft fritt.

B

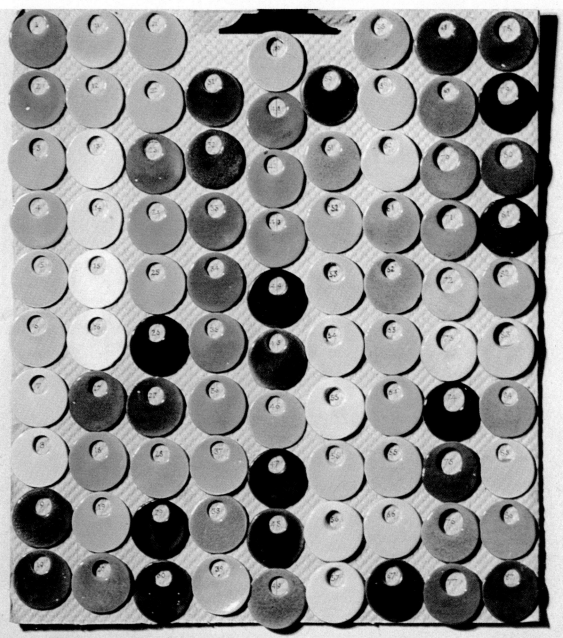

to change its form. Clay can still be joined, but it is advisable to score and slip, or to work up a slip with a little moisture by rubbing the two parts together. For absorbent clays (which include most of those made up by merchants) raw clay glazing *(once-fired ware)* is best done at leather-hard.

## LEPIDOLITE

A mineral with the ideal formula $(LiNaK)_2.(F.OH)_2.$ $Al_2O_3. 3SiO_2$, 472, m.p. 1170°C. A typical analysis by weight:

| | | | | | |
|------|------|-----------|------|---------|------|
| $K_2O$ | 8.3 | $Al_2O_3$ | 25.5 | | |
| CaO | 0.4 | FeO | 0.16 | $SiO_2$ | 54.0 |
| MgO | 0.08 | MnO | 0.06 | | |
| $Li_2O$ | 3.6 | F | 5.33 | | |

A *lithium* mica, with a lower melting point than feldspar. Difficult to grind. A source of lithium for bodies and glazes, but its use is complicated by the release of fluorine as a gas during firing, which can cause bloating in a body and bubbles in glaze.

## LEUCITE

A mineral $K_2O.Al_2O_3.4SiO_2$. Potash feldspar melts incongruently into a liquid plus leucite, which is an explanation of its high viscosity. Leucite can be formed when alkalis attack fireclay. Known as a feldspathoid. It is found in *lavas* (Australia, USA etc.).

## LEVIGATION

Defined in the Oxford Dictionary as to 'reduce to a fine powder', but in pottery it is taken to mean the separation of particles in a flowing stream (of slip), the finer ones remaining in *suspension,* the coarser sinking to the floor of the vessel or channel. China clay is levigated to remove the relatively coarse micas etc., the dumping of which produces the 'white mountains' of St. Austell.

C.PP illustrates a levigating trough 12 ft. (3.5 m.) long, with 1 in 14 slope and a 2 in. (50 mm.) high check-gate at one end. Slip is fed in at the higher end, heavy particles sinking below the 'gate' level while the fine ones flow over it. The natural levigating action of rivers has led to the accumulation of fine clay particles in their estuaries.

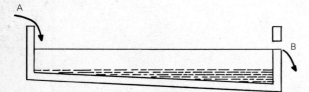

*A long shallow trough with a sloping floor. The liquid mixture flows in at (A) and out at (B) which should be at a slightly lower level. During the slow passage between (A) and (B) the coarse particles will sink and the finer ones remain in suspension to flow out at (B).*

## LIAS CLAY

A calcium-contaminated brick clay.

## LIDS

The covered pot is a comparatively sophisticated object, and we do not find ceramic lids in general use until after the craft had graduated from *coiling* to *throwing.* Those who have tried to make a well-fitting lid on a coiled pot will appreciate the difficulties.

The design of a lid depends as much on the method used to stop it falling off as on its formal relationship with the pot. The diagrams below show several ways of securing a lid. Apart from F, each involves a horizontal surface for the lid to sit on, and an upright wall or flange to prevent sideways movement. The tapered lid will automatically accommodate a tighter or looser fit but its success depends on the maintenance of two perfect circles—not always achieved in pottery!

The simplest way of throwing a lid is flat on the wheel head. A domed lid is thrown upside-down as

*Seven types of lid seating.*
*(A) shows flange on both lid and pot and is typical of teapots, etc. (B) has flange on lid only, and is useful where the maximum aperture is needed in the container, but it must be a good fit and the lid normally overhangs the sides of the pot. Can be used without knob if smaller than a handspan. (C) has flange on pot only and is typical of casseroles. (D) an inset lid (see photograph of throwing method). (E) has flange formed by outward twist of rim. (F) a tapered lid and flange. Self-adjusting to a degree but requiring true circles for a snug fit. (G) a lid for a small-mouthed pot or for a bottle shape.*

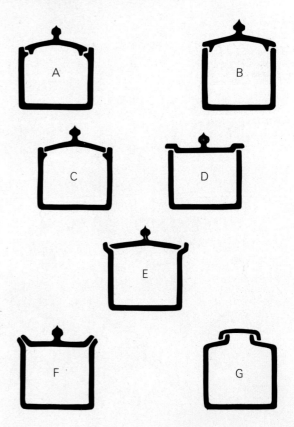

in photographs 1-5, either as a simple curve or a more involved flanged lid as shown. The knob may be turned from the stem of clay left at the base. An excellent example of lid type G in the diagram is shown in the porcelain jar. (See also *calipers, knob.*)

*Various types of thrown lid. The clay can be brought up into a cone from the top of which an inverted lid is thrown (1. 2). Three stages (3-5) in throwing an inset lid (D in diagrams). The diameter would be roughly measured with calipers at a stage just prior to (4), the flange then forming a short upright wall, and finally the completed lid (5). A narrow square-ended turning tool can be used for trimming, and a pointed one for cutting a short bevel at the base. See under knob for an intermediate action.*

4

1

5

*A porcelain jar (lid type G) by David Leach.*

2

3

135

Plate 11. Above, left. A porcelain hand-built bowl by Sheila Fournier. The orange-peel glaze, resembling salt glaze texture, is composed of equal parts feldspar, china clay, and dolomite fired in an electric kiln to 1270°C. David Leach porcelain body.

Plate 12. Below, left. Rich iron reds derived from the body color staining through a high lead and tin glaze — earthenware (see litharge). Teapot by Michael Casson.

Plate 13. Right. A goblet in a red-brown luster by Alan Caiger-Smith. Derived from silver chloride, red ochre, and copper carbonate.

Plate 14. Below. Majolica brushwork in ferric iron, oxide of manganese and mixtures of copper and cobalt oxides. Painted with a broad brush. Fired in a wood kiln.

*An ingenious knob on a charming casserole by Sheila Casson. The lid illustrates type E.*

## LIME

Lime, strictly speaking, is a burnt limestone CaO, an unstable *anhydrous* material (quicklime) which may be slaked with water to produce $Ca(OH)_2$. In ceramics the word is used, imprecisely, to indicate whiting, $CaCO_3$, or a calcium material which will be converted into CaO in the glaze or body melt, as in 'lead-lime-potash glaze.' (See *calcium*.)

## LIME-BLOWING

Pellets of lime in clay will be turned into quicklime in the firing. Moisture will subsequently slake the lime which expands and breaks pieces of pot away. If lime is suspected in a pot, dip it into water and put aside for checking in a day or two.

## LIMESTONE

The sedimentary rock of calcium carbonate or *calcite*. Formed from lime in solution or from organic deposits (fossil shells), and sometimes as pure as 98% calcite. There are mixtures of calcite and clay *(marls)*, and sandy (quartz) limestones. Chalk is an earthy variety. Marble is an 'altered' limestone.

## LIMIT FORMULAS

A term used by Rhodes (R.CGP 104-5) to indicate the minimum and maximum amount of any oxide which can be used in a particular formula. These are 'normal' limits: it can sometimes be instructive to exceed them.

## LINE BLENDS

A method of working out intervals in a series of mixtures of two different colors, glazes, etc.

The simplest blend is:

| A—100 | 75 | 50 | 25 | 0 —A |
| B— 0 | 25 | 50 | 75 | 100—B |

each vertical pair being tested.

The principle can be extended to any number of intervals. For a slightly different approach discussed in practical detail see *color trials*, also *glaze trials* for working blends back to a recipe.

## LINE TAP

A form of connector for thick electric wires, especially useful to potters for joining kiln *elements* to their connecting wires, and for joining the neutrals in a *three-phase star* system. The sheredized finish does not corrode. If difficult to buy, ask your Electricity Board.

## LIP

There is some overlapping and confusion over the use of this term to describe a part of a pot. It is sometimes applied to the upper termination of a pot or bowl, also variously called the 'edge' or the 'rim'. For the purposes of this entry 'lip' is taken to mean the pouring lip of a jug, mixing bowl, etc.

The lip can be formed immediately after throwing by a steady out-and-over pull or a side-to-side stroking motion with one finger, while the finger and thumb of the other hand support the rim at each side. Alternatively a somewhat crisper type of lip can be beaten out with the side of a rigid finger, after the pot has been turned or at soft-leather stage. Moisten the clay and give full support with a crooked finger under the lip as it is formed. Finish with smooth sweeps round the curve.

A lip which curves slightly downwards at the very edge is more likely to pour well than one which finishes with an upward slope. The last drop of liquid will fall from the end of the lip rather than round it (to dribble down the side of the jug). Similarly a sharper edge will cut the flow more efficiently than a rounded one, though there are obvious limits.

Two other forms are:

1   The ewer type in which a flared rim is cut down for the greater part of its circumference, the section of the original rim acting as a raised lip.

2   Lips made separately, either thrown as a small inverted cone which is cut in two, or molded, and luted onto the rim. The rim behind the lip can be cut away entirely; a bridge can be left across the top; or it can be perforated.

Whichever method is used, make the lip generous and well-defined. It will then be aesthetically attractive as well as efficient in directing the flow of liquid.

*The supporting and pulling positions of the fingers when pulling a lip from a wet, just-thrown jug. Other potters may vary the position but the principle of two supports and one, often side-to-side stroking-out motion is common to most methods.*

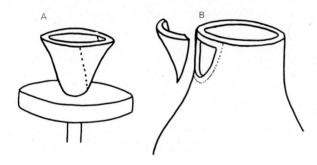

*An applied lip. A small flaring cup shape is thrown (A) and a segment sliced off with a wire. An equivalent area of the neck of a jug is either cut right away, left with a bridge as shown (B), or pierced with holes. The segment of the thrown shape is then luted onto the jug.*

1

2

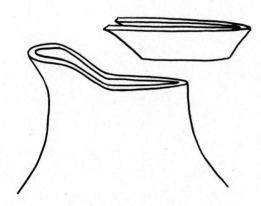

*A section cut away from a jug neck to form a raised lip.*

*Tapping or beating a lip from soft leather clay. The lip must be supported below so that the clay is pressed between two surfaces and not stretched or it will split (1). A wipe of water on the rim before starting will help. Finish with a sideways movement (2).*

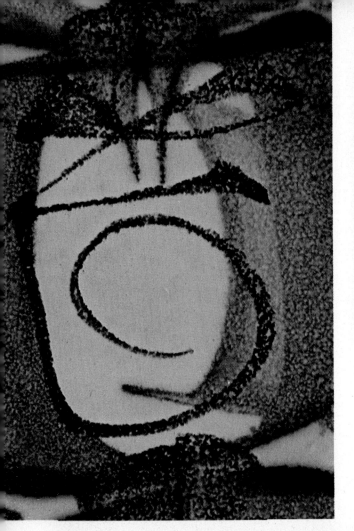

Plate 15. Above. Detail of a mosaic table top using a basic design motif varied by the use of mixed cobalt and copper transparent earthenware glazes.

Plate 16. Left. A detail from a majolica dish by Alan Caiger-Smith. The broken color results from the natural brief reduction during stoking of a wood kiln. The glaze settles again during subsequent oxidation. (Photograph: Alan Caiger-Smith).

Plate 17. Below. Ceramic modeling by Brian Newman. The dryish ochre-colored finish is typical of refractory ash glazes.

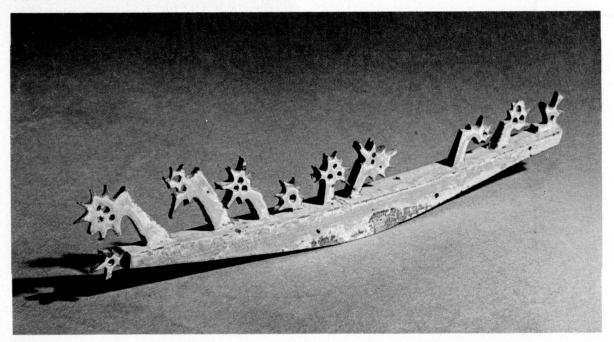

Plate 18. Above. The back of a raku dish showing the many colors from a single copper oxide glaze (alkaline fritt) due to degrees for oxidation and reduction — green, turquoise, red, and metallic luster.

Plate 19. Below, left. Sgraffito combined with washes of color. By Sam Haile.

Plate 20. Below, right. Slip colors. Red clay; buff clay with two per cent cobalt; red clay with ten per cent manganese dioxide; buff clay with one and a quarter per cent each of copper oxide and chrome, all covered with a honey glaze. Bowls by Sybil Houldsworth.

141

## LIQUID PETROLEUM GAS

L.P.G. (See *bottled gas*.)

## LIQUIDUS

The line on an equilibrium or *phase diagram* above which the components become a liquid or, conversely, below which a liquid begins to precipitate solids.

## LITHARGE

Lead monoxide PbO, 223. A yellow or orange powder which like all lead compounds is toxic if taken into the body. Potters working on their own may use litharge but in factories and schools a *fritt* must be used.

Litharge produces a rich, transparent glaze very suitable for slip-trailed ware. A typical recipe:

Litharge 50, china clay 17.5, flint 32.5, firing at 1080-1100°C.

Litharge-tin glazes, with high lead content and 12-15% of tin oxide, used over a red clay, will break on the edges to a brick-red. Lead/soda glazes will also work well for this technique, e.g.:

| | |
|---|---|
| Litharge | 46 |
| China stone | 52 |
| Bentonite | 2 |

For a black or dark brown glaze use 9% manganese and 1% tin. Avoid litharge glazes if contact is likely to be made with acids, vinegar, or ferments. See *raku, lead, green glazing, once-fired.* Color plate 12, p. 136.

## LITHIUM

An alkaline metallic element Li, 7.
Oxide $Li_2O$, 30, lithia.
Carbonate $Li_2CO_3$, 74, an insoluble form.

Acts in a glaze like soda or potash, i.e. with a strong fluxing action, and has the added advantage of a low *thermal expansion*. Will brighten colors.

Lithium compounds have been expensive and are still around six times the price of feldspar. Lithia, however, is light in weight (the lightest of the metals) and the addition of only 0.5-2.0% markedly affects glaze *fusion*. Its use is frequently suggested by Behrens in all types of glaze and in amounts up to 20% of the batch. Even *raku* recipes may contain 10% lithia (with very soft fritt, clay, and flint). 3% lithia in a stoneware glaze can bring its melting point down two or three cones.

Lithium has been tried in porcelain bodies. The common lithium minerals have certain disadvantages, e.g. the fluorine content of *lepidolite*. See also *petalite, spodumene, amblygonite.*

## LITHOGRAPHY

In ceramics, a method of making transfers printed in lithographic oil, the color being dusted onto the oil. They are applied to ware coated with a tacky varnish. Now generally replaced by slide-off transfers. Called 'decalcomania' or 'decals' in the USA.

## LOAM

A clayey earth, with sand and gravel.

## LOCAL CLAY

It is fun, and always instructive, to dig clay from the ground but you are not very likely to find good, workable deposits in regions where they are not already known. The study of local industries of the past may reveal clay workings, also the names of fields, etc. Few geological books deal specifically with clays. In America the State Geological Departments may be able to help; in England the Geological Survey. Also organizations such as CoSIRA (Council of Small Industries in Rural Areas).

If you have access to any local rock-formation studies take note of Cardew's dictum that 'it is broadly true that the younger geological systems and strata are more likely to yield workable clays than the older ones'. Brick clays will seldom take a glaze satisfactorily. Details on the testing of clays may be found under *clay testing;* see also *clay, body, clay-winning.*

## LONDON CLAY

A brick clay (Oligocene period, ca. 25 million years ago) from the Home Counties (those counties around London). *Vitreous* at about 1000°C. 'Possibly 90% *illite*' (Cardew).

## LOSS ON IGNITION

The loss in weight when strongly heated (of a clay or mineral) through the dispersal of carbonates, etc. For clays the figure quoted in catalogs is the percentage of its dry weight lost at 1000-1100°C. With fritts the temperature will be below the fusion point.

## LOW SOLUBILITY GLAZES

Fritts which comply with the Pottery Health Regulations not to 'release more than 5% of its dry weight of soluble lead when subjected to specific tests in hydrochloric acid'. Often marked L.S. in catalogs.

## LUG

*Lugs used decoratively on a bread pot by Michael Casson.*

A small handle or pierced piece of clay on the side of a pot. Originally for suspending a pot on a rope, lugs are now often used purely decoratively. (See also *cane handles.*)

*Detail of a sturdy lug for a cane handle on a David Leach teapot.*

## LUMP WARE

In the industry 'defective ware of the lowest saleable quality'. The grades are: best; seconds; lump.

Rather too much 'lump' appears as 'seconds' in some studio potteries!

## LUSTRE, luster

Thin metallic coatings on glaze, producing *iridescence.* The metal is obtained by reduction either in a reducing atmosphere or by the addition of a reducing agent to the metal *salts.* The lustre is applied to an already fired glaze, preferably an *alkaline* one, and refired just hot enough to adhere the lustre to the pot, 650-800°C. They can be bought ready to fire, or reduced in the kiln from a paste of red ochre with silver sulfide or copper carbonate and a little gum. Bismuth can be used for 'mother-of-pearl' (B.TP).

An overall lustre glaze can be obtained by silver nitrate, bismuth sub-nitrate (R.CGP) or copper sulfate in concentrations of 1-3%. The pots must be reduced during cooling until the color has gone from the kiln. Soft 900-1000°C. glazes are used. Parmelee also mentions iron chloride dissolved in sodium resinate, or manganese and copper sulfates treated in the same way. Silver color is derived from platinum.

Lustre is a tricky technique and the result may not always be worth the care and time expended in experiment. The Arab lustres were made from silver sulfide, cinnabar (HgS), iron oxide, and alum in vinegar. Fired in a smoky kiln. The lustres from sixteenth-century Spain must, however, have been fired in a comparatively simple way and without sophisticated chemicals. R.K 40 shows a simple updraft 'Spanish luster kiln'. Lustres can be produced in reduction in an electric kiln with wood, moth-balls, etc. *Raku* frequently produces lustre from alkali/copper glazes. Lustre may need cleaning with a mild abrasive when taken from the kiln. See color plate 13, p. 137.

## LUTING

The joining of plastic or leather-hard clay with *slip* or water. Called 'sticking-up' in the industry. Clay models, especially children's work, often disappointingly fall to pieces as they dry. This may be due to poor or dry joining. Clay surfaces at any stage need a film of water or slip so as to adhere firmly. Scoring the joint is an extra precaution but a little liquid will usually suffice at the plastic or soft-leather stages. One can rub up a slip with one's finger or, better still, between the two surfaces to be joined.

## LYNN SAND

Or Llyn sand. Given by Billington as a ground quartz, and by Leach as a pure form of quartoze sand. Does not now appear in suppliers' lists.

# M

## MAGNESITE

Given by Dodd as the natural mineral of magnesium carbonate $MgCO_3$ with some $FeCO_3$. Widely distributed. Is the chief ore of magnesium. It can be substituted for talc in *ovenproof* bodies. Used also for basic *refractories.*

Ferro lists a calcined magnesite with an analysis: MgO 88.2, $Al_2O_3$ 1.0, $SiO_2$ 4.3.

## MAGNESIUM, oxide, compounds

An unstable metallic element Mg, 24.
Oxide MgO, 40, magnesia, m.p. 2800°C.
Carbonate $MgCO_3$, 84. Decomposes to oxide at 350°C.
Sulfate $MgSO_4$ $7H_2O$, 246.5. Epsom salts.

The ore of the mineral is magnesite. It is also derived from seawater. *Steatite* (soapstone) is an hydrated silicate of magnesia.

Although a refractory oxide it is *basic* and will, like calcium, act as flux in higher temperature glazes. It

Plate 21. Above. A Cypriot kebab pot fired in a simple up-draft wood-firing kiln as in illustration with text (see up-draft). Shows the passage of the flames and partial reduction of smoking. The potter considered it a failure because it was not red all over!

Plate 22. Left. A large thrown pot in temmoku reduced iron glaze by Bernard Leach.

Plate 23. Below. A Ying-ching type glaze on an engraved cup and saucer in 1275°C. porcelain. The subtle accents of form make the most of this delicate glaze. By David Leach.

is classed as one of the *alkaline earths*. The normal formula equivalent is around 0.3 parts of the *RO*. *Talc* and *dolomite* are most generally used by potters as a source of magnesia. They also, of course, introduce silica and lime respectively. 5% is an average weight in a recipe but it can be exceeded. Magnesia can give a pleasant 'buttery' surface to a glaze. The carbonate, either precipitated or as ground magnesite, is slightly soluble. Its effect on cobalt can vary: giving purple or even red (Rhodes), or, used as talc can 'quench' the blue to a blue-gray (Cardew). It is considered by many to be an essential ingredient in *chun*-type glazes, but it may turn celadons brownish. Used in *fireproof bodies (cordierite)* and as magnesia *refractories*.

## MAGNETITE

The *spinel* oxide of iron $Fe_3O_4$ (Feo $F_2O_3$). Also known as magnetic iron ore (loadstone), or black iron oxide. It may be prepared by roasting scrap iron in the kiln at about 1100°C.—'Blacksmith's scale'. Listed by Ferro.

## MAJOLICA

In the pottery industry and in merchants' catalogs, a 'majolica' glaze indicates a soft, *opaque*, colored glaze firing 980-1080°C. However the majolica technique, as understood by craft potters, is the painting with metal oxides on a white, generally tin-opacified *earthenware glaze*.

The art of majolica painting has suffered an eclipse but it still has unexplored potential and great satisfaction can be derived from its practice. It is very flexible and can be treated as broadly or as finely as you wish. The basic technique is simple enough. A pot or plate is evenly coated with an opaque glaze such as a lead-lime-potash glaze with 10% tin oxide. The use of a light *terracotta* body will give warmth to the glaze. The design is painted straight onto the raw glaze. One may start work as soon as the wetness has gone from the surface, which then accepts the color like a dampened water-color paper. Alan Caiger-Smith, however, works on the dry glaze. The timing depends partly on the physical strength of the dried coating (which will usually be rather powdery if *fritts* are used). *Gums* or other binders can be added to the glaze.

The oxides are ground with water, either in a mortar or with a palette knife on a glazed tile. See also *pigment oxides*. The depth of color will depend on the amount of water used. Most oxides will become transparent and each stroke will be revealed after firing even though they appear as a solid block of color when raw. Many of the oxides are black and this can lead to confusion. It will help to use those carbonates which have distinctive hues, though these will change in the firing. Carbonates may be slightly toxic. Cobalt and manganese are the most stable colors: copper is rather watery with blurred edges; lead antimoniate is refractory and needs softening with lead oxide or fritt, and careful application; iron is rather fugitive, varying from a pale amber to dark brown within a single stroke. Chrome is rarely used because of possible pink reactions.

With practice one can work with these particular properties and turn them to advantage. Oxides can be mixed. Rather firmer greens can be obtained with antimony/cobalt mixtures. Much of the older majolica painting uses a thin outline of cobalt or manganese to give definition to the washes of copper and antimony. See color plates 14 and 16, pp. 137 and 140.

A long-haired *brush* is traditional but all kinds may be used, care being taken not to abrade the glaze coating or to saturate it. Painting should be rapid and direct—it has more affinity with Eastern *calligraphic* styles than is often realized. The Italian majolica glazes were compounded of *tin-ash* with a lead-clay-sand fritt and after painting a thin coat of clear glaze was applied. The clear glaze would also have been mixed with the oxides to help them to *flux*. Colors will vary with the type of glaze and *opacifier*. Tin oxide is kinder to the pigments than zirconium: leadless glazes will develop more brash hues than lead ones. The glaze must be applied with care, runs or thick areas pared down with a sharp knife, and the firing carefully controlled. The high degree of opacity may cause some *crawling*. As mentioned the body may be a mixture of red and buff clays.

Painted majolica pots are difficult to handle when packing the kiln. One may use siccatives to fix the glaze or color, but if the painting is designed with this problem in mind, and if the piece is held firmly, the difficulty can be minimized. With top-loading kilns the pot can be held by the inside.

## MANGANESE, oxides, compounds

A metallic element Mn, 55.
Oxide MnO, 71.
Dioxide $MnO_2$, 87 (pyrolusite) loses oxygen at 535°C.
Tetraoxide $Mn_3O_4$, 229.
Carbonate $MnCO_3$, 115.

A coloring oxide, typically brown or purple-brown, but capable of variation. Used in concentrations of 2-10% in soft glazes and even higher in stonewares.

In a lower oxide state it is *basic* in effect, i.e. softens or fluxes a glaze. On heating, however, it alters to $Mn_2O_3$ and to $Mn_3O_4$. As the *valency* rises it acts as an *amphoteric* and then as an *acidic* oxide. In earthenware glazes, therefore, and especially in lead recipes it can be considered as quite a powerful flux: in oxidized stoneware it will behave more like alumina. The alteration or decomposition results in the release of gas which can lead to *bubbles* or craters in the glaze at around 1070°C. In high temperature *reduction* it should, theoretically, revert to its basic state. 2% has given a gray in reduction. Fully reduced MnO gives a green similar to chrome.

As well as a variety of purple-browns (often lurid in a leadless glaze), manganese can produce pink. I have seen a salmon blush on tin glaze over black (manganese) slip. A pink *stain* is prepared from manganese, alumina, and borax. It is used with other oxides for *blacks*. 10% and over will cause metallic surface deposits giving *iridescence* and other effects. Manganese and zinc have a low *eutectic* and the mixture is best avoided. Manganese and copper can give a dull gold surface on biscuit, but the mixture has a tendency to run. Manganese is sensitive to the presence of sulfur gases, which may explain why it bubbles in a glaze on some bodies and not on others. Painted onto raw clay or biscuit it will fire to a dull gloss at 1090°C. and can also be used on stoneware.

## MARBLING

Marbled or variegated slip patterns can be achieved in two ways:

1 Tiles, small pots, pottery figures, etc. can be dipped into a bowl of *slip* onto the surface of which contrasting colored slips have been dribbled or *trailed*. The traditional Sussex 'pig-bank' is decorated in this way.

2 Slip may be trailed directly onto a dish or pot which is then either shaken sideways or given a sharp twist. Use a minimum of movement—if the effect is not immediately attractive, continued shaking will only make it more muddy. The colors tend to become less defined after glaze firing, due to overlapping slip becoming slightly transparent and showing the color beneath. This effect can also be turned to advantage.

Marbled *bodies* result from layered clays of different colors. The clays should be of similar shrinkage—it is advisable to use a single clay variously stained. The layers are sharply smacked together, pressed into a convenient shape, sliced through, and then used for making pottery in the normal way but with a maximum economy of movement. The surface or thrown pots will be smudged but the design can be sharpened by turning or by scraping, when leather-hard, with a steel palette. (See also *agate ware*.)

*A slip-marbled dish by Jane Smith.*

## MARL

An imprecise term given to some iron-bearing secondary clays, generally with calcium impurities. Examples: Keuper marl, of variegated color and containing magnesium carbonate and gypsum; Etruria marl, however, is almost lime-free. Cambridge marl contains some 40% CaO. The term is applied to a low grade fireclay (e.g. saggar marl). Leach mentions the use of a marl with a finely dispersed lime content for slipware. Much traditional slipware must have been made with this type of clay, which is common all over England.

## MASSIVE FORM OF ROCK

The rocky, solid, or block form of a mineral, e.g. steatite.

## MASTER MOLD

Or block-mold. A fine quality copy taken from a hollow mold and from which case molds can be made. In the case of simple dish molds, the 'block' would be in the form of a solid inverted dish.

## MATRIX

The 'ground mass' of a mineral or ceramic material in which larger crystals are embedded.

## MATT, mat

A non-shiny surface. Term sometimes confused with *opaque*. Opacity is, in fact, involved, since a fully transparent glass does not have *crystalline* structure and does have a bright surface. The matt effect is due to the break-up of reflected light by minute variations in the surface level. A matt glaze will, therefore, tend to stain or mark more easily than a shiny one.

Matt glazes may be a result of under-firing but these are less satisfactory than those due to the development of very small surface crystals. Slow cooling in the upper temperature range (maturity down to 800°C.) will assist crystallization. Alumina in slight excess of the optimum balance with silica; high base glazes; titanium; barium in low boron glazes; zinc oxides; hematite; lime (below 1200°C.); will all tend to make a glaze matt. 3% of copper oxide may produce a rather ashy matt black. Lime matts are a result of the formation of wollastonite (S.SCP).

## MATURING OF GLAZES

The optimum condition of a glaze when it has fully melted or otherwise achieved its potential. Most potters believe that the involved physical and chemical changes need time fully to 'mature'. This is not always proved in practice. In the older kilns it was not possible to fire quickly and the idea of a long, *soaking* fire may be linked with this fact.

The same glaze will give quite different results in different kilns and firing schedules, and I have found that some of the most attractive and apparently 'mature' glazes have come from fast firings. The question is an open one, but the subtleties of a well-developed interface and other considerations will for many potters swing the balance in favor of longer firings. A twenty-minute soaking certainly helps *earthenware glazes* to settle down.

## MEASURING SPOON

These can be bought in various sizes from a $\frac{1}{4}$ teaspoon to a tablespoon. Scrape the surface of the material flat for accurate measurement. Useful for small tests and especially for line blends of glazes etc. Attempts have been made to translate weight recipes into spoonsful (see CM 15/10) by taking density into account, but it is much easier to weigh larger amounts of glaze and slip materials. The measuring spoon could find a use in schools.

## MELTED GLASS DECORATION

Ordinary commercial window glass will melt at around 1060°C.—above or below this figure according to its type. It will also stand heating up to 1270°C. or more without trouble. On cooling it has the very high contraction natural to soda glass. This may be powerful enough to tear stonewares apart.

Molten glass is very fluid and, if not contained in a well or cavity, will flow like water. This quality can be turned to advantage in certain freely modeled dishes or other pieces, giving a 'frozen fall'. Too thin a coating will *devitrify* to a dull powdery surface: this can also occur on any melted glass surface—forming a white powder (with the glass beneath it dull and faulted), which may even appear weeks after the glass has been fired. Refiring is more likely to scum the surface with bubbles than to cure the fault, unless further glass is laid on top. Colored glass is more liable to this fault than clear glass. (See illustration under *devitrification*.)

The glass will always be very 'shattered' in appearance through excessive *crazing* but, as the surface usually heals over the effect is decorative and mysterious. Glass can be colored by laying it over glaze or pigment and firing them together. It is best used in a well-broken but not powdered form—the latter may involve too much trapped air. Wrap the glass to be broken in thick newspaper, thick plastic (for flat sheets), or a cardboard box, and hammer it from the outside. You can usually get a supply of broken pieces from a local builder's glass cutter. Window glass is easier to handle and more reliable in melting than bottle-glass.

Melted glass. Broken pieces of window glass are dropped onto the unfired glaze surface of a slab dish. After firing, the glass has melted together and the pigment in the glaze has stained it. Not all glazes are suitable for this technique—only trials will show which will work. Note the fierce crazing just below the surface which is, itself, miraculously smooth. (See also example under box.)

## MELTING POINT

The point of change from a solid to a liquid *phase*. In some cases this takes place completely at a given temperature (and pressure) and without change in composition. This is known as congruent melting. Many pottery materials, however, go through mixed solid and liquid *phases* i.e. they melt incongruently.

This behavior is of great service to the potter, allowing the development of *vitreous* stonewares and porcelains without collapse and assisting the *viscosity* of glazes. Reference books will often quote the melting points of the metals and oxides we use, but the knowledge is of limited use. To take magnesium, for instance: the m.p. of the metal is 651°C., that of the oxide 2800°C. Apart from the startling difference between these two figures, neither of them tells us much about their behavior in a glaze or body. It is more important to know where it stands in relation to the *Seger formula*, and its habits and effects in conjunction with silica.

Melting points in reaction with other materials will always differ from those of the oxide or minerals on its own—this is the limitation of the *button test*, instructive though that can be. The study of ceramics is the study of *eutectics* rather than of individual melting points.

## MENDING CLAY AND BISCUIT

'Mending' is used in the industry to mean the luting or joining of clay, as in the assembly of porcelain figures. Leach mentions the mending, in the more usual sense, of kiln props, etc. with powdered fireclay and *water-glass*. Repairs to unfired clay, can be made with slip up to the hard-leather stage but joins in dry clay or biscuit are unreliable. One may sometimes get away with the use of vinegar to repair dry clay, but one cannot be certain that it will hold: it should not be used for broken handles, for instance. Stress cracks will mend only temporarily.

Certain high temperature cements are advertised for dry or biscuit pots, which, the makers claim, can be glazed over without showing. One type is called 'Alumide': the name is a clue to its content. However if a pot is badly broken or cracked it will never fire very satisfactorily. (See also *stopping*, and *repairing broken pottery*.)

## METAL

A metallic *element* will generally unite with oxygen to form a *base*. Tin, titanium, zirconium, germanium, and aluminium are exceptions, forming acidic and amphoteric oxides.

## METALOID

An element with some metallic and some non-metallic characteristics. The oxides are *amphoteric* (U.DS), though two metaloids which occur in glaze formulas, arsenic and antimony, are glass-formers and listed with the *acidic* oxides. The metaloids belong to the fifth group of the *periodic table*.

## METAL RELEASE

The tendency of some heavy metals (high atomic numbers) to dissolve out of a glaze and into vinegar, fruit juices, or any strong alkali or acid. The most dangerous are lead (see *soluble lead*) and cadmium. Copper is also involved, especially in the presence of lead oxide. Cadmium is used mainly in orange and red enamels. Neither these nor cadmium glazes should be used on the inside of tableware, storage jars, or kitchenware. Some merchants are now rating their colored glazes and fritts on a metal release scale, those with high potential danger to be used on decorative ware only. Associated more with earthenwares than stonewares. Barium carbonate is mentioned as suspect. One need not panic over possible metal release. Pots involved should be well-fired and glazes should have a well-balanced formula—the great majority of pots would then be less dangerous than detergents!

## METAMORPHIC ROCK, mineral

A rock which has undergone transformation by natural agencies. *Igneous* or *sedimentary* rocks subjected to great heat and pressure are 'altered' and change their texture and appearance and sometimes their mineral composition. Limestone, for instance, re-crystallizes to form marble. Silliminite is a metamorphic mineral.

## METHANE

A *hydrocarbon*, $CH_4$. The principal constituent of natural gas. (See *gas fuel*.)

## MICA

A general term for a group of minerals composed of hydrated *silicates* of alumina, with other silicates e.g. of the *alkalis*. The characteristic mineral of schists, and the glittering crystals or scales in granite. Some deposits will readily cleave into sheets. Feldspars are altered to *kaolinite* and mica in the formation of china clay. The shallow troughs which *levigate* the china clay are known as 'mica drags'.

Biotite mica contains iron and magnesium and is sometimes present in feldspars and other ceramic minerals. Muscovite is white mica, ideal formula: $H_2KAl_2(SiO_4)_3$ or, $K_2O.3Al_2O_3.6SiO_2.2H_2O$ with fluorine sometimes given as an element. There may be wide variations from this formula. It can be used as a 'natural *fritt*' in bodies, especially for ovenware, where it will strengthen the fabric against thermal shock. Mica will begin to decompose into *mullite* and liquid at 1050°C.

The lamellar structure of mica has affinities with clay, though it is not plastic. This structure also makes mica difficult to grind. In the past the alkali fraction in clay has been attributed to feldspar in a *rational analysis* but it is now generally given to a mica percentage *(mica convention)* which leads to a re-assessment of the kaolinite content. Sheet mica is sometimes used as a heatproof window for furnaces.

## MICA CONVENTION

In a *rational analysis* of clay the assumption, for many years, was that the bulk of the mineral could be described as kaolinite, feldspar and quartz. It is now considered that the alkali content can more accurately be discussed in terms of mica. The new computation alters the proportions of the other compounds. See C.PP 292-3 for details.

## MICHIGAN SLIP-CLAY

A red fusible clay similar to *Albany slip*.

## MICRON

One-millionth of a meter. Symbol µm. A millionth may be written $10^{-6}$. Used in the discussion of light wavelengths, and very fine clay particle sizes. 1 micron= 10,000 ångström units.

## MICROPORE

A very efficient heat insultating material for the outer skins of kilns. One half inch (12.5 mm.) is reputed to replace 3 in. (75 mm.) of brick. (See also *insulation of heat*.)

## MILL

To grind finely, or, a machine for grinding materials to a powder. (See *ball mill, jar mill*.)

In CM 19/5 it was suggested that one could shake marbles and glaze in a glass jar to mill glaze materials. This sounds energetic and a little dangerous!

## MINERAL

In the process of the earth's cooling, and of its subsequent weathering, breaking down and re-combining, combinations of *elements* have formed with distinctive physical and chemical properties and, in the present environment, a degree of stability. In some crystal structures, *ionic* substitutions can occur causing variations in the detailed make-up of the mineral. Since the *electron* charges and the *atomic radii* must be similar to the displaced ions, the overall characteristics of the mineral remain within a certain range. *Rocks* consist of various minerals. Most minerals are of *inorganic* origin. The mineral is deemed to have an *'ideal' formula*: the actual material used will be the nearest approach in nature to this formula. Thus china clay or kaolin is often 98% kaolinite mineral. The principal rocks, ores and minerals of interest to potters are:

Alabaster. A pure form of micro-crystalline gypsum.

Albite feldspar. $Na_2Al_2O_3.6SiO_2$, 524. Igneous.

Amblygonite. Variable. Lithium, alumina, phosphorus, with a little silica.

Anorthite feldspar. $CaO.Al_2O_3.2SiO_2$, 278. Igneous.

Andalusite. $Al_2O_3.SiO_2$, 162.

Asbestos. Variable silicates of calcium, iron, and magnesia. Serpentine, amphibole.

Asbolite. Impure cobalt ore.

Barytes. Rock of barium sulfate, $BaSO_4$.

Basalt. Basic rock, high in iron. Volcanic.

Bauxite. Ore of aluminium. Residual.

Beidellite. Alumina-rich montmorillinite clay mineral.

Bentonite. Clay mineral of montmorillinite group.

Biotite. Mica mineral with iron and magnesium.

Borax. $Na_2O.2B_2O_3.10H_2O$, 381.5. Evaporate.

Boro-calcite. $CaO.2B_2O_3.6H_2O$, 304.

Brucite. Ore of magnesia, $MgO.H_2O$.

Calcspar.
Calcite. Crystalline $CaCO_3$, 100. Deposit.

Carolina Stone. See *china stone*.

Cassiterite. Ore of tin, $SnO_2$.

Chalcopyrite. Ore of copper. $CuFeS_2$.

Chalk. Soft limestone. $CaCO_3$, 100. Deposit.

China Stone. $Na_2O.Al_2O_3.8SiO_2$, 644. Igneous.

Chromite. Ore of chrome. $FeO.Cr_2O_3$. Ultrabasic, metamorphic.

Colemanite. $2CaO.3BO_2O_3.5H_2O$.

Cobaltite. Ore of cobalt, $CoAsS$.

Copperas. Ferrous sulfate, $FeSO_4$.

Corundum. Crystalline $Al_2O_3$. Igneous, Ultrabasic, or limestone rock.

Cuprite. Ore of copper, $Cu_2O$.

Crocus Martis. $Fe_2O_3$, 160.

Cryolite. $Na_3AlF_6$, 210.

Diaspore. Clay high in alumina.

Diatomite. Mainly $SiO_2$. Organic deposit.

Diopside. $CaO.MgO.2SiO_2$. Solid solution, Pyroxene, metamorphic.

Dolomite. $CaCO_3.MgCO_3$, 184.

Feldspar. See *albite, anorthite, orthoclase.*

Flint. Micro-crystalline $SiO_2$, 60. Boulder pebble in chalk.

Fluorspar. $CaF_2$, 78.

Galena. $PbS$, 239. Ore of lead.

Ganister. Fine-grain silica rock. Coal seams.

Garnet. Various, $RO.R_2O_3.3SiO_2$.

Gerstley Borate. See *colemanite.*

Gibbsite. $Al_2O_3.3H_2O$.

Granite. Variable; bases, alumina, silica, phosphorus, iron, titania, etc. Igneous, intrusive.

Gypsum. $CaSO_4.2H_2O$.

Halloysite. Clay mineral with a rolled plate structure.

Heavyspar. See *barytes.*

Hematite. Mineral of $Fe_2O_3$.

Horneblende. Silicates of calcium, magnesium, iron, and sodium. Amphibole, intermediate.

Illite. Micaceous clay mineral.

Ilmenite. $Fe_2O_3.TiO_2$, 152.

Ironstone. A hard iron ore.

Kaolinite. The ideal clay mineral, see *clays* as main dictionary entry. Igneous.

Kieselguhr. See *diatomite.*

Kyanite. $Al_2O_3.SiO_2$.

Lava. Basic rocks of variable composition.

Lepidolite. $(LiNaK)_2.(FOH)_2.Al_2O_3.3SiO_2$, 472.

Leucite, $K_2O.Al_2O_3.4SiO_2$. Feldspathoid, lavas.

Limonite. Ore of iron, $2Fe_2O_3.3H_2O$.

Limestone. Rock of calcite, $CaCO_3$. Sedimentary.

Magnesite. Mineral of $MgCO_3$, with some iron.

Magnetite. Magnetic iron ore, $Fe_3O_4$. A spinel.

Marble. Altered limestone.

Mica. Variable; hydrated silicates of alumina, with alkali silicates.

Monothermite. $0.2R_2O. Al_2O_3. SiO_2. 1.5SiO_2$. Weathered Mica.

Mullite. $3Al_2O_3.2SiO_2$. Dissociation of kaolinite.

Muscovite Mica. $(NaK)_2O.3Al_2O_3.6SiO_2.2H_2O$. Alkaline, igneous.

Nepheline Syenite. $Na_2O.Al_2O_3.2SiO_2$, but variable with some potassium, Feldspathoid.

Ochre. Earthy iron oxide.

Orthoclase Feldspar. $K_2O.Al_2O_3.6SiO_2$, 556. Igneous.

Perlite. Fine-grain acidic laval rock. Rhyolite.

Pegmatite. General granitic or feldspathic rocks. Sometimes a synonym for china stone.

Petalite, $Li_2O.Al_2O_3.8SiO_2$, 612.

Petunze. Chinese equivalent of china stone.

Plagioclase. Feldspar series between albite and anorthite.

Pitchblende. Ore of uranium.

Pyrites. Metal sulfide minerals, e.g. $FeS$, $CuS$, $CoS$.

Pyrolusite. Ore of manganese, $MnO_2$.

Pyrophyllite. Clay family substance, $Al_2O_3.4SiO_2.H_2O$.

Quartzite. Rock of crystalline silica, $SiO_2$. 60.

Rutile. Crystalline titania, $TiO_2$. Polymorphic.

Salt. $NaCl$. Deposit.

Sand. Various coarse rock particles.

Sandstone. Rock of silica minerals, cemented with clay, lime and iron.

Shale. Lithified clay.

Sienna. An hydrated iron-manganese earth.

Silliminite. $Al_2O_3.SiO_2$. A clay mineral. Metamorphic.

Smaltite. Ore of cobalt, $CoAs_2$.

Soapstone. 'Massive' impure talc.

Spangles. Magnetic iron, $Fe_3O_4$.

Spodumene. $Li_2O.Al_2O_3.4SiO_2$, 372. Pyroxene, granitic.

Steatite. See *soapstone*.

Stibnite. $Sb_2O_3$. Ore of antimony. Replacement deposit.

Talc. $3MgO.4SiO_2.H_2O$. 379. Metamorphic magnesium-rich rocks.

Tridymite. Theoretical form of silica.

Umber. A ferruginous earth. Hydrated.

Vermiculite. Biotite mica altered by hydrothermal solutions.

Volcanic Ash. Variable basic rocks, with iron.

Witherite. Rock of barium carbonate.

Wollastonite. $CaO.SiO_2$, 166.

Zincblende. Ore of zinc, $ZnS$.

Zircon. $ZnSiO_4$. Occurs as sands, etc.

## MINERALOGICAL CONSTITUTION

The type and proportions of minerals present in a material, as distinct from its chemical constitution.

## MINIUM

Red lead $Pb_3O_4$. (See *lead*.)

## MISHIMA

A form of inlay originating in Korea and now practised in Japan. The design, usually in fine lines, is stamped or impressed into clay at the *soft-leather* stage, and then filled with brushed-on slip which may or may not be scraped flat. (See also *inlay*.)

## MIXING CLAYS

Most commercial bodies are combinations of clays, each chosen for a particular quality. These are rendered into *slip*, combined in *recipe* proportions, *filter-pressed*, and *pugged*. A similar routine but with the filter-press replaced by weathering and drying in troughs is practiced by Leach and others.

In the last few years many potters have bought dough mixers from old bakeries to mix clay powder and water to a plastic state. For most potters, however, it is a case of pugging already plastic bodies, or hand-layering and *wedging*. Cardew warns against wedging *short* clays into plastic ones, the whole mix tending to assume the lowest level of plasticity. He recommends a slop mix, at least for china clay.

It is also possible to spread layers of dry clay onto a sheet of thick plastic in a wooden frame, slaking with water at each layer. The corners of the sheet are then folded in and the whole left to soak for a few days before kneading.

## MODELING

The sculptor models from the outside, generally applying clay to a solid core. The figure cannot be fired without the intermediary of *a mold and cast* (see *press mold*.) In this book discussion is limited to techniques which allow of direct firing, e.g. modeling by *pinching, coiling, slab-building, throwing*, etc.

An amusing 'choir' modeled from simple basic forms which could have been slab built but, in fact, were pressed from cone-shaped molds and varied by modeling, by adding and cutting away. By George Martin.

With some skill, practice and ingenuity most forms can be constructed by these methods, although, in general, the pottery figure will be stylized, compact, and self-supporting. Clay is an amiable and versatile material but imposes its own limitations. Some of the most fundamental of these are:

1 It shrinks during drying and firing—if soft clay is applied to stiff clay, tensions and cracks will result.
2 Clay will not adhere to itself simply by being pressed together: moisture or slip must be used.
3 Air and water will expand on heating and can destroy the fabric if trapped in it.
4 Clay will become *pyroplastic* during firing.

An open, grogged clay, and a maximum wall thickness of $\frac{1}{2}$ in. (12 mm.) will help in all cases.

Simple models may be made from thumb pots and slabs. For a more involved slab figure, but one still within a student's capabilities, see F.CC 32-37. The superb coiling technique of Rosemary Wren can be studied with advantage by all interested in building larger pieces. (See film Creatures in clay.) All her figures are totally self-supporting both during building and firing. Inverted-T shaped coils are used.

If a large piece has more than one support, e.g. the legs of an animal, it is advisable to biscuit and glaze fire on a flat slab made of the same body; the slabs will therefore contract at the same rate as the figure. The slab should be bedded on alumina, as should any wide-based construction. Any horizontally extended parts of the model may need separate support in the kiln. Coil a hollow supporting cylinder from the same body.

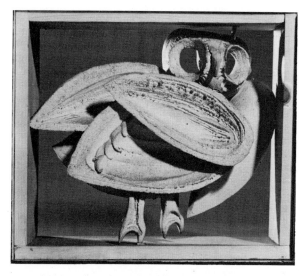

A modeled section of a screen, by Michael Casson.

A modeled pottery head or mask by Ruth Duckworth.

Rosemary Wren coiling a large figure. From the film Creatures in clay.

A 'chest of drawers' by Ian Godfrey. Rich modeling decorating a simple form. See also color plate 17, p. 140.

A coiled model of an anteater by Rosemary Wren. The form has been brilliantly stylized and worked out in ceramic terms so that the whole structure is self-supporting during building (and firing). About 32 in. (800 mm.) across.

## MODELING CLAY

The so-called 'modeling clay' listed by many pottery merchants is, too often, a characterless white body with low plasticity and poor dry strength. A red or buff clay with good plasticity, opened with a fine grog, makes the best body for modeling.

Many attempts have been made to prepare a clay body which will have high dry strength without firing. (See Newclay.) These are not, of course, ceramic materials in the true sense.

151

## MODELING TOOLS

The most useful clay modeling tool is a spatula-ended hardwood tool such as Anger's 'B' series. Other shapes are available but many of them are too lumpy and insensitive for good work. Flexible steel palettes are invaluable for large surfaces and built-up forms. 'Surform' tools and clay planes do a similar job. An ordinary penknife or a small fettling knife can be used as the clay hardens. Good metal tools are made in a variety of spatula and saw-tooth shapes. One can cut one's own tools from hardwood or even wooden meat skewers if nothing better is available, or from bamboo. Several splendid bamboo tools are now on the market. For hollowing-out a strong wire-ended tool is essential.

A few familiar tools are more valuable than a wide range of expensive purchases.

*A range of wooden potting and modeling tools. See also spatula tools. (Photograph: Wengers.)*

## MODULUS, elasticity, rupture

A constant factor for converting units or indicating relationships between one system and another.

There are equations for arriving at the breaking point (the modulus of rupture) of a kiln shelf; these are essential to a manufacturer. See D.DC for details.

The modulus of elasticity is the extent to which a material may be distorted under stress without failing. The industry calculates glaze-body relationships in these terms. For the average craft potter however, insufficient data is available to put these equations to practical use. (See also *conversion factor.*)

## MOH'S SCALE

See *hardness scale.*

## MOISTURE CONTENT

There is always some moisture in powdered minerals, though few of them suffer deterioration from damp. An appreciable or uneven moisture content can, however, cause error when weighing up a *recipe,* and one should keep all materials as dry as possible. If one of your materials is noticeably damp, dry off a weighed amount and note the loss in weight. The equivalent percentage can then be added to the *batch weight.*

## MOISTURE CRAZING

Crazing due to the adsorption of water into the body after firing, causing it to swell very slightly. More likely in earthenware. Can take place days or weeks after firing. (See *crazing, adsorption.*)

## MOISTURE EXPANSION

See *adsorption, moisture crazing.*

## MOLD, mould

In its widest sense a mold is any former over or in which clay can be shaped. Molds such as one's own elbow, a sand-filled bag, or a stone, are dealt with under *formers.* More specifically a mold is a biscuit or

*A very simple dish mold or former, using a square of cloth suspended from each leg of an inverted stool.*

plaster of paris 'negative' of the shape required and is normally used for repetition work. Virtually all industrial pottery is made by means of *press molds* or *slip molds.* (See also *jigger* and *jolley.*)

Molded work will, inevitably, be more mechanical in appearance than hand-built or thrown pottery. The *cast,* however, can be treated merely as a starting point, to be worked on or beaten into a more original and creative shape. Of the types of mold used by craft potters the commonest is the dish mold, especially when decoration is the main interest. A square of cloth or canvas can be suspended from the corners to make an 'instant' mold. A *rolling pin* is a handy tool which can be utilized for molding or forming cylinders.

Of the true molds, the press-mold is fairly widely used (some of Leach's large square bottles, for instance) and is often combined with coiling or throwing e.g. the neck of an oblong bottle. *Slip-molds* are not very relevant to the craftsman, although again simple basic forms can be utilized as a base for further work or in larger constructions.

The limitation of the mold is that it cannot deal with 'returning' forms unless it is split into sections.

There is a limit to the number of pieces a mold can be divided into. Involved shapes are cast in sections in separate molds, the pieces being *luted* together.

See *hump molds, hollow molds, dish molds, slip molds, press molds, formers, plaster of paris,* etc.

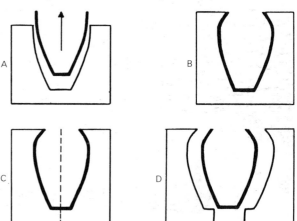

*The principle of molded forms. The beaker shape (A) can be lifted directly from a one-piece mold (as in jigger and jolley work) but any shoulder or returning shape (B) will prevent its removal. Such a mold must be separable at the dotted line (C) so that it can be parted to release the cast (D).*

## MOLECULAR FORMULA

See *formula.*

## MOLECULAR WEIGHT

The sum of the *weights* of all the atoms which make up a *molecule,* or in the case of minerals, the whole *ideal formula.*

Examples:

Ferric $Fe_2O_3 = (56 \times 2) + 16 \times 3) = 112 + 48$ = molecular weight 160.

Dolomite $CaCO_3.MgCO_3 = 40 + 12 + (16 \times 3) + 24 + 24 + (16 \times 3) = 184$.

As mentioned under *molecule*, the term is used for convenience, and is not strictly accurate. In cases where the first oxide or molecule mentioned in the formula is more or less than unity, an equivalent correction must be made before it can be used in glaze calculations. (See *equivalent weight.*)

## MOLECULE

The smallest particle into which a substance can be divided while retaining the properties of the original substance. Molecules are built up of *atoms* united by electrical bonds. (See *atomic theory.*) Strictly speaking, only those atoms united in a covalent bond are true molecules; most *salts* and metallic *oxides* are *electro-valent* compounds and thus aggregates of *ions*. The true molecule is considered to exist in the *gaseous* state only. However, for convenience and simplicity, it is applied (as in *molecular weight*, for instance) to any well-defined combination of more than one atom.

## MOLECULAR WEIGHTS OF COMMONLY USED GLAZE MATERIALS

For molecular weights of *oxides* see under that heading.

| | | |
|---|---|---|
| ALBITE FELDSPAR | 524 | |
| ANORTHITE FELDSPAR | 278 | |
| BARIUM CARBONATE | 197.3 | |
| BONE ASH | 310 | (103) |
| BORAX | 381.5 | |
| BORO-CALCITE | 304 | |
| CHINA CLAY | 258 | |
| CHINA STONE | 644 | |
| COLEMANITE | 412 | (206) |
| CRISTOBALITE | 60 | |
| CRYOLITE | 210 | (420) |
| DOLOMITE | 184 | |
| FLINT | 60 | |
| FLUORSPAR | 78 | |
| GALENA | 239 | |
| ILMENITE | 152 | |
| LEAD MONOSILICATE | 283 | |
| LEAD BISILICATE | 343.5 | |
| LEAD SESQUISILICATE | 313 | |
| LEPIDOLITE | 472 | |
| LITHARGE | 223 | |
| LITHIUM CARBONATE | 74 | |
| MUSCOVITE MICA | — | |
| NEPHELINE SYENITE | 292 | |
| ORTHOCLASE | 556 | |
| PETALITE | 612 | |
| POTASSIUM CARBONATE | 138 | |
| QUARTZ | 60 | |
| RED LEAD | 685 | (228) |
| SILLIMINITE | 162 | |
| SODIUM CARBONATE | 106 | |
| SPODUMENE | 372 | |
| STRONTIUM CARBONATE | 147.5 | |
| TALC | 379 | (126) |
| WHITE LEAD | 775 | (258) |
| WHITING | 100 | |
| WOLLASTONITE | 116 | |
| ZIRCON | 183 | |

Numbers in brackets indicate equivalent weights for glaze calculation.

## MOLOCHITE

A pre-fired china clay made by English Clays, St. Austell. P.C.E. 1770°C. Used as a *refractory grog.*

## MONOTHERMITE

A mineral mentioned by Shaw (S.CP) as $0.2R_2O.$ $Al_2O_3.$ $3SiO_2.$ $1.5H_2O$ produced by the weathering of hydrated mica and present in fireclays.

## MOP

A large round *brush* without a point. Does not leave brushmarks to the same degree as do flat *dusters.*

## MONTMORILLINITE

A group of minerals allied to *kaolinite* and included in the clay 'family'. They differ from kaolinite in being of a much finer grain and having a slightly different cell structure (details in C.PP and W.C). The bonds between the layers are weaker, allowing more water to penetrate. The outer layers of *electrons* exhibit a negative charge which together with a less stable structure allows the substitution of *bases* (Ca, Mg, Na, Fe, especially) for some of the alumina.

The composition is therefore very variable. The weaker 'bonds' also mean that they sheer easily and this gives the material an exceptional kind of plasticity. However its very high shrinkage and the release of silica during firing preclude its use alone or in any great quantity in a pottery body. The usual form of the mineral used by potters is *bentonite,* and the proportion in a body or glaze 2-3%. There are montmorillinites with little or no plasticity, e.g. fuller's earth.

It is thought possible that most secondary clays contain some montmorillinite in their make-up. The mineral is usually the result of the decomposition of basic rocks such as *basalt,* rather than acidic granite.

## MORTAR

Bricklaying mortar for kiln-building is usually a mixture of 10-30% fine grog with fireclay or china clay. A little soda silicate, about $\frac{1}{8}$ of a pint to 10 lb. of dry clay (or 0.07 liters to 4.5 kg. may be added to give a degree of dry setting. The mortar is used in an almost liquid state and is spread thinly—'buttered'—on. It is less a jointing material than a levelling bed.

Normal bricklayer's mortar is composed of lime and sharp sand. This may be used for exterior work exposed to the weather. Sand/cement is not generally recommended. Cardew warns against the use of mortar in the foundations of a kiln.

Commercial mortars or 'cements' are available, e.g. Sairset, which can also be used as a *kiln wash*.

## MORTAR AND PESTLE

Mortars, thick-walled semi-circular bowls generally made of biscuit porcelain, and pestles of the same material on a wooden handle, are used together for grinding materials; however they are used much less frequently, now that most minerals are supplied in a finely ground form. For experimental quantities they are still useful, for grinding a rock sample, for instance. Do not overfill the mortar—a teaspoonful at a time will grind more efficiently than a larger quantity. All materials must first have been broken to at least sand-size with a hammer. For general workshop requirements a *ball* or *jar mill* can replace the mortar and pestle.

*Grinding a teaspoonful of color in a mortar with a pestle.*

## MOSAIC

Small pieces of stone or ceramic fitted together to form an overall pattern or design. The traditional mosaic is flat, or with the pieces very slightly tilted to catch the light. Modern mosaic or wall-decoration includes the use of impressed, textured, and three-dimensional effects. See color plate 15, p. 140.

Small tiles or 'tesserae' can be cut from slabs of clay and finished either separately or in blocks. In the latter case a fairly coarse (wide) cut is taken not quite through the clay, the tesserae being broken apart at a later stage. With care they can be glazed as a block. Mosaics can be built up from random pieces; from more formal units such as a square or triangle; or from pieces shaped to fit the design. The last involves drawing the design full scale on a sheet of thin paper and dividing it into conveniently shaped pieces which are numbered on the reverse side. The design is then laid on a slab of clay, the shapes and numbers traced through with a suitable tool. If too large to be conveniently handled as whole it can be cut into sections, each laid on a slab of clay. The clay pieces are cut apart when at soft-leather stage, and trimmed. They must be glazed individually and reference can again be made to the original design as regards color. Glazed tesserae should be set on alumina for firing. The tedious work of glazing can be avoided by the use of vitrified *colored bodies*. *Egyptian paste* and *enamels* are other possibilities. The breaking of glazed slabs or tiles into pieces is not very satisfactory. A tile cutter could be used but this is also a long job.

*Transferring a design from the drawing to clay tesserae for building into a mosaic. The design is made on tracing paper and each piece numbered (1). The sheet of paper is then reversed onto a slab of clay, and the design and numbers traced through with a pointed (but not sharp) tool (2). The numbers will now be on the back of the tesserae which, with the paper removed, are cut apart with a knife (3).*

1

2

3

The pieces can be assembled in several ways:

1 As the Byzantine mosaics were set; piece by piece into a cement background e.g. a *lime mortar* (or a retarded *plaster of paris* could be used).
2 If the tesserae are of even thickness or an uneven surface is acceptable they can simply be glued onto a wooden base.
3 If the face needs to be quite flat, e.g. for a table top, the pieces must either be assembled face down, or a sheet of 'Contact' or other adhesive plastic laid over the glazed face and smoothed on. Sandwich the whole mosaic between two boards and turn it over. Level the back with a fairly liquid cement (no sand) or with a proprietary tile cement. Battens fastened alongside the mosaic can help in achieving a level. The whole can be adhered to a wooden base either with a bonding glue or even with a layer of Polyfilla or similar cement. The mosaic must be turned face-up before the cement has quite set (usually three or four hours later) so that the design can be cleaned off and grouted with a similar material. To grout, wipe over with a liquid mixture, working it into all the cracks, then wipe the tesserae clean with a rag. An edging, preferably of metal, is needed to finish off a table. This can either be made to size and dropped over the finished mosaic, screwed to the wooden base, or it can be made in angle iron and fitted over the back while the mosaic is reversed, and previous to the final grouting.

Mosaics can also be built up on plastic clay by pressing pellets of colored body on to the dampened surface. This is very suitable for mosaic tiles in schools.

## MUFFLE

In a kiln, an internal shell or box which protects pottery from the effect of flame or hot gases, these being directed between muffle and kiln wall. A saggar is a kind of muffle. Some gas kilns are semi-muffle: protected at the base and about half way up the walls.

## MULLER

See *glass muller*.

## MUG

See *beaker*.

## MULLITE

A compound of alumina and silica, $3Al_2O_3.2SiO_2$, m.p. 1880°C., which results from the *dissociation of kaolonite* at high temperatures. This leaves a proportion of *free silica* which is steadily converted into *cristobalite* up to 1660°C. Some mullite begins to form at 1000°C., and most of the alumina is in this form at 1340°C. The crystals are needle-shaped and are believed to have a 'felting' effect, strengthening stoneware and porcelain bodies. Mica at stoneware temperatures produces mullite (C.PP)

## MULTI-WIRE CLAY CUTTER

See *harp, bow*.

## MUSCOVITE

A mica with the theoretical composition $(Na_2K_2O).3Al_2O_3.6SiO_2.2H_2O$. The form of mica considered to be a constituent of most clays. (See *mica*.)

## MUSHROOM MOLD

A convex dish mold on a stem or stand, over which plates and dishes can be formed. (See *hump mold*.)

# N

## NAPLES YELLOW

A color derived from antimoniate of lead with a little ferric iron for use at temperatures up to about 1090°C. Use as a pigment, or add 5-10% to glazes.

## NATURAL GAS

Gas derived from wells or bore-holes in the earth's crust. (See *gas fuel*.)

## NECK

The narrow terminating section, often more or less elongated, of a bottle-shaped pot. A long neck may be thrown separately and luted on, or thrown from a coil (see *two piece throwing*).

## NEEDLE AWL, pricker

'Pricker' is the American term. A fine awl for cutting clay. A simple type can be made by pushing a coarse needle through a cork, but this will snap off rather easily. Commercial awls are stronger and are set in a wooden handle. Use 'Fine' grades for clay cutting, especially for the rims of thrown pots; thicker awls with a blunt point for less delicate work.

*Using a needle awl to cut the top of a thrown pot. Note the obliquely angled cut (to avoid rucking the clay, not to mention spearing the inside finger), and the position of the other fingers ready to whip away the ring of clay as soon as the cut is complete.*

## NEGATIVE EXPANSION

Only one oxide, that of boron, expands on cooling, i.e. has a negative value for its coefficient of expansion. (See *coefficients of expansion*.)

## NEPHELINE SYENITE

Nepheline is theoretically $Na_2O.Al_2O_3.2SiO_2$ but as it almost invariably contains some potash it may be written $K_2O.3Na_2O.4Al_2O_3.8SiO_2$, 1168, equivalent weight 292, m.p. 1200°C. Syenite is a crystalline rock of feldspar and *horneblende*.

The natural material is variable in constitution but always high in alumina and soda when compared with feldspar. It usually contains some iron which can be extracted magnetically. Deposits in Canada and Norway.

It is an interesting material to use in glazes, making possible formulas which are difficult to convert with feldspar. It is also used in small quantities in porcelain bodies.

A typical analysis by weight (Podmores):

| | | | | | |
|---|---|---|---|---|---|
| $Na_2O$ | 8.1, | $Al_2O_3$ | 24.9 | | |
| $K_2O$ | 9.0, | $Fe_2O_3$ | 0.1 | $SiO_2$ | 56.3 |
| $Cao/MgO$ | 1.7, | | | | |

Compare with a feldspar percentage analysis. It differs from spar in tending to have a more defined *melting point* and at a lower temperature. In stoneware glazes it can be used empirically to replace some of the feldspar. Rarely used in earthenware but a recipe was given in CM 19/6 (Behrens):

| | |
|---|---|
| Nepheline syenite | 69 |
| Fritt (3134) | 20 |
| Whiting | 10 |
| Bentonite | 1 |

## NERIAGE

A form of decoration used in Japan. Slabs of contrasting clays are laid one on another, cut into strips, and rolled or folded into a block. These are sliced end-on so that a whorl or other design of marbled color is obtained. The pieces are pressed into a mold side by side to form a continuous skin.

## NETWORK FORMERS, modifiers

A three-dimensional pattern of linked atoms; a lattice. In glass this pattern has a certain underlying regularity of formation but is random in detail (*amorphous* or non-crystalline).

Only a few acidic oxides can initiate a glass network (see *glass-formers*); the chief of these is silica. On its own, silica needs a very high temperature to vitrify or develop a glassy nature, but the atomic pattern can be loosened, or modified by other oxides so that a fluid material is formed at a lower temperature—as low as 650°C. The larger atoms intrude into the network and, themselves having weaker electrical *bonds,* lower the cohesion of the whole structure. Sodium and potassium have the ideal *ionic valency* and radii for this purpose. Calcium is interesting in that small quantities will modify a glass above about 1050°C., and the glaze

(or the body, in the case of bone china) will tend to be stable and viscous. At higher temperatures and concentrations, however, this behavior may be reversed and 20% or more at 1290°C. can make a glaze very fluid.

## NEUTRAL ATMOSPHERE

A kiln atmosphere which is neither strongly oxidizing nor reducing. The flame uses all the available oxygen without forming carbon monoxide—a state of perfect combustion. An electric kiln is usually neutral although the combustion of impurities in body or glaze causes a slightly reducing atmosphere in a tightly closed kiln.

## NEUTRON

The electrically neutral particle in an atomic core. (See *atomic theory*.)

## NEWCLAY

A proprietary name for a clay containing nylon fibers which give it a degree of dry strength. For use in junior schools where it is not intended to fire the work into ceramic. Its principal use is in modeling. Hardeners can also be added to form cements as the clay dries. Supplied by Newclay Products Ltd., Overston House, Sunnyfield Road, Chislehurst, Kent.

## NICKEL

A metallic element Ni, 59.
Black or green nickelous oxide NiO, 75, s.g. 6.7.
Black nickelic oxide $Ni_2O_3$, 166.
Also quoted as $NiO_2$ (Harrison Mayer). Black nickel decomposes into the monoxide at 600°C.

A fairly refractory oxide, producing in oxidation muted browns, grays, and greens, of a not usually very exciting nature.

1-3% is soluble or partially soluble in a soft glaze, the lower percentage tending to gray, the higher to brown, but with varying effect in different types of glaze; at its least attractive in *borax glazes*. It often contaminates cobalt to which it is a near neighbor in the *periodic table*. Will tend to increase glaze mattness. Gives uncertain and sometimes unexpected colors in *reduction:* Rhodes mentions yellow and purple; Podmores, blue. The tendency towards blue in any type of glaze will be increased by the addition of zinc oxide. A formula quoted in W.CNS:

| | | | | |
|---|---|---|---|---|
| ZnO | 0.33 | | $SiO_2$ | 2.5 |
| Pbo | 0.32 | $Al_2O_3$  0.2 | $B_2O_3$ | 0.2 |
| $N_2O$ | 0.35 | | | |

Lithium has also been recommended for nickel glazes.

Nickel is most often used to 'quench' or modify other coloring oxides. 'Nichrome' resistance wire is nickel/chrome.

## NON-VITREOUS, non-vitrified

A pottery body in which the *glass phase* is absent or has barely begun, e.g. soft earthenware or any porous biscuit. In the USA the official definition is 'a water absorption above 10% for pottery or 7% for tiles.

# O

## OCARINA

From 'goose-shaped'. An ovoid pottery musical wind-instrument, traditionally of porcelain but can be made from any pottery material. (For details of the mouthpiece, see *whistle*.) There should be eight finger-holes. To quote Scholes: 'the pitch is affected by the number of holes left open, i.e. if one hole is left open it does not much matter which, and so with more than one'. The range of the notes will rise as the clay shrinks in drying and firing and it is difficult to get a particular pitch. It has, however, a charming sound when properly used and played professionally. CM 19/2 gives advice on making.

## OCHRE, yellow ochre

A natural hydrated earthy *ferric* oxide, $Fe_2O_3.H_2O$, 178, together with impurities and often some clay. Can be *calcined*, or used raw, for slips, pigments, or in glazes. Produces a yellower color than pure ferric iron. Leach recommends calcined ochre for celadon glazes (L.PB 174). He also quotes Old Seto Yellow containing 25-40% ochre used thinly and oxidized. Yellow ochre contains *hydrated* iron: red ochre *anhydrous* ferric oxide.

## OHM

Symbol R or $\Omega$. A unit of electrical resistance, named after G.S. Ohm, the German physicist (1787-1854.)

The equation useful for potters is:

$$\frac{E}{I} = R \text{ where R is the resistance in ohms,}$$

E the voltage, and I the current in amperes.

*Example:* To obtain 30 amps at 240 volts in an electric kiln we need a wire resistance of 240 (E) ÷ 30 (I)=8 (R) ohms. Element wire is rated at ohms per foot. Thus if the wire you are using has a figure of 0.07 ohms per foot length then you will need 8 ÷ 0.07 =114 feet.

## OIL, fuel, burners

Various grades of petroleum oil can be used in the firing of pottery, the more unrefined oils producing more smoke. A medium grade has been quoted at 135,000 Btu per gallon (3.12 MJ per liter).

Oil must be transformed from a liquid into a mist or vapor before it will burn efficiently. This can most simply be done by *drip-feed* onto a hot metal plate; more controllably by atomizing the oil by means of a jet of air at the burner. This involves the provision of air-pressurizing equipment. Rhodes (R.K 69-75) describes several types of burner. The domestic heating burner would be adequate for 2 cu. ft. (0.06 cu. m.) chamber but lacks control and would probably give too rapid a heat rise. The 'Swirlamiser' burner is reasonably priced and has had good reports. All oil

kilns will burn more effectively when hot.

The advantages of oil over other fuels are its relative cheapness and the ease with which its temperature and atmosphere can be controlled. On the other hand it tends to be noisy and smoky, while the flame is not kind to kiln *refractories*. It is more suitable for high-fired pottery than for earthenware. (See also *forced draft*.)

## OIL-FIRED KILNS

Oil is most efficient in medium and large kilns—10 cu. ft. (0.3 cu. m.) and upwards. Built on the site, they are often constructed by the potter. Some detailed instructions were given in CR 16. Kilns plans are available from CoSIRA and from Homer, St. Agnes, Cornwall. An article in PQ 38 gave plans by Roy Cowan. R.K deals quite extensively with oil kilns, also several other books (C.PP, L.PB, etc.).

Oil-fired kilns are very variable in performance and need a reasonably isolated site because of the noise and smoke—not to mention a 600 gallon tank some 12-16 ft. (3.5-5.0 m.) above the ground. A low, stable flame is difficult to maintain, and some potters practise pre-heating with *bottled gas*.

## ONCE-FIRED POTTERY, glazing

Also known as 'green-glazed' ware. Glazing on the raw clay and firing both together by passes the biscuit fire. The hazards of raw-glazing on the average commercially supplied body are considerable: collapse or blistering due to rapid penetration of liquid from the glaze; the scaling away of the glaze due to shrinkage differences; the bubbling of the fired glaze.

However, a majority of the world's ceramics have been once-fired and the technique is practised by some present day potters including Colin Pearson on stoneware, Lucie Rie on porcelain, and Alan Frewin on slipware.

Some plastic clay must be added to the glaze batch to allow for the necessary shrinkage. The glaze can be applied at the leather-hard stage although some clays with a high dry strength and low absorption will take it when quite dry. It is advisable to leave an interval between glazing the inside and outside of a pot, especially if the body is sandy. Dry handles can be moistened before dipping. *Spray* equipment is useful for large structures. Green-glazed ware needs careful and thorough drying and a steady firing with plenty of ventilation to allow the easy escape of *hydrocarbons* from the body. The cycle must combine the typical *graphs* of a *biscuit* and a *glost* firing and it may therefore take a longer firing than either alone. Inter-action between body and glaze is greater than when the glazing is done on the biscuit. Some of the body surface will combine with the glaze to assist its maturity, especially in earthenware. *Slips* and *engobes* must be of adequate thickness or they will become transparent or disappear completely.

The traditional once-fired earthenware glaze has a high lead content together with some plastic clay. It is also possible to use leadless and of course stoneware glazes. A 1100°C. glaze based on suggestions by Alan Frewin is:

(CR)   Lead sesquisilicate   58
       Body clay             38
       Whiting                4

used on a slipware body of: 45 red clay, 45 buff clay, 10 grog.

Experiment will always be necessary to achieve a glaze which will match the shrinkage and other characteristics of the body you are using. To adapt a stoneware glaze one can start with a normal biscuit-glazing recipe and replace the china clay with ball clay. e.g. 50 feldspar, 20 whiting, 20 ball clay, 10 flint. A little bentonite will increase shrinkage if the glaze peels. Zinc oxide has a high drying shrinkage if it can be accommodated in the formula. (See *Bristol glaze*.)

## ON-GLAZE

Color applied to a pre-fired ceramic, generally at a low temperature. (See *enamels*.) A very wide range of color is available at 700-900°C. It is a more explicit term than 'over-glaze' which may also include majolica painting. True on-glaze color adheres to the surface of a glaze but barely penetrates it.

## OPACITY, opacifiers

When light cannot pass through a glaze but is reflected back from its surface, the glaze is termed opaque. Opacity is caused either by reflective matter suspended in the glaze, or by an uneven (matt) surface. (See also *translucent*.) All glazes will become transparent or nearly so if fired to a high enough temperature.

The principal opacifying agents operate by remaining as suspended, white, undissolved particles distributed through a glaze. They are the oxides of tin, zirconium, titanium, and zinc; the average addition to a *soft glaze* being 10-12% and rather less for stoneware. Chrome is an opacifying coloring oxide. Refractory oxides such as alumina can be increased in a glaze to give an opacity which is linked with mattness of surface. Bubbles which have been unable to escape from a glaze (generally caused by too thick a coating) will appear as white milky patches. Very slow cooling, with the formation of crystals (low alumina glazes) will induce opacity.

## OPALESCENT

Applied to a semi-translucent, cloudy glaze showing *iridescence*. Like an opal. A high boron content can induce opalescence (Rhodes) and it is a quality sometimes found in reduced *raku* glazes. The so-called *Chun* glazes (relatively high in MgO and low in $Al_2O_3$) show opalescence. (See *optical color, color*.)

## OPEN BODY

A body with large pores. Usually contains *grog*. Normally applied to unfired clay mixtures. At stoneware temperatures an open body may *vitrify* but the surface texture will remain characteristically rough or coarse.

Very fine-grain clays need 'opening' with *fireclays*, calcined china clay, or grog. Grog is more efficient in assisting drying than the addition of *sand*. An open body will usually have a lower wet/dry shrinkage and greater standing strength, but also faster water absorption. A low-fired open body will have high resistance to *thermal shock*. Modeling clays are usually open to allow for possibly excessive wall thicknesses.

## OPTICAL COLOR

Certain glazes without coloring oxides will nevertheless give an appearance of color e.g. *Chun*. The effect arises from very fine particles which approximate to the wavelengths of light e.g. around 0.5 *microns*. A very thin coating on a glaze can also produce color, like oil on water; bismuth mother-of-pearl lustre is an example The colors are frequently bluish. Cardew mentions the hypothesis of the suspension of one glass or glaze within another to explain Chun blues.

## OPTICAL PYROMETER

Commonly the 'disappearing filament' type, where the temperature is measured by the comparison of two light sources: firstly the light from a lamp filament, which is adjustable and secondly the light radiated through the kiln spyhole. Both are viewed through a red filter which renders them monochromatic. The system takes advantage of the fact that the intensity of light at any one wavelength depends on the temperature of the 'hot body'. The brightness of the filament is adjusted until it matches that of the kiln when it will apparently disappear. The setting on a connected *ammeter* reads on a scale as a temperature. The device needs recalibrating at intervals. If your kiln has a small spyhole some sort of stand or tripod is essential. It has been found to produce somewhat subjective results.

*Using an optical pyrometer. The hot interior of the kiln is sighted and focussed through the spyhole. The knob on the side is then turned until the glowing filament inside the pyrometer disappears. The temperature can be read on the dial below the eye-piece.*

## ORANGE-PEEL GLAZE

A finely crinkled surface texture often associated with sprayed-on glaze. *Salt glazes* also exhibit this texture.

## ORGANIC CHEMISTRY

The chemistry of substances produced by living organisms. More recently confined to the study of *carbon* compounds, excluding the metallic *carbonates* and the oxides and sulfides of carbon (U.DS). The term is useful in a general sense but can be imprecise in particular instances.

## ORTHOCLASE

Potash feldspar $K_2O.Al_2O_3.6SiO_2$, 556. (See *feldspar*.)

## ORTON CONES

American *pyrometric cones*. They are numbered in a similar way to Staffordshire and Seger cones but their temperature equivalents differ and there are complicated tables for speed of heat rise and size (length) of cone. As with all heat measuring devices, experience is a better guide than lists of temperature equivalents. (See also *cones*.)

The range for standard 63 mm. cones at a temperature rise of 150°C. per hour is given as:

ORTON CONES Temperature at which the point of the cone has curved over level with its base.

| Cone No | Temp. °C. | Nearest Staffs. | Temp. given in R.CGP |
|---------|-----------|-----------------|----------------------|
| 020 | 635 | 021 | |
| 018 | 717 | 018 | |
| 016 | 792 | 015 | |
| 015 | 804 | 014 | |
| 013 | 852 | 012 | |
| 011 | 894 | 010 | 875 |
| 010 | 894 | 010 | |
| 09 | 923 | 09 | 930 |
| 08 | 955 | 08a | |
| 07 | 984 | 06 | 974 |
| 06 | 999 | 05 | |
| 05 | 1046 | 03a | 1030 |
| 04 | 1060 | 02 | |
| 03 | 1101 | 1 | 1080 |
| 02 | 1120 | 2 | 1095 |
| 01 | 1137 | 3 | 1110 |
| 1 | 1154 | 3a | |
| 2 | 1162 | 4 | 1135 |
| 3 | 1168 | 4a | 1145 |
| 4 | 1186 | 5a | 1165 |
| 5 | 1196 | 6 | |
| 6 | 1222 | 6a | 1190 |
| 7 | 1240 | 7a | 1210 |
| 8 | 1263 | 8a | 1225 |
| 9 | 1280 | 9 | 1250 |
| 10 | 1305 | 10 | 1260 |
| 11 | 1315 | 11 | 1285 |
| 12 | 1326 | 11 | 1310 |
| 13 | 1346 | 12 | 1350 |

It will be seen that the equivalents given in R.CGP are variations on the temperatures quoted by suppliers of the cones, especially in the 7-11 range. His glaze recipes presumably refer to his cone chart, e.g. cone 9 glaze melting at around 1250°C.

## OVAL SHAPES

Oval dishes may, of course, be pressed in oval molds (see note below), or they may be derived from circular thrown bowls either by beating, or by the following method. Cut a leaf-shaped sliver from the center of the base (which must be thrown with a reasonable and even thickness). Only about $\frac{3}{16}$ in. (5 mm.) at the widest point need be removed. Make the cuts at an angle, both sides sloping the same way, damp the faces with slip and ease them together by pressure from each side of the dish. The work should be done at the soft-leather stage. Another method is to cut out two sections near opposite walls of the dish and to press the faces together again. These joins tend to be stronger than the center cut illustrated. Oval pots are usually pressed into shape; beating may destroy the surface quality.

To draw an oval for the basis of an oval mold:

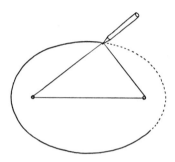

Lay a sheet of paper on a drawing board or wooden surface. Fix two drawing pins at a distance from one another $1\frac{1}{8}$-$3\frac{7}{8}$ in. (30-100 mm.) less than the breadth of size of oval you require. Make a loop of string which, when held taut, from one pin, extends $\frac{5}{8}$-2 in. (15-50 mm.) beyond the second pin. With the loop over both pins, hold the string taut with the point of a pencil and the oval can be drawn by moving the pencil round the loop of string. The larger the loop compared with the distance between the pins, the nearer the shape will approach a circle.

*An oval plant pot by Joanna Constantinidis.*

*Making an oval dish from a circular thrown one. A narrow leaf shape is marked in (1) and cut away at an angle (2). The faces of the slot are slipped and pressed together, the angle allowing them to ride a little one over another so that a firm join can be smoothed over (3).*

*A glaze-trailed oval oven dish by Ray Finch.*

## OVEN WARE

There are a number of factors governing the efficiency of ceramic cooking vessels. Our chief concern is with the expansion and contraction which occurs at oven temperatures. A low-fired open body like that of African cooking pots, and some Mediterranean and European wares, can accommodate these strains within the fabric of the pot (see also *flameproof ware*). At harder earthenware temperatures some *cristobalite* will form in the body. This helps to prevent crazing, an important factor in hygiene (though Cardew maintains that a case of food poisoning due to a crazed cooking vessel has still to be proved), but cristobalite also has an *inversion* within the oven range. A reasonably open-bodied earthenware dish fired below 1050°C. and with a low-expansion glaze (see *coefficients of expansion*) is, theoretically, the most likely to be successful. Against this is the fact that porous ware has low conductivity and heat applied to one point will not rapidly be dispersed through the fabric. Oven heat, however, is reasonably even; it is when taking the dish from the oven and putting it down on a metal or conductive surface that trouble may occur. This depends as much on the cook as on the potter.

A well-fired stoneware casserole has a good chance of resisting the thermal shocks of cooking, with the proviso above. Advice from various sources for increasing this resistance includes: a minimum of free silica in the body; the use of high alumina clays, such as high-grade fireclays, which will help the development of *mullite* without a release of excessive silica; an *open* stoneware body, not quite vitrified, which may be less brittle than a glassy one; *mica* minerals and zircon sand have been mentioned as suitable additions to the body; the increase of thermal conductivity can be increased with *silicon carbide* (but this poses glazing problems); and the addition of silliminite.

Finally, the form of the piece can help; a well-rounded casserole approximating to the sphere being under less strain. A wide, flat base is not recommended for ovenware. See the curved form illustrated under *flameproof ware*.

The glaze should, of course, be in slight *compression*. If lead is used, the glaze must be well-balanced in its formula and adequately fired. A low-solubility or a leadless glaze might be advisable.

High magnesia bodies and glazes are mentioned by Behrens, and he gives the recipes:

|  | Body | Glaze |
|---|---|---|
| Ball clay | 25 | 44.6 |
| China clay | 35 | 18.7 |
| Talc | 36 | 25.8 |
| Bentonite | 4 | |
| Penco fritt | 54 | 10.9 |

Bodies containing grog, and lithium glazes are also listed.

## OVER-FIRING

Over-firing means firing above the temperature at which the desired result would obtain. Thus an over-fired tin glaze will go *translucent;* a matt glaze, shiny. The fluidity of the glaze is increased and with it the possibility of the glaze running onto the kiln shelves. *Volatilization* will lead to blistering and a thin 'starved' glaze. An over-fired glaze will always show a different color and appearance. Earthenware tin glazes will often stand considerable over-firing without disastrous results. *Oxidized* stonewares are more liable to violent change in a short temperature range than are reduced ones. Very occasionally desirable characteristics may emerge. An over-fired body will vitrify, probably *bloat,* distort, and eventually melt and collapse. Prolonged soaking may have the same effect as higher temperature. Excessive over-firing will severely damage the kiln and kiln furniture. Elements should be used with a maximum temperature rating at least 50°C. above the firing temperature. (See also *flashing.*)

*An impressive heap of melted and vitrified pots and kiln furniture from a very obviously over-fired kiln which continued burning over a week-end, the 'automatic' controls failing to switch it off.*

## OVERGLAZE

Colors applied on top of the glaze. In its widest sense it includes *enamels,* though these are better described as *on-glaze.* It is possible to paint onto a fired glaze with the pigment oxides or stain thickened with gum or fat oil, but overglaze color is more easily applied by the *majolica* technique on the *raw glaze.*

## OXFORD CLAY

The raw material of many English bricks, e.g. the Peterborough Flettons. Carbonaceous material burns in the brick during firing, which therefore requires a minimum of fuel.

## OXFORD FELDSPAR

A feldspar from Maine, USA. More siliceous than English spar and approximating nearer to *stone.* Wengers recommend mixed feldspars as an English equivalent.

Analysis by weight quoted in D.DC:

| | | | | | |
|---|---|---|---|---|---|
| $K_2O$ | 7.9 | $Al_2O_3$ | 17.0 | $SiO_2$ | 69.0 |
| $Na_2O$ | 3.2 | $Fe_2O_3$ | 0.1 | | |
| CaO | 0.4 | | | | |

## OXIDATION, oxidize, oxydize

The combination of a metal or other element with oxygen to form an oxide. All pottery materials are used in the oxide form. Although one may refer to the metal as, for instance, in 'an iron glaze', it is the oxide that is always implied. The abbreviation occurs quite frequently in this book.

Heat is generated during the process of oxidation. The burning of fuel is the rapid oxidation of *carbon* into *carbon dioxide,* $CO_2$. Most elements oxidized during the cooling of the earth. Metals etc. can be oxidized in a workshop or factory.

Oxygen is present in the atmosphere in *molecules* of two oxygen atoms which can receive transfer of *electrons* from another *element* according to its valency. Thus $2Mg + 2O$, $4K + 2O$, etc. are generally written MgO and $K_2O$ respectively. Elements may have more than one oxide form, one of which will be more stable than the others.

## OXIDE

A compound of an *element* with oxygen. The combination may be in various ratios, e.g. 2:1 as in potash, 1:1 in lime. The ratios mentioned represent the RO group of the *Seger formula* where the middle group of oxides is in 2:3 proportions; and the last group in 1:2 ratio. There are other, less common, ratios such as 3:4, e.g. magnetic iron $Fe_3O_4$.

Elements may combine in more than one ratio although one of these will be more stable and normally only one enters into combination in a glaze.

The suffix -a is often applied to the root name of the element to indicate the oxide. Thus: aluminium—alumina; titanium—titania; silicon—silica. The suffix -ic indicates the higher (most oxygen) ratio (the stable form) and -ous, the lower more unstable proportion. For instance: ferric—ferrous (iron); cupric—cuprous

| Oxide entering fusion | Molecular wt. | Name | Materials commonly used to supply oxide |
|---|---|---|---|
| $Al_2O_3$ | 102 | Alumina | Clay Minerals, Feldspars, Alumina Hydrate. |
| $B_2O_3$ | 69.5 | Boric Oxide (Boric Acid) | Borax, Colemanite, Fritts. |
| $BaO$ | 153.3 | Baria | Carbonate, Barytes. |
| $CaO$ | 57 | Calcia, Lime | Whiting, Dolomite, Anorthite Feldspar, Wollastonite, Wood and Bone Ash, Fluorspar, Colemanite. |
| $CoO$ | 75 | Cobalt Oxide | Black and Gray Oxides, Carbonate. |
| $Cr_2O_3$ | 152 | Chrome, Chromic Oxide | Green Oxide, Iron Chromate. |
| $CuO$ | 79.5 | Copper Oxide | Black Oxide, Carbonate, Red Oxide, Oxalate. |
| $Fe_2O_3$ | 160 | Iron Oxide, Ferric | Hematite, Red Ferric, Black Magnetite, Spangles, Ilmenite, Ochre, Sienna, Copperas, Red Clay, Synthetic Red Iron. |
| $K_2O$ | 94 | Potash | Orthoclase Feldspar, Pearlash (Carbonate), Nepheline, Stone, Wood Ash. |
| $Li_2O$ | 30 | Lithia | Oxide, Carbonate, Petalite, Spodumene, Amblygonite. |
| $MgO$ | 40 | Magnesia | Carbonate, Talc, Dolomite. |
| $MnO$ | 71 | Manganese Oxide | Dioxide, Carbonate. |
| $Na_2O$ | 62 | Soda | Albite Feldspar, Nepheline, Borax, Alkaline Fritts, Salt, Carbonates, Silicates, Stone. |
| $NiO$ | 75 | Nickel Oxide | Black or Green Nickel Oxide. |
| $(P_2O_5)$ | 173 | Phosphoric Oxide | Bone and wood ash. |
| $PbO$ | 223 | Lead Oxide | Litharge, Galena, Red and White Lead, Silicate Fritts. |
| $SiO_2$ | 60 | Silica | Flint, Quartz, most Clay and Feldspathic Minerals, Talc, Silicate Fritts, Lithium Minerals. |
| $SnO_2$ | 151 | Tin Oxide | Oxide. |
| $SrO$ | 103.5 | Strontia | Carbonate. |
| $TiO_2$ | 80 | Titania | Precipitated Oxide, Rutile. |
| $U_3O_8$ | 842 | Uranium Oxide | 'Depleted' Oxide, Sodium Uranate. |
| $V_2O_5$ | 182 | Vanadium Oxide | Oxide, Ammonium Metavanadate. |
| $ZnO$ | 81 | Zinc Oxide | Oxide, Calcined Oxide. |
| $ZrO_2$ | 123 | Zirconia (Zircon) | Zirconium Oxide, Zircon (Silicate), various prepared forms to assist dispersion. |

(copper); cobaltic—cobaltous.

Water is hydrogen in 2:1 combination with oxygen. It will be seen that oxides bear no obvious physical relationship to the elements which make them up. (See *compound*.) Carbonates are oxides in combination with $CO_2$. They are written not as $RO.CO_2$, but $RCO_3$ (R being the element in combination). Oxides in combination with one another form more elaborate compounds such as *minerals*.

Each oxide used in pottery is discussed under the entry for *element*. To save continual reference, however, the principal oxides are listed below with their molecular weights or *equivalents*.

## OXIDIZED STONEWARE

Stoneware fired in a clear atmosphere with plenty of air. Electric kilns will normally have an oxidized or at least a neutral atmosphere. Many potters regard reduction as the apex of achievement in stonewares, but there is still a wide field to be explored in oxidation. In the latter the 'interest' must be integral to the glaze itself, and the potter's handling of it. Janet Leach, describing Hamada's Mashiko pottery, says that all 5000 pots in his eight-chamber climbing kiln were oxidized, except those in the first chamber.

In my experience, manganese and copper are more useful than iron as coloring oxides, but potters are deriving *kaki* and other iron stonewares from oxidized firings. *Ochre* is a useful material and 20% more can be used in a glaze. The maturing range of glazes seems to be shorter than in reduction, making careful and precise firing essential. The firing can be rapid—7 to 8 hours. Up to 20% red clay can be included in the body. 'Stepped' *firing graphs* i.e. *soaking* or even dropping the temperature at certain points in the firing (Japanese 'fire-change') may be essential for certain effects.

## OXIDIZING FIRE

A clear fire with plenty of air intake, in which *oxides* remain unaltered and any *elements*, such as carbon, will find sufficient oxygen in which to oxidize freely. In a closed electric kiln organic matter may consume the oxygen early in the firing and give rise to a slightly *reducing* atmosphere. In a fuel-burning kiln plentiful *secondary air* must be admitted.

Earthenware, with the exceptions of *copper reds*, *lustres*, and some *raku*, is fired in a fully oxidizing atmosphere. (See also *stoneware glazes*.)

## OXYGEN

A gaseous element 0, 16. An odourless invisible gas essential to life, and to combustion. The most abundant element in the earth's crust. Composes about 21% of dry air. Present in the atmosphere as *molecules* of two oxygen *atoms*. Combines with elements to form *oxides*.

# P

## PACKING KILNS

An evenly and reasonably closely-packed kiln is not only economical but is also likely to fire better than a half empty one. Kilns and pots vary too widely to give more than a general guidance. In fuel burning kilns space must be allowed for the proper circulation of hot gases, and the pack or setting will control the behavior and efficiency of the firing. Keep the density as balanced as possible, especially in an electric kiln. Do not crowd closely packed shelves into one side of the kiln but try to disperse them.

Large kilns may be packed with a combination of *saggars* and *shelves*. (See L.PB.)

In the biscuit fire, pots may be piled in *bungs* (see *boxing*) but it must be remembered that clay has a degree of *pyroplasticity* at all firing temperatures and will warp under any uneven strain. An oval shape set in a round one may deform both. The rim of a jug is seldom flat and a thin tile bat should be inserted if pots are to be set on top. (See also under *biscuit firing*.)

In the gloss pack, glazed surfaces must not touch each other, although they can be set very close for high-fired stoneware, since the shrinkage during firing will further separate them. (See also *bat, bung, kiln furniture, prop*.)

In an electric kiln tall pots, especially slab pots, will incline towards the elements if packed too close to them, due to the greater shrinkage on that side.

A                                    B

*Packing of close shelves and large pots in a kiln. In arrangement (A) the density is unbalanced and although (B) would entail tall props it is preferable from the point of view of even firing temperatures, especially in an electric kiln.*

*Packing a top-loading kiln. It is easy to see whether the pots are laterally separated but the height must be checked to avoid rims sticking to the undersides of kiln shelves. This is done by laying a strip of wood across the supports, seeing that all rims lie below it.*

## PADDLE, paddling

A beater or bat-shaped wooden tool (see *beater*) which can be used either for shaping or decorating pots, or for stirring glazes and slips. In America the term 'paddling' may be used for beating.

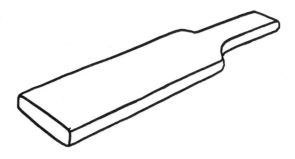

*A paddle: a beating or stirring bat cut from a piece of 1 x 4 in. (20 x 100 mm.) timber and about 14 in. (360 mm.) long.*

*A truck packed for an industrial continuous kiln.*

## PAINTING ON POTTERY

Pots can be decorated with brushed color at any stage from wet clay to fired porcelain as follows:

1 On the raw clay with pigment oxides or *underglaze* colors.
2 On biscuit with oxides or underglaze *stains* (but see *hardening on.*)
3 On the unfired glaze with oxides or suitable glaze stains.
4 On the fired glaze with *enamels*.

All can be used on earthenware, stoneware, or porcelain, although the range of possible pigments decreases as the temperature rises. For further discussion see *decoration, brushwork, majolica, wax resist, paper resist, calligraphic, brushes.*

## PALETTE, knife

The Oxford Dictionary defines 'pallet' as 'a flat wood blade with handle used by potters.' A palette knife, however, is of flexible steel with a round-ended blade in a wooden handle, and is used for grinding and mixing colors in water or enamels in oil, working the knife from side to side on a glazed tile.

A *steel palette* is a thin, very flexible piece of sheet steel—a valuable tool.

*The use of a palette knife for grinding and mixing colors on a tile. A sideways motion is used, tipping the knife to compress and grind the color at each stroke. Use a minimum of color at a time.*

## PAN MILL

A primitive grinding mill in which hard stones (chert) are dragged over a paved area by rotating paddles. Used until recently in English country potteries.

## PAPER RESIST

A technique of decoration with characteristic bold, open patterns. As with all resist methods it is the background which is colored with slip or pigment, the design being reserved in the original surface color. Of especial value to the beginner or student who is usually more fluent with scissors than with a brush.

The design can be altered and developed at will before its actual application to the dish or pot.

*Method:* paper resist can be practised in association with *glaze on glaze* but is most useful on leather-hard clay. Cut or tear the design in a thin, fairly absorbent paper such as typing copy paper and apply it to the surface of the pot or dish with a little moisture. Designs can be built up of a number of pieces of paper which may overlap. Sponge over the surface of the paper when finally in position, and work the edges gently but very firmly onto the clay. The coloring material should have been prepared previously and be ready to apply. As soon as any excess moisture has dried from the surface, brush your *pigment* on with broad, even strokes, or flood the surface with *slip*, pouring gently to avoid floating the paper. Put aside until the surface has dried to leather-hard and then remove paper with a needle or fine knife, making sure that you have found all the pattern!

When designing for paper avoid large areas: they will look very blank on the finished piece. A large shape can be given interest by cutting smaller design elements within it. A simple but effective idea is to cut a single shape, a fish for instance, and then to slice it into several sections placing these a little apart. The result will be an 'exploded' shape broken up with lines of color. One can also mask off larger areas and use a second color.

*Paper resist. A thin-paper design is adhered to the pot with a little water and a sponge (1). The color is then brushed over with firm, broad strokes over clay and paper (2). The paper is peeled away to show the resist design (3).*

2

3

## PARALLEL WIRING

Many pieces of electrical equipment can be taken from a *single phase* (2 wire) mains input. The number is limited only by the ability of the input wires to carry the load. To maintain full voltage, however, each must be wired directly to a line and neutral connection. (See diagrams under *series*.)

## PARTS OF A POT

Just as we use the word 'body' for the clay fabric of a pot so the pot itself is described in human terms: foot, belly, shoulder, neck. Leach also calls the termination of a pot the 'head' but this term is less commonly used. The top edge is the 'rim'. A pot may also have a 'waist' e.g. a diabolo shape. 'A Potter's Portfolio' (Leach) includes an analysis of pottery form in these terms. They are more easily applicable to the traditional full-bodied pot forms.

## PASTE

A term often used by archaeologists and historians to indicate any *body* mixture. To a potter it suggests a body with low plasticity and smooth, e.g. porcelain or bone-china, and especially the artificial, prepared mixtures used for the old *soft-paste* wares.

## PASTRY CUTTER

Circular metal cutters sold at large kitchen equipment shops. Invaluable for cutting circles and rings of clay from slabs. (See *coiling, slab pots*.) At one time the cutters were sold in sets of up to 16 sizes but these are now difficult to find.

## P.C.E.

Abbreviation for *pyrometric cone equivalent*.

## PEARL ASH

Potassium carbonate $K_2CO_3$. Billington gives potassium oxide as 'pearlash'; 'made from wood ashes' (U.DS). *Deliquescent* and *soluble*. Unsuitable for raw glaze but used in *fritts*.

## PEBBLE MILL

A *ball mill* using flint pebbles.

## PEELING OF GLAZE

Often attributed to a very low thermal expansion *(c.o.e.)* with consequent compressive strain, although this could be better described as *shivering*. Glaze can peel away from the pot during drying, or early in the firing, and this is often caused by excessive shrinkage of the glaze (e.g. from a *flocculated* ash batch) or from too thick a coating. An over-plastic slip can peel and crack. Zinc and colemanite, as well as ash, can cause shrinkage. The use of calcined materials or the substitution of china clay for plastic clay will help. Glaze which has begun to peel in drying will *crawl* in the firing.

*A pinched form by Sheila Fournier glazed with an ash glaze which has flocculated in the bin, causing excess shrinkage as it dried. The peeling has been used as a deliberate decorative effect in the well of the piece.*

## PEGMATITE

Geologically the term is given a very wide connotation, from granitic minerals to nearly pure quartz, and branching into lithia-micas and the syenite group. Pottery books will, however, often use 'pegmatite' as a synonym for Cornish granite or *china stone* with a formula of RO (made up of soda, potash, and some lime and magnesia). $Al_2O_3$. 7.0-7.5 $SiO_2$.

## PENCIL

A pointed sable brush, also listed as majolica pencils.

## PERCENTAGE COMPOSITION

.The percentage by weight of the elements or oxides in a compound. (See also *analysis.*)
To derive percentage composition from a formula:
1  The percentage of elements in an oxide.

$$\frac{\text{Total atomic weight of the element}}{\text{molecular weight of compound}} \times 100$$

*Example:* the amount of oxygen in $MnO_2$

$$\frac{2 \times 16 \text{ (atomic wt. oxygen)}}{87} \times 100 = 36.8\%$$

leaving 63.2 of manganese metal.
2  The percentage of an oxide in a compound.
*Example:* the amount of calcia in whiting, $CaCO_3$

$$\frac{\text{Molecular wt. calcia, 56}}{\text{Mol. wt. calcium carbonate 100}} \times 100 = 56\%$$

Some 44% of the recipe weight will therefore be lost when the *carbon dioxide* is driven off during firing. The equation can be extended to work out the percentages of *oxides* in *minerals*.

## PERCENTAGE RECIPES

A recipe can be listed as *batch weights* with a random total, or as parts of a hundred. It is much easier to compare recipes in the latter form.
*Example:* two batch weight recipes,

|             | A     | B     |
|-------------|-------|-------|
| China stone | 74.0  | 128.4 |
| China clay  | 116.1 | 185.7 |
| Whiting     | 90.0  | 144.0 |
| Quartz      | 105.0 | 168.0 |

If we bring each of these recipes to percentages, we find that they have the same proportions (to the nearest whole number: stone 20, clay 30, whiting 23, quartz 27).

It is therefore worth bringing all batch weights to percentages both for easy comparison and also to get an immediate impression of the proportions, and thus the sort of glaze or body likely to result.

*Method:* Total the batch weights and divide each of the items in the recipe by this total, then multiply by 100.

i.e. $\frac{\text{Item}}{\text{Total}} \times 100$

*Example:*
From the above batch A. Total 385. To work out the whiting percentage:
90 ÷ 385 = 0.2337
0.2337 x 100 = 23.37%.

## PERIODIC TABLE

A table or chart in which the elements are arranged in order of their *atomic numbers*, and grouped according to their electron configuration and *valencies*. As far as their behavior in ceramics is concerned the groupings are often appropriate. In Group 1 (one electron in the outer shell) we find lithium, potassium and sodium vertically adjacent, as are the slightly less 'efficient' fluxes calcium, strontium and barium. However another important base—lead—is found in Group IVA with the glass-formers, silica, and germanium. Many of the colors are contained in the Group 23-29 and are called the *transitional* elements.

The table's practical value is limited but the information it contains can give some explanation and forecast of behavior.

## THE PERIODIC TABLE OF THE ELEMENTS

| IA | IIA | IIIB | IVB | VB | VIB | VIIB | VIII | | | IB | IIB | IIIA | IVA | VA | VIA | VIIA | 0 |
|---|---|---|---|---|---|---|---|---|---|---|---|---|---|---|---|---|---|
| 1 H | | | | | | | | | | | | | | | | | 2 He |
| 3 Li | 4 Be | | | | | | | | | | | 5 B | 6 C | 7 N | 8 O | 9 F | 10 Ne |
| 11 Na | 12 Mg | | | | | | | | | | | 13 Al | 14 Si | 15 P | 16 S | 17 Cl | 18 Ar |
| 19 K | 20 Ca | 21 Sc | 22 Ti | 23 V | 24 Cr | 25 Mn | 26 Fe | 27 Co | 28 Ni | 29 Cu | 30 Zn | 31 Ga | 32 Ge | 33 As | 34 Se | 35 Br | 36 Kr |
| 37 Rb | 38 Sr | 39 Y | 40 Zr | 41 Nb | 42 Mo | 43 Tc | 44 Ru | 45 Rh | 46 Pd | 47 Ag | 48 Cd | 49 In | 50 Sn | 51 Sb | 52 Te | 53 I | 54 Xe |
| 55 Cs | 56 Ba | 57 La | 72 Hf | 73 Ta | 74 W | 75 Re | 76 Os | 77 Ir | 78 Pt | 79 Au | 80 Hg | 81 Tl | 82 Pb | 83 Bi | 84 Po | 85 At | 86 Rn |
| 87 Fr | 88 Ra | 89 Ac | | | | | | | | | | | | | | | |

| RARE EARTHS Lanthanides | 58 Ce | 59 Pr | 60 Nd | 61 Pm | 62 Sm | 63 Eu | 64 Gd | 65 Tb | 66 Dy | 67 Ho | 68 Er | 69 Tm | 70 Yb | 71 Lu |
|---|---|---|---|---|---|---|---|---|---|---|---|---|---|---|
| ACTINIDE Series | 90 Th | 91 Pa | 92 U | 93 Np | 94 Pu | 95 Am | 96 Cm | 97 Bk | 98 Cf | 99 Es | 100 Fm | 101 Md | 102 No | 103 Lw |

## PERLITE

A fine-grained *acidic* laval *rock* (rhyolite type) which swells when rapidly heated. Used for making heat insulating bricks.

## PERMEABILITY

The rate at which one substance (a liquid or a gas) can pass through another. In pottery, the rate at which water will pass through a ceramic body. It gives some idea of the size of the pores as distinct from total pore volume, which is demonstrated by *porosity* tests. Scientific tests for permeability are beyond the potter's range but simple comparative trials can be made. *Example:* sit several similarly sized but differently fired biscuit containers in saucers and fill them with water; the rate at which the saucers fill will be a comparative test of permeability.

## PETALITE

A mineral $Li_2O.Al_2O_3.8SiO_2$, 612. A *fluxing* mineral with a rather high melting point. Can be used as a source of lithia in glazes and porcelain bodies. Should be pebble-ground. A sample analysis by weight:

$Na_2O$ 1.1
$MgO$ 0.3
$CaO$ 0.2
$Li_2O$ 4.3
$Al_2O_3$ 16.0   $SiO_2$ 77.2

Related to spodumene, which has half the amount of silica in its formula. Lithium minerals are recommended by Cardew for flameproof bodies, using as much as 60% petalite to 40% plastic clay for very low *thermal expansion*.

## PETUNZE

The Chinese equivalent of *china stone* or *feldspar*.

## pH FACTOR

The number of hydrogen ions in a solution, denoting relative acidity or alkalinity; pH 7 is neutral i.e. pure water. Higher numbers are increasingly *acidic*, lower ones *alkaline*. Used in testing casting-slips.

## PHASE DIAGRAMS

A diagram or graph showing changes in the physical state or composition of various mixtures of two materials at increasing temperatures. Shows *eutectics* and the degree of *vitrification* or glassy liquid likely to be present at a given temperature. The diagram for alumina and silica is important to potters, especially in the manufacture of refractories.

There follow two simplified diagrams based on McMurdie and Hall's Phase Diagrams for Ceramists (American Ceramic Soc. Inc. 1956).

1   Mixtures of potash and silica in the range between 60/40 and 10/90 $K_2O/SiO_2$, and between 700 and 1300°C. There are two eutectic mixtures at 55/45 and 33/67.

2   Mixtures of calcium feldspar (anorthite) and

silica. Here there is a eutectic at almost equal parts with solid solutions either side. It can be seen that additions of quartz or flint to anorthite feldspar will lower its melting point.

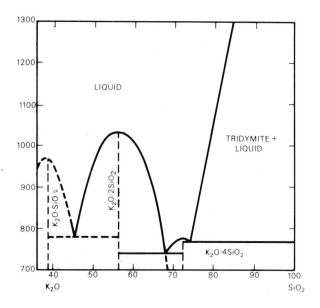

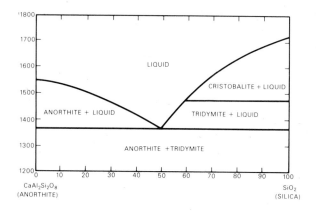

## PHASE, electrical

A line of electricity supply. (See *single phase, three phase.*)

## PHASES OF MATTER

Distinct physical states which include *states of matter* and also changes within solids and liquids. Thus alumina and silica compounds at high temperatures have phases where liquids are present within solids. Most phase changes occur at a definite temperature, but ceramic materials are very involved and the process is 'dynamic' or continuous with overlapping phases. One can discuss, for instance, 'glass phases' in a pottery body. (See also *phase diagrams.*)

## PHOSPHORUS

Element P, 31. Pentoxide $P_2O_5$, 173.

One of the glass-forming elements (i.e. high valency, 5, and low ionic radius, 0.35 A). Wood ash for example usually contains 2-5%. The element occurs only in the combined state: in ceramics the main source is bone-ash, $Ca_3(PO_4)_2$, calcium phosphate. Small amounts of calcium phosphate are considered a help in Chun glazes. It probably has a subtle effect on glazes (and on bone china body) which is not fully understood.

## PHOTO-ELECTRIC PYROMETER

A heat measuring device in which the light given off by a 'hot body' in a kiln is measured and transformed into an electric current which will operate a pointer on a dial. Similar to a photographic light-meter. Generally used for high temperatures.

## PIGMENT OXIDES

The various metals whose *oxides* provide *color* or *opacity* to glazes are dealt with in detail under their individual headings. Ordinary oil paints and other painting pigments will provide color in fired pottery only to the degree to which they contain these metals as all organic materials burn away.

Their number is few but there are many variations and combinations. It is somewhat misleading to give a tidy list of colors resulting from the use of the oxides. Cobalt, for instance, can confidently be quoted as providing a strong, stable blue, but it can also give viridian green with zinc, or even purple and red with magnesia under certain conditions.

It is well-known that a range of colors from red to blue can result from the use of iron, while copper can give apple-green, turquoise, purple, red, or copper lustre. The final hue, the result of the absorption of certain wavelengths from white light, is dependent on the material in which it is dissolved or suspended and on the particular oxide or compound which has been formed in the glass.

The fired color will bear little resemblance to the raw oxide unless it is undissolved in a glaze e.g. painted onto the biscuit when it will be largely unaltered from the unfired oxide. In this case copper and manganese, though of different qualities, will remain black, iron will lose its brightness but remain red-brown to black, and cobalt may develop a gray-blue.

The principal oxides are those of the metals:
1 The common coloring materials:
   copper, cobalt, chromium, manganese, iron, nickel antimony, and their variants such as ilmenite, ochre, rutile, etc.
2 The rare or precious metals:
   vanadium, cadmium, selenium, uranium, gold, silver, platinum.
3 The opacifiers:
   tin, zirconium, titanium, zinc.

To minimize the confusion when using oxides for painting, slightly different chemical forms can be used e.g. the *carbonates* of copper or cobalt which, at least, are distinguishable from manganese!

Some carbonates are poisonous. The prepared colors listed in suppliers' catalogs are *fritted* mixtures of oxides with other ceramic materials. Chrome is often included to give stability to the darker colors and in reaction with tin to give pink. Oxides are stained to give an approximation to their fired color. The hues listed may not be true for all glazes; they are not immune to the variations mentioned above.

*Temperature* is another factor in the quality of color. In general, the lowest temperatures produce the brightest colors, e.g. a bright red can be obtained from iron or chrome at below 900°C. It is also true, however, that cobalt in stoneware can be pretty lurid, as can high temperature reduced copper. Finally, the kiln atmosphere is crucial, whether *oxidizing* or *reducing*.

Reference books list theoretical maximum percentage proportions of pigments in glazes and slips. These are good guides to the relative coloring power of oxides but it is instructive to exceed the limits in test batches. In some cases, copper for instance, an excess will destroy the glaze surface, producing an ashy black, but very considerable proportions of iron or manganese can be used.

Some generally recommended maxima are: copper 3%, iron 12%, chromium 5%, nickel 3%, rutile 10%, ilmenite 5%, manganese 10%, iron chromate 3%, antimoniate of lead 5%, cobalt 2%, the opacifiers 10%. The impure and 'diluted' ochres, etc. can be as high as 25%.

There is no harm in trying combinations of any pigments. (See *color trials, line blends*, etc. R.CGP 138 and 206-7 gives useful lists of mixtures.) The colors mentioned, however, are those which are likely to develop in a 'neutral' glaze; the actual results may be different under your particular conditions. A few mixtures can generate *volatile* particles which will affect other glazes. Copper has this tendency (see also *chrome-tin pink*.) Dolomite and zinc glazes may produce a similar mushroom pink reaction in stoneware. (See also *color*, under the individual *element* headings, *painting on pottery, majolica, enamels, colored glazes*, etc.)

## PINCH POTS

Also known as Thumb pots. Pressing one's thumb into a ball of clay and squeezing it up into a hollow shape is the most instinctive and intimate way of handling clay. It is often presented to the beginner as the first and not very important step towards making 'real' pots, but this is to seriously underestimate the technique. Not only can one's fancy run free but, with practice, quite large thin-walled shapes with subtle organic qualities can be achieved. The technique is soothing and satisfying.

Simple pinched pots are especially suitable for sawdust, raku, and other primitive firings.

*Method:* As the clay will dry fairly rapidly during the process, moist plastic material should be used—

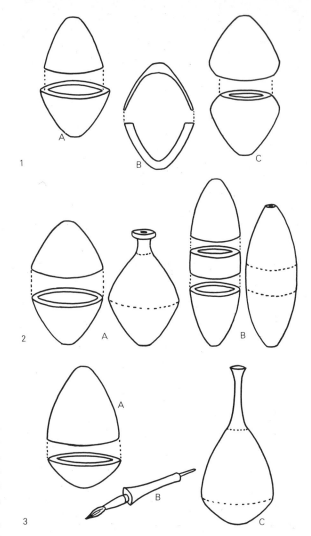

*Pinch pots. The first diagram shows three common faults which occur when pinching the parts of multiple pinch pots. In (A) the openings are of different sizes; the walls of (B) are uneven and the top half too thin to make an adequate join; (C) shows inward curving pots which are almost impossible to join together. The second diagram shows double pinch pots. In (A) an aperture can be cut after joining and shaping, and a neck modelled or coiled on. In type (B) a short cylinder or collar is inserted to give a taller form. The third diagram shows how, by varying the proportions of the parts, a high or low bellied form can be obtained. A tall neck can be formed round a paintbrush or other suitable rod and luted on to give a bottle form shape as (C).*

normally a red clay. Grog may be added but if used in excess the necessary plasticity is lost. If cracks appear on the surface smooth them over immediately. To make a single pot roll the clay into a ball, the rounder the better for a symmetrical shape. Hold in one palm and start to press the thumb of the hand centrally into the lump, turning with short movements as the thumb penetrates. When down to within ½ in. (10 mm.) of the base grip the pot between the thumb inside and the fingers outside and begin to squeeze the walls to an even thickness, revolving the pot about $\frac{1}{2}$ in. (10 mm.) between each pinch. Do not try to thin the wall haphazardly; keep up a steady and rhythmic series of movements. Work round and round in an ascending spiral towards the neck of the pot. If a shoulder is required on the finished shape, keep the mouth as small as possible.

When two pinched pots have been well joined together, the shape can be perfected by rolling the 'egg' on the bench as shown. This is done before cutting any aperture. The pressure must be gentle or the wall may split.

1

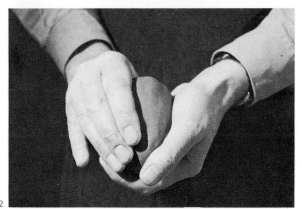

2

3

Pinching a pot from a ball of clay, showing the entry of the thumb (1), the grip in the palm which prevents excessive outward spread (2) and a similar grip when completing the shoulder of the pot (3).

A lively pinch pot in earthenware by Alex Watson. 'Fins' have been modeled onto the basic shape.

Do not stand the pot on its base while soft; rest it on its rim or in a suitable hollow support. To control the spread of the shape hold it sideways in the palm and squeeze slightly round the circumference after each 'pinch'.

The pinch-pot can be used as a unit or basis for future work. Examples are illustrated. Multiple pinch pots luted mouth to mouth, or with a 'collar' between, can be built up to quite respectable sizes. Oval balls of clay can be pinched into asymmetric forms. The finished pots can *be burnished*, or colored, slipped or glazed in the usual way.

For large bowls the initial pinching can be done with all the fingers inside the bowl, while a combination of pinching and stroking is used for the walls. See illus. under *handbuilt pots*.

## PINHOLING IN GLAZE

A particularly aggravating glaze fault, found most often in *viscous* stoneware glazes. According to most authorities, pinholes result from blisters or bubbling in a glaze which has not quite settled down. Recommended as precautions: a thinner glaze coating; a more fluid glaze; the avoidance of *over-firing;* a heat *soak* at melting temperature. Rhodes also mentions over-zealous *reduction* early in a firing as a contributory cause. Even 'perfectly' fired pieces, especially plates, can show pinholes. I have noticed that the holes are often quite deep, suggesting pits in the body over which the glaze refuses to flow, rather like paint over cracks in woodwork. In these cases they show no signs of a burst bubble. Clean clay and the careful smoothing of 'flatware' will help; you may well find the same glaze to be perfectly smooth on a vertical surface. Sulfur released from the clay (made very evident to the nose by some bodies) may also be a cause. Air trapped between particles of glaze powder is suggested by Dodd. Glaze which regularly pinholes is difficult to cure without adding more *flux* which will change its character. Try altering the body clay.

## PINT WEIGHT

The weight of solid matter in a slop glaze or slip. Usually quoted in oz.: 26-28 being the average for casting slips; 28-30 for glazes. (See *Brongiart's formula.*)

## PIPECLAY

A white clay of the type used for tobacco pipes. According to some authorities it was un-plastic and siliceous, but W.C describes it as plastic and fusible. Leach applies it to a wide range of marls and fireclay. The term was probably applied to any discovered pocket of white-firing, possibly *calcerous*, clay.

## PITCHER, pitchers

In the singular the word is applied to a large water *jug*. (In USA any jug e.g. cream pitcher.) In the plural it applies to broken pots, generally biscuit, which may be crushed and used for *grog*. Electrical porcelain factories grind glazed pitchers to add to the body. (See also *jug*.)

## PLACING

The setting of pots in a kiln (see *kiln packing*, etc.). *Wads* of clay are 'placed' between *saggars* for ventilation and stability.

*The method of placing a piece of pottery with more than one base or 'leg'. It should be set on a slab of the same clay as the body of the piece which, in turn, is set on a generous layer of sand or calcined alumina to allow it to shrink without splitting.*

## PLACING SAND

Fine white or 'silver' sand used for *setting* earthenware. May be used under large pots or multibased ceramics, providing tiny 'rollers' over which the piece can move as it shrinks. For most setting purposes, however, *alumina* is replacing sand.

## PLAGIOCLASE

A series of feldspars between albite and anorthite, i.e. with variable amounts of soda and lime as the base oxides. The mixtures occur because of the similarity in *ionic radius* of the atoms of soda and calcium. Although the series is continuous it is divided, for convenience, into half a dozen mineral types. These are listed in C.PP 47.

The two types of feldspar are considered to be 'melted' into one another (see *solid solutions.*)

## PLANE

A clay plane is similar to a woodworking plane but has a somewhat larger aperture in front of the cutter. Alternatively the Surform type can be used. Clay, particularly with grog, is highly abrasive and no metal edge will last long. If used with discretion the clay plane can be a valuable item of equipment, especially for the hand-builder.

*Using a Surform plane on a grogged surface.*

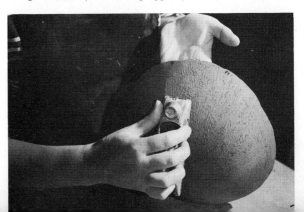

## PLASTER OF PARIS

A partially dehydrated gypsum known as a demi-hydrate ($CaSO_4.\frac{1}{2}H_2O$) which, when mixed with water, recombines to form a soft porous stone. It has the quality, partly by reason of a slight expansion during setting, of reproducing in great detail the shape and surface texture of any material or object onto which it is poured and allowed to set. It was known to the ancient Egyptians and to the Greeks but its name derives from the fact that the original modern material was prepared from deposits in the Montmartre district of Paris.

*Mixing plaster of paris. It is sprinkled into a bowl of water (1) until small islands stand above the surface (2), or the measured proportion of plaster is used up. Do not stir at all until all the plaster is in the water. Allow it to soak for a minute or so and then mix by swinging the hand to and fro beneath the surface of the mixture (3).*

1

2

3

Plaster-of-paris is made in various qualities, from a coarse, yellow-pink builders' plaster to a very fine-grain white 'dental' plaster. There is a special type supplied for pottery molds. The so-called 'dental' plaster is quick-setting and rather too close and hard for our purposes. Plaster of paris is prepared by roasting crushed gypsum in a revolving retort to 120°C. Commercial pottery of all kinds is formed in or on plaster molds, the shape being as much conditioned by the plaster as by the clay. Its main use in a school or pottery will be for non-circular dish molds, or in the form of slabs or bowls which will absorb moisture from very wet clays. Pieces of plaster in clay will cause it to split or bloat in the kiln. If it is heated to 150°C. or above it will become 'dead-burnt'—weak and powdery—so do not put molds to dry directly onto a hot kiln.

*Method* for mixing plaster. Once plaster has been stirred into water it is difficult to add more without forming lumps or even nodules of dry powder. Start, therefore, with up to half a bowl of water, as required, and sprinkle handfuls of plaster into it, without stirring, until the powder is heaped into 'islands' just above the surface. Leave these to soak for a few minutes and then stir vigorously, keeping the hand beneath the surface to avoid aeration. A proportion of $2\frac{1}{2}$-3 lb. to 2 pts. (1.25 kg. to 1 liter) of water will give about 80 cu. in. (1000 cu. cm.) of a reasonably hard mix.

Materials can be added to alter the performance during setting: lime added to the plaster will lessen expansion; dextrin, milk, vinegar, sodium carbonate, and size have been mentioned as setting retardants and/or hardeners; warm water, salt and alum can accelerate setting but may also aerate. Molds should not contain additional materials.

## PLASTIC

Capable of being easily molded. (See *plasticity.*)

## PLASTICITY

With reference to ceramic materials, especially clay, it is the property which permits the shape to be altered by pressure and yet retain the given shape when the pressure is removed. The 'yield point' of a clay will vary with the type and with the amount of water present.

The sheet structure of clay is a possible explanation of this behavior. Between each leaf or sheet of clay material (which is molecular thin) a layer of water will lubricate movement relative to one another, while the electrical attraction is sufficient to hold the leaves in place when not under pressure. This simplified view has not been definitely proved and the movement may be between larger particles. *Colloidal* gels from bacterial action have also been suggested as a contributory factor. Clay is unique in possessing true plasticity allied to dry strength. S.SCP illustrates the distinction between the flat plates of *kaolinite* and the curled or tube structure of *halloysite* which has otherwise similar constituents.

173

In common use the term is widened to include general workability, but excess plasticity can render a clay unworkable. The *bentonites (montmorillinites)* cannot be used alone and, like the *ball clays,* are valued for their very plastic nature but are used as additions to a body rather than as a working clay. Plasticity involves a high water content with fine grain and consequently high shrinkage and, frequently, *fusibility.*

Clays may be arranged, as a general rule, in the following order of increasing plasticity: *china clay, fireclay, stoneware clay, buff secondary clays, ball clays, red clays, montmorillinite clays.* (See also *thixotropy, aging, weathering,* etc.)

## PLASTICS

A series of synthetic resinous or other 'organic' polymerized substances shaped in a liquid state and allowed to set. Low melting point. (See *polythene.*)

## PLATES

Making hand-made plates creates problems of throwing, warping, 'humping', and uneconomical packing in the kiln. Therefore they are not widely produced. Some potters jigger and jolley their plates but this is tantamount to failure on the part of a craft potter. With practice, care and the use of large circular *throwing bats,* it is not difficult to make plates on the wheel. The illustrations show some of the stages.

After centering (by the *annular* method) the block of clay should be pressed down to a wide, shallow block before actual throwing starts. Leave plenty of clay for the rim which should be firm and well-defined. Avoid a ridge or hump just before the wall of the rim begins to rise, and also any suggestion of a dip in the middle. A slight rise is preferable towards the center—the cutting wire will tend to rise as the plate is cut off. Use

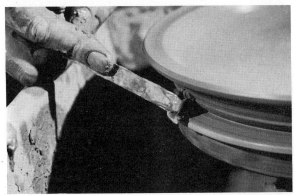

*Throwing plates. The first down and outwards pressure, using a sponge (1). The rim is formed, taking care not to make a depression just inside the rim (2 and 3). A kidney shaped tool is used to level the central area of the plate (4). Plates are most easily thrown on a circular bat and lifted off when somewhat stiffer. The angle between the base and the bat trimmed to a bevel with a turning tool prior to cutting off (5). (See under cutting-off for wire pattern under a plate, and Sindanyo for method of lifting bat.)*

the wire with the wheel turning very slowly. Trimming with a pointed tool close to the wheel head will help to keep the wire flat and low. Leave the plate on the bat until it is *soft-leather*. If adequately thrown it will need no turning but if a foot ring is turned leave a second ring nearer the center to support it. At the hard-leather stage, plates can be inverted to dry on their rims.

Ray Finch *once-fires* large plates to minimize *dunting*. In the biscuit fire the heat-retention of the kiln shelf can cause trouble and some potters biscuit their plates and flat dishes on clay pellets to allow air under them. I have not found this necessary when using shelves up to $\frac{1}{2}$ in. (12.5 mm.) thick. Plates may also be glazed in the well only and fired *boxed*.

*Plates can be left as cut from the bat, or turned as shown. The second inner ring helps to prevent sagging during firing.*

## PLATINUM

Used as the salt, platinic chloride, to obtain silver *enamel* for overglaze painting. Bought as a liquid pigment. Platinum and its alloy are used with rhodium in the *thermocouples* of high temperature *pyrometers*.

## PLUCKED WARE

Scars caused by glazed ware touching the kiln wall or supports etc. during firing. Very evident on old *salt-glazed* pots.

*Salt glazed ware is often plucked and this detail shows the scar where the bottle was in contact either with another pot or part of the kiln. The very thin glaze makes such marks visually acceptable and even a virtue.*

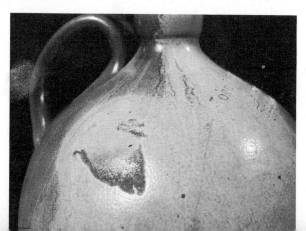

## PLUNGE POTS

A name given to the technique of making pots by pressing a batten of wood into a block of clay. The walls can be thinned by stroking and easing the clay upwards against the wooden former, or by slicing away surplus clay with a wire. Very direct and lively pots can be formed.

*Thrusting a roller into a block of clay to form a plunge pot (1). The clay is being eased along the roller to thin the wall and produce a taller pot (2). The wall is brought to reasonable thickness by cutting the faces with a wire (3). This cut can be a decorative feature.*

1

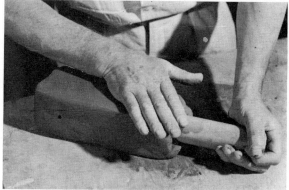

2

3

*A carved plunge pot by Leslie Pearson.*

## POISE

A unit of *viscosity*. Occasionally quoted when discussing glazes at the melting stage. The viscosity of water at 20°C. is 0.010 poise; molten glass varies widely, of course, but its viscosity is at least 5000 times as great.

## POLISHING CLAY

The actual application of furniture or other polish to pots after firing can have undesirable effects, especially if the pot is wetted. Use sparingly, if at all, on burnished pots.

The Elers brothers were reputed to have polished their red stonewares on a lapidary's wheel. Some faults in glazed ware can be polished using an electric drill and a very fine abrasive. (See *burnishing.*)

## POLYTHENE

A synthetic material (the polymerization of $C_2H_4$, if it interests you!), useful, cheap, and at once a bane and a blessing to potters. Because it is chemically inert it is suitable for glaze and slip containers, while in its sheet form it has eased the potter's problem of keeping pots moist, doing away with the rotting rags and the usually inefficient *damp-cupboard,* not to mention the rusting biscuit tins. On the other hand it has, more than any other material, been responsible for the rapid decline, almost to the point of extinction, of the traditional country potter throughout the world.

## PORCELAIN BODY

In China the definition of porcelain (T'zu) is wider than is generally accepted in the West; it could be any fine, pale body of primary clay with a distinctive ring when struck, fired to *vitirfication* but often too thick to show the *translucency* which we expect today. Essentially porcelain is kaolin and silica with a little *flux,* fired to vitrification point. This is 'true' or hard-paste porcelain and requires a high temperature in the region of 1350°C. An increase or multiplication of the bases (or of the acids, boron or fluorine) can lower the melting point and it is possible that the Eastern kilns averaged no more than 1270°-1300°C.

Richard Parkinson asserts that 1360°C. is needed fully to develop the 'felted mass of mullite needles bonded in a glassy cement' by which he defines true porcelain, and that the lower temperature mixtures such as David Leach's 1270°C. body, give a white stoneware. To a degree, this is a matter of words and preferences. Certainly the bentonite porcelains lack the white purity of the harder types and one must learn to counter what Harry Davis calls their 'evil properties', but they throw pleasantly and thinly up to 9 in. (22 cm.) high or so. It can also be used for pinching, but the joins tend to show in slab pots. The color is better in reduction.

The basic recipe for porcelain is: 50% kaolin (china clay), 25% feldspar, 25% flint or quartz. It is wise to leave the feldspar at 25% although this may be replaced in small part by nepheline: silica can be reduced to a 15% minimum. This leaves the clay. English kaolins lack plasticity, limiting the development of porcelains in England and frightening off studio potters. By swapping a proportion of kaolin for ball clay the throwing qualities are improved but the translucency diminished. Rhodes suggests up to 15% ball clay. 2-5% 'white' bentonite will make a body throwable but will increase shrinkage and impurities. Bentonite will also greatly increase *thixotropy,* apparently stiff or even leather-hard clay may soften suddenly and alarmingly under pressure or when turning. Practice can overcome the dangers here. More serious is the tendency to warp in drying and firing.

Mixing the body needs to be thorough for complete fusion of the particles. Parkinson recommends a 300 screen (lawn). For many potters, however, the simple compounding of already finely ground materials, followed by efficient hand kneading and a week or so of 'resting', will suffice. (See *clay preparation*.)

Two recipes: David Leach.

| | |
|---|---|
| Grollegg china clay powder | 53 |
| Potash feldspar | 25 |
| Water-ground quartz | 17 |
| White bentonite | 5 |

Firing to translucency 1260-1280°C. Substitute some quartz for china clay if *crazing* is persistently encountered.

Parkinson (published in CR.3)

| | |
|---|---|
| EEC JM china clay | 51 |
| Potash feldspar | 18 |
| EEC BB ball clay | 7 |
| Fine (300 mesh) quartz | 24 |

Firing 1320-70°C.

A traditional commercial earthenware body, fired to 1280°C. or more, can also be used. This yields a low translucency 'proto-porcelain'. (See also *electrical porcelain*.) There are also dolomite porcelains. The English porcelain equivalent is bone *china*. Bernard Leach's recipe given in PQ 1 is near to the 'earthenware' body type: china clay 25, black ball clay 33, feldspar 30, quartz 12.

*A porcelain hand-built pot covered with a partly-washed ash glaze, by Sheila Fournier.*

## PORCELAIN GLAZES

Hard paste porcelain glazes have a very high silica equivalent. Parmelee quotes 7.0 $SiO_2$ with bases $0.3K_2O/0.7CaO$, for 1320°C. and even as much as 12.0 with $0.5K_2O/0.5CaO$ for a high-gloss glaze at the same temperature. These very nearly correspond to the Seger cone formulas. The alumina equivalents in the above examples are 0.8 and 1.3 respectively. At the other extreme, the low temperature bodies (1270°C.) may have glazes with as low as 2.0 parts silica. This proportion has been found in analyses of Chinese glazes, and also features in a formula given by Victor Margrie in CR 2 for a barium semi-matt glaze:

$$\begin{array}{lll} K_2O\ 0.32 & & \\ BaO\ 0.34 & Al_2O_3\ \ 0.4 & \begin{array}{l} SiO_2\ \ 2.0 \\ SnO_2\ \ 0.1 \end{array} \\ CaO\ 0.34 & & \end{array}$$

This has been translated into raw materials by Wengers Ltd. (see CR4 which also contains other recipes):

| | |
|---|---|
| Potash feldspar | 58.1 |
| Barium carbonate | 22.0 |
| Whiting | 11.1 |
| Alumina hydrate | 4.1 |
| Tin oxide | 4.7 |

Feldspar is the principal mineral in most porcelain glaze recipes. It will melt into a viscous glaze at cone 10 and over, and so needs only the modification of additional alumina, usually as china clay, with perhaps the diversification of the fluxes with lime or zinc. Magnesium can give a milky quality and a slightly subdued surface. Glazes for the lower-fired porcelains can be similar to those for stoneware.

One glaze for David Leach's body has been quoted as:

| | |
|---|---|
| Feldspar | 12 |
| Dolomite | 12 |
| Quartz | 22 |
| China clay | 14 |
| Ball clay | 9 |
| Petalite | 28 |
| Bentonite | 3 |

My standard white stoneware glaze works quite well, although it may craze.

| | |
|---|---|
| Feldspar | 40 |
| Nepheline | 20 |
| Whiting | 15 |
| China clay | 10 |
| Talc | 10 |
| Flint | 5 |

## POROSITY

Used by potters in a general way to indicate both water *absorption* and *permeability*. Defined as the proportion of pores, both open and sealed, compared with the total volume, and normally refers to the fired body of a ceramic. The open, connected pores allow water to seep into and through a pot; the closed pores simply increase heat insulation (and marginally decrease strength). Earthenware biscuit is porous and must be covered with an unfractured (uncrazed) glaze in order to be rendered watertight. Porosity declines as molten materials fill the pores i.e. with an increase in *vitrification*. There is no sudden change from one state to the other; stonewares are porous to a small degree. An increase in *fluxes*, such as a little red clay, will aid vitrification.

A rough test for porosity is to weigh a dry pot, immerse it in water for twelve hours and re-weigh; the difference being the weight of water absorbed.

## POT, potting

A vessel, generally rounded, for holding liquids or solids. The development of *'ceramic sculpture'* has led to a blurring of the definition but if a hollow fired clay shape has any sort of hole near the top it may be considered to be a 'pot'. The word is also used as an adjective in place of 'pottery' and as a verb 'to pot' i.e. to make pottery.

## POTASH

The common term for potassium oxide, as in 'lead-lime-potash glaze' etc.

## POTASSIUM, oxide, compounds

A metallic element K, 39.
Oxide $K_2O$, 94. Potash
Carbonate $K_2CO_3$, 138. Pearl ash

A base, strongly *alkaline*, and a powerful *flux* in glazes and bodies. Both the oxide and carbonate are *deliquescent* and *soluble* and can be used only in a *fritted* form. There are a number of 'natural' fritts (minerals) containing potash, including: orthoclase fledspar, wood ash, nepheline syenite, china stone, and to a smaller degree, many other vitrifiable materials, e.g. clay. Potassium is frequently associated with sodium, so much so that the *RO* for some minerals may be written KNaO indicating a variable mixture.

Potash occurs in all but the simplest glazes and at all temperatures. Equivalents vary between 0.1 and 0.5 of the RO group. Its effect on the coloring oxides is more 'neutral' than soda or zinc.

## POT GAUGE

A tool used to assist in the repetition throwing of pieces of a similar size and shape. It consists of one movable arm which is set with its point just clear of the rim of the pot, or with two arms the second of which indicates the widest point of the circumference.

In its simplest form the pot gauge can be merely a stick set in a wedge of clay; this is all that most of the old country potters would have used. Two modifications of the jointed arm type now in use by craft potters are recommended: a stiff rubber end to the pointer, and a means of swiveling the whole gauge to one side so that it does not inhibit *centering*. It is brought into position again when the pot is well under way. (See also *card measure*.)

The simplest form of pot gauge, a rod stuck into a wedge of clay.

1

2

A more sophisticated form of pot gauge (1), each arm adjustable in length and vertical movement, and with a rubber end. The disadvantage is that the arms can inhibit centering and it may be knocked out of true. If the whole thing can be swung aside (2) it can remain set but be out of the way. The use of a single screw in the base allows this movement.

## POTSHERD

A broken piece of pottery. (See *pitchers.*)

## POTTERY

Fired clay objects. The term is narrower in its application than ceramics and may be used for the less sophisticated types of earthenware or, sometimes, for hand-made ceramics in general. As its root 'pot' suggests, it is applied mainly to containers, though these may be asymmetric and purely decorative. May be used as an adjective as in 'pottery modeling' i.e. modeling carried out by means of recognized pottery techniques such as coiling.

## POWER WHEEL

A potter's wheel driven by a motor. The simplest system for transmitting the power of an electric motor to a wheel head is where a rubber or leather leather drive is brought into contact with the flywheel of a traditional kick wheel by foot pressure, springing back when the foot is removed. In a sophisticated version in general use in England, the drive wheel can be moved to any position from the center to the circumference of the flywheel, thereby controlling the speed of the wheel head.

In the typical industrial wheel the speed is modified by two slightly convex cones which can be swiveled on their axes relative to one another. Other systems are: the expanding pulley, and the variable speed motor.

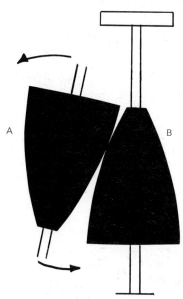

*The double cone principle of transmitting power and varying the speed of a power wheel. The left hand cone is driven from a shaft or motor and so mounted that it will swing in the direction of the arrows whilst remaining in contact with the second cone, to the shaft of which the wheel head is attached. As the comparative diameters in contact vary, an infinitely graduated speed is transmitted to cone (B) from the fixed speed of cone (A). In the diagram position the speed of (B) would be near its maximum.*

The latter is now available without any great loss of torque at lower speeds and is thus likely to supersede other methods which are generally noisier and lose power through friction. At the present state of development the motor has a high-pitched whine which some potters may find unacceptable. The average commercial wheel limits the thrower to about 10 lb. (5 kg.) of clay. It is important to try various wheels before purchasing: if the potter and his wheel are not in 'sympathy' it is difficult to do good work.

*A simple drive from a motor via a leather wheel to the perimeter of the large flywheel of a traditional Mediterranean kick-wheel.*

## PRASEODYMIUM, oxides

A metallic element Pr, 141.
Oxides $Pr_2O_3$, 330; PrO, 157.

One of the 'rare earths' or 'lanthanides' group. Fulham Pottery quote a zircon/praseodymium yellow for use up to 1280°C. Considered to be a more stable yellow than *vanadium*.

## PRESSED DISHES

Dishes formed by pressing sheets of clay into molds. (See also *dishes.*)

*Making a pressed dish. The clay slab is cut to the approximate shape of the mold (1), carefully lifted, supported with the hand as shown (2) and dropped into a hollow mold. The worst of the surplus clay is cut away (3) before sponging the slab snugly into the curve of the mold with gentle strokes from the centre towards the perimeter (4). The edge is trimmed flat in two stages, the first (5) holding the wooden spatula tool at a slight upward angle (use the outer edge of the mold as a guide) and cutting with sweeping movements away from the center of the dish in order to avoid parting the clay from the mold. The final cut (6) is made with the tool held parallel to the top face of the mold. A final smoothing of sharp corners (7) and the dish is left to dry a little. Cover with a board and invert mold and board together. The mold can then be lifted away (8) and the outer edge of the dish sponged or planed (9).*

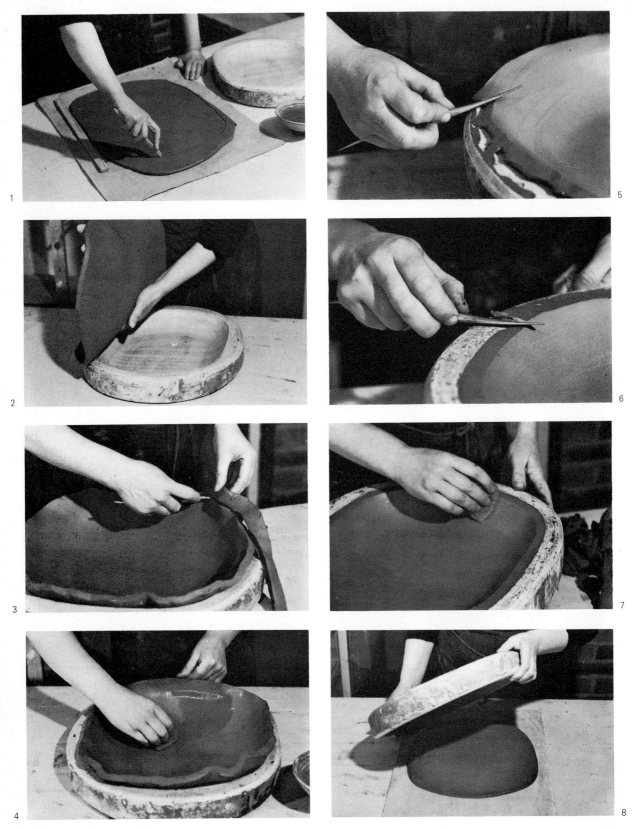

fireclay. Rigorously extracted by the industry, but the dark, slightly ashy spots which they develop on a reduced glaze are considered decorative by many craft potters. There are also tin pyrites and cobalt pyrites (smaltite).

## PYROLUSITE

An ore of manganese dioxide.

## PYROMETER

A device for measuring high temperatures, as distinct from low temperature mercury thermometers. The commonest type consists of two parts. Fused, silica or *silliminite* tube containing wires of dissimilar metals, the thermocouple. For high temperatures the wires must be made of platinum alloys. and are therefore expensive; for soft glazes they may be of base metals, chromium, nickel, etc. It follows that you must not use a pyrometer for firings above those specified by the manufacturers. When the tube is inserted into the kiln a minute current of electricity is set up, proportional to the temperature. This is measured on the second part of the instrument, a galvanometer or a potentiometer, and transmitted to a dial calibrated in degrees of temperature.

The pyrometer will, of course, measure only temperature and not *heat-work*. Its main value is in indicating intermediate stages of firing: for the 'end point' *pyrometric* cones are very reliable. Pyrometers are very delicate instruments and are not infrequently damaged in transit or by other means. The calibration can be inaccurate and it is wise to check against cones. However, once the difference between a reading and a cone indication has been established it can usually be applied over the whole scale. Instruments are made with automatic switch-off or 'soak' mechanisms; these can be very useful but do not trust them absolutely. The electronic devices are reputed to be more reliable than the motorized ones.

Other forms of heat-gauging devices are the photo-electric pyrometer and the *optical* or disappearing filament type. The latter has the advantage of portability. The pyrometer is a useful but by no means essential aid to firing and if economy is necessary there are more valuable tools on which to spend money. (See also at *thermocouple*.)

## PYROMETRIC CONES

Head indicators in the form of sticks or elongated pyramids of ceramic materials which deform at a given temperature. (See *cones, Orton cones, Holdcroft bars*.)

## PYROMETRIC CONE EQUIVALENT

Often written P.C.E. The measurement of *refractoriness* of a clay or ceramic material obtained by firing a test of the material with *cones*. The cone number nearest the softening temperature of the test is the P.C.E. of that material.
*Example:* a high duty fireclay (USA) has a P.C.E. of 33; cone 33 melts at 1730°C.

## PYROPHYLLITE

A clay-family substance with the formula $Al_2O_3.4SiO_2.H_2O$. Used in some bodies and naturally present in many clays.

## PYROPLASTIC DEFORMATION

Long words to describe the warping or bending of ceramics as they 'soften' at high temperatures. Applied especially to the bending of *kiln shelves* under load.

*A case of extreme pyroplastic deformation from the same kiln as illustrated under over-firing.*

## PYROSCOPE

A general term for heat-work recorders which operate by change of size or shape. (See *cones, Buller's rings, Holdcroft bars*.)

# Q

## QUADRIVALENT

A valency of 4, as silica, tin etc. Oxides reading $RO_2$. The *acidic* oxides.

## QUARTZ

A natural crystalline silica, $SiO_2$. Occurs as visible crystals (rock crystal) or as silica sand, quartzite or *ganister*, and in most clays.

Ground quartz is allegedly purer than flint and is preferred by many potters although the difference is difficult to detect in the fired body or glaze. Fused quartz is very resistant to chemical change and has a low *thermal expansion;* it is used for crucibles, etc.

## QUARTZ INVERSION

A volume change in the crystal of silica due to a 'straightening out' during heating into a state of greater symmetry of the $SiO_4$ lattice. It occurs instantaneously at 573°C—the increase in size being given variously at between 0.45 and 1% linear expansion. On cooling the crystals revert to their previous squeezed or deformed state at the same temperature with a corresponding contraction. These changes are in addition to the normal coefficient of expansion of silica.

If the silica is heated beyond 1050°C. it begins to change into cristobalite which has its own inversion at a lower temperature. The forms of crystal are known as alpha (sub 573°C.) and beta quartz (above 570°C.). Flint is, of course, also affected in the same way. The inversion occurs only in 'free' silica and not in silicates (glasses) or in altered silica; cristobalite, tridymite, mullite etc. which behave in different ways. More than about 25% of silica as crystals in a cooling body can shatter it, but smaller additions can give the contraction necessary to put a glaze into compression (see *crazing*). The inversion of flint is said to be less abrupt and taxing than that of quartz, because of its microcrystalline structure. The failure of a kiln at around the inversion point can lead to severe shattering of pottery.

## QUARTZITE

A *metamorphic* rock, formed from quartz sandstone cemented by silica.

## QUICKLIME

The unstable form of burnt limestone. (See *lime.*)

# R

## R

There is no element with the symbol R and so the letter is useful to denote any appropriate element of an oxide, as in the *Seger formula* $RO.R_2O_3.RO_2$.

## RADIATION, heat

The heat given off by a 'hot body'. *Electric elements* give radiant heat. In a fuel burning kiln, most of the work is done by hot gases, but radiation from the walls and from pot to pot plays an increasing role as the peak temperature is reached, levelling out the heat through the setting. This is one of the chief values of *soaking.*

## RAKU

A low temperature earthenware technique involving a very rapid glaze firing cycle, the pots being placed into and removed from a red-hot kiln. The ware may or may not be *reduced.*

It was raku that brought Bernard Leach into ceramics. Its Japanese symbol means 'enjoyment'— a 'conscious return to the direct and primitive treatment of clay' (Leach). Eastern raku was usually oxidized, often painted, and air cooled. Modern western techniques have developed along the lines of sawdust reduction and quenching in water.

Raku may be made in any style but the typical piece is fairly thick, asymmetric in form and hand-built. The often remarkable richness of color and surface obtained from plain or painted glazes, and the contrast with the gray or black of the body in reduction, can be weakened rather than enhanced by excessive texturing or modeling of the clay. See color plate 18, p. 141.

The symbol for raku firing.

The reduction (often, more correctly, *carbonization*) is achieved by covering the pot when it is still red-hot with sawdust, peat or leaves. Variation will result from partial immersion. The firing chamber or saggar should be kept free of coke or fuel. Wally Keeler (CR 1) states that, whatever the kiln atmosphere, pots will oxidize on removal. This has not been my experience: if coke falls into a saggar it is very difficult to get an oxidized glaze out of it. In Japan the system is sometimes reversed: the pots are carbonized in random patterns by biscuit firing in an open trough with charcoal dropped amongst them. The smoked pots are then covered with a clear glaze and cooled in air.

*Method:* the body must be open and *grogged* but need not be coarse-textured. Buff clay is usual but red clay and mixtures can be tried. The pots are normally biscuit fired to about 900-1000°C. in an ordinary kiln. Pots could be biscuited in the raku kiln, packing before firing starts, but this limits the pieces available for glazing; there should be sufficient available for a firing every twenty minutes or so for two or three hours. Once the kiln has reached cone 016 (Staffordshire) or 750-800°C., the lid or front is removed and completely dry, glazed pots which have previously stood on the kiln to get warm are quickly placed in the chamber with long tongs. They are loosely packed to allow for expansion but may be laid directly on one another. An inspection after about twenty minutes will show whether the glazes are shiny and fluid, and if this is the case, the pots are removed one by one with tongs and either laid in sawdust or plunged directly into water (use a metal not a plastic bowl!). After a few moments the reduced (sawdust) pieces are also transferred to the water. When cool the glazes will need scrubbing with a nail brush to reveal their surfaces. The muffle is re-packed as soon as one batch has been removed and the cycle recommences. See the film 'Raku English style' for a complete raku session in detail.

1

2

*A very direct method of making a dish for raku firing. The hollow is carved out of a block with a hoop turning tool, (1). The Japanese raku dish (2) shows gouge marks suggesting that it may have been made in a similar fashion.*

## RAKU GLAZES AND PIGMENTS

Almost any glaze which will melt below 900°C. is suitable for raku. L.PB lists some recipes using white lead. Low temperature *fritts*, e.g. the *lead silicates*, can be mixed with a little clay to provide some alumina (5-15% clay). Other fritts are complete in themselves (Harrison Mayer have a good list) and include borax and high-alkali types. 2-4% of bentonite will assist

*suspension* and glaze coating. These glazes will *crystallize* after a few weeks and it is advisable to dry them out after use. Alkaline (soda) fritts develop exciting glaze colors especially from copper.

Any coloring oxides can be used. 2% each of $CoO$, $MnO_2$, $Fe_2O_3$ for black. 5% of tin will opacify and can produce a mother-of-pearl sheen in reduction. Always glaze reasonably thickly. Areas or strips of un-glazed body will give an attractive contrast but should not be overdone. Enamels and gold can be used for painting, in addition to the ordinary oxide pigments, and can contrast with the rough clay in a stimulating way.

Some typical raku recipes:

| | | | | | |
|---|---|---|---|---|---|
| 1 | Red or white lead | 55 | 2 | Lead sesquisilicate | 50 |
| | Clay or china clay | 6 | | Soft borax fritt | 50 |
| | Flint | 33 | | China clay | 2 |
| | Soft borax fritt | 6 | | Bentonite | 2 |
| 3 | Soft alkaline fritt | 93 | 4 | A simple and unusual | |
| | China clay | 4 | | recipe from CM 15/10 | |
| | Bentonite | 3 | | Gerstley Borate | |
| | Copper oxide | 3 | | (colemanite) | 80 |
| | (for turquoise) | | | Feldspar | 20 |

Special raku pigments can be made up for:
blue: a lead fritt, flint, and cobalt.
white: alkaline fritt with china clay, and zircon or tin oxide.
iron-red: equal parts fritt and white lead with 0.5 red iron oxide and 10 parts of yellow ochre (fire as low as possible).
green: equal part of fritt, white lead, and copper oxide.
yellow: lead fritt with 3:1 ferric and antimony.

## RAKU KILNS

A raku kiln must satisfy the following conditions: it must reach 800°C. and maintain that temperature for several hours; the chamber or muffle must be readily accessible and easily opened and closed with the kiln at full temperature; reasonably oxidizing conditions must prevail. There must be no danger (e.g. from shock in an electric kiln) when inserting metal tongs into the chamber.

One of the most popular and easily built is the *brazier kiln*. The Japanese type kiln, illustrated in R.K, R.RAT, and L.PB resembles the Roman kiln, a long firemouth feeding into a circular chamber via a perforated hearth. Flame throwers, oil burners, ace-tylene burners, etc. have all been utilized by modern western potters. Wood and coke fuels are commonly used. Electric raku poses problems. Firstly the kiln must be absolutely protected from damp or rain, but the pots must be reduced in the open if everybody is not to be choked and blackened; secondly the elements must be completely shrouded from any possible contact with the tongs; thirdly a complete *muffle* within the kiln is essential. CR 1 describes one type and the illustration overleaf shows another. In P.Q 36, John Chalke has advice and a series of drawings for raku kilns. R.RAT gives kiln types very full coverage.

A special muffle or saggar for a top loading kiln to enable it to be used without danger for raku firing. The refractory box, built of slabs and coils (1). The wide rim or flange round the top holds the walls about 1½ in. (35 mm.) from the kiln elements. The box is in position and the lid is shown (2). The idea could be adapted to an upright kiln. Under no conditions should tongs be put into a kiln with unguarded elements.

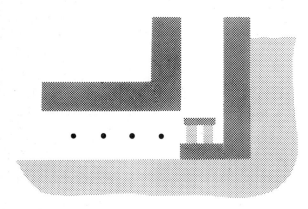

A diagrammatic section through a simple raku or other low-fired ware kiln, set in a bank. The black dots represent firebars on which logs of wood are burned. The pots are set on the shelf which is built up on brick columns.

## RARE EARTHS

Actually these are neither very rare nor 'earths' (they are true metals); they are the elements numbers 57-71 in the *periodic table*. A few are coming into use in ceramics, though mainly as prepared pigments. Praseodymium yellow will fire to 1300°C. Others are used in optical glasses but may well become available to craft potters.

## RASORITE

Listed in Ferro catalogue as $B_2O_3$ 66.3, $Na_2O$ 30.0 i.e. a form of borax.

## RATIONAL FORMULA, analysis

The description of a material in terms of its *oxides* in a *formula,* or its *minerals* in an *analysis*. From a rational formula one can associate the mineral with the *Seger formula* to arrive at some idea of its reaction in the fire. A rational or 'calculated' analysis will list the probable minerals present, and is used for rocks and clays. C.PP Appendix 10 gives the method for arriving at a calculated analysis from an 'ultimate' or oxide one. Shaw considers rational formulas to be of little value to craft potters but the information helps to build up an overall picture of the material.

## RAW CLAY

Green clay; unfired clay.

## RAW GLAZE

A glaze in which none of the constituents are fritted. In the active sense, 'raw glazing' is often confusingly applied to *once-fired* ware, where the term raw-clay glazing is more accurate.

## RECIPE

A list of materials, with proportional physical weights, which make up a specific slip, glaze, body, or color. Distinct from the *formula* which is expressed in theoretical atomic or *molecular parts*. *Percentage weights* are preferable to batches for comparing one weight with another.

Beginners in pottery are often hopeful that a good glaze recipe will solve their problems. However the recipe is only one (albeit a prime one) of the variables which affect the fired glaze. Others include the particular samples of raw materials used and the speed of firing.

Trials and alterations may be necessary to arrive at a mixture which will suit your unique conditions. Some knowledge of the principles on which the recipe is based will prove invaluable: the first step towards preparing your own individual glazes. (See *chemistry of pottery, glaze.*)

## RECIPE-INTO-FORMULA

A recipe will give some idea of the possible behavior of a glaze but the *Seger formula* will be more instructive and may be compared with those of known glazes.

The chart used for the computation is the reverse of

## RECIPE-INTO-FORMULA—Chart A (Reverse of formula-into-recipe, Chart A)

| % | Material | Parts | ÷ Mol. wt. | = Mol. parts | PbO | $Al_2O_3$ | $SiO_2$ |
|---|---|---|---|---|---|---|---|
| 50.2 | Litharge | 50.2 | ÷ 223 | = 0.225 | 0.225 | | |
| 17.4 | China clay | 17.4 | ÷ 258 | = 0.0675 | | 0.0675 | 0.1350 |
| 32.4 | Flint | 32.4 | ÷ 60 | = 0.540 | | | 0.540 |
| 100.0 | | | TOTALS | | 0.225 | 0.0675 | 0.675 |
| | Molecular equivalents | | | | 1.0 | 0.3 | 3.0 |

## RECIPE-INTO-FORMULA—Chart B (Reverse of formula-into-recipe, Chart B)

| % | Material | Parts | ÷ Mol. wt. | = Mol. parts | PbO | $Al_2O_3$ | $SiO_2$ |
|---|---|---|---|---|---|---|---|
| 70.5 | Lead sesqui-silicate | 70.5 | ÷ 313 | = 0.225 | 0.225 | | 0.377 |
| 17.4 | China clay | 17.4 | ÷ 258 | = 0.0675 | | 0.0675 | 0.135 |
| 12.1 | Flint | 12.1 | ÷ 60 | = 0.202 | | | 0.202 |
| 100.0 | | 100.0 | TOTALS | | 0.225 | 0.0675 | 0.674 |
| | Molecular equivalents | | | | 1.0 | 0.3 | 3.0 |

## RECIPE-INTO-FORMULA—Chart C (Reverse of formula-into-recipe, Chart C)

| % | Material | Parts | ÷ Mol. wt. = | Mol. parts | $K_2O$ | CaO | MgO | $Al_2O_3$ | $SiO_2$ | $TiO_2$ |
|---|---|---|---|---|---|---|---|---|---|---|
| 48.47 | Feldspar | 48.47 | ÷ 556 = | 0.087 | 0.087 | | | 0.087 | 0.522 | |
| 14.53 | Whiting | 14.53 | ÷ 100 = | 0.145 | | 0.145 | | | | |
| 5.34 | Dolomite | 5.34 | ÷ 184 = | 0.029 | | 0.029 | 0.029 | | | |
| 1.5 | China clay | 1.5 | ÷ 258 = | 0.006 | | | | 0.006 | 0.012 | |
| 25.52 | Quartz | 25.52 | ÷ 60 = | 0.425 | | | | | 0.425 | |
| 4.64 | Titania | 4.64 | ÷ 80 = | 0.058 | | | | | | 0.058 |
| 100.0 | | 100.0 | TOTALS | | 0.087 | 0.174 | 0.029 | 0.093 | 0.959 | 0.058 |
| | Molecular equivalents | | | | 0.3 | 0.5 | 0.1 | 0.32 | 3.3 | 0.2 |

that used in *formula-into-recipe* and, for simplicity, the formulas used are the 'ideal' ones. The results are therefore approximate. Greater accuracy would demand an analysis of your particular samples, and would involve much more arithmetic although the principle still holds good. There are several variations on the system. See also C.PP Appendix 10.

In the first column we list the recipe figures followed by the mineral or oxide they represent. This figure is then divided by the *molecular* (or unit) *weight* of the material; the resultant figure representing the unity figure in the formula, the alumina in clay for instance, or the potash in feldspar. This figure is entered in the appropriate column and multiplied in the others according to the formula ratio, e.g. clay, 1 alumina to 2 silica; feldspar, 1 alumina to 1 potash to 6 silica.

In the illustrative charts the examples dealt with under *formula-into-recipe* are reversed.

To bring the figures to the Seger formula:

1 Total the bases.
2 Divide each of the totals in the base line by this figure.
3 Arrange as $RO.R_2O_3.RO_2$.

## RECORDS, workshop

Some records, such as the total sales of work produced, are required by law and you will also need proof of expenditure to set against income from sales (see *costing*.) The extent of your additional records depend on your temperament and style of work. Kiln logs are useful and can save worry and spoilt firings. Tests and trials of materials and glazes will be a waste of time without adequate records. One's memory is fallible and one doubts it most when the unexpected occurs.

It is not practicable to record all the factors which influence a result but the mere note of recipe and temperature is not quite enough. The following data will enable a fair appraisal to be made:

1 A test number for identification; a running number with or without a prefix. Codes are apt to get muddled or forgotten.
2 Percentage recipe and the amount actually weighed. The batch can be divided into fluid measures to facilitate future additions, line blends etc.
3 Type of test piece—cylinder, tile etc. and whether fired flat or upright.
4 Body color and texture.
5 Glaze thickness; a vital factor in the appearance of the glaze.
6 Position in kiln.
7 Kiln and firing as *kiln log*.

For the recording of clay tests see under *clay testing*. Briefly the record should be of: plasticity and workability; soluble materials; shrinkage; raw and fired colors; absorption; deformation and faults and the behavior of glaze on sample. Other useful records can be kept of weights of clay for reproduction items, with their size and shape. (See *card measure*.)

## RED CLAY

An iron-bearing *secondary clay*. Includes brick clays. Although called 'red' clay its fired color is brown or terracotta. It is present in vast quantities and a great variety of qualities all over the earth's surface.

A potter needs a plastic but not sticky clay, fairly smooth and with a shrinkage within 12% plastic-to-fired. It should contain negligible 'free' impurities such as lime fragments and soluble alkalis.

The fine particle size adds to the plasticity but also lowers the *fluxing* temperature, and red clays are normally used only for earthenwares, notably slip-wares. In England the Etruria marls are well-known high-iron clays some of which, from the Staffordshire region, will stand up to 1260°C. in an oxidizing fire without serious trouble. They are vitrified and 'self-

glazed' at this temperature. In *reduction* red clays will generally fail or melt.

Red clay may be added to other clays, and also to glazes to provide iron in an ultra-fine form. In stoneware glaze it also provides valuable fluxes, and up to 50% can be used. 'Slip-glazes' are high-clay glazes or are composed mainly of very fusible clays such as *Albany clay*. Local red clays may be useful as pigments.

## RED COLORS AND GLAZES

Reduced copper reds are the only true reds available to the studio potter at 1100°C. or over. Various red glazes appear in merchants' catalogs for lower temperature firing under careful conditions up to about 1050°C. Most are opaque.

Selenium is a comparatively new oxide and with cadmium will give orange and red but the compound is difficult to stabilize and is subject to *volatilization*. Research is improving the performance of these fritts. Chromium oxide at around 900°C. in a high-lead low-alumina glaze will produce red. A possible recipe: white lead 66%, china clay 10%, flint 21%, soda ash 3%, with 3% chrome or 5% potassium bichromate. Until recently uranium has been unobtainable but is now appearing again as 'spent' uranium. It is a source of orange-reds up to 1020°C. A *chrome-tin* reaction will give pinks, as will zircon-iron compounds at higher stoneware temperatures (Dodd).

Iron reds rely on undissolved crystals of $Fe_2O_3$ which are difficult to maintain in the fired glaze. Cardew recommends a pure nepheline in the batch (C.PP 145) with a high-alumina, low-calcium formula. Rhodes reverses this advice. In Cardew's type however the color is from an undissolved suspension within the glaze, while the latter is derived from precipitated surface crystals. The glazes need applying fairly thickly. Formulas quoted (C.PP) include:

$$K_2O \quad 0.8 \quad Al_2O_3 \quad 1.17$$
$$Na_2O \quad 0.2 \quad Fe_2O_3 \quad 0.05 \quad SiO_2 \quad 5.35$$

Difficult to transform into a recipe. The use of an alkaline fritt may help.

A recipe suggested by Peter Smith, and which approaches the formula is:

| | |
|---|---|
| Nepheline | 42% |
| Potash feldspar | 35% |
| Fremington red clay | 20% |
| China clay | 3% |

Another recipe for iron red appeared in PQ 37/20 (John Reeve). The calcium content controls the ability of the glaze to dissolve the iron oxide.

Soaking and slow cooling to 1000°C. are reputed to help. The aesthetic attraction of a bright red on craft ceramics is open to doubt even if it becomes easily available. Of course it is always possible to use *enamels* which exhibit a very fine range of reds. Geoffrey Whiting has produced a persimmon red at 1200°C. in an electric kiln by varying the temperature rise, a method known to the Japanese as 'fire change'. Details have not been published. Titanium is reputed to enhance the redness of iron in very fluid glazes.

## RED LEAD

Lead peroxide $Pb_3O_4$, 685 (equivalent weight 228). Also known as 'minium'. Poisonous. A strong flux in a glaze. Although forbidden in schools or potteries where assistants are employed, it can still be used by the studio potter. Traditional slipware glazes use red lead and it figures in several raku glaze recipes.

## RED PIGMENTS

Similar considerations apply to red pigments as to red glazes: they are plentiful in the enamel range and below 1000°C. Underglaze reds include the ubiquitous *chrome-tin*, sometimes with vanadium. Above 1050°C. most compounds revert to brown.

## RED SLIP, body

Like red clay this is brown rather than red and is normally a simple liquid red clay. Lighter colored slips and bodies can be stained with iron oxides or with prepared body *stains*, often iron-based, to give red-browns, pinks, and 'coral' up to as high as 1280°C. (Harrison Mayer). These are more suitable for industrial pottery and need a very white body to develop their color.

## REDUCTION

The extraction of *oxygen atoms* from *oxides*. The most startling color changes in reduction are those of the iron and copper oxides. More subtle alterations take place in other oxides, in the glaze quality and in bodies. The reduced oxides are usually unstable and will revert to their 'higher' oxide unless protected from the air by dispersal in a glaze. Precipitated iron will re-oxidize (see *kaki*, and *red glazes*).

Reduction is generally considered to be the result of starving the fuel of oxygen during the firing, creating *carbon monoxide* and *hydrocarbon gases*. CO is a very poisonous gas and kiln rooms should be well ventilated. David Ketteridge (CR 12) mentions reduction by hydrogen as it forms water with oxygen 'stolen' from the glaze oxides, e.g. $2Fe_2O_3 + 3H_2 = 4Fe + 3H_2O$, or elemental carbon by a simple equation yielding the metal and CO. This contradicts several accepted theories including that of the negative role of smoke. Searle in PQ 8 lists CO, H, coal gas, incompletely burned oil and finely divided carbon in luminous flames as the chief reducing agents. The wide variety of results from 'reduction' suggests that more consideration should be given to the fundamental chemistry. The $CO/CO_2$ and the $H_2/H_2O$ ratios control the degree of reduction (together with elemental carbon) and it is possible to measure the atmosphere with instruments placed in the chimney flues.

The reduction in a kiln is normally sufficient to produce the lower oxide, FeO, only. Copper oxide, however, can be reduced to the metal. The moisture given off by burning fuel helps to develop celadons. It has been noticed that a humid day is better for reduction than a dry one.

Reducing atmospheres are built up by the adjustment of *primary* and *secondary* air controls, judicious use of the *damper*, and sometimes the extraction of chimney bricks to cut down the draft. Reduction started before 800°C. may stain the glaze gray or black which subsequent firing will fail to burn away. During reduction the fuel is inadequately burned and the temperature may fall; reducing periods are therefore interspersed with clear-fire conditions. With wood or coal firing, each stoking tends to set up reducing conditions willy-nilly. Alternatively a semi-reducing atmosphere can be maintained from about 1000°C., so long as the temperature can be steadily increased.

Other cycles have been recommended: Ray Finch reduces for 55 minutes of every hour from 1000-1240°C. but not sufficiently fiercely to prevent a steady rise in heat, then continuously until the peak temperature is reached, soaking for half an hour in *oxidation*. Some potters maintain a neutral atmosphere from 1050°C. with a reduction at the end; or give half-an-hour of reduction at 1000, 1100 and 1200°C. Shaw mentions reduction starting at top temperature and continuing during cooling to 800°C.

The weather has its effect. I have found that a still, bright fine day is more conducive to success than a dull or windy one. It does not seem to matter whether or not one 'cleans' the kiln at the close with an oxidizing fire. When a kiln is reducing, flame may appear at cracks and spy holes wherever the gases come into contact with free oxygen. Any sign of 'escape' should be ignited to reduce the danger from carbon monoxide. Beware gas burners 'blowing back' into the pipes: turn off and re-light if this happens.

Glazes can be reduced in a neutral atmosphere, e.g. in an electric kiln, by means of local reducing agents incorporated into the glaze batch itself. Soot, charcoal, animal charcoal, and silicon carbide can be used, the last mentioned being the least effective. A fairly viscous glaze is needed to prevent re-oxidation. The more fluid the glaze the more reducing agent is needed. The amount will vary with the kiln as well as the glaze and experiments should be made with additions of between 10% and 20% to the batch. Copper and iron will respond to this type of reduction (Peter Smith).

*Kiln furniture* will be affected by reduction and it is advisable to check with the manufacturers that it is suitable. Cast props are very vulnerable. Shelves need to be thicker: $\frac{3}{4}$ in. (18 mm.) for alumina or silliminite bats, slightly less for silicon carbide. Obviously a *refractory* body must be used for pots, often a ball clay strengthened with fireclay, china clay, and flint. Few red clays will stand up and all are more liable to fail during reduction than in oxidation. A proportion of red clay—usually about 5% though this varies widely— can aid vitrification and warm the body color, a darker body often giving improved glaze color. In glazes the red ferric iron is most commonly used: 2% or less for celadons; up to 12% for other effects (see *red glazes, temmoku, kaki*). Red clay, black iron oxide, crocus martis, ochres, and other forms of iron have also been used with good results. Reduced iron may be the spinel

$FeO.Fe_2O_3$ (the formula for 'magnetic' iron).

Reduction is a skill which can be learned only with practice in your particular kiln. A kiln log is essential. In an electric kiln reduction is usually a trial activity only, although the development of *silicon carbide elements* widens the scope. Porcelain has responded to small sticks of wood about 5 in. (30 mm.) long and $\frac{1}{4}$ in. (5 mm.) square inserted into the lower spyhole during the last half hour of firing, giving a gentle greeny-buff color to a $1\frac{1}{2}$% iron glaze at 1270°C. *Kanthal* wire will stand occasional reduction without damage.

Copper reduction will take place at lower temperatures than iron: 600-800°C. for producing copper-red *enamels* and *lustres*. It may be taken to the extreme of producing the metal by the same method as on-glaze painting and in *raku* firings. One-half % of copper, or less, is added to a glaze for high temperature reds. See *copper red*. Cobalt is not altered; manganese may produce a gray, or green.

Peter Smith has kindly made available the following recipes for reduction glazes in a neutral atmosphere.

| | | |
|---|---|---|
| Feldspar | 72 | |
| Whiting | 13 | |
| China clay | 7 | A green matt |
| Flint | 8 | tableware glaze. |
| Calcium phosphate | 5 (bone ash) | |
| Charcoal | 8% of total | |
| Ferric iron | 3% of total | |

Use animal charcoal if available as it contains calcium phosphate. This recipe gives a celadon type glaze without the calcium phosphate.

| | | |
|---|---|---|
| Fremington red clay | 28.2 | |
| Cornish stone | 28.2 | A viscous celadon |
| Whiting | 21.1 | type glaze. |
| Flint | 7 | |
| Ball clay | 14.1 | |
| Ochre | 1.4 | |

plus 10% of charcoal, coal-dust, or graphite.

The above glaze is viscous but can be made shiny by the addition of 10% flint or quartz. The reducing agent should then be increased by 5-10%.

Add extra iron for temmoku.

## RE-FIRING

A second glaze firing for faulty ware is seldom successful. The glaze may change its whole character on re-fire, only very occasionally for the good. In all cases it is advisable to re-coat the pot with glaze, or to rub it well into crawling etc. Use a thick glaze mixture, and warm the pot before re-dipping. Repeated re-firing will destroy the fabric of a pot.

## REFRACTORIES

Heat-resisting materials used in those parts of the kiln which must stand high temperature and reduction without deforming or spoiling: bricks, tiles, shelves, supports, saggars, etc. The term is most often applied to the bricks.

High grade fireclays, high alumina bodies, and silicon carbide are some common materials. Special types are made from chrome ore, etc. The official rating of a refractory is a P.C.E. of 18 or above. Ciment Fondu is a refractory cement for use up to 1320°C. Some refractories are also designed to insulate—the lightweight bricks used in electric kilns for instance—others such as silicon carbide shelves to conduct heat.

Study of the alumina-silica *eutectic* will show why high alumina refractories are preferred. Even though a material whose make-up approaches the eutectic is way above our working temperatures, a certain degree of *pyroplastic* movement is always likely because of small amounts of impurities which lower the melting point. Refractories need a long soaking fire to develop a mat of *mullite* needles throughout the fabric. (See also *bricks, fireclay,* etc.)

## REFRACTORY MATERIALS

Applied to oxides or minerals which are heat-resistant in their own right or which tend to raise the firing temperature of a glaze. The *acidic* oxides are considered refractory, especially silica, tin oxide, titania, chrome, zirconia and antimony. Zinc and boron have ambiguous positions. Alumina in molecular proportions greater than 1-8 compared with silica has a refractory effect. Lime has a very high melting point (2615°C.) but acts as a base in high temperature glazes. Barium has a similar role.

## REGENERATIVE PRINCIPLE

In kiln design: the use of heat given off by cooling ware to pre-heat other chambers. The *climbing kiln* is very efficient in utilizing heat. A regenerative brick kiln is illustrated in R.K 53.

## REPAIRING POTTERY

For broken pots the most commonly used glue is Araldite. Equal amounts from two tubes are mixed on a wooden surface with a wooden tool. As the glue takes several hours to harden, some method must be found to hold the join tight together meanwhile. Adhesive tape, string, clamps, and rough 'molds' are possible depending on the size and shape of the piece. If several breaks are involved it is better to do the job in two or more stages.

Wash, dry, and dust any loose pieces from the break before sticking. When the join comes together make absolutely certain that the faces are flush with one another; run your finger gently along the join to feel for any step. The glue must be used thinly and care should be taken not to let it set on the surface. Contact glues are less satisfactory as there is no second chance once the pieces are pressed together.

A good join will scarcely show but if the surface is broken then it will need filling with Polyfilla or something similar. The colors can be matched in water paint and touched in. For glazed ware the join can be

## ROULETTE

A tool for producing a repeat decorative impressed pattern. The technique is of great antiquity. A roulette is an engraved wheel or cylinder which, when rolled over clay, produces the pattern. It was much used by Roman potters. 'The edges of old English ovenware dishes were notched by this means' (Leach). In the film 'Isaac Button, country potter', Isaac Button is seen impressing the name of his pottery as a continuous band round flower-pots. Ladi Kwali rolled a carved roulette round the shoulder of her pots, combining it with free pattern (see also the film 'Ladi Kwali').

The most readily available roulette 'blank' is a piece of blackboard chalk, which can easily be carved with a simple pattern. Biscuit rollers can be mounted onto a wire handle or onto a forked twig with a piece of thick wire. Roulette wheels can be shaped for concave and convex surfaces.

*An engraved stick of chalk used as a roulette: rolled over a clay surface to produce a repeat pattern.*

*A large roulette wheel with a full address both advertises the Pottery and decorates the pot.*

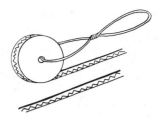

*Roulette. An impression of a simple roulette wheel which could be of pottery, plaster, or wood, and mounted on a wire or other form of axle so that it can be rolled over clay to impress a repeated pattern or motif.*

## RUN SLIP

One of the slipware techniques. The *slip* is trailed in blots around one edge of a dish or on the shoulder of a pot, usually on a wet base-slip of a contrasting color. A shake will run the blots across the dish or down the sides of a pot, giving pleasant, liquid shapes. In a bowl, a sideways twist can give variety. Some practice is required and the shaking should be restrained. The comparative consistencies of the background and trailed slip will directly influence the resulting pattern.

*Run slip on a dish. The leather-hard dish is flooded with slip and immediately trailed round one edge with a contrasting color (1). The dish is held vertically and the lines given two or three sharp downward shakes (2). A completed dish (3); John Shelley. The side of a pot bowl can be similarly treated. Triangular dishes are especially suitable.*

1

2

3

## RUTILE

One of the crystalline forms of titania. To a chemist rutile is synonymous with titania, $TiO_2$, but to a potter it indicates the impure iron-bearing ore of titanium, an accessory mineral of *igneous rocks*. Also occurs as ilmenite beach sands, $FeTiO_3$.

The distinctive mottled appearance of rutile in borax glazes has led to its use ad nauseam on commercial tiles, etc. The titanium content will opacify a glaze. Small amounts (1-3%) of rutile are useful in modifying other pigments in earthenware and stoneware glazes. In reduction, rutile may give a blue glaze.

# S

## SADDLE

An item of *kiln furniture*. A bar of *refractory* material used to support tiles, etc. during firing. In section it is a concave triangle. Supplied in sizes 1-11 in. (25-280 mm.) long by $\frac{3}{16}$-$\frac{3}{4}$ in. (10-20 mm.) across.

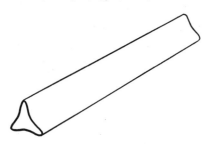

*A saddle. Used to support tiles, etc. in the kiln.*

## SAGGAR

A clay box in which pottery is fired to protect the ware from flame and ash. Used in larger kilns as the unit of a bung. The box is made of well consolidated refractory clay with up to 50% graded grog. It can be coiled, slab built round a drum, formed on the wheel using soft clay and a rib, or by a combination of thumping and

throwing. Industrial saggars may also be jolleyed or slip-cast. Wall thickness averages $\frac{3}{4}$ in. (20 mm.). Saggars may be oval, circular, oblong, or square (but always with rounded corners). The industrial norm is a 17 x 23 in. (420 x 575 mm.) oval but they come in all sizes and thickness of wall. For some purposes they have holes in the sides. With the coming of cleaner fuels, smaller kilns, and 'continuous' firing the use of the saggar has declined sharply and it is becoming difficult to purchase them.

## SAGGAR CLAY

A *refractory* mixture of clay and grog, the latter may be in proportions of 50% or more. The inclusion of grog from broken used saggars is useful. The 'dust' should be removed from the grog. The clay content is generally fireclay but the inclusion of some vitrifiable clay will set up a liquid phase which will help the growth of *mullite* crystals. *Silliminite* is a useful addition. Up to a point saggars will get stronger with firing. Cardew discusses the problems involved in making saggars in C.PP 158-60.

## SAIRSET

A commercial name for an *air-setting* kiln *cement* or mortar for jointing bricks or facing walls. Available from A.P. Green Refractories.

## SALT

Common salt is sodium chloride, NaCl, a colorless, *soluble, crystalline* substance. It is believed to assist glaze *suspension* but its main use in ceramics is in the production of *salt glaze*. The re-crystallization of salt in cruets can cause trouble: a *crazed* earthenware glaze will allow dissolved salt to permeate the body and it may lift the glaze away.

A chemical salt is a compound: the reaction of an *acid* with a *base*, e.g. sodium sulfate, barium chloride, etc. A glaze may be considered as a salt, or as a salt into which additional material is dissolved. Salts are, in general, more stable than their separate constituents.

## SALT GLAZE

Stoneware ceramics, generally once-fired, with a glaze achieved by throwing common salt or rock salt onto the hot fuel at 1200°C. and upwards. The NaCl decomposes into chlorine gas and sodium, the latter reacting with the silica of the clay to form a thin, slightly orange-peel textured glaze which is very hard and resistant to corrosion. Developed in Germany, it went out of favor for tableware around 1760, its use since confined mainly to cheap jars, bottles, and drainage materials. Several craftsmen potters are now reviving the technique, which produces a very integrated and interestingly variable finish.

A *siliceous* clay or a wash of silica slip has been recommended, although alumina is also needed. More complete glazes, or *ash*, can be applied, the salt being used as an additional flux. Borax additions will produce a thicker and more lustrous glaze but at the

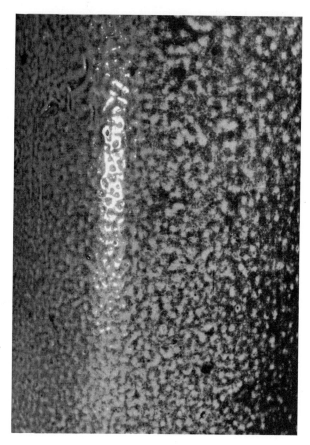

The typical orange-peel texture and varied color of a salt glaze surface.

Three salt glazed bottles by Wally Keeler.

expense of the typical texture. Carbonates of copper, etc. thrown onto the fire have been reported to produce psychedelic color!

The flashed and uneven color of salt glaze is very suitable for creative work. The Wren family have developed small coke and gas kilns to produce excellent salt glaze. Hamada has used the technique for several years. Once a kiln has been used for salt glaze it cannot be used for *feldspathic* glaze firing, as the deposited salt will be released on to other glazes. All *lid* flanges etc. should be washed with pure alumina or silica to minimize sticking. Be generous with alumina on shelves, tops of props, etc. The technique is hard on refractories but high-alumina shelves, etc. stay reasonably free from glaze. Firebrick takes a thick coat. Nevertheless the Wrens have fired their gas kiln for salt glaze some 90 times without serious damage. Rosemary Wren recommends slightly damp salt (table-salt, rock salt, or 'water-softener' salt) at 1 lb. to every 3 cu. ft. (50 kg. to 1 cu. m.) of kiln space, applied in three doses, starting at the highest temperature. The temperature will drop after salting. Bowls will glaze all over but mugs and bottles may need a thin wash of a suitable glaze inside.

### SALTPETRE

Sodium nitrate $NaNO_3$. Soluble and normally used only in *fritts*.

### SAMPLING

Natural materials may vary slightly throughout a batch. A true sample must be made up from small amounts taken from various parts of a batch. A lengthier system is to divide the batch into four, discarding two parts and remixing the rest, continuing the process until only a sample amount remains. (C.PP).

### SAND

Coarse particles of rock: generally impure silica. 'Sand-size' is given as 0.065-2.0 mm. Some sands contain heavy mineral impurities such as zircon, rutile, ilmenite.

The use of a pure silica sand as a *placing* material has largely given way to alumina. The grain shape varies and some sands are much more rounded than others. Some potters prefer smooth granules but sharper types are more likely to increase standing strength. Its addition to bodies will give 'bite' to throwing clays; will assist drying (though not as efficiently as grog); and decrease shrinkage. However it introduces *'free' silica* which may give trouble at the inversion point if used in large quantities. Builder's sand is supplied in 'sharp' and 'soft' qualities, the former being washed sand. The impurities in builder's sand can add interest to a body. Beach sands are variable and will need washing to remove salt, etc.; river sands are preferable. Zircon sand has been recommended for *saggars*, *refractories*, and for *ovenware*. Sand additions can lead to pitted glazes especially in oxidized stoneware.

### SAND SIZE

Given as 0.65-2.0 mm. Rocks or minerals must be broken at least to sand size before grinding in a mill or mortar.

## SANDSTONE

A rock of silica (quartz or sand) particles cemented with clay, lime, and iron oxides. White clays may be found in association with sandstone.

## SATIN GLAZE

A semi-matt glaze—usually with zinc, tin, and titanium —listed by many merchants.

## SATURATED GLAZE

A glaze with the maximum color content which it is capable of dissolving. Liquids can hold more material in *solution* at high temperatures than at lower ones: some metal or oxide may therefore be precipitated onto the surface of the glaze during cooling. Pigment/ glaze ratio varies with the oxide and, to a lesser extent, with the glaze formula. 3% of copper in a lead glaze can produce a black metallic matt but it will still be shiny with 10% and more of manganese oxide. Some stoneware glazes can dissolve as much as 25% MnO. In general, the more fluid the glaze the more color in solution it will accommodate.

A list of 'saturation points' is therefore misleading but as a comparative guide the following list may be useful. Average for *soft* clear *glazes,* color in solution:

    2% cobalt
 2.5% copper
    4% nickel
    6% chrome
    8% lead antimoniate
 10% iron
 10% manganese

Some types of *kaki* are examples of a super-saturated glaze where the surplus iron has been precipitated onto the surface, to *re-oxidize* on cooling.

## SAUCER

Its design must always be considered in relation to the cup which is to be set on it. Saucers tend to flatten during firing and should be thrown with a slightly generous curve or lift. The foot ring is placed outside the line of the 'well' both for stability and strength. Saucers are thrown either as short cylinders, the walls of which are then thrown outwards to the desired shape, or as a plate is thrown, the edge being shaped from a ring of clay after the well is formed. The well must be flat or slightly dipped or the cup may spin. One can finish the well at the turning stage. Saucers can be turned with a foot ring but this is time-consuming and they are often left as cut from the wheel, merely trimming the outer corner to a bevel.

## SAWDUST FIRING

The firing of pots in slow-burning sawdust is fun but as an educational exercise may be misleading. The heat generated is not often sufficient to turn clay into ceramic and the pots will disintegrate in water. A low initial biscuit fire will rectify this and the sawdust treatment will then be a mainly decorative one, subtle graduations of color resulting from *reduction* and *carbonization.* With practice and care, a measure of control can be exercised. In our so-called temperate climate the sun is rarely hot enough to avoid the all too common mishap of *dunting* as the piece is exposed during the firing. An *open* body helps but also increases the difficulties of *burnishing.* A rounded form with a sturdy rim is most likely to survive. The inclusion of sand or other silicas is not recommended, the firing always hovering round the *inversion* point.

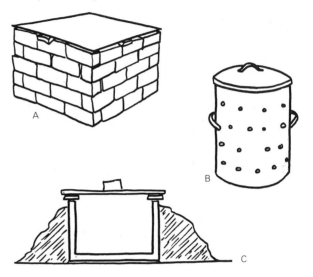

*Three types of sawdust kiln. (A): simple dry-built brick box with a sheet metal cover raised slightly on shards or brickbats. Burns efficiently and the draft can be controlled but pots are liable to dunt. (B): a dustbin perforated to allow air for combustion. This type can also be used for more controlled bonfire firing. (C): saggar or brick box insulated with soil. The lid is propped up as in (A).*

*Method.* A brick box is dry-built, usually about an 18 in. (450 mm.) cube. Ventilation holes can be left between bricks but these increase the incidence of dunting. In some designs earth is banked round the kiln for insulation or a dustbin is pierced with holes and used instead of a brick box. Galvanized metal may give off poisonous fumes when heated and should be avoided. Whatever type of kiln is used, an outer baffle wall or windbreak is useful. An easily removable and fireproof cover must be provided, set on three or four pieces of brick to allow air to enter. The box is filled with alternate layers of dry sawdust and pots until full, finishing with 3-5 in. (80-130 mm.) of sawdust. It is ignited from the top and burns downwards; a sprinkling of paraffin (kerosene) on top will facilitate lighting. There is little point in 'topping up' with sawdust and if this is done there is the slight danger that the sawdust, given sufficient air, may ignite with a mildly explosive force. As the sawdust burns down pots will be exposed and settle down onto those beneath. Put the strongest ones at the bottom. As mentioned above, success is most likely on a hot, still day.

*A pinched and coiled pot, burnished and fired in sawdust, by Sheila Fournier.*

### SCALES, weights

The most useful weighing balance for the small potter is a ½ oz.-2 lb. (15-1000 gm.) 'sweetshop' scales. A 15 lb. (7 kg.) set is also useful for weighing clay and larger glaze batches. The cheaper spring balances are rarely accurate enough, but dial scales working on a counterweight principle can be adequate for throwing clay lumps. Good quality 'beam' scales are suitable for 10 lb. (5 kg.). There is also a torsion balance with dial reading which is reputed to be very sensitive from 0.1 gm. to 2 kg., but with the disadvantage of being expensive (£75 or more).

Gram weights are sold in sets from ½ gm. to 1 kg., graded in such a way that all weights between can be measured. The set is 1 x 1 kg., 1 x 500 gm., 2 x 200 gm., 1 x 100 gm., 1 x 50 gm., 1 x 25 gm., 2 x 10 gm., 1 x 5 gm., 2 x 2 gm., 1 x 1 gm., 1 x ½ gm.

### SCEWBACK

A sloping-faced brick (see *springer*).

### SCRAPER

The ordinary triangular paint scraper with the sharp corners filed away provides the best scraper for cleaning tables, etc. A cook's rectangular plastic scraper is also excellent and is less likely to damage polythene bins etc. The steel palette can also be brought into use and is the best tool for shaping and finishing *hand-built* pots. (See illus. under *hand-building*, *former*.)

### SCREEN

A wire mesh or perforated plate for sieving materials. The term is often applied to the coarser meshes. (See also *lawn, sieve, silk screen, vibratory sieve*).

### SCUMMING OF CLAY

A white efflorescence which can mar the surface of fired terracotta. It is due to soluble basic salts, often calcium sulfate, being brought to the surface while working on the drying clay. It is almost impossible to remove. If a salt-free clay cannot be found, the addition of 1-2% of barium carbonate will help. This however is a toxic material. Barium sulfide (barytes) can also be used. (See *efflorescence*.)

### SEAL, stamp

All potters, whether amateur or professional, should have their own stamp with which to identify their pots. A seal is usually about ½ in. (10 mm.) across and must be simple in design—initials, a monogram, or a cipher. More information (the name of the pottery for instance) can be shown on a *roulette* seal.

The design may be either in relief or recessed (intaglio). The former is useful for pots that have become rather dry but the latter is more impressive. If you have a steady hand the seal can be cut directly into leatherhard clay; otherwise it is cut into a wood or *plaster* block from which casts can be taken. One can paint or scratch one's signature straight onto the pot—these are 'marks' rather than seals. A stamp pressed onto a little pellet of clay gives a raised seal which is attractive and can be a decorative item of decoration on a plain pot. It also minimizes the risk of pushing the stamp right through a thin pot wall.

*A seal with a raised monogram (1) as distinct from the intaglio type which gives the impressions in (2).*

1

2

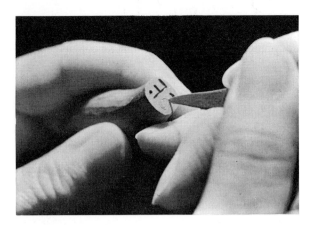

*Cutting a seal directly into leather-hard clay.*

*A seal used as an item of decoration on a box.*

## SEAT EARTH

The material immediately beneath a coal seam—often *fireclay*. 'The seat earth for vegetation' (W.C).

## SECONDARY AIR

The air supply allowed into the kiln to assist the *combustion* of the fuel beyond the actual source of the flame, i.e. to *oxidize* any unburned carbon or gases given off by the fuel. Manipulation of secondary air can control kiln atmosphere. Secondary air will be more efficient if it is pre-heated. Kiln design should take this into account, directing it through a hot zone before it enters the chamber.

## SECONDARY CLAY

A clay which has been transported from the site of its formation by water, wind, or glacial action. The clay is thus ground and *levigated* to a fine particle size which increases its plasticity but, inevitably, it picks up impurities in the process. Some may be very pure (e.g. English ball clays) but most are fusible and fire to a *terracotta* color. In some cases (*fireclays* for example) the impurities have been leached out again later, the clays becoming more refractory.

## SECONDS

Given by Dodd as 'pottery ware with small not readily noticeable blemishes', a definition which some potters would be advised to study. (See also *lump*.)

## SEDIMENTARY CLAYS

Sometimes confused with primary clay, these are very variable in character and origin. The common factor is that they have been deposited in depressions in the earth's crust (lake basins, etc.) and most of them have been formed by the decomposition of feldspar. They are weathered clays often containing *micas*, hydrated iron oxide, lime, *'free' silica*, etc. English *ball clays* probably have their origin in a *primary clay* which has been washed away and re-deposited as a fine-grain but reasonably iron-free material.

## SEDIMENTATION

Although all solid particles will eventually settle in a liquid in which they have been suspended, the heavier and larger ones will settle first. Thus the finer particles carried by rivers tend to travel the furthest, finally coming to rest in estuaries or lake basins, forming reasonably pure clay beds. Sedimentation is used to separate heavier minerals from lighter, e.g. mica from china clay. (See also *levigation*.)

## SEGER CONE

A *pyroscopic* device in the form of an elongated pyramid of ceramic material graded and numbered to 'squat' at a given temperature. The mixtures represent a logical series of steps originated by Hermann Seger, a nineteenth century German ceramic chemist. (See *Seger formula*.) Modifications have been made for the lower temperatures but the principle on which the series is based still holds.

The RO group is made up of 0.3 $K_2O$. 0.7 CaO, while the alumina is kept at one-tenth of the equivalent of the silica. A No. 6 cone is: RO. $0.6R_2O_3$. $6.0RO_2$; a No. 9 in the ratio 1: 0.9: 9.0. The silica ratio will be seen to be higher than that used in stoneware glazes but some porcelain glazes have similar formulas. (See *cones*.)

## SEGER FORMULA

Originated by the German chemist Seger a century ago, this is still the standard procedure for representing a glaze formula. The system lists oxides as comparative molecular equivalents in three groups: *basic*, *amphoteric*, and *acidic*, written $RO.R_2O_3.RO_2$, R denoting any appropriate element. The RO group also includes $R_2O$ oxides, e.g. potash and the sum of all the basic oxides is taken as unity—1.0 equivalent. In this way the other constituents can be directly and immediately compared. The $R_2O_3$ is represented by alumina; ferric iron may also be included. When we come to the acid group certain ambiguities creep in. The principal acid and the foundation of all ceramics, $SiO_2$ fulfils the role, as do $TiO_2$, $SnO_2$, etc. but boric acid, antimony, and others have amphoteric type formulas: ($B_2O_3$

etc.) and are still listed with silica. The symbol $RO_2$ is therefore not to be taken literally but as including all the *glass-formers*.

The placing of $B_2O_3$ continues to be questioned since it acts more like a *base* or flux and falsifies the silica proportion (see *leadless glazes, glaze formula*, and under the oxides of individual elements.)

## SEGER RULES

Hermann Seger's rules for dealing with *crazing* and *peeling* of glaze.

For crazing adjust body thus:
1 Decrease clay content
2 Increase flint
3 Replace some clay with kaolin
4 Raise biscuit fire
5 Decrease feldspar

(Nos. 1 and 5 refer more specifically to industrial bodies.)

For crazing adjust glaze thus:
1 Increase silica base ratio
2 Replace some $SiO_2$ with $B_2O_3$
3 Replace high molecular weight bases with low weight ones.

For peeling, reverse these adjustments.

## SELENIUM

A non-metallic element Se, 79. 'Resembling sulfur in its chemical properties . . . ; occurs as selenides of metals' (U.DS). A 'metalloid'.

Used in combination with cadmium, as sulfides, to produce low temperature orange and red glazes and enamels. Quick cooling helps to retain color. Normally only available as a complete fritted glaze. A quoted fritt is:

soda-ash 15.0, nitre 2.0, cryolite 6.0, fluorspar 14, borax 29.0, sand 34.0, with 3% selenium.

At the present time the maximum firing temperature of selenium reds is around 1040°C. (See *red, glazes*.)

## SEMI-MUFFLE

A muffle in a kiln which does not completely protect the ware. In effect a double *bag wall*. (See *muffle*.)

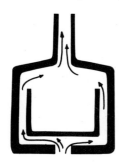

*A semi-muffle kiln. The example shown is an up-draft type but it can also be adapted to a down-draft kiln. The gas kiln photographed under that heading is a semi-muffle down-draft, the half walls acting like bag walls.*

## SEMI-PORCELAIN

According to the Brussels Nomenclature it has: 'The commercial appearance of porcelain without being really opaque like earthenware or truly translucent like porcelain. These products may be slightly translucent in the thinner parts such as the bottoms of cups (and) . . . can be distinguished . . . because the fracture is rough grained, dull, and non-vitrified . . . a fracture clings to the tongue'. Some studio porcelains come into this category.

## SERIES WIRING

A number of conductors wired one to another. This reduces the voltage to each one and the total resistance will be the sum of all the conductors in the circuit. Thus two similar lamps in series will reduce the power by a factor of the square of half the voltage—in other words you will get a very dim light! The various kiln elements in a circuit are wired in series and so must be calculated as if they were one unbroken length, but the various circuits are wound in parallel. Series/parallel switching is used for slow/medium/fast kiln controls.

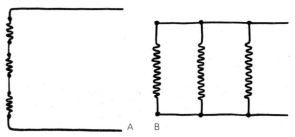

*(A) three conductors connected in series.*
*(B) the same equipment wired in parallel.*

## SETTERS

Supporting refractories for pots during firing which closely follow the contours of the ware. Dishes can set in sand or alumina (as *bone china* biscuit).

Tile setters are thin, flat shelves sometimes called 'cranks'.

## SETTING, density

A *kiln* pack, including *shelves* and *furniture*.

Setting density will influence kiln behavior, a full kiln generally firing better than a half empty one (see *radiation*). However, problems of heat transfer can arise from too solid a pack, of very close tiles for instance. The professional potter will arrange his work with the kiln setting in mind so that the space can be fully utilized, yet allowing for variety. (See *packing kilns*.) Setting density can be recorded in terms of weight (see C.PP), number of pieces or market value, or at least in general terms ('very full', 'loose pack' etc.) which will be some help in assessing *kiln graphs*.

## SETTLING OF GLAZES

The settling of solid material in slips and glazes, often to form a hard cake on the bottom of the container, is a perennial headache for the potter. *Fritts* are especially prone to settling. Attempts to stir up a hard, settled glaze are often a hopeless task and the only way to deal with it effectively is to pour off all the liquid. The cake of glaze will then usually come away quite cleanly and can be cut and broken up with the hands and reworked little by little into the liquid.

The suspension of glazes depends on several factors (see *suspension, suspender*).

## S.G.

Abbreviation for *specific gravity*.

## SGRAFFITO, sgrafiato

Decoration in which slip or other coating is scratched or cut away to reveal the clay body beneath. A variety of tools can be used: the fingers for very wet slip (also called 'finger combing'), a stiff brush, a knife, or more traditionally, with a bamboo or cane tool cut to a flat end resembling a very broad pen nib. The condition and thickness of the slip at the time the design is cut will also affect the result. Glaze and pigment, as well as slips, will respond to sgraffito treatment: glaze should be applied in a broad and simple way, while pigment can be worked with finer lines that can slip.

*The typical sgraffito cut in soft leather clay. The chisel-ended cane tool is also shown.*

*A simple use of sgraffito on a Waistel Cooper pot.*

*A brilliant use of sgraffito by a schoolboy. Note the reversals of light on dark and dark on light as in the creatures eye.*

Designs are too varied to discuss in a short article. Compare, for instance, a Leach bottle with a decorated Greek amphora for extremes of sgraffito styles. The line should be fluid and yet taut, rapidly executed and, once cut, left alone. Backgrounds can be cut away leaving textured areas which will throw more solid shapes into relief. Do not become carried away by the fascination of the work and do not forget the vital correlation between the decoration and the form of the piece, which is as important for dishes and bowls as for pots. 'Sgrafiato' is sometimes used for designs in which the background is cut away, as opposed to linear pattern. (See also *finger combing, wax resist, combing*.) See color plate 19, p. 141.

## SHALE

As the water was squeezed out of clay in geological time by strata movements, pressure and heat, it hardened or 'lithified' into mudstone and shale. Slate is a further, metamorphosed stage. *Fireclays* are often shaley and need grinding for use.

## SHATTERING

The break-up of the pot fabric after glaze firing, happily a rare phenomenon. It is almost always due to an excess of fine, *'free'* silica in crystalline form and to the shock of its *inversion*. This not only strains the body itself but can also put a glaze into a state of such extreme *compression* that it splits the body. Associated with *peeling* (see also *Seger rules, crazing, quartz inversion*). A large dish glazed on one side only is at especial risk; a thick glaze coating more dangerous than a thin one. Glass, melted in a ceramic piece as a decorative effect, can break the piece through excessive contraction and tension.

To cure compression-shattering use less flint or quartz in the body and/or higher contraction bases in the glaze. Cool rapidly to about 950°C. in order to minimize crystal formation, and increase body fluxes to form silicates, which do not 'invert'. Geoffrey Whiting found that 5% of a red clay cured bad shattering. A clay with a high incidence of the trouble may be best discarded. (See also *shivering.*)

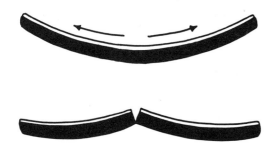

*Shattering. A glaze in high compression on the top face of a dish can exert sufficient outward thrust to break the body.*

## SHELF, kiln

See *bat, kiln shelves.*

## SHIVERING

The action of glaze breaking away from the body, especially on rims and edges. It is usually suffering from *over-compression* associated with a poorly developed interface. The treatment generally recommended is as for *shattering* or *peeling*. The replacement of some of the feldspar with nepheline and also some of the china clay with ball clay may help, especially with ash glazes. Rim crawling is a similar complaint, the glaze lifting away from the body at a sintering stage. It is difficult to cure (see *crawling*).

Slip can also 'shiver', especially a white slip on a red body, and this is most often caused by unequal slip/body shrinkage. Add more plastic clay to the slip,

a fusible ball clay for instance. If shivering happens during drying, apply the slip to rather stiffer clay, or apply it more thinly. Slip shivering during the cooling of the kiln may be caused by quartz inversion and can be avoided by the addition of about 5% of flint.

## SHORT CIRCUIT

See *circuit, fuse.*

## SHORT CLAY

Clay with poor plasticity or workability, also known as 'lean' clay. Large-grain, pure clays are short; ball clays are *fat* or plastic. Most bodies contain both types. 2-3% of bentonite in a short body will impart some of the qualities of plasticity. Shortness can result from *over-wedging* or *pugging*, or from too small a water content. A few days' rest in a damp atmosphere will restore a normally plastic clay, and a week or two will help a short one.

## SHOULDER

The upper part of a pot where it turns in towards the neck or rim. It is the most eye-catching area of a pot and generally takes the most important part of the decoration.

## SHRINKAGE OF CLAY

Progressive lessening of clay in length and volume during both drying and firing. Firing shrinkage is non-reversible, and is not to be confused with the heat expansion and contraction which all materials undergo or with *inversions*.

There are two phases. First, wet to dry shrinkage caused by the evaporation of films of water of plasticity from between the particles of clay. This varies with the fineness of grain; a red surface clay or a bentonite may shrink too much to be any use to the potter at all. English *ball-clays* have a high wet/dry shrinkage. The

*Shrinkage. (A) shows plates or particles of clay held apart by layers of water as in plastic clay. As the water evaporates, the particles come closer together. The interstices can still hold some water and (B) can represent either hard-leather clay or dry clay. Hence the comparatively high shrinkage between (A) and (B) compared with (B) with water in the pores and bone dry clay. It will be seen that rewetting one side of (B) (the outside of a pot, for instance) will force some of the particles apart quite violently and put strains on the fabric which cause it to disintegrate. See also the next stage under sintering.*

maximum for a useful body should not exceed 10%. The shrinkage is reduced by the addition of flint, sand, or grog. (See *clay tests* for shrinkage test.)

Second, firing. There is little or no shrinkage from leather-hard clay to a low biscuit, in fact there may even be a slight expansion. However, as soon as glasses begin to form in the body through heat reaction between basic impurities and silica, the un-melted particles pack closer together and an overall lessening in volume occurs and continues at an increasing rate to complete *vitrification.*

Some approximate shrinkage rates:
Etruria and brick clays wet/fired to 1000°C. average 12%.
Fireclays dry/fired average 3%.
China clay, low wet/dry shrinkage, if fired up to 1300°C., 12%.
Ball clays wet/dry up to 12%.

*Showing the shrinkage of similarly sized slab boxes at various stages. From left to right: wet plastic clay; leather-hard clay; dry clay; biscuit; stoneware. It is obvious that the greatest shrinkage occurs between the first two and the last two. (See text.)*

## SIENNA

A hydrated iron-manganese ochrous earth. Similar to umber but with less $MnO_2$. (See also *ochre.*)

## SIEVE

Regular mesh or perforations which will control the grain size of a material which is passed through the sieve. Made of metal, metal wire or nylon.

Useful sieves (screens or lawns) for potters are $\frac{1}{2}$ in. (12 mm.) garden sieves for removing the worst roughage from ash, stony clays etc.; 8 or 16 mesh cooking sieves usually of nylon, which can be used for the first breaking down of a slip or glaze batch and for grog; 60 or 80 phosphor bronze lawns for slips and stoneware glazes; 100 or 120 for earthenware glazes; and 200 mesh for colors. The number indicates the

wires per linear inch (see *lawns*). In practice some slightly larger particles will pass through because of unevennesses in the weave (which may be forced apart by clumsy usage) and oblong particles which slip through endways. Grog is graded by sieve range.

Use only a brush for working material through a sieve, not tools or fingers! The most accurate grading is probably given by a vibratory sieve, but this sort of precision is rarely required in craft work.

*Using a sieve supported on two sticks over a bowl, the glaze worked gently but firmly through with a nylon washing-up brush.*

## SIEVE FRAMES

Lawns must be mounted on frames. These are usually circular and vary in size from 3 in. (75 mm.) cones to 12 or 14 in. (300 or 350 mm.) wooden or poly-propylene frames. The standard frame is about 4 in. (100 mm.) high and is designed to be used with the deeper wall upwards so that it will hold the maximum quantity of liquid (many students use sieves upside down). 8 in. (200 mm.) is a good average diameter for a frame. Wooden (ashwood) frames inevitably overlap at the joins and are difficult to clean completely and it is advisable to keep one sieve for each major class of work: for transparent glaze, white opaque, and colored for example. The more recently developed plastic frames in which the lawn can easily be replaced should be an improvement.

## SIEVE, use of

It is easier, and quicker in the long run, to use more than one sieve size when preparing a slip or glaze, working from coarse mesh to fine. For slips and glazes made up from commercially supplied materials sieving is more a question of breaking down loose aggregates rather than separating particle sizes. Use a 'cooking' sieve of nylon for the first break-down and then the appropriate lawn for the resultant slurry (see *sieve, lawn*). Sieve a glaze at least twice through the finest sieve if it is to be used immediately, to assist the inti-mate mingling of particles. A newly made-up slip will improve if left to rest for a day or so.

Slips should be sieved every time they are used, but only the amount required, of course, not the whole batch. Glaze needs re-sieving every so often: bits of pot, grit, and other rubbish will fall into it. It is advisable to pour the glaze from its container to ensure that a 'cake' does not form on the bottom; this will alter the constituents of the remaining mixture (see *settling*).

In persuading the mixture to pass through the lawn use an appropriate brush—never a rigid tool or your fingers—and do not work it too hard. Use plenty of water—it can always be poured from the settled mixture later. A thick sludge will form a coating on the lawn and never pass through. The ideal is to use little or no direct force and in this respect the *vibratory sieve* may not be a complete luxury. If slips or high-clay glazes are forced thickly through a sieve they will only re-unite on the other side and the result will be nearly as lumpy as the original. More water, as mentioned above, will make easier work, more effective screening and prolong the life of the sieve which, with care, should last many years.

## SILICA

Silicon dioxide $SiO_2$, 60, m.p. 1610-1713°C. Normally oxides are discussed under the element but silica is such a fundamental material in ceramics that an exception is made for it. All ceramics are based on silica both in the body and glaze, except for a few specialized industrial products. It is the principal *glass-forming* oxide.

Used as a white powder, it is derived from *calcined* and ground flints or ground quartz. Many *sands* are mainly silica. It is more often used to produce *silicates* than on its own (see *fused silica*). Crystalline silica has an *inversion* point at 573°C., changing from alpha to beta forms with a linear expansion of about 1% (given variously at 0.45-1.0), with an equivalent contraction on cooling. It ceases to be stable at around 870°C. and will begin to convert to *cristobalite* from 1050°C.

However most of the silica in a glaze, and to a lesser extent in the body, will unite with bases to form silicates, in which case the reverse beta to alpha inversion does not occur. Silica also combines with alumina and these have a *eutectic* at 1595°C. (see also *phase diagrams*) and form *mullite* and *corundum* at different temperatures according to their respective proportions.

## SILICA REFRACTORY

Refractory bricks and other materials containing 93% or more silica. They are resistant to deformation under load but, as might be expected, are subject to *thermal shock* in the *inversion* ranges. Potters' *refractories* are therefore more usually *aluminous*.

## SILICATE

A compound of a *base* or bases with silica, that is, a salt. Many pottery minerals and all clay and glazes are silicates, many of them very complex. A silicate may be written $RSiO_3$ or $RO.SiO_2$ and is described according

to the other element involved e.g. aluminium silicate. Clay includes combined water in its formula and is thus a 'hydrated aluminium silicate'. The fritt, lead mono-silicate, is one part lead oxide to one part silica, $PbSiO_3$ or $PbO.SiO_2$.

## SILICEOUS

Rich in silica. Applied to refractories, sometimes to ball clays, etc.

## SILICON, oxide

A non-metal element Si, 28. Oxide $SiO_2$, 60. (See under *silica* for general information.)

## SILICON CARBIDE

SiC, 40, s.g. 3.2. Low thermal expansion, 5.0 (see *coefficient of expansion*). Made by fusing coke and sand.

Silicon carbide's excellent thermal shock resistance, *refractoriness*, and thermal *conductivity* make it a useful material for *kiln shelves*. It is also a conductor of electricity which makes the bats dangerous for use in an electric kiln, but the property has been utilized as *silicon carbide* heating *elements*. It is also in common use as an *abrasive* (carborundum).

It has been used in a powdered form as a glaze ingredient to produce 'crater' glazes (it bubbles with the release of the carbon), speckled red copper glazes, and as a local *reducing* agent.

## SILICON CARBIDE ELEMENTS

*Kiln elements* in the form of straight hollow rods. Middle range diameter just over $\frac{1}{2}$ in. (14-18 mm.). The performance of these elements has been greatly improved since their introduction in the nineteen-thirties. They no longer need an expensive transformer, which once cost more than the kiln. Crystal growth within the rod increases its resistance to the passage of electric current by about 10% every thousand hours, the kiln consequently taking longer to fire. An ingenious system has been invented by Peter Taylor (Labheat, Ironbridge, England), by which the wiring, on three phases and neutral, can be modified to compensate almost indefinitely for this loss by increasing the voltage through each element from 60 through to 120 volts.

The rods are self-supporting, the working area producing the bulk of the heat. The ends, which must be $\frac{1}{2}$ in. (12 mm.) longer than the kiln wall thickness, are designed to offer less electrical resistance. Connections are made with braid and clips. The use of modern refractory insulators can reduce the wall thickness to 6 in. (150 mm.). The cost of these elements is still several times that of equivalent wire ones, but they should have a very long life and are less affected by reduction. They are fairly brittle and need the protection of a board against the possibility of damage when packing the kiln. Details of a silicon carbide kiln were given in CR 17. Materials and advice from Labheat.

*(A) shows a simple silicon carbide element: the ends which are enclosed in the kiln wall are rated at only 0.5 ohms of resistance compared with 4 ohms in the working portion. (B) shows the end of a bar through a kiln wall. The hole must be equal to at least to 1.25 d. compared with the rod. The braid and clip connection are shown diagrammatically. The clip can be against the kiln wall. (C) represents the element inside the kiln. It is self-supporting from the points where it enters the wall. The kiln face is grooved at (X) so that the bars need not stand out too far into the chamber, but the distance from any part of the rod to the wall must be 0.5 d. while the rods must be a minimum of 1.5 d. distant from one another.*

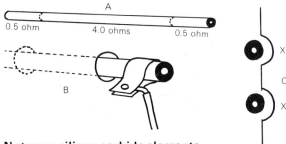

## Notes on silicon carbide elements

Wiring systems for resistance alteration compensation (by kind permission of Peter Taylor, Labheat, Ironbridge, England).

Using 12 elements or multiples of 12; three phase supply:

A. 3 series of 4 in star connection. 60 volts per element.
B. 4 series of 3 in star connection. 80 volts per element.
C. 3 series of 4 in delta connection. 100 volts each across phases.
D. 6 series of 2 in star connection. 120 volts per element.

Change when firing time has increased by 25%, e.g. from eight to ten hours. Average resistance increase 10% per thousand hours.

No support is needed if the correct size is used for the length of span.

Up to 32 in.—14 mm. diameter
Up to 39 in.—16 mm. diameter
Up to 50 in.—18 mm. diameter

## SILICONE

A series of *organic* compounds of *hydrocarbons* with silica $(R_2SiO)_n$ some of which will stand temperatures up to 300°C. Used as sealers and water-repellents, they have been mentioned as a last-ditch method of waterproofing the bases of leaking or scratchy pots.

## SILICOSIS

A disease caused by fine *silica* dust inhaled over a long period. The dust cannot be eliminated from the lungs and so builds up to a solid substance. The studio potter is not at special risk unless he is in the habit of sandpapering dry clay. Reasonable hygiene and cleanliness are essential, working as far as possible with liquid or

damp materials especially in handling glazes, ash, etc. *Alumina* can replace silica for *setting*, for spreading on kiln shelves, etc.

## SILIT

A trade name for SiC heating elements which can maintain a constant resistance over a period.

## SILK SCREEN

A decoration technique, especially useful for tiles. A stretched piece of silk or other fine mesh material is marked with a design and those areas not required to be colored are varnished or otherwise made *impermeable*. The 'screen' is then laid flat on a tile and color (generally an *enamel*, but possibly other pigments) is brushed through or pressed through with a squeegee or roller.

## SILLIMINITE

A brown or grey metamorphic mineral $Al_2SO_5$ $(Al_2O_3.SiO_2)$. A highly refractory material (melting point around 1900°C.) found as a type of fireclay. Its heat resistance and high thermal *conductivity* makes it valuable for *kiln furniture*. Chief sources S. Africa and India. There is a silliminite zone in N. Scotland. Kyanite and andalusite are similar in composition but have different properties. It is also made into bricks suitable for bag walls.

## SILVER

A metallic element Ag, 108. A clear yellow is derived from silver salts for temperatures up to 1000°C. Silver-colored *enamel* is made from platinum. Silver sulfide with *ochre* can be used for lustre, with *reduction* near the top temperature of 700-800°C.

## SINDANYO

A type of very hard and durable asbestos sheet. It has a special use for *throwing-bats*. Expensive but almost everlasting and unmarked even by steel turning tools. Obtainable from Bell's Asbestos.

*Wheel bats (Sindanyo in this case) can be held steady on the wheel head by two pins as described in text, or bedded on a ring of clay with a single pin in the center, as shown (2). The handle of a turning-tool can be used to exert sufficient leverage to break the seal without jerking the pot (1).*

2

## SINGLE FIRED WARE

See *once-fired ware*.

## SINGLE PHASE SUPPLY

The normal household electricity supply, conducted through a live and a neutral wire. Usually 60 amps, with 30 amps the maximum for any one piece of equipment, e.g. a 7 kW kiln of about 3 cu. ft. However, some electricity authorities are now allowing 40 amps or more on a reasonably new line and it is worth contacting your local electricity authirity for advice. Single phase motors are dearer and marginally less efficient than *three phase*—the alternative form of supply.

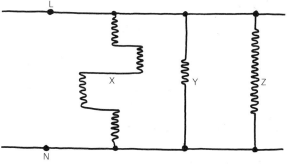

*A single phase supply. Between the live (L) and neutral (N) various items of equipment can be connected so long as the total load does not exceed the strength of the mains wires to conduct it without producing heat. In the diagram X might represent a 5 kW kiln, Y a 200 watt lamp, and Z a 2 kW electric fire. The total load if all were on together would be 7.2 kW.*

## SINTERING

An intermediate stage in the firing of a ceramic, either glaze or body, where the *liquid phase* has not yet begun but 'solid state reactions or intercrystallization' (Dodd) or the beginning of a reaction between two solids has fused the material causing a decrease in porosity and an increase in strength. The sintering temperature of a material is called the *Tamman* temperature, being between 0.55 and 0.6 of the K.

temperature of fusion (Cardew). If the melting point is 1500°C., then the material will sinter at about 0.6 of the K. temperature, in this case 1773 (1500+273; see *absolute temperature*).

Thus, $\dfrac{1773}{0.6}$=1106 K. or 833°C.

A certain expansion takes place in clays up to sintering temperature.

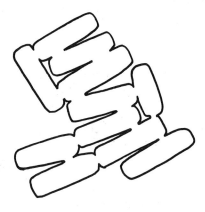

*Sintered particles of clay or other material. The points of contact have fused together giving a stronger fabric but resulting in very little shrinkage. In practice, the particles would have begun to assume a more spherical shape.*

## SKIPPING

Sometimes used to indicate the *peeling* or *shivering* of glaze or slip on the rims of pots or bowls.

## SLAB POTS

Pots built up from slabs of clay can be very diverse in form and character. They may have the sharp clean lines which result from cutting the pieces from leather-hard clay, or the squashy, rounded forms of plastic clay building.

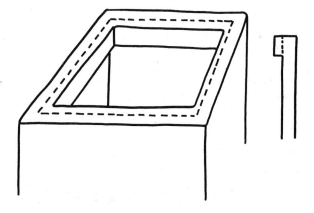

*As mentioned in the text, straight lengths of wall in slab pots tend to warp during drying and firing and should be strengthened by the addition of a strip attached at right-angles to the wall as shown in diagram.*

Leather-hard slabs are cut with a fine bladed knife held quite vertically, scored at the edges and luted together with slip made from the body clay. Press well home with a wooden spatula. The surfaces can be decorated before or after assembly by *impressing, beating, applied* clay etc. or by *wax resist, brushwork* or *poured glaze*. Several pourings of thin ash glazes will give an attractive and appropriate finish.

The proportions of a slab pot are all-important. Rules cannot be laid down but a rectangular plan tends to be of more interest than a square one. The clay is usually fairly well grogged for stoneware, but there is a wide field in earthenware. If the technique is used for open containers, the rim needs to be strengthened with an additional strip forming an inward or outward angle in order to counteract the almost inevitable warping. Cylindrical slab pots are described under *rolling pin pots*. The inside corners of larger slab pots will need reinforcement with thin clay coils worked well into the angle.

Slab pots make good lamp bases. Large composite pots can be built up from smaller ones. Curved surfaces can be partially dried over a former before assembly.

*Building a slab pot. The sizes of the various pieces are worked out (remember to allow for the extra wall thicknesses on top and base, for instance). Cut the sections from soft leather clay, keeping the awl, or spatula tool, or knife quite upright (1). The neck aperture can be cut with a pastry-cutter (2). All joints are slipped (3). Use slip made from the body clay or it will show at the joins. The first pieces are put together (4) and the inside joint is sealed and cleaned with a square-ended tool (5). The outside is also worked in vertically (6). When an open box is complete the joins are pressed together with a firm stroking action (7). The top (8) and base are applied to the walls. The base can be set inside the walls when only three walls have been joined together. The top and base can be made and finished in various ways: the pot can be made with thick walls and left open (see under beaten decoration); a true slab neck can be made as shown on p. 210; see also the flat grooved top with a rim on p. 210. Many others will occur to you. A foot will give a certain lightness to the pot if this is required. A neck (or a foot) can be thrown and luted on when half-dry (9, 10). The corners may be left sharp or bevelled or rounded (11). A biscuit form being used to give a curved clay wall for a shaped pot (12).*

6

7

8

9

10

11

12

*A fine large slab pot 18 in. (460 mm.) high, by Ian Auld.*

*A slab pot by Shoji Hamada.*

*An original way of using slabs to build a pot. Each layer is cut from a slab with circular cutters and then laid, with a little slip, one on another.*

## SLAG

The product of the reaction between *fluxing* materials e.g. ash, and a *refractory* kiln lining. Also applied to a non-metallic fusion which floats on metal during its extraction, or to any encrusting, semi-molten material—'our slipware body . . . would turn to slag at 1300°C.' (L.PB). (See also *basic slag*.)

## SLICK

The movement of a metal blade over clay tends to bring water and fine particles—a 'slick'—to the surface. It sometimes causes lamination in pugged clay.

## SLIP

Any clay or body mixed with water to a smooth consistency. Originally used to provide a thin coating, over a red body, of the then rare light-firing clays, now mainly used for decoration and for slip-casting. The ingredients of commercial bodies are mixed together in the slip condition. Decorative slip techniques are dealt with under *trailing, run slip, feathering, sgraffito, hakame* etc.

The term 'slip' is generally reserved for liquid

'natural' clays or bodies used for decorative pottery. Those which contain significant proportions of non-clay materials are known as 'engobes'. 'Slip-casting' is an exception. (See various colors of slip, e.g. *black slip, blue slip, green slip,* also *slip making, slip recipes, engobes.*) See color plate 21, p. 141.

*A quick way of making the occasional special slip, when making slab pots for instance. A piece of leather-hard clay is rubbed over a Surform plane as in illustration.*

*The method of flooding a plate, dish, or bowl. Adequate slip is poured into a dish which is tipped and revolved, spreading the slip just up to the rim. The movement is almost complete in the picture. Surplus slip is poured out as neatly as possible.*

## SLIP CASTING

The making of pottery in *plaster* molds using liquid body or slip. The *mold* is filled with slip: the absorption of the plaster causes a thin wall of clay to be deposited on the inner surface. Surplus slip is then poured off and the cast is left to dry and shrink away from the mold, when it can be removed (see *molds*). Casting-slip is made up of a clay with up to 75% china clay, stone and flint. Nevertheless it is still too *viscous* to be used for casting and must be *deflocculated*. A perfect cast is not easily obtained. The seam left by the

mold is almost impossible to eradicate. Even if trimmed quite flat it will rise again during firing. Some of the faults which may occur are dealt with in the table issued by the British Ceramic Research Association (under *casting-slip*). Detailed instructions for slip casting for the craft potter were given in CR 9 by William Hall.

## SLIP DECORATION

Slip may be used as a complete or partial covering on a pot or dish. A 'bib' can be dipped, or contrasting colors poured over. Other techniques include *brushed slip, sgraffito, trailing, feathering, marbling, run-slip* and *hakame,* and they are dealt with under those headings.

Slip decoration at its best is very direct and free. Essentially an earthenware technique, it is also sometimes used on stoneware using special *engobes.*

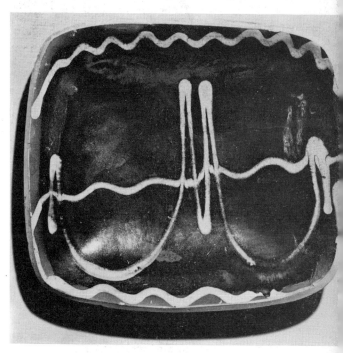

*Slip decoration. An English slip-trailed dish—possibly Tickenhall.*

## SLIP GAUGE

An instrument for measuring the consistency of slip or glaze. (For details see under *hydrometer.*)

## SLIP GLAZE

A very fusible clay which will melt to a sort of glaze at stoneware temperatures. *Albany clay* is commonly quoted.

In a glaze one can use 50% of red clay and more. The difficulties lie not in the actual melting of the glaze, but in countering the effects of high shrinkage during drying and *sintering* stages. Dolomite, feldspar, cole-manite or a fritt will lessen shrinkage and increase *fusibility.* Additions of iron, rutile, or spodumene (Rhodes) will alter its behavior.

Any red or surface clay may have the necessary qualities to make a glaze, and experiments with local materials are always worthwhile. Slip glazes are useful for *oxidizing* conditions, though not so variable as in *reduction.* They will always be dark brown, red-brown if you are lucky, or black. It is possible that *temmoku* and other dark-colored Oriental glazes were slip. If a slip-glaze shows bubbles or blisters, a slightly higher or longer firing may help.

## SLIP MAKING

For plain colors, the clay is broken into small pieces and soaked in water. When well saturated, the *slurry* is brushed through a coarse *sieve* and then through a 60 mesh. Brush lightly with plenty of water.

If pigments are to be added, the ingredients must be weighed dry. The clay must therefore be used as a powdered body, or thoroughly dried and broken into small pieces. The appropriate proportion of pigment oxide is ground separately and passed through a 200 *lawn.* The liquid color can be added to the clay at the slurry stage before all is passed through a 60 or 80 mesh two or more times. Newly made slips should be 'rested' for a few days before use.

## SLIP RECIPES

For slip trailing etc. (all dry weights):

White or buff slip    100% buff clay (throwing clay)
Red slip    100% red clay
Black slip    100 red clay+9% manganese dioxide. Cobalt 0.5% can be added for a blacker slip
Blue slip    100 buff clay +0.5-1.5% cobalt oxide
Green slip    100 buff clay +1.25% chrome and 1.25% copper oxide

If slip crazes or *shivers (peels or flakes)* see under these headings for possible remedies. Stoneware slips are generally iron slips, variation being obtained by reduction. (See also under *casting slip, engobes.*)

## SLIP TRAILERS, tracers

These vary considerably in shape, but are all designed to direct a controlled stream of slip onto a surface.
1   The commonest type is a soft rubber bag with a glass or plastic nozzle. The bag is filled with a funnel.
2   Stiff rubber bulb containers have the advantage that slip can be drawn in by suction, but the control is not so delicate as with the first type.
3   A rigid container with a direct outlet—sometimes a quill. A pottery tracer can be made which fits snugly into the palm. It will have two holes: one is for the quill or nozzle, and the thumb fits over the other to control the entry of air and thus the outflow of slip. Two or more streams of slip have been used.
4   A rigid container with a rubber tube. Slip can be forced out of the nozzle by blowing down the tube. A baby's bottle is a possible container.

*Filling a soft rubber bag slip trailer. The funnel is filled with slip which, if thick enough for trailing, will probably need 'milking' into the bag by gripping the top of the neck and sliding the fingers downwards. This is repeated until the bag is full. It is not always easy to insert the funnel into the neck of the bag. The inside of the bag can be damped but keep the outside quite dry in order to get a grip.*

*A more involved slip trailer designed by Peter Smith. The flow is controlled at the mouthpiece.*

5   Cloth icing bags. These tend to drip after some use.

6   Paper containers, wrapped over like a sweet bag. Used by Odney Pottery, who published details in PQ 2. These are made of waxed paper or soft plastic. A segment of a circle is held point downwards and wrapped over the hand. Fastened with a pin or dab of clay.

7   A cup or container with one or more holes in the base. This method needs free, sure and rapid movement. Hamada uses a ladle with a hole for trailing slip and glaze.

## SLIP TRAILING

A decorative technique. (See *trailing*.)

## SLOP GLAZE

A *suspension* of glaze materials in water: a glaze ready for use, in fact.

## SLOP WEIGHT

The weight of solid material in a slip or glaze. Industrial pottery materials are measured and combined as slop weights. (See *pint weight* and *Brongiart's formula*.)

## SLUMPING

The collapse of a pot in the kiln due to *pyroplastic* deformation, i.e. in a semi-molten state. Impure clays and porcelains will slump if over-fired, as a result of the high degree of glass formation in the fabric. (See *over-firing*.)

## SLURRY

A thick, half-mixed slip, or a rough, wet, sandy mixture used for *clamming* etc.

## SMALT

A fused mixture of cobalt, silica and a flux. A sort of cobalt fritt or glass, sometimes used as a pigment or for staining.

## SMOKE

Unburnt particles of fuel, mainly carbon, caused by insufficient air in the combustion-chamber of a kiln. Smoke coming from the chimney is a sign of wasted fuel, but in the firing-chamber elemental carbon assists *reduction*.

## SMOKED WARE

A body or glaze discolored by a smoky *reduction*-fire. Early reduction, below about 900°C., can stain pots with carbon which will not burn out. The black body of *raku* and *sawdust* firings is a mixture of reduction and smoking or carbonization. *Celadons* are rather liable to smoking.

## SOAKING, heat

Maintaining a glaze or body in a kiln at a certain temperature, generally at the maturing-point. Many potters believe that a soaking period is essential to the maturity of a glaze. A slower firing from about 1000°C. will have similar results. A kiln graph, with its steadily flattening rocket-like curve, will show that most kilns slow down considerably after 1200°C. and give a soaking effect with little deliberate control.

Time must be allowed for the glaze in its fluid state to release gases, and for the resultant bubbles to smooth out, but an excessively long firing can set up secondary reactions which aggravate the trouble. The act of reduction will slow down or reverse the temperature rise, and this 'stepped' firing may be crucial to the development of some iron colors (see *kaki*).

Most *earthenware glazes* benefit from a soak of about 20 minutes, but it must be remembered that the glaze is fluid and may be slowly running down the pot. A *controlling pyrometer* is needed to soak an electric kiln efficiently. A degree of soaking can be achieved by switching on and off at intervals of one or two minutes. Use a second cone one number above the optimum temperature to ensure that the kiln does not get too hot. Alternatively one can set the 'medium' control if the kiln is wired in this way; this will retard the cooling rate.

Stoneware is more subtle in its reactions, and it is difficult to lay down rules. *Oxidized* glazes are often very susceptible to even ten degrees of over- or under-firing and I have found a soak to be a mixed blessing. Very fast firings in a test kiln have produced more exciting and silky-surfaced glazes than have the same recipes in larger, slower kilns. Triple *cones* are useful for soaking without a pyrometer, the higher number warning if the optimum temperature is being exceeded.

## SOAPSTONE

Or steatite. An impure, 'massive' form of *talc*. Frequently used in *'soft paste'* recipes. Now used in electroceramics and in *cordierite* bodies.

## SODA

Refers, in pottery, to sodium oxide $Na_2O$. Used to describe glazes which contain sodium oxide, e.g. lead and soda glaze. Pure forms soluble but contained in many minerals. (For fuller discussion see under *sodium*.)

## SODA ASH

Anhydrous sodium carbonate $Na_2CO_3$, 106. *Deliquescent* and soluble. Used in alkaline fritts, also as a *deflocculant* for *casting-slips*.

## SODA GLAZE

Soda alone can produce a glass with silica, but this may be so soft that it will dissolve in water (water-glass). The turquoise soda and copper glaze was used by the ancient Egyptians and though considered to be unstable has lasted for three thousand and more years! (See also *copper, turquoise, Egyptian paste*.)

A majority of glazes contain some soda which must be introduced as a *fritt*, the raw compounds being soluble, or as a *mineral* (see *sodium*). The molecular equivalent of soda is usually kept at a maximum of

0.3, on account of its high thermal expansion. High-soda glazes will nearly always *craze*. Soda is inextricably mixed with potash in many minerals, so that the symbol NaKO may occur denoting random proportions. Piccolpasso mentions the calcining of wine lees with sand to produce a soda silicate for *majolica* glazes (marzacotto). Pigments will give brighter colors in soda glazes.

## SODA, washing

Hydrated, or hydroxide of, sodium carbonate $Na_2CO_3$. $10H_2O$. Crystalline.

## SODIUM, oxide, compounds

A metallic element Na, 23. (Natrum).
Oxide $Na_2O$, 62. 'Soda' (Caustic soda).
Other compounds are listed below.

An *alkali*. A large *atomic radius* similar to potassium, with which it is often found in combination giving rise to the compound symbol KNaO. A very powerful *flux* (network modifier) with silica. All soda glasses need some lime or alumina to prevent their becoming soluble in water. Very high *coefficient of expansion* (37.0).

All simple compounds of soda are soluble and must be used as *fritts*, or as 'natural' fritts, e.g. the *feldspathic* minerals. Small amounts of soda figure in the analyses of most clays and of many other pottery materials. The high thermal expansion leads to the crazing of glazes, and the molecular equivalent is normally kept to within 0.3 parts. Brightens most colors, turning copper turquoise if in a high concentration.

Soda compounds and minerals used in ceramics:
Sodium carbonate $Na_2CO_3$, 106. Soda ash.
Sodium bicarbonate $NaHCO_3$, 107.
Sodium chloride NaCl, 58. Common table salt.
Sodium silicate $Na_2O.SiO_2$, but in practice variable $Na_2O.2\text{-}3.5SiO_2$. Water-glass, i.e. a glass which will dissolve in water. A deflocculant. Used also in *air-setting cements*.
Washing soda $Na_2CO_3.10H_2O$, 286.
Caustic soda, the oxide $Na_2O$, 62. An unstable form.
Sodium tannate. An efficient deflocculant. Prepared from NaOH and tannic acid.
Sodium uranate (see *uranium*).
Sodium borate (bi-borate) $Na_2O.2B_2O_3.10H_2O$, 382. (See *borax*.)

Chief soda minerals:
Albite feldspar, $Na_2O.Al_2O_3.6SiO_2$, 524. Also some soda in nominally orthoclase feldspar.
China stone $Na_2O$ (or NaKO)$.Al_2O_3.8SiO_2$, 644.
Nepheline syenite $Na_2O$ ($0.75Na_2O. 0.25K_2O$)$. Al_2O_3. 2SiO_2$, 182.
All are variable within certain limits.

## SOFT GLAZE

A glaze which matures at around 1150°C. or below, and includes in its formula lead or boron. *Earthenware* (and *bone china*) are covered with a 'soft' glaze. The term is comparative in the sense that the glaze can be scratched with a steel knife. The converse term 'hard glaze' is not, however, in general use.

## SOFT LEATHER STAGE

Used in this book to indicate clay slightly damper than leather-hard—that is, at the point where it has stiffened but can still be deformed manually without breakage.

## SOFT PASTE

A general term for all the experimental and glassy bodies which were developed in Europe from the time of the Medicis to the end of the eighteenth century, in an attempt to imitate oriental porcelain. The factories of St. Cloud, Bow, Chelsea etc. used soft paste. The material was immensely difficult to handle and fire, having little plasticity and a rapid and very fluid glass phase at maturity. Soapstone, bone ash, alkalis, tin oxides, white clays, are among the ingredients mentioned. Firing temperatures around 1100°C., but variable. The very soft glaze with which they were covered took *enamels* very well. The bone ash/china clay mixture finally triumphed in England around 1800 (Spode), and continues to hold its own against hard paste porcelain. (See *bone china*.) Some porcelain bodies in current use among craft potters hover between soft paste and true *hard paste*. A soft paste for low-fired (1020°C. or less) beads and jewelry can be made up from roughly equal parts of ball clay and fritt. Fire on a bed of alumina.

## SOFT SOAP

A potash soap which remains in a liquid or jellified state. Used to lubricate the surfaces of plaster molds to prevent plaster casts sticking, e.g. when reproducing dish molds. (See also *molds*.)

## SOLID SOLUTIONS

Materials dissolved one into another at high temperatures, reverting to a homogeneous solid mixture on cooling.

## SOLUBLE, solubility, solution

A soluble material is one which will dissolve in a liquid to form a solution, an intimate combination but without chemical change, e.g. sugar in water. Materials which are soluble will crystallize out of solution and are not suitable for raw glaze batches. Pouring the water from the top of such a glaze will also pour away dissolved materials, altering the constitution of the glaze. There may be slightly soluble elements in any mineral or material, and it is always a wise precaution to retain the poured-off water for re-use if necessary. Dusting of soluble glaze materials onto wet clay (even immediately after throwing) with a garden 'puffer' has been suggested (CM 18/2)—it would be advisable to wear a mask during this process—but the usual method of using them is in the form of *fritts*. The alkalis and boron are soluble in all their simple compounds; even colemanite is slightly soluble.

Glaze is a super-cooled liquid and we can therefore

refer to certain materials and oxides as being soluble in a glaze, e.g. most of the *pigment* oxides will, up to a certain concentration, yield transparent color. The *acidic* oxides are mainly insoluble. Tin, for instance, will remain unchanged in suspension, rendering the glaze opaque. Glaze will also form compounds, one of which will dissolve in the other (see *solid solutions*). Liquids, including glazes, will hold only certain proportions in solution, the excess remaining in its original form or being rejected (precipitated). Hot liquids will hold more than cold ones; certain oxides may therefore come out of solution as the glaze cools, especially if this takes place slowly. Iron may do this in stoneware (see *red glazes*). 3% or more of copper and 12% or more of manganese will have the same effect, the degree of precipitation varying with the *fluidity* of the glaze. In an 'under-fired matt' or a high-base stoneware glaze the oxide may not dissolve at all: copper, for instance, giving gray instead of green.

Soluble materials (soluble in water) used in pottery:

| | |
|---|---|
| Boric oxide | Most boron minerals including borax, calcined borax to a lesser degree. Colemanite is slightly soluble. |
| Soda | Most silicates and carbonates of soda, salt (sodium chloride), borax. |
| Potash | Oxide and carbonate, pearlash. Soluble form in many ashes. |
| Fritts | Very soft fritts may dissolve in part, to re-crystallize after a few days. |

## SOLUBLE ALKALIS

Plant ashes contain *soluble* and *caustic alkalis*. These may *crystallize*; invade the fabric of the biscuit; cause flocculation of the batch with attendant cracking of the glaze coating; and make it impossible to pour liquid from the batch without altering its behavior. Ash is therefore usually 'washed'. (For method see *ash preparation*.)

## SOLUBLE LEAD

Lead and lead oxides are soluble in the bloodstream, where they act as cumulative poisons. The lead in a fired glaze, unless it is very stable, may also be 'dissolved' by the action of strong acids, such as those in certain fruits and vinegar, and by fermentation.

Raw lead compounds are forbidden by law in all but a few situations, and their use in manufactured materials is controlled. The potter working on his own may use them but not his employee. Fritted *lead silicates* are powdered glass, which (in spite of detective fiction) is much safer in use. The *fritts* must be made to certain standards of solubility (not more than 5% must dissolve in a standard hydrochloric acid test). Those that pass this test are labelled low sol. or LS fritts. Monosilicate is too 'soft' to satisfy the regulations; sesquisilicate and bisilicate are usually satisfactory.

The dangers to the potter can be minimized by common sense and hygiene; the fired product presents a more involved problem. S.SCP states that 'lead glazes are brilliant, highly craze resistant and, if properly fritted, are absolutely safe in use.' He gives the rule that the *bases* plus *alumina* must equal at least 2.0 parts of silica in the molecular formula (see *Thorpe's ratio*).

Copper will increase lead solubility. According to F. Littlefield (CM 19/1):

Boric acid, Alkalis } increase solubility

Alumina, Silica, Lime, Zinc, Barium, Zircon } decrease solubility

There is, however, some doubt about the role of zinc oxide.

At high temperatures, lead is *volatile* and may be inhaled from a kiln. Do not open the kiln door when ware is very hot. It can also be deposited as a thin skin on leadless glazes, rendering them dangerous in use.

A test for the presence of lead was described in NZP 13/2. 2 oz. of vinegar are left in the test pot for 12 hours. The vinegar is then poured into a glass and 2 oz. of fresh vinegar poured into a second glass. One-eighth of a teaspoon of liver of sulfur is mixed with 2 oz. of hot water, and two teaspoonsful are added to each glass. If the test vinegar is tinged tan or brown compared with the fresh batch, then heavy metal is present.

## SOLUBLE SALTS

Sulfates and carbonates of calcium, magnesium, and sodium are present in some clays and may 'migrate' to the surface, especially when they are much handled in modeling. They are most apparent on red clays (see *scumming*). *Egyptian paste* relies on this phenomenon to develop its glaze. *Filter pressing* tends to eliminate salts. Soluble alkalis are also a feature of ash (see *ash preparation*).

## SOLUTION

See *soluble*.

## SOLUTION COLOR

Colors derived from metal oxides dissolved in a molten glaze. (See *color*.)

## SORTING TOOL

'Sorting' is the removal of the sharp points of glaze left by *stilts* etc. after glaze-firing. A sorting-tool is a type of cold chisel with a tungsten carbide or other very hard edge. To use it, hold the pot firmly in one hand and bring the tool down sharply and square onto the pot just behind the snag to be removed, so that the tool catches the snag as near to its base as possible. Repeat with short, sharp movements, working into and under the blemish. With skill the blemish will sheer off after very few jabs.

## SOURING

The aging of clay to improve plasticity and other qualities.

## SPALLING

The breaking away of flakes or larger pieces from the faces and corners of *refractory hot-face* bricks in the kiln. *Thermal shock,* crystalline *inversion,* inadequate expansion allowances and *slag* formation are among the causes. *Free silica* should be minimal in the refractory fabric. Sudden heating or cooling will alter the expansion of the face of the brick compared with its back, and can cause deep spalling.

## SPANGLES

Iron spangles, magnetic ferroso-ferric iron $Fe_3O_4$, 233. Magnetite. A coarse black iron oxide used to produce speckling in bodies and glazes.

## SPATULA TOOL

A tool with a flattened, curved and rounded end. It can be of wood or metal and is a most useful tool for potters.

*A wooden spatula tool.*

## SPECIFIC GRAVITY

The ratio of the density of a material to that of an equal mass of water at 40°C. A specific gravity (s.g.) figure of less than one will therefore indicate that the material is 'lighter' than water (i.e. will float). The s.g. of clays and most common ceramic minerals averages 2.6; feldspars slightly less, and quartz a little more at 2.65. This is useful when using *Brongiart's formula.* The mass or weight of a material divided by its volume will give its density. The equation must be either in lb./pts. or kg./liters. The figure obtained is divided by the s.g. of pure water, but since this is 1.0 the density and s.g. are the same.

The s.g. value will also control the setting speed of pottery materials in water. Lead, with a figure of 11.3, will drop quickly and such glazes must be stirred repeatedly. The high s.g. of zircon sand limits its use in refractories, saggars etc., for which it would be otherwise very suitable; high concentrations make these too heavy.

## SPECIFIC HEAT

The heat required to raise a unit of a substance through one degree. (See *British thermal units, calorie, joule.*)

## SPINEL

A mineral built up into regular *crystals* from a *bivalent* and a *trivalent* (tervalent) metal. The general composition is $MO.R_2O_3$, where M equals magnesium, ferrous iron, manganese, zinc, cobalt or nickel; and R equals ferric iron, chromium or aluminum. The typical mineral is magnesium aluminate, $MgO.Al_2O_3$. Magnetic iron oxide $FeO.Fe_2O_3$ is a spinel, and cobalt also forms spinels. They are considered to be the most stable form of oxides.

## SPINNER

A plate or saucer which has sagged or warped in the center of its base so that it will not sit firmly, i.e. it can be spun round. This may be caused by careless *turning,* or may develop during drying. Test before packing in the kiln and, if necessary, flatten with a pad of glass paper which can also be used on soft biscuit.

## SPIRAL WEDGING

See *wedging.*

## SPODUMENE

A *lithium* mineral $Li_2O.Al_2O_3.4SiO_2$, 372. Similar to *petalite* which has $8SiO_2$.

Undergoes an irreversible expansion from alpha to beta forms at 900°C. Used in bodies where a low *thermal expansion* is required. C.PP 76 discusses the compounding of an artificial spodumene body or the use of spodumene rock (60%, 60-200 mesh) with plastic clay for flameproof bodies. A very simple glaze recipe using 54.5% spodumene to 45.5% talc is given by Behrens in CM 20/3. (See also *lithium.*)

## SPONGE

Various synthetic sponges are now made, but none can equal a fine-grain natural sponge for sensitivity and working qualities. The ideal type is the 'elephant's ear' Turkey sponge, about $2\frac{1}{2}$ in. (65 mm.) across. Natural sponges are becoming rarer and more expensive. If you can visit a supplier to choose your own, so much the better. The 'grain' should lie all in one direction with no holes or tears. Once found, a good sponge is worth treasuring; wash it after use and avoid highly abrasive surfaces.

Synthetic bath-sponges with large holes are best for swabbing and cleaning. The type which dries stiff can more easily be cut to shape and used for throwing, but most of them become loaded with clay, which is difficult to wash out.

## SPONGE-STICK

A natural or polyester fiber sponge fastened to the end of a dowel or stick, and used for absorbing surplus water from pots during throwing. A small natural sponge stretched tightly over the end of a $\frac{1}{2}$ or $\frac{3}{4}$ x $\frac{1}{4}$ in. (say 15 x 7 mm.) stick can be used as a *throwing stick.*

## SPOUT

A tapering tube which conducts and controls the flow of liquid from a tea or coffee pot etc. It is useful to bear this definition in mind, especially with regard to 'control', when designing a spout. The object of the taper is to build up a pressure or weight of liquid so that it issues in a steady, arching stream. A large and clumsy spout will not do this efficiently. Nor will it pour well if the grid behind the spout will not allow more water to pass through it than can issue from the narrowest part of the spout.

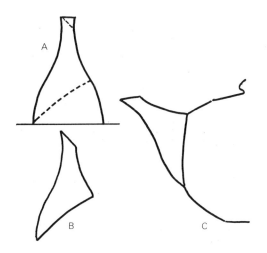

*If a teapot spout is thrown as shape (A) it can be cut with a wire along the dotted lines to give (B) and attached to the pot as (C), forming a teapot spout with a single curve above and a double curve below.*

Spouts are usually thrown, leaving sufficient extra clay top and bottom for trimming. The form can be straight-sided, concave, or slightly bottle-shaped. Trim the large end to fit the pot at the correct angle, about 45° to the vertical, and ensure that the other end is at least level with the lid flange, if not higher. If the lower part of the spout is too thick it can be trimmed inside with a knife. Mark the outline on the pot and drill grid holes before scoring, slipping, and luting it on.

Trimming the small end presents problems. Clay has what Cardew calls 'memory', that is, it will continue to twist during firing in the direction of the throwing strain. This means that the spout may be pointing sideways after firing if it has been trimmed horizontally. Slower, 'easy' throwing will help. Allowance can be made when trimming by facing the spout away from you and cutting it to slope slightly to the right and point a little to the left. Some potters avoid the difficulty by leaving the end of the spout as a right-angle, but the form must be very carefully worked out if this is not to look blunt and unfinished.

Spouts have been *press molded* and applied to thrown pots, but not with conspicuous success. Thrown spouts are usually applied at soft leather stage, but Michael Casson and others lute them on almost immediately after throwing. This demands great skill but at its best can be very fresh and integrated in its effect. A spout may be 'pulled' (see *handles*) into a curve when half-dry. The very tip of the spout should be reasonably sharp, and its pouring qualities will be enhanced by a slight downwards curve (see *lip*).

*Michael Casson applying a spout immediately after throwing. (1-5) show stages in the throwing. (5) is especially important: all trace of slip on the surface is removed with a rib so that it will be dry enough to handle. The spout is cut through (6) and set down, and the base angle cut through with a wire (7). The top of the base aperture is eased upwards with the finger (8), and the spout pressed onto the pot just firmly enough to make a mark (9, 10). Within this line the grid is cut through (11); the spout is placed in position and fastened on with a few careful but free-moving strokes (12, 13). The end of the spout is now cut. To allow for the twist which often occurs during firing, the wire is held sloping slightly downwards on the left when facing the pot as in the picture (14). The completed spout, only a few minutes after throwing (15). The teapot body is leather-hard.*

12

13

14

15

A modern Japanese teapot by Futoh of Tokoname with a slab spout.

## SPRAYING

The application of glaze or color by rendering it to a fine mist under pressure. Usually done with a spray-gun similar to those used for paint etc. The granular nature of ceramic suspensions will clog some types, especially the cheaper electric drill-sprayers. A more sophisticated and efficient set-up involves an air-pressure pump and pressure tank. Spraying is practiced in the industry, but has limited value in the small workshop. It is noisy, and an additional spray-booth with an exhaust fan is strongly advised. A mask should always be worn. Sprayed glaze is liable to uneven thickness and to *pinholing*. Although small amounts of glaze can be used, there is considerable waste. The minimum cost of equipment, with a booth, would be about £125 (England, 1973).

Spraying is useful for *once-fired* wares, especially large plates and other bulky pieces. Color can be sprayed onto *resist* or, from a finely controlled jet, 'drawn' on the dish or pot. It is difficult to avoid a mechanical, commercial appearance. A number of professional potters are, however, experimenting with sprayed decoration.

## SPRIG

A bas-relief or medallion made in a small press-mold and stuck with slip onto a pottery surface. Typified by eighteenth-century bi-colored sprigging, salt-glazed bellarmine masks, and in the industry by Wedgwood's cameos. The craft potter can still devise new and entertaining uses for the sprig.

The sprig-mold can be cut directly into clay and then biscuit fired; the design can be cut into a slab of plaster; or the sprig can be modeled separately and cast in plaster. To make a cast, work plastic clay firmly into the mold with a flat tool and flatten the back. It can be removed by pressing a damp metal spatula or *palette knife* onto the back and lifting sharply. Position the sprig on the damped surface of a pot and press gently with a wooden tool in the hollows of the design. Do not attempt too large a sprig; it is better to build up from smaller units.

219

*A simple sprig mold with casts.*

## SPRINGER
Or scewback. A brick with one sloping face from which an arch can be 'sprung' when building a kiln. (See *brick, bricklaying.*)

## SPUR
A small piece of kiln furniture with one point up and three down. For use at earthenware temperatures only.

## SQUARE LINER
Long slender brushes with the end cut square. For lining with the whole length of the brush.

## STABLE, stability
A stable glaze has a well-balanced formula, is adequately fired and will not react easily to acid or other corrosion. An excess of bases or coloring oxides may render a glaze unstable. Stability is always desirable, but especially so in lead glazes (see *lead solubility* and *metal release*). Adherence to the generally recommended ratios of the Seger formula will assist in computing stable glazes. (See also *Thorpe's ratio.*)

The physical stability of a pot is also a virtue. Tall shapes with very small bases are seldom good pot forms. The strengthening of a narrow-waisted pot with a metal rod is an acceptance of failure. An uneven base is aggravating, and all pots and bowls should be tested before firing. A slightly hollow or concave base may be achieved during making or turning by tapping with the finger when soft-leather. A wobbly base can be flattened by holding the pot hard down on to a wetted wheel head or whirler, which is then revolved. Dry pots can be sandpapered in the same way.

## STACK-THROWING
Term sometimes used to describe several small pieces of pottery thrown from one large block of clay. The top surface clay should be well compressed after cutting off each piece so as to minimize the chance of cracking because of excessive wetness remaining from the previous throwing.

*Throwing from a cone of clay (1)—stack throwing—in this case for glaze trial bowls. A method of cutting-off is shown, a needle awl held sloping slightly upwards towards the center of the base (2).*

## STAFFORDSHIRE CONES
A range of pyrometric cones made by Harrison Mayer Ltd. The numbers correspond within 10°C. to Seger cones. Graded in 10°C. steps above 08 (940°C.) up to 11 (1320°C.), except 1200-1215° and 1215-1230°. The numbers are prefixed by H. A nought in front of any number indicates a temperature below 1100°C. (See under *cones* for list.)

## STAIN
A term widely used in pottery, but without a specific meaning. It can indicate an organic identifying stain (used industrially for *electrical porcelain* bodies); or any oxide or prepared pigment used for coloring bodies, slips or glazes. The term might with advantage be restricted to fritted, prepared colors, in which sense it is generally used in merchants' catalogs.

## STAMP
An embossed or intaglio stamp can be used to build up a pattern on clay. *Impressing* is a type of stamping. It

can also indicate the printing of color onto the surface without involving impression. Sponge 'root', cut into patterns, has been used for stamping designs onto pottery. Some potters' 'marks' are rubber-stamped with pottery pigment. (See also *seal*.)

## STANDARD BLACK

A color derived from 4% each of cobalt, manganese, and iron oxides. (See *black glazes*.)

## STANNIC

Applied to a tin compound or to a glaze containing tin. More exactly, 'stannic' indicates quadrivalent tin $SnO_2$, as distinct from stannous *bivalent* SnO tin.

## STAR AND DELTA WIRING

Systems for wiring *three-phase* equipment.

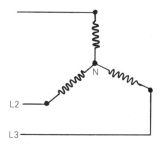
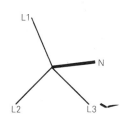

*Star wiring for a three phase kiln. Each line is connected back to neutral. This will give full mains voltage on each phase. See also under three phase.*

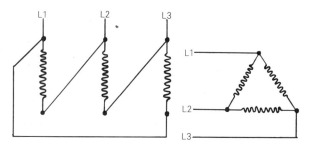

*Delta wiring for three phases. Element circuits are connected across phases giving 415 volts per circuit from a 240 volt supply. The neutral is not employed in this system.*

## STATES OF MATTER

The three most distinct states of matter are the gaseous, the liquid and the solid. No chemical change takes place between these states, but only the physical 'loosening' of the bonds between the *molecules*. Energy, usually heat, is involved in the changes.

## STEATITE

The massive form or rock of talc. Soapstone. One of the softest rocks and minerals. Can be carved into pot and other forms and is still known as 'pot-stone'. Also used as 'French chalk'.

## STEEL PALETTE

A very thin, flexible, sheet-steel tool, rectangular or kidney-shaped. Made in two thicknesses and several sizes, averaging 5 in. (127 mm.) across. Invaluable for scraping and smoothing plastic clay, especially for *hand-building*. Can be used as a throwing *rib* or, occasionally, for *turning*.

## STENCIL

Allied to *resist*, a stencil is a piece of shaped card, paper or other fairly stiff material laid onto a surface so as to control a design. It can have apertures cut in it, through which color can be applied; it can be used as a resist shape, producing a blank shape on a background of color; or to divide a surface into two areas. The comparative rigidity of stencils confines their effect to simple shapes and masses, often as a foundation for other decoration. Sponging or dabbing the color will give sharper outlines than will brushing; alternatively pigment can be sprayed on. Shallow dishes and tiles present no problems, but stencilling is more difficult on a pot. *Paper resist* is a form of one-off stencilling. Leach uses a stencil to divide his 'mountain' dish designs.

*Brushing color across a paper stencil on a dish.*

## STICKING-UP

The assembly of parts of a model, teapot, or similar construction, either at the leather-hard or a softer stage.

## STILT

An item of *kiln furniture*. It has three arms radiating from the centre, with vertical points, generally at the end of each arm. Glazed pieces are supported on appropriately sized stilts, the points about $\frac{1}{4}$ in. (6 mm.) in from the edge of the base. The point adheres to the glaze and breaks away when the stilt is removed. Stilts are therefore expendable, though they may last three or four uses. Designed for the industry with its thin, *fritted* glazes, a stilt can become firmly welded into thick or carelessly applied *raw glaze*. Glaze the base sparingly, therefore, or wipe some of the glaze away.

Do not jam the points into a *foot ring* or extend them beyond the ring. *Spurs* may be used in place of stilts for large dishes. Remember also that the pot will shrink, but the stilt will not. Remove stilts with a sorting tool.

Sizes are available from 25-100 mm. (1-4 in.) point to point. 'Egg stilts' are triangular in plan, with a hole in the center. Stilts are for use in *earthenware* firings only, and will fail in stoneware.

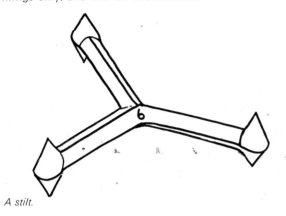

*A stilt.*

## STONEWARE

According to the Brussels Nomenclature—'dense, impermeable, and hard enough to resist scratching with a steel point . . . more opaque [than porcelain] and normally only partly vitrified'. Stoneware is distinguished from earthenware by:
1   Its higher firing-temperature. The generally accepted minimum is 1200°C., and the range is 1200-1350°C. Bodies with artificially lowered *vitrification*-points have been marketed.
2   Its degree of vitrification. A *porosity* of not more than 5%. The higher fired stonewares will also be *impermeable*. The surface has a close and glassy texture but may be rough.
3   A well developed reaction zone across the *interface*, giving greater integration and subtlety of glaze.
4   Low iron-content in the body. Red clay will not form a true stoneware, though it may be added to a *refractory* body.
5   Does not need either lead or boron in its glaze, although the latter is sometimes used in small quantities.
6   Iron can be *reduced* in stoneware.

In spite of stoneware's apparent advantages over earthenware, the qualities of the two types of ceramics are so different that neither has an inherent superiority.

## STONEWARE BODY

A naturally *fusible* but reasonably iron-free plastic clay is the basis for a stoneware body. Many *fireclays* and other *sedimentary clays* may be suitable either alone or as the major constituent. Sources of 'stoneware' clay are reported in the USA in Colorado, Wyoming, and New Jersey (Jordon clay).

Most stoneware bodies are mixtures of a number of materials, each chosen for their particular qualities.
1   For *plasticity*: ball clays and red clays, up to 40% of the first and 20% of the second.
2   For *fusibility*: natural fusibility from the ball and red clays. Additional non-plastic fluxes such as feldspar, stone, (5-15%), or 5% of talc have been mentioned.
3   Refractoriness and low shrinkage: china clay, quartz or flint (15-20%), sand, grog (ideally the body biscuit), or aluminous fireclay.
4   For color: red clay, or 5-10% of *ochre* (Leach).
5   Texture: *grog*, sand, coarse fireclay up to 25%.

Ilmenite will cause glaze speckle. The materials should be blunged to a slip for maximum efficiency.

Many potters buy a prepared plastic body which when bought is often too smooth and characterless, but which can be modified as above. (Cardew warns against wedging china clay into a plastic body.) Others buy dry powdered materials and work them together in a *dough mixer.*

## STONEWARE CLAY

A general name for plastic, refractory, *secondary clays* which are not as fine-grained as *ball clays* or as deep-seated as *fireclays*. In Germany and the USA, and in other parts of the world, grades of clay can be found which will fire to 1300°C. with few if any modifications. They have no massive commercial use and are therefore more difficult to obtain than kaolins and fireclays.

## STONEWARE GLAZES

A range of glazes firing between 1200°C. and 1350°C., with the great majority in the midway range, 1260-1310°C. The two oxides which feature so prominently in soft glazes (lead and boron) have little or no place in stonewares, which are generally based on feldspars or wood ash.

The average formula for a stoneware glaze is $RO.0.35Al_2O_3. 3.5SiO_2$, but there are numerous combinations outside this ratio, e.g. above 1300°C. the silica ratio can rise sharply, while formulas with only 2.0 parts of silica have been reported in analyses of Chinese glazes. At temperatures of 1250°C. plus it is difficult *not* to produce a glaze of some kind by mixing two or three ceramic minerals. The classic starting point is 40 parts feldspar, 30 flint, 20 whiting, 10 clay; but in other recipes the feldspar is much more dominant, e.g. 70 feldspar, 13 flint, 10 whiting, 7 china clay. Various *line blends* and *triaxial mixtures* can be tried with nepheline, dolomite, talc, barium and stone; with other more exotic minerals such as petalite, basalt, etc.; also with red clay and, of course, ash. It is useful to be able to translate any interesting result back to a glaze formula (see *recipe-into-formula*). The effects of the various oxides and minerals are discussed under their headings. (See also *oxidation* and *reduction*.)

Iron is the principal coloring oxide in reduced stoneware glazes, which seem to have a wider firing-range without violent character changes than do oxidized glazes. In the latter the range is wider but the effects, in general, are not so subtle. Manganese and copper have a place, the latter in matt glazes to prevent *volatilization*. Cobalt needs to be well 'quenched' with iron, red clay etc. if it is not to be strident.

## STOPPING

Mixtures for filling cracks in biscuit ware. Merchants list 'red', 'white' and 'stoneware' stopping—generally composed of china clay, flint and a little flux. If a biscuit pot has cracked, this suggests strain which may cause further damage in the glaze fire, and the piece is better discarded. With modeling there is more justification for attempting repair. A special new stopping called Alumide has appeared, which, the makers claim, can be glazed over.

## STORAGE OF CLAY

Clay improves with *aging*, and facilities for storing clay in a damp atmosphere are very desirable. For large quantities, some sort of clay 'cellar' with non-absorbent walls, a tile floor, no ventilation and a close-fitting door is ideal, but for most craft potters something more modest is called for. The *polythene* bags in which plastic clay is often delivered provide storage, if unpunctured, for many months. Similarly, plastic sacks, bin-liners and the like can be utilized for mixed and *wedged* batches, which should be rested for at least a day or two before use. Damp the interior of the bags with a sponge to avoid dry flakes of clay.

Clay bins present problems: drying layers of clay on the sides; the decomposition of zinc on galvanized surfaces; and the difficulty of extracting clay from a pressed-down mass. If clay has been pugged, try to keep the rolls separate so that they can be more easily lifted out; sheets of stiffish polythene between layers help. Pug your clay fairly soft. A full bin is more efficient than a half-empty one. Asbestos tanks will need filling with water first so as to saturate them. Plastic bins are effective as far as dampness goes, but are easily damaged with scrapers. They will also melt easily, and can crack in frost.

## STRAW ASH

A highly refractory ash, usually containing up to 75-80% silica. An exception is 'bean straw ash' (L.PB).

## STRONTIUM, oxide

A metallic element Sr, 87.5.
Oxide SrO, 103.5. Strontia.
Carbonate $SrCO_3$, 147.5.

An *alkaline earth*. The slightly *soluble*, non-poisonous but expensive carbonate is used as a glaze flux. Similar to calcium, which it can replace. Strontium glazes should be low in lime, however, if crystallization is not required. Parmelee states that good earthenware glazes can be had by replacing some other bases with strontia, and that colors also benefit. The oxide provides a long firing-range and is very craze-resistant. There

are no common strontia-bearing minerals. Strontium earthenware glazes are reported to be widely used in Russia, the oxide replacing lead.

## STUDIO POTTER

An artist-craftsman working alone, or with very few assistants, who takes part in all the ceramic processes so that the final piece has his or her individual stamp or character. It is not a very satisfactory term, and others have been suggested: craftsman potter; artist potter; workshop potter; hand potter; non-industrial potter; ceramist etc. As the industry becomes more and more remote from its craft origins, perhaps simply 'potter' will soon be sufficient.

## STUPID

An old term for a *wad-mill*!

## SULFIDES, sulfates

Many elements will form a salt or binary compound with sulfur. Its release during firing, however, can have ill-effects on glazes, and the form is rarely used. Galena is a sulfide of lead; barytes a sulfate of barium. Both liberate sulfur dioxide. Plaster of paris is $CaSO_4 \cdot (\frac{1}{2}H_2O)$. (See also *sulfuring*.)

## SULFUR

An element S, 32. Combines with metals to form sulfides. Sulfur is present in some fireclays.

## SULFURING

The dulling of a glaze surface through attack by sulfur. Parmelee discusses the effects at length (P.CG 308-11). Sulfur as sulfides—salts of sulfurous oxide $SO_2$—will burn away, but those of the higher $SiO_3$ sulfuric oxide are resistant to change by heat. Early ventilation is therefore necessary to clear fumes from the kiln, especially in *soft-glaze* firings. At higher temperatures a *reducing* atmosphere is more likely to drive out the sulfur in sulfates. *Leadless* glazes and those with a high calcium or barium content appear to be at greatest risk from sulfur gas. The sulfur gases liberated by some clays in an electric kiln are a nuisance, and the pottery room should be well ventilated.

## SUPERSATURATED GLAZE

A glaze with more coloring oxide than it can dissolve, the surplus being precipitated on cooling. (See *saturated glaze*.)

## SURFACE COMBUSTION

Fuel gases burn more readily in contact with hot surfaces. This will be obvious to anyone who has tried to start a *drip-feed* kiln from cold. Kiln design should take this into account; the heating of *secondary air* is important.

## SURFACE TENSION

An effect, resembling that of a stretched elastic skin, seen at the boundary or surface of any liquid. For instance, when gently pouring liquid from the surface of a glaze it will pile up on the rim before bursting through and running off. Glaze, in its liquid state, has a high surface tension value—some 200-300 as compared with 74 for water. This will be seen from the globules of glaze which hang at the foot of an over-fired or over-glazed pot. *Crawling* in its final stages is influenced by surface tension, the glaze failing to 'wet' the surface. The surface tension of the glaze is greater than the gravity effect which would otherwise spread it over the surface. Cracks in the glaze coating, the primary cause of crawling, increase the surface area and thus the tension. Dust under the surface will have a similar effect. Zinc and magnesium are reputed to lower the surface tension.

## SUSPENDER, floatative

A glaze or slip additive which will help to retard *settling* and aid *suspension*. This can be by physical means, using gums (tragacanth, dextrin, arabic), size, bentonite or ball clay; or by the electrical or molecular effect of salt, deflocculants or ammonia. All have intrinsic disadvantages. Organic materials (Parmelee also includes quince pips and blood!) decompose if glaze is kept for long periods and need the further addition of *formalin*. *Deflocculants* thin the mixture; salt introduces unwanted *soluble* ingredients. Dodd mentions calcium chloride to prevent settling—about 0.02%. Epsom salts have been mentioned.

All in all, perhaps the best suspender is a good wide paddle and a strong arm.

## SUSPENSION

All insoluble materials stirred up in a liquid will eventually sink to the bottom again. Fine particles will remain suspended in the liquid longer than coarse ones; those with a low *specific gravity* will remain longer than those with a high one. A lead fritt will thus have the worst of both worlds. *Colloidal* particles will remain longest in suspension, hence the use of bentonite. Suspension does not of course refer to *soluble* materials. Some glazes will stay in suspension for a longer period if the container is tightly sealed.

Glaze becomes liquid during firing. Certain oxides, generally *acidic* oxides, will fail to dissolve but will remain in suspension in a fundamentally unaltered state. These are the opacifiers, notably tin and zircon.

# T

**T°**

Symbol for degrees of temperature.

## TABLEWARE

A general term for pottery directly concerned with the serving of food and drink. See *plate, cup, saucer*.

## TAILINGS

The portion of a material which will not pass through a particular *screen*, for instance, coloring oxide in a 200 sieve. The tailings go back into the *mortar* for further grinding.

## TALC

A mineral, a hydrated magnesium silicate $3MgO.4SiO_2.H_2O$, 379 (convenient equivalent weight 126). Low *coefficient of expansion* (2.0).

The chief mineral of soapstone and steatite. Used as an insoluble form of magnesia in glazes. Dolomite is now more commonly used for this purpose. Typical analysis by weight:

| MgO | 32.0 | $Al_2O_3$ | 7.0 | $SiO_2$ | 56.5 |
| CaO | 3.0 | $Fe_2O_3$ | 1.5 | | |

Small amounts, 2% in the batch or up to 0.3 of the *RO*, will act as a *flux*; more than this will tend to make the glaze *viscous*, but can impart a pleasant sheen to the surface. Lowers the *thermal expansion* (see *cordierite*). It affects some colors—iron goes brown, cobalt a less intense blue. Can be mixed with cobalt when this oxide is used as a pigment.

Talc has a fine, powdery nature and is difficult to mix with water in a glaze batch, floating on the top and blowing away in the slightest breeze. It is advisable to mix it well with the other dry ingredients, and to slowly add the water to the batch.

## TAMMANN TEMPERATURE

The *sintering* point of range.

## TEAPOTS

A good teapot is difficult to make but, when successful, few things can give a potter more satisfaction. One of our most distinguished potters, Geoffrey Whiting, gave this advice in PQ 7:

'A teapot needs to be fairly broad and certainly stable. Throw as thinly as possible, and keep the opening as small as is compatible with easy filling and cleaning. Throw the spout on a fairly thick base, which should be wide enough to allow a grid the holes of which have a slightly greater cross-sectional area than that of the narrow end of the spout. Make the knob on the lid something worth getting hold of, and vent the lid with a generous $\frac{1}{10}$ in. (2 mm.) hole.'

It is vital to trim the spout so that it is at least level with the top of the teapot (see also *spouts*). Punch plenty of grid or strainer holes, each about $\frac{1}{8}$ in. (3 mm.) across, and leave the ragged edges inside the pot severely alone until quite dry, when they can be chipped away without blocking the holes. Mark and score the spout position and attach with slip. Geoffrey Whiting prefers a spout which grows 'smoothly out of the body of the pot and makes a continuous unbroken line with it', but other teapots show more articulation between spout and pot, as in the Michael Casson example illustrated.

The *handle* is very important. It must be efficient and comfortable, with room for three fingers on a

A teapot by Geoffrey Whiting with a typically smooth, flowing profile, all parts being physically as well as aesthetically integrated.

A more articulated approach to teapot form (Michael Casson). See also under spout.

medium pot and four on a large one. Its form and the area of void its loop encloses must balance the spout and the lid. Always attach the handle after the spout, and with the completed lid in place. 'You [may] find that, to form a comfortable efficient hold, the handle looks wrong on the pot . . . in which case you may have to redesign the whole thing. This sort of difficulty is implicit in the nature of design and craftsmanship and it is no good being afraid of it. Pencil sketches will help but do not allow yourself to become a slave to paper designs. They militate against the freedom and spontaneity the thrown shape should always have.'

Arched-over handles can be of *cane* or clay. They must be high enough for comfortable removal of the lid. The *lugs* of a cane handle should be sturdy; a good deal of weight depends from them. (See also *spouts, handles, cane handles, glazing, lids, knobs*.)

## TEMMOKU, tenmoku

The Japanese name for very dark colored *reduced* iron stonewares of the Chien Sung types, including 'hare's fur', 'oil spot' and other effects on a near-black glaze, which can also break to an iron-red. Quoted percentages of iron in the batch vary widely: 4.5-5% with slow cooling (Cardew); 10% burnt sienna, or a slip glaze of the Albany variety (Rhodes); up to 12% (Leach); a precise 7.6% from Dodd, who also gives this recipe: feldspar 50, whiting 10.9, magnesite 2.3, kaolin 5.9, quartz 23.0.

It obviously depends upon the type of glaze, usually a fairly fluid one, and on how much iron it will dissolve. A supersaturated glaze will tend to break with lighter browns. (See also *black glazes, red glazes, iron* etc.) S.WJC mentions manganese, chrome and cobalt in connection with temmoku glazes. See color plate 22, p. 144.

## TEMPERATURE COLORS

The optical effect of rising heat (in the absence of light) is a change from black to blue-white, through reds, oranges and yellows. It is difficult to give names to these 'colors' which will make them recognizable when peering through a kiln spyhole. G.EP gives a color chart, but the light reflected from an illustration is different in kind from the radiant heat color. With these reservations in mind, the following table may have some use.

| Seger cone | T°C. | T°F. | Color |
|---|---|---|---|
| 022 | 600 | 1110 | dull red |
| 015 | 800 | 1470 | red |
| 010 | 1000 | 1830 | cherry red, between red and orange |
| 1 | 1100 | 2010 | orange |
| 5 | 1180 | 2160 | light orange |
| 7 | 1230 | 2250 | pale yellow |
| 10 | 1300 | 2370 | yellow-white |
| 12 | 1350 | 2460 | white tending to blue |

Intensity of light, in fact, produces color effect.

## TEMPERATURE DEGREES

Heat produces internal activity in matter: 'hotness' or temperature is a measure of the kinetic energy of the *molecules* of which the matter is composed. Heat leads to fundamental alteration and rearrangement in the basic atomic structure. Certain reactions (e.g. *oxidation*) in themselves produce heat. Temperature is one factor in *heat-work*.

The degree of heat is indicated by a constant scale. Those in common use are based on the interval between the freezing- and boiling-points of water. The Centigrade or Celsius scale divides this interval into 100 degrees and commences at freezing point, 0°. The freezing point in the Fahrenheit scale is 32°, and the interval is divided into 180 degrees, giving 212°F. as the boiling-point. Conversion cannot therefore be made directly except by memory. The arithmetic is:
Centigrade into Fahrenheit—divide by 5, multiply by 9, add 32 to total.
Fahrenheit into Centigrade—subtract 32, divide remainder by 9, multiply by 5.

## Temperature conversion tables—Centigrade (Celsius) Fahrenheit, and Kelvin

| C. | F. | K. | C. | F. | K. |
|---|---|---|---|---|---|
| −273 | −477 | 0 | 1000 | 1832 | 1273 |
| −18 | 0 | 255 | 1050 | 1922 | 1323 |
| 0 | 32 | 273 | 1080 | 1976 | 1353 |
| 10 | 50 | 283 | 1100 | 2012 | 1373 |
| 50 | 122 | 323 | 1120 | 2048 | 1393 |
| 100 | 212 | 373 | 1140 | 2084 | 1413 |
| 120 | 248 | 393 | 1150 | 2102 | 1423 |
| 200 | 392 | 473 | 1180 | 2156 | 1453 |
| 225 | 437 | 498 | 1200 | 2192 | 1473 |
| 250 | 482 | 523 | 1220 | 2238 | 1493 |
| 300 | 572 | 573 | 1230 | 2246 | 1503 |
| 350 | 662 | 623 | 1240 | 2264 | 1513 |
| 400 | 752 | 673 | 1250 | 2282 | 1523 |
| 450 | 842 | 723 | 1260 | 2300 | 1533 |
| 500 | 932 | 773 | 1275 | 2318 | 1548 |
| 550 | 1022 | 823 | 1280 | 2336 | 1553 |
| 573 | 1063 | 846 | 1285 | 2345 | 1558 |
| 600 | 1112 | 873 | 1300 | 2373 | 1573 |
| 660 | 1220 | 933 | 1310 | 2390 | 1583 |
| 700 | 1292 | 973 | 1325 | 2417 | 1598 |
| 750 | 1382 | 1023 | 1335 | 2435 | 1608 |
| 800 | 1472 | 1073 | 1350 | 2462 | 1623 |
| 870 | 1598 | 1143 | 1380 | 2516 | 1653 |
| 900 | 1652 | 1173 | 1400 | 2552 | 1673 |
| 950 | 1742 | 1223 | 1450 | 2642 | 1723 |

## TEMPERATURE INDICATORS

If a sufficiently large aperture is available, pieces can be extracted from the kiln during firing as indications of its progress. These can be pieces of the actual body and ware in the setting, or lead-glazed pieces which will become darker and colder as the firing proceeds (these should be of red clay). If the pieces are in the form of a ring or hoop they will be easier to withdraw with a simple iron rod. (See *cone, pyrometer, Buller's rings, Seger formula* etc.)

## TEMPERING CLAY

Adding water to clay powder, or distributing it more intimately. This can be done with a *paddle* and bin, with a *dough mixer*, or, really professionally, by *blunging.* (See also *mixing clays.*)

## TEMPLATE

A sheet of card, metal or stiff material cut to the profile of a pot, plate, bowl or mold former, and used as a guide or to scrape the clay surface to a regular curve. (See *jigger and jolley, hollow mold.*)

## TEMPORARY KILN

The spate, in recent years, of large 'sculptural' ceramics has given rise to firing problems. When pieces are too heavy or too awkward to be packed into a standard kiln, simple dry-built kiln structures have been erected round them and the whole fired *in situ*. Firing is generally by oil, carried out through strategically placed burner apertures. More than one burner is needed. A simple *up-draft kiln* might be easier to fire. (See also diagrams in R.K) Raku and *sawdust* kilns are also temporary structures, erected and taken down in a few minutes. A more traditional structure erected as a temporary kiln can be very instructive with regard to kiln design and performance.

## TENSILE STRENGTH

The resistance a material exhibits to being torn apart by tension or pulling. The tensile strength of glazes and bodies is important, one or the other usually being in a state of tension. *Soft glazes* are reputed to be more 'elastic' or resistant than stonewares, but it is easier to get a stoneware glaze into *compression*. (See *crazing, shattering*.)

## TENSION

A state of tensile or 'pulling' strain. Glazes under tension will *craze*.

## TERRACOTTA

Literally 'cooked earth', the term most commonly indicates unglazed red clay modeling or architectural ceramic. It is also applied to the color of fired *red clay*. Rhodes equates terracotta with a low-grade open *fireclay*, but this would not be a widely understood meaning. Cardew describes a 'terracotta' wood-firing kiln for temperatures up to 950°C. (C.PP 174-6).

## TERRA SIGILLATA

A reddish-brown, slightly glossy surface found especially on Roman pottery. Probably a very fine *(colloidal)* red slip. Potash additions (wine lees) have also been mentioned. Behrens suggests: clay 40, water 100, soda ash 4. Allow the slip to settle, pour water from the surface and use only the top one-third or so—the finest grain (see *suspension*). Colors in the form of carbonates and also zinc or titanium can be added before sedimentation.

## TERTIARY AIR

An infrequently used term for a supply of pre-heated air to the chimney of a kiln to assist combustion of smoke and to minimize pollution. The chimney can be large enough to accommodate pots for biscuit-firing; it will then act like an up-draft kiln.

## TESSHA

A Japanese glaze of the temmoku family but more metallic and breaking to iron reds. The standard 4.3.2.1. glaze (see *stoneware glaze*) with the addition of 26% quartz and 13% iron, in reduction, is given in L.PB for tessha. The firing schedule will radically affect the glaze. Quick cooling to 900°C. is recommended.

## TEST-KILN

The value of very small trial kilns is limited. By their nature they fire and cool more quickly than a production kiln and this, together with other factors, will give misleading results. They are more useful in earthenware, the results approximating more closely to those from larger kilns than in *stoneware*. On the credit side, they can give a general impression at *various temperatures* and can reveal gross errors in glaze mixes before a full pack is spoiled. Tests are always more valid, however, when worked in with the general run of production in normal kilns.

Electric test-kilns can be built quite cheaply and quickly, although the limited *element* lengths will necessitate a thinner gauge wire than is normal for high temperatures. 90 ft. (27 m.) of 17 s.w.g., producing 2.5 kW, can generally be housed in a test-kiln.

## TEST-PIECE

See *glaze trials*.

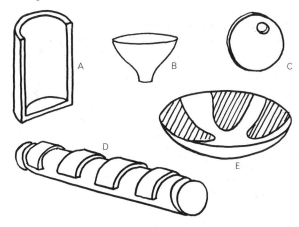

*Test pieces for glaze tests, etc. (A) a thrown cylinder can be cut in two as shown or, if wider, into four or six segments. Each will give an upright, curved surface simulating a pot. (B) is a small bowl thrown on a 'stack' (see photographs). (C) a ring with a hole is useful for hanging either on a board, or stringing together. (D) shows strips of clay drying on a rolling pin so that each piece will stand on a curved edge. (E) is a shallow dish from the center of which several glaze tests have been poured, keeping a series together for reference and comparison. It is sometimes instructive if the tests overlap.*

## TEXTURE

The same root as 'textile'. The *Oxford English Dictionary* gives 'an arrangement of threads'. In general usage the term indicates fine markings or irregularities of the surface, or the degree of smoothness of the surface, as apparent to sight and touch.

With the increase in *hand-building* and the decline in *brushwork* and pattern-making, texture is often the main interest provided by the surface. Sand or grog is either beaten into the surface or exposed by working it over; coarse metal oxides (e.g. ilmenite) or even fragments of metal (e.g. copper filings) produce varied texture on a surface. More consciously controlled markings are made with hacksaws, fine combs etc., or by beating with engraved or string-bound bats etc. (See also *impressing*.)

*A heavily textured surface. The body is grogged and various materials beaten into the surface: copper and iron metal filings, larger grog including red clay grog, and builders' sand.*

lators'. The variation between common ceramic materials can be startling, e.g. silicon carbide is given a factor of 120, while a white porous insulating brick may be as low as 0.8. The factor is arrived at by computing the Btu's per square foot of face area per hour per degree Fahrenheit per inch of thickness, written $Btu/ft^2/h/°F./in$. Other measurements can replace certain items, such as square meters for $ft^2$, or °C. for °F., but it is the comparative figures derived from any one factor which are of practical interest. The diagram for conductivity through a brick shows a section through the thickness (through the kiln wall); the *hot-face* temperature is marked on one side by dividing the upright into degrees (like a *graph*). The outer face is also similarly divided and the temperature indicated is that which is maintained when the brick has reached full *heat storage*. The flatter or more horizontal the line, the more complete is the thermal conductivity and the poorer are the *insulating* qualities.

Two bricks of different constitution are often used in a kiln, the inner one chosen for strength and physical heat resistance, the outer one for low thermal conductivity.

It will be seen that, as the hot face temperature rises, the initial heat input into the kiln will go to warm the brick itself (heat storage); when this is complete the outer temperature will rise in direct relationship with the inner one. At a certain temperature the radiation (which increases with the difference between the outer face and the *ambient* temperatures) will equal input into the kiln, and the chamber temperature will become static. (See also *heat loss*.)

Air, except when in free movement (*convection*), is a poor conductor of heat. The inclusion of pores in a material will therefore lower its rating, and it follows that dense, heavy materials have a much higher factor than lightweight 'open' ones.

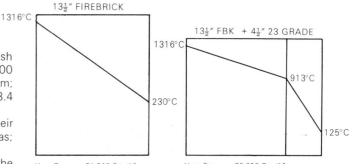

13½″ FIREBRICK
1316°C — 230°C
Heat Storage: 51,500 Btu/ft²
Conduction Loss: 1,450 Btu/h/ft²

13½″ FBK + 4½″ 23 GRADE
1316°C — 913°C — 125°C
Heat Storage: 78,050 Btu/ft²
Conduction Loss: 540 Btu/h/ft²

## THERM, thermal unit

A unit of quantity of heat equivalent to 100,000 British thermal units or 29.3 units of electricity. Around 100 cu. ft. of *natural gas* are needed to produce a therm; one gallon (4.55 liters) of *propane*; or ¾ gallon (3.4 liters) of fuel oil.

A 'therm' unit is used by Gas Boards to price their product based on the calorific value of a cu. ft. of gas; 200 cu. ft. of gas produce one therm. (See *gas fuel*)

Even the best-designed kiln will not utilize all the heat produced, and the 'useful therm' is reckoned at about two-thirds of the 'true therm'. *Electricity* is direct conversion and there is almost no loss. One gas therm is therefore equated with about 20 kWh. In *joule* units one therm equals 105 mJ.

## THERMAL CONDUCTIVITY

The rate at which heat passes through a material. High conductivity is required in kiln furniture, a low rate in kiln walls. Materials with low conductivity are 'insu-

## THERMAL EXPANSION

The expansion which all materials undergo when heated, and which is normally reversed on cooling. (See *coefficients of expansion*.) Not to be confused with *inversions*, or with the structural changes which occur in a clay body and are not reversible (see *shrinkage*).

## THERMAL SHOCK

Bodies and glazes as a whole, or some oxides within them, undergo changes in volume during firing, some of which are reversible on cooling. If expansions and contractions cannot be accommodated within the structure, then damage will occur. The *inversions* of quartz and cristobalite will cause thermal shock. The latter, which spans cooking temperatures, is the more important in ovenwares. Quartz inversion is instantaneous and can damage a high-silica ceramic in the kiln. Alumina rather than silica refractories are therefore preferred. Limit *'free' quartz* or flint additions to bodies to 20%, and cool reasonably slowly over the 600-150°C. range. Rapid cooling of a glaze can cause shock and *crazing*, especially if it is high in alkalis.

## THERMOCOUPLE

The activating part of a *pyrometer*. Two strips of slightly dissimilar alloys—chrome/alumel for sub-1200°C., platinum/platinum-rhodium for higher temperatures—are joined at one end. This junction is housed in a *silliminite, fused quartz* or *fused alumina* sheath, and inserted into the kiln, protruding about an inch (25 mm.) beyond the *hot-face*. The other ends of the strips are joined to leads of normal base-metal wire, which are again connected, making a single *circuit*. As the alloys get hot a small electric current is set up in the circuit, which increases with the rise in temperature. The current is passed through an instrument which will measure its strength and record it by means of a moving arm which travels across a dial calibrated in T°. The length of the connecting wires will affect the reading so do not shorten or lengthen these once the pyrometer has been set.

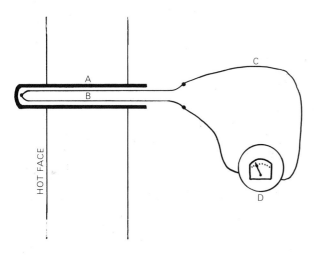

*A thermocouple. The silica sheath (A) houses a bi-metal strip (B) which is joined at one end. It is passed through a kiln wall to protrude 2 in. (50 mm.) or so beyond the hot-face The cold ends of the metal strips are connected through a wire (C) to form a complete circuit. The current induced by the heat in the kiln is registered on a galvanometer introduced into the circuit (D).*

## THIMBLE

An item of *kiln furniture,* now more rarely listed by merchants. One thimble fits into another, and each has a short horizontal arm. Three piles, set into bases, provide support for similar sized plates or tiles. Used for *earthenware* only. The term *'cranks'* is applied to similar constructions listed in suppliers' catalogs.

## THIXOTROPY

A factor of *plasticity.* A clay body 'softens' momentarily under pressure (e.g. of the fingers when throwing) and solidifies again when released. It controls standing strength. The *lamellar* structure of clay with strong electrical bonds between the layers seems to hold the key to this behavior but other explanations have been suggested, e.g. 'house of cards' or 'scaffold' structures. In general scientific terms, thixotropy indicates an increase in *viscosity* with the passage of time, as in thixotropic paints.

Excess *electrolyte* can produce thixotropy in slips, causing them to 'set', becoming fluid only when stirred.

## THORPE'S RATIO

An equation controlling the *base* (especially lead/silica ratio) in a glaze. A simplified version given by Kenneth Shaw in CR 11 (after Mellor) to help computation of safe lead glazes (*low solubility*) reads:

$$\frac{RO+R_2O+Al_2O_3}{RO_2 \text{ (mainly } SiO_2)}=\text{a maximum of } 0.5$$

*Examples:*

Formula 1. $\begin{matrix} PbO\ 0.8 \\ K_2O\ 0.2 \end{matrix}$ $Al_2O_3$ .25.$SiO_2$ 2.0

gives $\dfrac{0.8+0.2+0.25}{2.0}=\dfrac{1.25}{2}=0.625$

Formula 2. $\begin{matrix} PbO\ 0.8 \\ K_2O\ 0.2 \end{matrix}$ $Al_2O_3$ 0.3.$SiO_2$ 3.0

giving $\dfrac{1.3}{3.0}=0.43$

Formula 1 is in excess of the maximum and is therefore likely to be outside the allowed solubility limits; Formula 2 is a better figure.

This is to be taken as one guide only in working out glazes: the alumina/silica ratio and other factors must also be considered. (See *glaze, Seger formula,* etc.)

## THREE PHASE SUPPLY

An electrical mains input through three 'lives' and a neutral. A high load can be equally distributed over the lives each supplying a third of the wattage, or they can be connected in such a way as to increase the voltage. It enables the Electricity Board to balance its supply and also reduces the cable size necessary for each phase. The normal domestic supply is on one live and neutral only—*single phase*—and this may be limited to a total load of about 60 amps.

For wiring diagrams on three phase supply see *star and delta*.

Kilns of over 4 cu. ft. (1.2 cu. m.) capacity will need more than one phase. Sometimes a two phase supply may be installed. The cost depends on the distance from the mains cables to the meter position and to your kiln. In England it appears to be fairly arbitrary and negotiable—anything from £15 to £100 or more. Electric motors are marginally cheaper and more efficient on three phases. See *electric kiln, element, electrical*, etc. Some authorities will allow up to 70 kW on one phase, especially where three phase is not available.

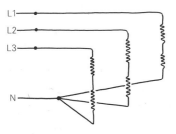

Diagram of a three phase supply. Each circuit in a kiln or other piece of equipment is taken from one phase back to neutral. See also star and delta. More than one resistance piece of equipment can be taken from each phase. See diagram at single phase.

## THROWING

Stages in throwing a large flowerpot. Opening out, using both thumbs inside and squeezing the clay up to the fingers outside (1) into a thick collar (2) which is gripped and lifted. A slight change in position, the little finger crooked over to exercise control over the rim (3). Note that the extra thickness required on the finished rim is already apparent. The hands are in the usual position for thinning the wall, the knuckle outside, straight fingers inside (4). The still slightly narrow pot is brought up higher than the guide stick (5) so that, when brought out to full width, it is the correct height (6). The outside has been smoothed with a rib.

2

3

1

4

5

*Halfway stage in pulling up a 28 lb. (11 kg.) cider jar. The wheel is built so that the potter can stand on crossbars and be well above the pot.*

### THROWING BATS
See *wheel bats.*

### THROWING GAUGE
See *pot gauge.*

### THROWING STICKS
Called 'egote' in Japan where they are much used. Shaped wooden sticks used as interior *ribs* when throwing, especially narrow-mouthed vessels. (See illus. under *egote.*) The more usual Western method is to pull up a wider pot and throw the shoulder inwards. (See the film 'Isaac Button, Country Potter'.) Sometimes a stick with a sponge on the end is used.

### THUMB POTS
See *pinch pots.*

### TILES
The industrial tile, usually 4 x 4 in. (100 x 100 mm.) or 6 x 6 in. (150 x 150 mm.) is power-pressed from a barely damp powdered body in a die or metal mold. This minimizes shrinkage and warping (the latter being the main obstacle to making tiles from plastic clay) but it also destroys any quality in the finished ceramic. Thicker tiles may also be extruded from between rollers.

A number of potters use industrial tiles as surfaces to be decorated with brushwork, trailed glaze, etc. There is an account of pre-industrial tile making in B.TGH. Roughly cut rolled tiles were piled up to 'yearn' (even out their moisture content) before a final rolling and cutting using an iron-edged template. They were fired in pairs, upright, bedded in 'wads'. Throughout the history of the tile there has been a steady diminution in thickness from around $\frac{3}{4}$ in. (20 mm.) to $\frac{1}{4}$ in. (6 mm.). The average thickness of a hand-made tile is $\frac{3}{8}$ in. 10 mm.).

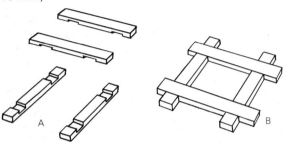

(A) tile frame, showing halved joints which can be fitted together as (B). Clay is beaten into the frame, which should be laid on a square of paper. The surface clay is scraped off with a ruler or smooth strip of wood. Sponge the surface for the final smoothing pull. It helps to make this a two potter job, one pulling while the other holds the frame.

Methods of making tiles:
1.   Slabs can be rolled out freehand or with the use of guide sticks: the tiles cut at leather-hard with a fine knife using a square template
2.   A block of clay cut into appropriately sized slabs with a multi-wire 'harp' and then treated as above.
3.   Wooden frames or plaster molds: a two-piece mold with a separate base needed for the latter. Clay is beaten into the frame with the palm of the hand and the surplus is scraped off with a ruler, wetting the clay for the final smoothing movement. Turn the frame 45° between each pull. Lay the frame on a square of paper before commencement to avoid the clay sticking to the table.
4.   Metal tile cutters, with ejection plates, can be purchased. Usually made for 4 in. (100 mm.) squares or circular tiles. The tile is cut from a rolled-out slab.
Drying tiles:
Methods:
1.   Tiles can be dried in the open, turning them over frequently to correct warping.
2.   Between absorbent bats, such as asbestos sheets or several thicknesses of newspaper.
3.   Leach suggests that tiles cut from a large sheet of clay should be not quite separated so that they hold each other flat.
4.   Smaller or thinner tiles can be dried very rapidly on a hot surface such as a kitchen range, or the top of a hot kiln. Lay them on a kiln shelf and cover with another.
    Tiles can be biscuited in piles of five with a *setter* on top. They are glazed by skimming the surface over a well-stirred glaze; or they can be sprayed.

Tilework has always included other shapes than square, and has often had relief treatment. There is a greater variety today than ever before, in shape, size, and finish. On the walls of our rather dim modern buildings they can add a touch of gaiety and interest, but their use is seldom really understood or fully exploited, and there is a wide open field for the potter to explore.

Cutting a tile with the aid of a card template.

Using a tile cutter.

## TIMER

A one-hour or five-hour cooking timer is an invaluable aid when firing. In a classroom, or when engrossed in other work it is easy to forget the passage of time. The warning ring has saved many a pot from disaster!

## TIN, oxide

A metallic element Sn (stannum), 118.5.
Stannic oxide $SnO_2$, 151. s.g. 6.7.

A useful *opacifier* at all temperatures, with unique qualities which cannot be matched by zircon, etc. It is *acidic* and *refractory,* and does not *dissolve* to any great extent in a glaze but remains suspended as a white powder. A tendency to cause *crawling.*

Its principal use is in *soft glazes* for *majolica* painting or colored glazes. the latter often rather misleadingly called tin enamels or majolica glazes in suppliers' catalogs and by historians. Tin gives a pleasant texture, and a soft clear color from oxides. Make additions of 9-10% in a lead glaze; up to 15% in a soft litharge glaze on red clay; 3-5% in stonewares. Beware *chrome-tin pink* reaction (see also *tin glaze*). A little tin oxide is reputed to assist *copper reds.*

## TIN ASH

Tin *calcined* with lead, used as a more fusible white pigment than tin oxide alone. The early majolica potters used mixtures varying between 2:1 and 4:1 lead/tin, calcined and ground as one of the ingredients of their glazes.

## TIN GLAZE

Any glaze which owes its opacity to tin oxide. An adequate glaze coating is needed to achieve *opacity* but not so thick as to crack and subsequently crawl. *Calcined* clay or the use of *tin ash* will help to prevent crawling. (See *tin* for percentage additions.)

Ideally a tin glaze will include around 0.5 RO equivalents of lead oxide. The tin will increase the *viscosity* of a glaze, which is an asset in *majolica,* helping to prevent the running of colors. High-lead glazes with 15% or more of tin will break red on the edges of red clay pots. Michael Casson's early and immensely attractive work used this technique. Alan Caiger-Smith in PQ 35 states 'a glaze deriving . . . alumina and silica from stone or feldspar is likely to have richer color-carrying properties than one dependant on china clay'. Much other useful information is to be found in this article.

## TIN OVER SLIP

A useful and versatile technique for earthenware. A lead glaze with 10% of tin oxide is used over slips which have rather more than the normal pigment content, e.g. black slip with 15% $MnO_2$, or blue slip with 2% $CoO$. The slip is used as a vehicle for dispersing the oxide evenly over the surface of a dish or pot—a difficult feat by brushing or any other method. The iron in red clay will produce only a faint gray if any color at all; the chrome in green slip will have little effect but the copper will give a watery green. We are, therefore, largely limited to blue and black slips but a great variety of shades will result from varying thicknesses of glaze and with practice this can be used to great advantage. The technique is used in combination with *sgrafitto, paper resist,* and *wax resist.*

Strangely, a lower tin concentration in the glaze does not necessarily lead to stronger color from the slip, the effect being watery and much less striking than with the full *majolica* type glaze. The color will also be directly affected by the firing temperature and degree of *soaking.* A slightly higher fire, or a softer glaze, than normally used for over-glaze painting will give improved results. Do not glaze too thickly.

*A flask built up from two shallow thrown bowls and decorated with sgraffito and tin over slip. Note the dark lines on edges where the glaze is thinner, giving a degree of emphasis to the form.*

## TITANIA

Oxide of titanium $TiO_2$.

## TITANIUM, oxide, compounds

A metallic element Ti, 48.
Titanic oxide $TiO_2$, 80, titania, m.p. 1850°C.
Sesquioxide $Ti_2O_3$, 144, c.o.e. around 16.

Precipitated titania is white but the rutile and anatase forms are brown. It will tend to produce a cream color when used as an *opacifier* in a glaze. Produces rutile mottle (ad nauseum on commercial tiles, etc.) with pigments. It is an agent in *crystalline* glazes. Tends to give yellows with chromium. In some *Bristol* glazes titania can turn iron green according to Parmalee who quotes 0.1 of titania to 0.9 of iron. In *reduction,* various colors from blue to red have been reported. 'Rutile', though strictly a form of titania, is used to describe the iron-bearing mineral.

## TOKI

According to Dodd, a Japanese name for a high-fired earthenware of the composition: 70% clay; 10% pegmatite; 20% grog.

## TONGS

Tongs are required for *raku*. Not usually listed by merchants but can be made from flat or round iron. Iron rod will need beating flat at the hinge. About 3 ft. (1 m.) long, they should open 5 or 6 in. (125-150 mm.) at the working end. They must be light and easy to use; wooden handles will help grip and insulation. A distinction is made between the shape of the gripping ends for red and black raku (W.WJC). A more elaborate type are 'accordion' tongs. Kemper Manufacturing Co., California, make raku tongs.

*Typical raku tongs made from two ¼ x ¾ in. (5 x 20 mm.) metal strips. The jaws are twisted at right-angles to the handles. The whole can be about 3 ft. (say 1 m.) in length. Wooden handles at the 'cold' ends will insulate and give a better grip.*

## TONGUE TEST

If the tip of the tongue is touched against a biscuit pot one can get an idea of its porosity by the extent to which the tongue sticks to the pot momentarily. The more porous the biscuit the more it will adhere. If the surface feels slippery and the patch stays wet or absorbs only slowly, the biscuit is partly vitrified and will take up very little glaze when dipped.

## TOOLS

*Some useful pottery tools from a potter's kit. A nylon or metal wire on wooden handles, a natural sponge, a scraper, a hoop turning tool (see also used for scooping out at raku), a wooden spatula, a fine needle awl, a small knife, and a plane.*

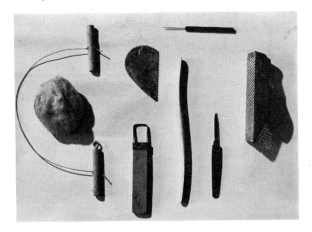

There are as many tools as there are potters but one can list half a dozen or so essential ones. Some of these are shown in the photograph; these and others are discussed under *steel palette, beater, turning tool, chamois, spatula.*

*A fine group of bamboo tools: a trimming, turning or scoring tool; a comb; a grooving tool (see fluting; a Japanese type-cutting off thread with a bamboo handle which is spear ended for making the initial groove; and two ribs. (Photograph: Wengers.)*

## TOP LOADING KILNS

While most pottery kilns open in the front, some are packed from above. Both types have advantages. Top loaders, usually *electric kilns* (though *raku* is often top loaded), are easier for the potter to build, and they can be heated all round. Pots can be tightly packed laterally. When firing, the top is at a convenient level for the supervision of drying pots and it can also provide an extra working surface in a small workshop. The height is limited by the potter's ability easily to reach to the floor of the chamber; the width by the available roofing bats which support the top bricks or slabs. The maximum capacity is therefore in the region of 12 cu. ft. (0.36 cu. m.) e.g. 2 ft. (60 cm.) high x 2 ft. (60 cm.) deep x 3 ft. (80 cm.) wide, although the width is not so crucial.

## TOWING

The industrial term for the act of smoothing the outer edges of plates, etc. on the wheel, traditionally with 'tow' but also with glasspaper or scrapers.

## TOWN GAS

Gas fuel produced from coal at a gasworks, as distinct from *natural gas.*

## TRAIL AND FEATHER

*Slip trailed lines* and dots which are feathered through, generally at right-angles. The decoration is done on a flat slab of clay, the plate or dish being formed over a hump-mold when the surface is partly dry. (See also *feathering, trailing.*)

## TRAILER, tracer

See *slip trailer.*

## TRAILING

Decorating by means of slip or glaze extruded through a nozzle onto the surface of a piece of pottery. A similar technique to cake-icing but with a more fluid material.

The trailing may be done straight onto the body clay, as was practised in the seventeenth century notably on the fine 'Toft' and other large platters. 'Dry' trailing is linear in character—masses may be filled in with washes of brushed slip.

Trailing onto a wet-slip surface allows a more flowing style. The design can be trailed onto a flat slab of clay, the dish being formed when the surface has dried somewhat. The piedish illustrated appears to have been made in this way. The clay can be eased into a *hollow mold* from the edges of the slab, or made over a *hump-mold.* The back must be kept damp with sheets of damp newspaper or the clay will crack. Alternatively the dish can be made first, covered with slip when stiff enough to handle, and the design applied immediately. This is easier as far as making the dish goes but more difficult in the actual trailing. Drop the dish back into the mold as a support when trailing.

*A trailed dish by Michael Cardew.*

Contrasting slips can be spooned into roughly sponged-off areas on the surface of the dish to give some solidity to the background. *Finger combing* can be combined with trailing. The consistency of the slip will affect the style of the design—the thinner the slip the faster and freer will be the trailing movement. A very thick slip will give lumpy results, physically and aesthetically! A sure and unhesitating movement is

called for, the design growing as much from the immediate behavior of the slip as from premeditated ideas. A sharp blow on the work-table, or lifting the corner of the mold a fraction and letting it drop again, will spread and unify the trailed line with the background. Trailing on pots is possible but difficult, the face to be worked is generally held nearly horizontal. (See also *slip, slip trailers, glaze trailing, feathering,* etc.)

## TRANSFERS, decalcomania—USA

Designs, printed onto special paper backgrounds, which can be applied to biscuit or glazed ware, the paper peeling or soaking away. (See *lithographic transfer.*) They have little place in craft pottery although *silk screen* printed transfers have been used effectively on tiles.

## TRANSITIONAL ELEMENTS

The elements nos. 23-29 in the *periodic table* together with some of the *rare earths.* These elements form coloring oxides.

## TRANSLUCENT

Transmitting light, but not *transparent.* Objects between the translucent object and the light source will be seen through it as shadows. It is one of the properties of porcelains and occasionally of thin stoneware. The term is also applied to semi-transparent soft glazes with 3-6% tin oxide, cooled slowly to promote crystallization.

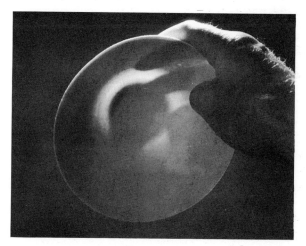

*Showing the translucency of a porcelain bowl by Lucie Rie. Oxidized fired in an electric kiln.*

## TRANSPARENT

Transmitting light without diffusion so that objects behind the transparent material can be plainly seen. A majority of glazes, if taken up to full fusion, will be transparent or nearly so. Transparency is a characteristic of glass. Lessened or destroyed by *opacifiers,* and by *underfiring*, by the development of *crystals* during slow cooling, by trapped bubbles, and by the opalescent effect of mixed glasses within the melt. Also, of course, by coloring oxides, especially the *acidic* or refractory ones. The ratio of 0.1 $Al_2O_3$:1.0 $SiO_2$ should be maintained for transparency in glazes.

## TRI-AXIAL BLENDING

Or ternary system. A diagrammatic method of studying the effects of the various mixtures possible with three materials or colors. (See *line blends* for two materials.) Four variables would require the construction of a pyramid.

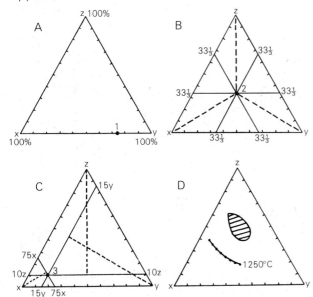

Each corner of the triangle represents 100% of the material, a point half way along the side represents 50% and so on. Each side, therefore, can be considered as a line blend of the materials mentioned at either end of it. Point 1 in fig. A would indicate 25% of material X and 75% of Y.

As soon as we enter the area of the triangle, however, we are dealing with all three materials, Thus in fig. B point 2 is at the center of the triangle. The lines which intersect at this point cut the sides at $33\frac{1}{3}$ on each face. Another set of lines drawn to bisect each angle will indicate to which material the percentage refers: in this case all refer to $33\frac{1}{3}\%$. An off-center point 3 in fig. C makes this clearer and 3 would indicate a mixture of 75% of X, 15% of Y, and 10% of Z.

A line drawn within the triangle represents any mixture at any point on the line. It might be labelled 1250°, meaning that all the mixtures within that range would melt at that temperature. An area marked within the triangle would similarly indicate all the possible combinations within the area. For instance, it might show all the mixtures of three materials which would be craze-free, those outside the area being liable to crazing. See fig. D. Tri-axial diagrams are also used for phase diagrams.

## TRIDYMITE

A theoretical form of silica, probably with a disordered crystal *lattice*, with several *inversions* between 117°C. and 870°C. Stable up to 1470°C. It seems likely, however, that the involved make-up of plastic bodies prevents the formation of tridymite.

## TRIVALENT, tervalent

Elements which combine with three atoms of hydrogen. The oxides (since oxygen is bivalent) are written $R_2O_3$, e.g. alumina, ferric iron, boric oxide.

## TRUE POROSITY

The sum of open and closed or sealed pores in a fired body.

## TUNGSTEN

A metallic element W (wolfram), 184.
Trioxide $WO_3$, a yellow insoluble powder, m.p. 1473°C.
Could be used for high temperature yellow pigment, possibly with molybdenum (Billington). Also used in very hard steel alloys.

## TUNNEL KILN

A kiln in which ware is transported through a hot zone in the middle of a long tunnel. The firing is a continuous process. The nearest a studio potter can approach the tunnel kiln is with a kiln with doors back and front, the ware being packed on trolleys and wheeled in. This is still, however, an intermittent firing. (See *continuous kiln*.)

## TURNING

The trimming of a thrown pot on the wheel. This can be done immediately after *throwing* but more generally when *leather-hard*. Excessive turning will destroy the lively effect of throwing. However very short bodies such as *porcelains* are sometimes thrown thickly and turned to a thin wall. It is obvious that the Chinese

*Supporting small-necked or tall pots for turning. (A) shows (in section) a thrown, diabolo-shaped supporting chuck in leather-hard clay: (B) a cup head used in turning a smaller pot. The chuck is adhered to the wheel head with a little slip. The pot in (B) is centered and held in place by means of a coil of clay as shown. Note: the pot in (A) drops in as far as it will go but does not touch the bottom of the chuck; in the cup-head the neck of the pot is set firmly down before the coil is fixed (B).*

practiced a good deal of turning. The little industrial ware still thrown is turned on a horizontal lathe like a piece of wood, the *short* body making very high turning speeds possible.

Jugs, bottles, and most pots can be trimmed as the final action of throwing; alternatively they can be turned at a drier stage but still right way up, re-adhering them to the wheel head with a little water. If a flat base is given a sharp tap with the fingers to make it slightly concave, the pot will have more stability.

If a *foot ring* is required the piece must be inverted. For tall pots a hollow *chuck* or a *cup head* and *wad* can be used. A solid chuck is generally used for bowls or squatter shapes. Bowls and many pots can be adhered to the wheel head simply by moistening the rim. The clay should be leather-hard, the parings coming away crisply like wood shavings. If it is too soft it will stick to the tool. If too hard the work will be slow and tedious. See also *chatter* for the method of dealing with the corrugations which sometimes develop when turning; also *plates, knob.*

*Turning or trimming the base of a pot with a bamboo tool.*

Turning the foot ring on a bowl. The rough flange left from cutting-off is removed by an upward cut with the pointed tool (1), giving a true surface to work on. The outer wall of the ring is cut with the square tool (2). The inner face of the ring is incised (3) and the interior cut away with the square tool, working from the center to the ring (which should be left wider than finally required to allow for accidents) (4). The curve of the bowl is perfected, the ring cut to size and bevelled on the outer edge (5). The bevel gives a pleasant line of shadow beneath the bowl and prevents chipping.

1

2

3

5

Turning in the Industry. Where the wheel is still used, bodies are thrown thickly and turned at speed on a horizontal lathe. The great insulators (electrical porcelain) are turned.

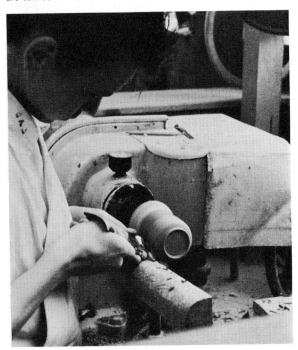

## TURNING TOOLS

The only essential feature of a turning tool is a short, firm cutting edge which can be held at a right-angle to the rotating pot. The actual design varies widely. The standard tool is made from a 7 x ½ or ¾ in. (180 x 12 or 20 mm.) iron strip. A 1 in. (25 mm.) length at one end is bent to 90° and cut either to the shape of a rectangle, a triangle, a rounded end or a 'leaf' shape. A V-shaped nick cut away at the angle makes for cleaner working. The cutting end of the tool is then bevelled to a sharp edge all round. Loop tools are also made, using a thinner steel strip and a wooden handle, and there are other designs. Each potter will recommend the type to which he has become accustomed.

Clay is abrasive and tools need regular sharpening. They should not, however, be honed to a knife edge, which is as liable to *chatter* as is a very blunt one. A slight burr seems to help. A *steel palette* can be used for turning a large plain area. A bamboo tool is a pleasant tool to use for trimming the foot of a pot immediately after throwing.

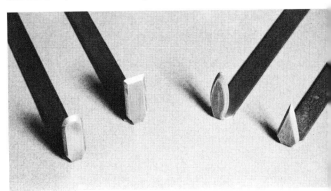

The four shapes most useful for turning tools. See also hoop tool under tools.

## TURQUOISE GLAZES, color

Generally derived from copper oxide. For the purest color, soft glazes must be virtually free from alumina while soda must predominate in the RO. Such a glaze lacks stability (pure soda-silicates are soluble in water) and is very liable to *crazing*. A recipe of one part sodium silicate to one part quartz with 0.5% copper carbonate would make a turquoise fritt, but in practice small additions of alumina or lime would have to be made. Published formulas include equal parts of CaO and $Na_2O$ with no alumina and 2.6 $SiO_2$. 0.6 $B_2O_3$, and more involved glazes which include small proportions of alumina, lime, and zinc. A *fritt* is always needed for this type of glaze. (See also *Egyptian paste*.) Any type of turquoise fritt will work better on a *siliceous* body or slip. The Egyptian bodies are reported to consist of up to 90% silica by analysis.

Turquoise stoneware glazes are rare but can be developed from formulas high in calcium and barium, using dolomite to introduce some magnesium. None of the rules governing soft glaze turquoise seem to apply. Use about 2% copper carbonate. A quoted turquoise glaze is nepheline 56, barium carbonate 25, ball clay 6, flint 7, copper carbonate 3. It is my experience that the color in stoneware is very dependent on a precise firing temperature and on the thickness of the glaze. It is always variable.

Small amounts of vanadium and zircon are reputed to produce turquoise in an alkaline glaze.

## TWADDLE DEGREES
Symbol °Tw. A system for denoting the *specific gravity* of a liquid.

$$°Tw = (s.g. - 1) \times 200.$$

Used for solutions of sodium silicate in casting slips.

## TWO PIECE THROWING
Large pots may be thrown in two or more sections (the method is also useful when working with porcelain or other short bodies). A neck can be thrown from a coil or squat cylinder stuck to a half dry base as illustrated. It is possible to build up very large forms section by section, throwing from a fresh coil as each previous one stiffens. Shrinkage of the last thrown section must be taken into account. Leach shows a considerable outward bulge immediately above the join in his diagram in L.PB.

Alternatively the two sections of a pot may each be shaped on the wheel, luted together when stiff enough, and the join worked together on the wheel, perhaps with a throwing stick inside. The rims to be joined must be broad and fairly flat and, of course, of similar diameters. (See also *amphora*.)

*Pots by Robin Welch. The simple, uncompromising shapes are softened by textured stoneware clays and variagated ash glazes in reduction. (Photograph: Robin Welch.)*

*Two piece throwing in Cyprus. Water jars—the partly dried bases are shown on the right—have their necks thrown from a thick coil to the finished shapes seen in the foreground.*

## TYPES OF POTTERY
Firing temperatures and categories of pottery:

| Temperature (°C.) | Type |
| --- | --- |
| 700–800 | *enamel* colors |
| | *raku* |
| 800–1000 | soft *earthenwares* |
| | *bricks* |
| 950–1150 | *soft paste* porcelains |
| 1000–1140 | range of most craft earthenwares |
| 1150–1200 | hard earthenware (industrial) |
| 1160–1180 | *Bristol* glazed ware |
| 1200–1250 | *bone china* (biscuit firing temperature) |
| 1220–1320 | *stonewares* |
| | *salt glaze* |
| 1255–1275 | low-temperature *porcelain* |
| 1320–1350 | porcelain |
| 1350–1430 | *hard paste* porcelain |

# U

## ULTIMATE ANALYSIS
The chemical breakdown of a material into its constituent oxides (see *analysis*). Also called an 'element analysis'.

## ULTIMATE FORMULA
The arrangement of atomic symbols as the total numbers present in the formula e.g. $Al_2Si_2H_4O_8$, as distinct from the rational or oxide formula $Al_2O_3.2SiO_2.2H_2O$.

## μm

Pronounced mu. The symbol for a *micron* or 0.001 of a millimeter (one-millionth of a meter). Many clay particles are less than 0.5 microns in size.

## UMBER

A natural *ferruginous* earth or *hydrated* iron oxide with some manganese oxide. Allied to ochre and sienna. *Calcined* as burnt umber.

## UNDER-FIRING

Under-fired biscuit will be very porous and breakable. The word will have a different meaning in terms of temperature for different materials. In general the more fluxes and impurities there are in the clay, the lower will be its optimum firing temperature. For stoneware, *biscuiting* is simply a method of making it possible to dip the pots into glaze without disintegration, but for earthenware other factors are involved and a very low-fired biscuit is not recommended. (See *crazing, cristobalite*.)

Badly under-fired glazes will be *opaque*, with rough *matt* surfaces and probably with a quite different color to the mature glaze. Slightly under-fired tin glazes are liable to *crawl*.

## UNDERGLAZE COLORS

Pigments applied to the raw clay or biscuit and covered with a glaze. When used on biscuit they must either be fixed in a *hardening-on* firing, or a gum or other binding material must be mixed with the color. The latter will tend to influence glaze take-up. The binder generally used for stoneware underglaze painting is simply a little clay. Underglaze colors are limited to those oxides, mixtures, or prepared *fritted* pigments which will withstand the temperature of the glaze which is to be put over them.

If simple oxides are used on raw clay it may be found that some color is still loose after the biscuit firing. This must be washed off under a tap and the pot thoroughly dried before glazing. A little *flux*—a fritt, china stone, etc.—mixed with the oxides will help them to adhere, especially cobalt which often fails to *sinter*. An addition of a plastic clay, as mentioned above, will at least prevent the color from blurring when dipped in glaze.

Most pigment oxides yield *transparent* color (chrome is an exception). Opacity can be increased by the addition of tin, zinc, etc. or china clay and flint. (See also *pigments*, and under the individual *elements*.) Commercially prepared underglaze colors are fritted compounds with various 'fillers', flint, clay, etc. and opacifiers which may include chrome for the darker colors. Leadless or low lead glazes are usually recommended. In the workshop, a *jar mill* is useful for preparing underglaze colors.

There is an optimum thickness of application for all colors. The oxides, especially copper, need careful handling. Practice and experience are needed to get the best from them.

## UNFIRED CLAY, bricks

Clay will not become a ceramic until it has been subjected to a temperature of at least 550°C. A cooking oven (max. circa 275°C.) is obviously insufficient, as is sun heat. Some clays, however, dry very hard, perhaps because of a particular grain structure or the presence of cementing materials. A great number of the houses in the Mediterranean countries and elsewhere are built of unfired bricks or slabs reinforced with straw and chaff, sometimes called *adobe*. Several attempts have been made to produce a material with the plastic advantages of clay but which will not easily break on drying, using fibres of nylon, etc. to form a sort of felting throughout the body, or the addition of resins as setting cements. (See *Newclay*.)

## UNITS OF ELECTRICITY

The units of immediate interest to potters are discussed under *volt, ampere, watt, ohm*.

The 'unit' on which the pricing of electricity supply is based is one *kilowatt-hour*, symbol kWh, the amount consumed by a 1000 watt appliance (e.g. a single bar electric fire) in an hour. The same fire would consume 5 kW in 5 hours; if rated at 1.5 kW then it would consume $7\frac{1}{2}$ kW in 5 hours, and so on. To estimate the cost of firing an electric kiln:

Kilowatt rating x hours of firing x cost per unit, thus a 6 kW kiln x 10 hours firing x 1.5p per unit = 90p.

The sum is slightly complicated by the fact that the kiln may not be running at full all the time, or there may be a standing charge in addition to the unit cost, but a little common sense can allow for these. Reckon one-third the rating if you have a 'slow' setting and two-thirds for a 'medium'.

## UP-DRAFT KILN

The simplest form of true kiln: a fire beneath the floor, the hot gases and flame rising through the ware to a chimney or vent at the top. The heating tends to be uneven—hot at the base—and a great deal of heat is wasted.

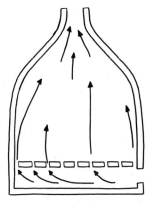

*An up-draft kiln, the flame and hot gases travelling through a perforated floor and up through the pots to a short chimney or simple vent.*

Nevertheless it was the type in use for thousands of years and is still fired. Interesting variations are found; in Cyprus a perforated hollow dome is built inside the kiln, and the pots stacked in the space between it and the outer wall. A wood fire is burnt inside the dome which is reached by a low tunnel. There is no chimney—merely vents in the top. Sometimes bottomless pots are stuck over holes in the upper part of the kiln, often pointing downwards. The form of the kiln itself acts as a chimney.

In up-draft gas kilns a *semi-muffle* may be used, or the jets injected horizontally through separate flues, greatly extending the life of the floor refractories. See many illustrations of up-draft kilns in R.K.

*A simple wood-fuelled up-draft kiln in Cyprus in which the coiled pots shown under that heading were fired. It is stoked in a pit beneath the floor through a hole at the left of the kiln in picture. Built of brick and local stone. Minimal chimney, and yet pots fully odixized.*

## URANIUM, oxides, compounds

A metallic element U, 238.
Oxide $UO_2$, 270.
Sodium uranate $Na_2O.2UO_3.nH_2O$.
'Depleted' oxide $U_3O_8$, s.g. 7.3.

The radioactive potentialities of uranium are well known and it has not been available since 1944. However, the depleted oxide is now appearing in the catalogs, albeit still expensive.

The use of uranium as a pigment oxide is generally limited to *soft glazes*, giving reds and oranges up to about 940°C. and turning to a cool yellow at higher temperatures. A high-lead glaze is recommended, with a little tin oxide. Boric oxide and whiting are to be avoided. At stoneware temperature L.PB gives a recipe for Kawai's yellow which uses 2% uranium oxide in the traditional 4:3:2:1 recipe (see *stoneware glaze*) with an additional 15% of feldspar. Uranium is liable to turn gray or black above 1260°C.

# V

## VACUUM FILTER

An idea developed by Harry Davis. The usual method of squeezing the water from slip is reversed, a semi-vacuum being used to draw it out. No heavy machinery is required and the equipment is neither bulky nor costly. A similar system has also been developed in the USA.

## VACUUM PUG

See *de-airing pug*.

## VALENCY

The way in which *atoms* combine. The inert gases contain 8 *electrons* in their outer shell (helium has 2) and other atoms with different configurations aspire to this stable state, borrowing or sharing electrons with neighboring atoms. Shared electrons take part in '*covalent*' bonds.

The transfer of electrons results in an unbalanced electrical charge on the nucleus (electrons being negatively charged) and the formation of '*ions*' (see also *electrovalent*). Chemical action, the formation of *compounds* and new materials, is the result of one or other of these bonds or a combination of them.

The ratio in which atoms combine is thus in terms of simple whole numbers, and the valency is the number of hydrogen atoms with which an atom of an *element* will combine (or which it will replace). A *compound* or *molecule* must balance these numbers if it is to be stable. Thus tin has a valency of 4 oxygen 2 (as in $H_2O$) and they combine in the ratio which will balance them—bring them both up to 4—i.e. two oxygen atoms with valency 2=4, one tin atom with valency 4=4 or one tin (Sn) to two oxygen (O) written $SnO_2$. Many elements can be made to combine in different ratios i.e. have more than one valency, but there is often a single stable combination, or oxide, e.g. $TiO_2$, $Al_2O_3$. The transitional elements in particular occur in nature in more than one combination, e.g. iron as $Fe_2O_3$ and $Fe_3O_4$.

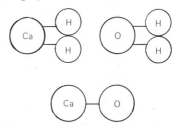

*Valency. calcium, Ca, will combine with two H atoms and is thus bivalent. Oxygen, O, is also bivalent and the two can therefore combine in the ratio of 1:1 (having equal valency values) giving the oxide CaO. Potassium, K, is monovalent and two of its atoms must be present to balance the bivalency of oxygen, giving the oxide $K_2O$. See also electron shells, atomic theory, trivalent.*

## VANADIUM

A metallic element V, 51.
Pentoxide $V_2O_5$, 182 m.p. 685 °C.
Ammonium metavanadate $NH_4VO_3$, 117.

A fairly rare mineral found in *bauxitic* clays and also recovered from fuel oil soot. Both forms listed above can be purchased. It is used in proportions of 5-10% for a yellow color, rather weak in a clear glaze but stronger in combination with titania and tin oxide.

Zirconia-vanadium blues have also been quoted and have been suggested as a substitute for copper in lead glazes in order to avoid the latter's tendency to increase *lead solubility*. Also gray colors with tin under certain conditions. The metavanadate is reported to be refractory to 1300°C. and to be unaffected by reduction (Fulham Pottery Catalog) although Behrens mentions blue from reduced vanadium, and heavy reduction may turn the oxide gray. The pentoxide may be used in oxidized firings.

## VELLUM GLAZE

A merchant's term for an *opaque* glaze with a dulled or satiny sheen. Tin-zinc-titanium combinations often used. Magnesia in the glaze will also help to promote a less shiny surface.

## VENTURI BURNER

An inspirating gas burner with a constricted flow just beyond the point where the gas exits. This increases the speed of the gas flow and draws air in from behind. The principle was formulated by the Italian scientist Venturi. See R.K 76 for illustrations.

## VERMICULITE

An expanded (exfoliated) mica. Fairly refractory. Main use as a heat insulator for temperatures up to 1000°C. Has also been mentioned as a type of grog for lightweight brick and, finely ground, for other bodies. From S. Carolina and Montana.

## VIBRATORY SIEVE

A sieve or lawn which is shaken rapidly in a lateral direction by an eccentric drive on an electric motor. Marketed by various suppliers. Something of a luxury for most potters but the action gives a more even particle separation and is kinder to the lawn than is brushing through. (See *sieve, use of*.)

## VINEGAR

Contains 3-6% acetic acid. It has a deflocculating effect on clay and can be used to repair dry pots or modeling (so long as the damage is not a result of strain). Work the vinegar with a brush onto both surfaces and press them together. It has been successful with large coiled pots but must not be used for handles. Odors reminiscent of fried fish shop during firing!

## VISCOSITY

Resistance to flow offered by a liquid, due to internal frictions. A very fluid glaze would run from a pot at peak temperature (and sometimes does!) but the presence of alumina increases viscosity, distinguishing *glaze* from *glass*. Viscosity also prevents glaze from soaking too readily into the body of a pot, and inhibits crystal growth. The unit of viscosity is the *poise*.

Magnesia increases viscosity, as will zircon and tin oxide. The alkalis have the opposite effect and are vigorous in promoting *fluidity*. Lime has an ambiguous role. It will increase viscosity at low temperatures and, in certain proportions, in stoneware. The point of maximum fluidity will vary from 15-35% at 1250°C. and over. *Celadon* needs high viscosity (Cardew).

*Water* decreases in viscosity as it is heated to a factor of 3 between 0°C. and 40°C., hence the greater efficiency of hot water in various processes. It is known that the temperature of the water affects clay during throwing.

## VITREOUS

Glassy, or containing glassy materials. Vitreous bodies will have low *porosity*. 'Vitreous' slip or *engobe* is one with a high *base* content and is fired to fusion point. Vitreous silica, or *fused silica*, has been heated to translucency (see also *thermocouple*). Any pottery body or associated mineral will become vitreous if heated sufficiently.

## VITRIFY, vitrification

To assume the nature of a *glass* (glaze) or to form glassy melts within a fabric which flow into the pores and allow the particles to become more closely packed. It involves the breaking down of *crystalline* structures. A vitrified body will be non-porous and *impermeable*, although in pottery this is rarely completely achieved (see *porosity*).

Vitrification—the progressive fusion or glassification of a clay—is accompanied by shrinkage and leads eventually to deformation and collapse. The temperatures at which it occurs will vary with the *fusibility* of the clay (the number and type of fluxes) and the alumina content. The 'vitrification range' is the temperature interval between the initial glass formation (beginning of shrinkage) and eventual deformation. The first figure is around 850°C. for plastic clay and varies between 1030°C. for a very impure red clay to 1450°C. for the most refractory kaolin porcelains. Aluminous fireclays will have an even greater range.

Porcelain is a mixture which will vitrify to *translucency* without collapse.

## VOLATILIZATION

The passing into vapor of materials at high temperatures. Copper is liable to become *volatile* at 1200°C. and can stain neighboring pieces, especially in *reduction*, or can be seen to stain right through a body. The fluorine from fluorspar will volatilize and can cause glaze pitting. Lead will volatilize to a small degree slowly coating kiln walls and furniture when used with regularity, as will other bases from stoneware glazes. The volatilization of sodium from salt is the basis of *salt glazing*.

The term is also used to denote the removal by heat of $CO_2$ and other components of a glaze batch but this is better described as *decomposition* or *dissociation*.

*The wall of a large earthenware kiln, used mainly for firing galena glazed pots, thickly coated with volatilized lead.*

## VOLCANIC ASH

Volcanic lava frequently produces *basic* rocks which can eventually decompose into clay of the *montmorillinite* type. The typical volcanic rock is *basalt,* which can be used for dark colored stoneware glazes.

'Volcanic ash' is available cheaply in the USA and has been quoted as roughly equivalent to 70% feldspar, 30% flint. It is probably more fusible than this sounds for it is also said that 25% volcanic ash with 75% red clay will *vitrify* at earthenware *temperatures*. It can be combined with Gerstley borate as a glaze. Not generally available in England but basalt is listed. Wenger's latest list (1973) includes volcanic ash with an analysis by weight:

| | | | | |
|---|---|---|---|---|
| MgO 0.35 | $Al_2O_3$ 13.0 | $SiO_2$ 73 | $Cl_2$ | 0.03 |
| CaO 1.0 | $Fe_2O_3$ 3.0 | | $H_2O$ | 1.5 |
| $Na_2O$ 3.6 | | | | |
| $K_2O$ 4.5 | | | | |

They suggest 10% for use as a secondary flux and up to 50% for a clear, fluid glaze.

## VOLT

The unit of electromotive force, e.m.f. The force that would carry one ampere of current against one ohm of resistance. Voltage is e.m.f. expressed in volts, symbol E.

Useful equations for potters:
$E = W$ (watts) $\div A$ (amperes)
$E = A \times R$ (ohms)

## VOLTAGE DROP

If more than a certain amount of current is taken from an electrical supply, the 'pressure' or voltage will drop and all appliances will become less efficient, e.g. lights will dim, kilns take longer to fire. The percentage loss of power will be equal to the square of the voltage drop; thus 240 V to 230 V is a $4.1^2$ or 16.4% drop in power.

# W

## WAD, wad mill, wad box

A coil or extruded column of clay. Short coils of *fireclay* used for placing saggars, for separating boxed pots, etc.

A wad box or wad mill is a simple hand-operated screw plunger enclosed in a cylinder with a die at the aperture and is used to extrude plastic clay in coils or wads. Can be utilized for *coiling*. Some catalogs suggest that it is a sort of *pug*, which it is not.

## WARPING

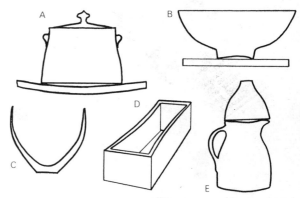

*Common causes of warping during firing: bent shelves (A); uneven foot-rings or bases (B); very thin rims (C); long, straight, unsupported sides — see under Slab pots for remedy (D); the boxing of uneven or dissimilar pieces (E).*

Deformation which can take place at any stage in the making of a pot. Few fired pieces escape totally—try spinning a commercial saucer on the wheel. Warping will be aggravated by:

| During making and drying | High wet/dry shrinkage |
|---|---|
| | Uneven clay walls |
| | Very thin rims |
| | Poor *wedging* |
| | Unsupported weight, including open slab boxes |
| | The joining of clay of different consistencies |
| | Unlevel bases or *foot rings* |
| | Uneven *drying* |
| | Plastic 'memory' |

| | |
|---|---|
| During the biscuit fire | Close proximity to kiln wall |
| | Unsupported weight |
| | The *boxing* of pots on jugs |
| | 'Bungs' too high |
| | Bent kiln shelves |
| During the glaze fire | Uneven bases |
| | Unsupported weight |
| | Bent kiln shelves |
| | *Overfiring* |
| | Inefficient *stilt* support (earthenware) |
| | Molded dishes which are too flat or thin |

Pots which are deformed during drying may revert even if the fault has been corrected in time. Wooden cones are useful for rounding out cups etc. An extreme case of unsupported weight is the handle of a porcelain cup pulling it out of true during firing. The industry beds bone china in alumina (its high fire is its biscuit fire) but the craft potter must design self-supporting ceramics. (See *kiln furniture*.)

*Badly placed stilts and spurs, causing warping (unsupported weight).*

## WASHING ASH

To remove *soluble alkalis*. Steep the ash in plenty of water and stir well. When the solid matter has settled, pour off the clear liquid. Refill with clean water and repeat the process. Three washings are usually sufficient. At the first wash the liquid may be sufficiently *caustic* to harm the hands, so wear gloves. (See also *ash*.)

## WASTE HEAT DRYING

Optimum use is made of very little of the heat generated by kilns. It is worth planning your Pottery so that heat liberated during cooling has some work to do, either as space heating or to dry pots. *Top loading* kilns are very useful in this respect. Fans and ducts can distribute heat: more simply it can be directed through a gap to an upper floor. Kiln exhaust gases can first be directed beneath a drying cabinet before reaching the chimney. See film 'Isaac Button, Country Potter'.

## WASTER

A spoiled pot which is discarded, often on the site of the kiln. Archaeologists owe a great debt to wasters.

## WATER

The 'oxide' of hydrogen, $H_2O$, 18.

The normal water supply contains impurities and these can, to some extent, affect the behavior of clays and glazes. Water impurities have been mentioned as a cause of *crawling* after a pot has been sponged with very 'hard' (high calcium) water.

Water in pottery can exist in a number of forms:
1 In its familiar liquid state, mixed with clay to promote plasticity or in excess of this to produce slip. This water is drawn or driven off at temperatures up to 100°C. (see *drying*).
2 As *adsorbed* water, not obvious as a liquid and more tenacious in its hold and can only be completely dispersed by heating to 120-200°C.
3 The $H_2O$ which is built into the molecular structure of clay, sometimes known as 'combined water'. This needs considerable heat—500°C. plus—before it will separate as vapor, with fundamental and irreversible changes in the fabric.

Other *hydrated* minerals may lose their $H_2O$ at different temperatures, *plaster of paris* for instance at a much lower heat. Water decreases in *viscosity* as it is heated and hot water will have a different effect from cold on many materials including clay. (See also *adsorption, absorption, hydration*.)

## WATER GLASS

Sodium silicate $Na_2O.SiO_2$, with grades from 1:2 to 1:3.5 soda/silica ratio. Used as a *deflocculant*, and in *air-setting cement. Soluble* in water. (See also *mending*.)

## WATER SMOKING

The evolving of vapor at temperatures beyond 100°C. 'Bone dry' clay will still contain *adsorbed* and mechanically held water which will continue to vaporize up to 250°C. in bentonite type clays especially. Care must be exercised throughout this range. The term probably arose because the combination of steam and burning carbons early in firing combine in a steamy smoke.

## WATER OF PLASTICITY

The water content of a clay in the range between soft plastic and leather-hard. Clays vary in the percentage of water needed to attain plasticity, the average being about 40% of the dry weight.

## WATT

An *electrical* unit of power. It is the rate of working in a *circuit* where electromotive force is one *volt* and the intensity of current is one *ampere*. Symbol W. Named after the English scientist. Useful equation for potters:

$$W = A \text{ (amperes)} \times E \text{ (volts)}$$

The load or power of a kiln or other electric appliance is stated in watts, as in a 60 watt electric lamp. Multiples of 1000 watts are called kilowatts or kW, e.g. a 4.5 kW kiln—4500 watts.

## WAX

Used in a fluid form for *wax resist* decoration or resisting glaze when glazing. Candle melted on its own is not satisfactory since it sets hard before it can be properly applied. Mixtures of paraffin wax, or candle with paraffin are very inflammable. Equal parts of candle and a thin oil makes a very useable mixture, kept warm over an electric or gas ring in a double saucepan or old fashioned glue-pot.

There are several proprietary cold wax emulsions and resist materials on the market. They are generally less workable and some must be left to dry and have poor 'resist' qualities. A liquid latex resist is now sold: it can be removed from the surface at any time and one can envisage interesting decorative possibilities. Very low temperature paraffin waxes are also available.

Wax can be applied by using sticks of candle like crayon (see *wax resist*).

Do not leave your brush in the wax: it may burn during heating or may develop a permanent bend. On the other hand, do not attempt to clean it with water. Stroke the hairs flat and leave to set either hanging or lying flat. Take care not to drip the wax where it is not required—it is difficult to remove. Turpentine removes a certain amount, but absorption is still affected. Badly waxed pots may need refiring to remove the wax.

## WAX RESIST

For decoration. Wax designs are applied to a pottery surface in order to repel liquid pigments, thin slips, or glazes. The wax is usually applied as free *brushwork*, but a design can also be drawn with a wax crayon or piece of candle. The work can be done at various stages:
1    On the raw clay, generally when leather-hard. The wax design is applied and color or slip is spun on or laid over the whole surface with a brush, or poured or dipped. The waxed parts will be left in reserve against a painted background. The wax rarely repels the overlaid color completely and the small blobs and dots of color within the resisted areas give the technique its attractive and distinctive character.
2    A reserved biscuit design will result from waxing on the raw clay for once-fired pottery, or on the biscuit before glazing.
3    The unfired glaze surface can be waxed and painted as on the raw clay or covered with a second glaze coat of contrasting type for *glaze over glaze* techniques.

*Wax resist painting. The wax/oil mixture is being applied with rapid strokes onto leather-hard clay (1). Immediately the design is complete, pigment is spun over the whole surface (2). Detail (3) shows the resisted pattern before firing. A close-up (4) of the plate by Harry Davis shown under brushwork, showing the typical lively wax effect— the open areas broken with small blots of color.*

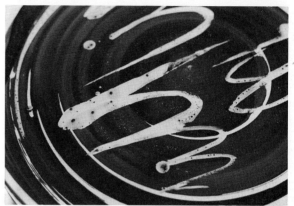

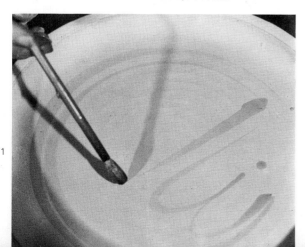

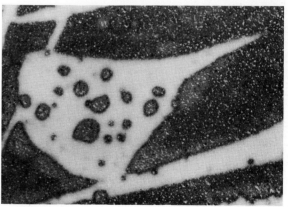

Wax resist is more often used on stoneware but there is no reason why it should not be a valuable supplement to *majolica* and other earthenware techniques. The kiln will need ventilation as the wax burns off.

A more mundane but extremely useful and time-saving application of wax resist is to coat bases, foot rings, lid flanges, and all those parts of a pot which are to be free of glaze. The whole piece can then be dipped or poured. A heavy *whirler* or banding wheel is essential for the efficient waxing of thrown pieces. (See illus. under *glazing*.)

## WEALD CLAY

A variable brick clay from S.E. England.

## WEATHERING OF CLAY

Exposure to rain, sun, and frost will improve the working qualities of most clays, breaking them down and oxidizing pyrites and other metals, leaching out soluble alkalis, and by the development of an intimate and uniform water content. Long weathering, over geological time, has probably been a major factor in the plasticity of clay. The minimum useful period for weathering, usually done in outside troughs with some protection from excessive rainfall and dirt, is a year.

Weathering is a different process to *aging* or *resting* but they all assist workability.

## WEDGING

The hand-mixing of clay either to combine different materials or to work clay into a consistent, bubble-free mass.

There are two stages:

1   Layering. The clays are cut into thin slabs which are slapped down alternately on one another. If grog is being added it can be spread between the layers. Harder and soft conditions of the same clay can be alternated. The whole pile is then cut vertically; one half lifted and brought smartly down on the other, taking care that the layering remains horizontal. Repeat until the layers have merged.

2   The mass of clay is cut into balls of 3-6 lb. (1.5-3 kg.). These are kneaded either by the forward and inwards thrust of the 'bull's head' method or by the spiral method.

*Wedging and kneading clay. The blocks of clay (light and dark, hard and soft, etc.) are sliced into layers about ½ in. (10 mm.) thick (1) and slapped down alternately one on another (2). The mass is then cut through vertically (3), each half looking like (4). These blocks (it is possible to cut four or more from a large mass of clay) are again combined (5), bringing one smartly down on the other while taking care to keep the layers always horizontal—this is crucial. The block is compressed (6), recut (7) and the process continued until the layers merge together. It is almost complete (8). The final mixing is done by kneading and two allied methods are used. For up to 7 lb. (3 kg.) of clay the 'bull's head' method is suitable, so called because the typical overlapping layers resemble an animal's head (9). The main block is lifted (10) and then forced down and back with the pressure of the palms (11), the hands also enclosing the sides to exert a certain inwards pressure at the same time to prevent undue sideways spread. The base of the clay must grip the bench so that the whole mass is spread over itself as it is forced away from the potter's body. Keep the arms fairly straight and use your body weight to exert pressure. This will be less tiring than working from the elbows. A pellet of a colored clay placed on the 'forehead' of the 'bull' should travel downwards and under the base as the process continues. Spiral kneading is shown (12-15). The basic movement is not very different from the above, but it is applied to one corner of a large mass forming a spiral shell pattern shape as the work proceeds. The clay is again lifted, rolled a little forwards, gripped and thrust down and away. The spiral*

*is being worked into a suitably compact shape by slapping and rolling it on the bench (15). Ideally the throwing should follow the direction of the kneading, that is, the point of the cone at the right hand of the potter (15) (for an anti-clockwise wheel).*

1

2

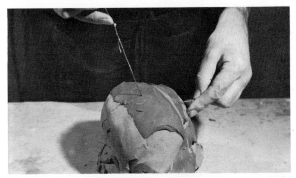

3

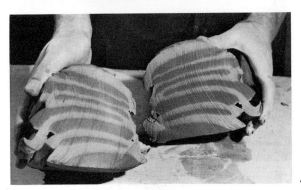

4

5

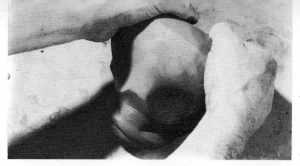

10

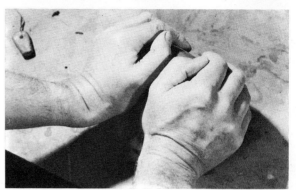

11

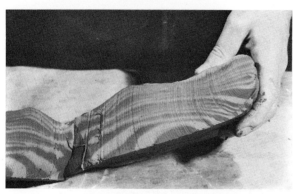

6

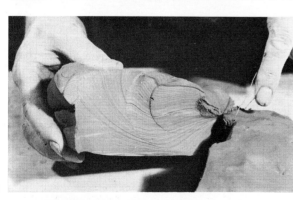

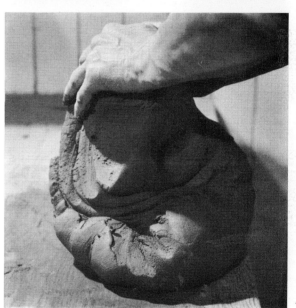

7

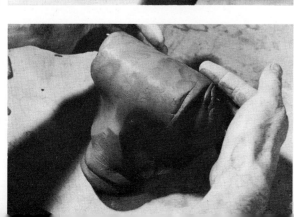

8

12

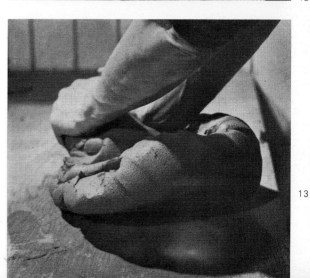

9

13

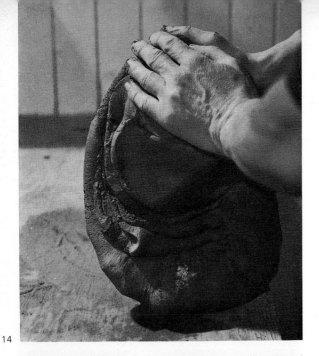

14

15

stores energy and ensures a steady and even movement. It probably evolved from a slow wheel used for coiling etc. In the Far East a stick is inserted into a hole in the rim of the wheel head which is spun round by this means and then withdrawn, the throwing being done before the impetus is lost. The European wheel has a wide stone flywheel which is spun by the sole of the foot on its surface. Manually powered wheels using pulleys and ropes featured in the eighteenth century factories. The traditional English wheel is the cranked wheel described under *kick wheels*.

Wheels are now frequently powered by a self-contained electric motor. (See *power-wheel*.)

## WHEEL BAT

A circular bat which can be removed from the wheel head complete with the thrown pot. Useful when making plates, large pots, shallow bowls, and for repetition throwing.

They can be of wood, plaster, or asbestos. (See *ejector head* for plaster type.) Wood is 'sympathetic' to the touch and has good clay-release properties but can warp or soften in use. Waterproof plys are available. The Lotus Pottery supply $11\frac{3}{4}$ in. (300 mm.) bats and special wheel heads. Of the asbestos materials, *Asbestolux* is easily shaped but is too absorbent and needs partial sealing, for example with a polyurethene varnish, to make it usable. *Sindanyo* bats are expensive but very hard and durable. Bats can be fastened to the wheel by means of two short lengths of metal rod set into the wheel head, one in the center and one about $2\frac{1}{2}$ in. (70 mm.) from it. The bats are drilled to fit over these 'pins'. Alternatively they can be adhered to the wheel head by a ring or thin slab of clay. (See illus. under *sindanyo*.)

## WHIRLER

A hand operated turntable also called a *banding wheel* although this term has a narrower application. Used for decoration, waxing, or glazing and for modeling and hand-building. There are many types and designs: in some the base will fall away if the whirler is lifted by the head. These are dangerous and should be avoided, especially in schools. The head may be of aluminium or cast iron—the latter gives greater stability and momentum. You should choose as heavy a model as you can handle. Weights vary from 4 - 36 lb. (2-15 kg.) 15 lb. (6.5 kg.) is a useful average.

## WHISTLE

Richard Dunning in PQ 13 gave full instructions for making clay whistles. A pinched or thrown pear shape is formed as shown (A) with an initial hole cut through it. The mouthpiece and the aperture through which the note is formed are shown in the second drawing. The 'whistle stick' (C) is thrust through the mouthpiece and out at the top of the bulb. A small pad of clay has been luted over the initial hole (D), which was made large enough to trim the inside shape of the bulb. A small wedge of this pad is now cut away

## WET FIRING

A rather controversial system of drying clay during the actual firing. CR 1 gives particulars. The method resembles that of raku in some respects. The newly thrown, wet pot is inserted into the red-hot kiln. Cooling by rapid evaporation, the principle of refrigeration, may be the factor at work. Even as described by an enthusiast the technique seems hedged about by provisions, exceptions, and some uncertainty though it sounds fun as an exercise in the unlikely.

## WHEEL, THROWING

A potter's wheel is, essentially, a flat circular slab of wood, metal or stone so mounted as to revolve on a vertical axis. There is generally a heavy flywheel which

(E) back from the point where the stick emerges, as in the second drawing. The stick is very carefully withdrawn. The sixth drawing shows how the points 1, 2, 3, and 4 should lie in a straight line while 3 should present a sharp edge. Point 1 to point 2 should be about $\frac{1}{2}$ in. (10 mm.).

The whistle can now be tried—it is often helpful to 'tongue' the breath, as when playing a recorder. If it does not produce a clear note the aperture is probably at fault and careful trimming may put it right. The one error which cannot be put right easily is too wide an aperture, due to miscalculating in the first place the angle of the stem to the body; too much air escapes. It is better to start again. Tuning holes are made, when the whistle has stiffened, with the handle of a paintbrush (5 and 6). Each successive hole gives a note of higher pitch; see *ocarina*.

The whistles can be decorated, or bird and animal forms constructed. Make sure that the tuning holes are where your fingers can easily reach them.

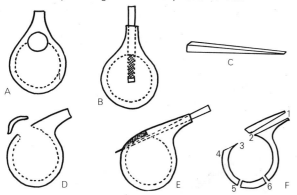

The basic form of the whistle (see text). The whistle stick is $\frac{1}{2}$ x $\frac{3}{4}$ in. (12 x 16 mm.) at the widest end of the wedge and about 8 in. (200 mm.) long.

## WHITE, glazes, body, pigment

Tin oxide will give the purest and best quality white *opaque* earthenware glaze. Zircon is also efficient but harder and shinier. Use 8-12% of either in a *soft glaze*. Titania will opacify but tend to produce a cream. Zinc and *Bristol* type glazes can be very white. Stoneware glazes are often naturally white and opaque: barium, zinc, and lime can assist, the last, perhaps, in the form of bone-ash.

A white body will always be a *short* one. Kaolin and flint are used to whiten bodies in the industry. Small quantities of cobalt are sometimes added to impart a certain spurious whiteness. Porcelain is normally very pale in color and will have a whiter appearance if fired in reduction, the iron traces being bluish instead of cream. White *engobes* are mixtures with very little ball clay and various fillers: see recipes in R.CGP 161.

*Tin-ash* may be used as a white pigment or tin oxide mixed with a little fritt.

## WHITE LEAD

'Basic' lead carbonate $2PbCO_3.Pb(OH)_2$, 775. Con-venient equivalent weight 258 (see also under *lead*).

Poisonous, use with great care. A very active *flux* in soft glazes and gives clear transparent glaze for use with tin oxide for *majolica*. Now forbidden in schools or where labor is employed. White lead was formerly the standard material for lead-lime-potash glazes. Specimen recipe:

White lead 43, feldspar 30, whiting 5, china clay 8, flint 14.

## WHITING

Finely ground cretaceous chalk, practically pure—97%—$CaCO_3$. (See *calcium carbonate*.) Decomposes to oxide at 825°C. The most commonly used glaze material for the introduction of *lime* into bodies and glazes.

## WICKET

The door of a kiln. Usually bricked up for firing.

## WIRE

See *resistance wire, element, electric kiln wiring, cutting wire, harp, bow*.

## WITHERITE

A comparatively rare rock of almost pure barium carbonate.

## WOLLASTONITE

Calcium metasilicate $CaO.SiO_2$, 116. m.p. 1540°C.

There are natural and synthetic forms with thermal expansions of 11 and 6 respectively. Sometimes used as a part substitute for feldspar in low temperature vitreous bodies. Can be used as a source of calcium in glazes. Wollastonite with barium and about 20% of clay is used for the very strong bodies of electrical porcelain. Whiting and flint mixtures give a cheaper equivalent.

## WOOD ASBESTOS

A type of asbestos sheet. A cross-ply material which will not crack if used for a kiln outer skin. Takes self-tapering screws. Available 8 x 4 in. (2.4 x 1.2 mm.) and $\frac{1}{4}$-1 in. (6-25 mm.) thick. Costs slightly more than Asbestolux but also superior in some ways.

## WOOD ASH

See *ash*.

## WOOD FIRING

Wood firing, at its best, gives a quality to both earthenware and stoneware which is unmatched by other fuels. It entails long and continuous work both in the preparation and firing. It is a fuel of comparatively low specific gravity and a great volume of material is required to fire a kiln: $4\frac{1}{2}$ cords of wood (about 580 cu. ft.) were used by Michael Cardew to fire his large (100 cu. ft.) kiln to stoneware. The calorific value is less than half that of oil. The Chinese potters are said to have been largely responsible for vast tracts of desert through their rapid destruction of the forests. This role is now taken over by newsprint, although a more conscious effort is made to replace the trees. Nevertheless, wood of the right type, condition, and size is not easy to obtain and comparatively few potters rely on it as their only or principal fuel. It is more often used as a boost towards the end of a firing, fed through subsidiary fireholes. Its long clear flame makes it an ideal fuel in many ways, especially for stoneware.

Leach specifies dry pine 3-8 in. (75-200 mm.) in diameter and 2 ft.-2 ft. 6 in. (600-750 mm.) long. At the height of the firing up to twelve such logs are burned every four minutes. Common deal off-cuts from timberyards can be used but are likely to come in small and odd-shaped pieces which makes the use of the semi-automatic grate impossible and thus increases the time taken up in stoking and surveillance. Advice on wood firing can be found in L.PB 190-7, C.PP and R.K 202-10.

## WORKABILITY

'An evasive synonym for plasticity' (Dodd). Nevertheless the word sums up the various qualities which a potter requires in his clay: plasticity, standing strength, low water absorption, together with the less tangible qualities of 'feel' and texture.

## WORKING SURFACE

The working surface for potting should be slightly porous, so that clay comes away cleanly, but not so porous as to dry it too rapidly. Nothing fulfils these requirements as well as a sound wooden bench, preferably, though not necessarily, a hardwood. Education Authorities are 'hooked' on plastic surfaces on which it is impossible to *wedge* or work with damp clay with any comfort. They are not even particularly easy to clean and they damage easily with metal scrapers.

## YELLOW, glazes, pigments

The sources of yellow color in ceramics are antimony, uranium, vanadium, iron and cadmium, and the compounds zircon/praseodymium and chrome/titania have been mentioned. An ochre yellow stoneware glaze given in C.PP is: AB clay (a red-firing African clay) 55, limestone 26.25, quartz 18.75.

Uranium will give a cool yellow at medium temperatures and is mentioned in a stoneware recipe in L.PB. Antimony must be fritted with lead and used in a high-lead soft glaze for its best color, see lead antimoniate. A yellow pigment fritt recipe is: red lead 15, antimony 10, tin oxide 4. Vanadium is used as the pentoxide or as ammonium metavanadate for high temperatures (to 1280°C.). Cadmium is used only at low temperatures and is even then difficult to stabilize. Iron yellows are cream or brown-yellows. See under the various materials mentioned for percentages in a glaze, etc. and *antimoniate of lead* for use on *majolica*.

## YELLOW OCHRE

See *ochre*.

## YING CH'ING

Translated as 'shadow blue' or 'sky blue', the term is used to cover a large family of pale blue-green reduced iron glazes from the East, usually on engraved porcelain. The term is now in some disfavor among ceramic historians but remains a convenient description for similar glazes used by craft potters today. David Leach's recipe:

    25 Feldspar
    25 Whiting
    25 China clay
    25 Quartz
     1 Ferric iron

gives a close approximation when fired on *porcelain* in reduction to about 1275°C. See color plate 23, p. 144.

## ZAFFRE

An impure cobalt arsenate, or a roasted mixture of cobalt ore and sand. Now largely obsolete as a pigment, but it sounds as if it might yield a more attractive color than the present vivid cobalt blues.

## ZETTLITZ KAOLIN

A Czechoslovakian kaolin, high in alumina.

## ZINC, oxide

A metallic element Zn, 65.
Oxide ZnO, 81, c.o.e. 6.5, s.g. 5.6.

In small quantities, up to 2%, it acts as a flux in many glazes and increases *craze* resistance. Larger additions tend to opacify and promote a *matt* surface. Used in both earthenware and stonewares. The *Bristol* glaze was an attempt to replace lead with zinc. The $ZnO.Al_2O_3.SiO_2$ eutectic is high at 1360°C. but the inclusion of other bases will lower this figure. Zinc has a balancing effect in glazes.

The raw material has a high shrinkage which gives trouble in a glaze on biscuit, though it is advantageous on once-fired ware. Shrinkage is reduced if the ZnO is calcined. An example stoneware formula:

    0.4 KNaO
    0.3 CaO. 0.6 $Al_2O_3$. 3.5 $SiO_2$
    0.3 ZnO

Zinc has a strong effect on pigments: poor color with iron, brighter with copper (sometimes a pink!), brown with chrome, with cobalt mauve or even an intense green have been obtained—these reactions all in oxidation. A versatile oxide but somewhat unpredictable and must be handled with care.

## ZIRCON

See *zirconium*.

## ZIRCONIUM, oxide, silicate

A metallic element Zr, 91.

Oxide $ZrO_2$, 123, *zirconia*, m.p. 2700°C.

Silicate $ZrO_2.SiO_2$, 183. 'Zircon'.

The oxide has an *inversion* of about 2.5% at 1200°C.

Zircon sands occur abundantly in Australia. Very refractory. Used as a glaze *opacifier*, replacing some or all of the tin oxide, giving a harder, shinier, more scratch-resistant surface. Less favorable reactions with pigments which are, however, very stable in a zircon glaze over a wide range of temperatures. The zircon needs to be well mixed with the batch either by grinding or very thorough stirring if it is not to show white specks. Special coated zircon is made to assist dispersion. Up to 12% is required in a soft glaze for opacity, but up to 30% can be added to promote crystalline and broken color effects in a soft glaze. Zircon has a low *thermal expansion* and will increase craze resistance, at the same time making a glaze more *viscous*.

Used in the manufacture of *refractories*, e.g. platinum melting crucibles, sparking plugs, etc. Can be used as a bat wash and kiln wash: 10 zircon to one clay.

## ACKNOWLEDGEMENTS

My thanks are given to John Anderson for his patient work on the photographs and to Peter Smith and my wife Sheila who checked every word and gave valuable help and advice. Peter Smith also gave generously from his recipes and research. The various publishers and supply firms mentioned in the bibliography have kindly allowed me to quote from various authorities; Wengers Ltd. gave excellent photographs of tools and Eileen Lewenstein the pictures of Robin Welch jolleying. South West Gas Board supplied up-to-date information and the Electrical Development Association and the British Ceramic Research Association allowed adaptations of their diagrams to be used. To these and to potters Mick Casson, Alan Caiger-Smith, and others; to Leslie Savage who put me right on electrical matters; and to all who have made the book possible, my gratitude.

# BIBLIOGRAPHY

A.RE    Aldred, F. *Refractories in the Electrical Industry.* Electricity Council.

B.TGH    Berendsen, A. *Tiles, a general history,* London, Faber, 1967.

B.TP    Billington, D. A. *The technique of pottery,* London, Batsford, 1962

C.CMW    Chandler, M. *Ceramics in the modern world,* London, Aldus, 1968.

CM    *Ceramics Monthly,* Columbus, USA.

C.MPWW    Carlton Ball, *Making pottery without a wheel,* Van Nostrand Reinhold, New York & London, 1965.

C.PC    Clark, K. *Practical pottery and ceramics,* London, Studio Vista, 1964.

C.PP    Cardew, M. *Pioneer pottery,* Harlow, Longmans, 1969.

CR    *Ceramic Review,* London, Craftsmen Potters Association.

C.TT    Colbeck, J. *Pottery: the technique of throwing,* London, Batsford, 1969.

D.DC    Dodd, A. E. *Dictionary of ceramics,* London, Newnes-Butterworth, 1967.

F.CC    Fournier, R. *Ceramic creations,* New York, Sterling, 1972.

G.EP    Green, D. *Experimenting with pottery,* London, Faber, 1971.

H.IPC    Holderness, A. *Inorganic and physical chemistry,* London, Heinemann Educational, 1963.

L.PB    Leach, B. *Potter's book,* London, Faber, 1945.

NZP    *New Zealand Potter,* Periodical.

PQ    *Pottery Quarterly,* Tring, Hertfordshire, Great Britain.

R.RAT    Riegger, H. *Raku art and technique,* London, Studio Vista, 1970.

R.CGP    Rhodes, D. *Clay and glazes for the potter,* London, Pitman, 1967.

R.K    Rhodes, D. *Kilns, design, construction and operation,* London, Pitman, 1969.

R.SP    Rhodes, D. *Stoneware and porcelain,* London, Pitman, 1960.

S.SCP    Shaw, K. *Science for craft potters and enamellers,* Newton Abbot, David and Charles, 1972.

S.WJC    Sanders, H. H. *The world of Japanese ceramics,* Tokyo/Palo Alto, California, Kodansha International Limited, 1969.

U.DS    Uvarov, E. B. (ed.) *Dictionary of science,* Harmondsworth, Penguin, 1969.

W.C    Worrall, W. E. *Clays: their nature, origin and natural growth,* London, Applied Science Publishers, 1968.

W.CNS    Webb, *Cobalt, nickel and selenium,* Mond Nickel Company.

## Catalogs from the following companies:

Ferro (G.B.), Wombourne, Wolverhampton, Staffordshire.

Fulham Pottery, New Kings Road, London, S.W.6.

Harrison Mayer, Mier, Stoke-on-Trent, Staffordshire.

Podmores, Shelton, Stoke-on-Trent, Staffordshire.

Wengers Ltd., Etruria, Stoke-on-Trent, Staffordshire.

## FILMS MENTIONED IN THE DICTIONARY

CIC      *Creatures in clay*, black and white, sound, 16 mm., 22 minutes.

GWCP      *Geoffrey Whiting, craftsman potter*, black and white, sound, 16 mm., 32 minutes.

IBCP      *Isaac Button, country potter*, black and white, silent, 16 mm., 42 minutes.

LK      *Ladi Kwali, Abuja 1959*, color, silent, 16 mm., 10 minutes.

RES      *Raku, English style*, color, sound, 16 mm., 16 minutes.

All these films are available from:

Slides and Films, 12 Chase Hill, Enfield, Middlesex.

## SUPPLIERS MENTIONED IN THE DICTIONARY

| | |
|---|---|
| Acme Marls Ltd. | Clough Street,<br>Hanley,<br>Stoke-on-Trent,<br>Staffordshire. |
| Cement Fondu | Lafarge Aluminous<br>    Cement Co. Ltd.,<br>Fondu Works,<br>P.O. Box 13,<br>730 London Road,<br>Grays,<br>Essex. |
| Ferro (G.B.) | Wombourne,<br>Wolverhampton. |
| Harrison-Mayer Ltd. | Meir,<br>Stoke-on-Trent,<br>Staffordshire. |
| Hymus Engineering Co.<br>   (recommended pugmill) | West Station Yard,<br>Maldon,<br>Essex. |
| Labheat | Peter Taylor,<br>56 Hodge Bower,<br>Ironbridge,<br>Shropshire. |
| Newclay Products Ltd. | Overston House,<br>Sunnyfield Road,<br>Chislehurst,<br>Kent. |
| Podmores and Sons Ltd. | Shelton,<br>Stoke-on-Trent,<br>Staffordshire. |
| Potclays Ltd. | Albion Works,<br>Etruria,<br>Stoke-on-Trent,<br>Staffordshire. |
| Rayefco<br>   (recommended power<br>   wheel) | Longfield,<br>Bulstrode Lane,<br>Felden,<br>Hemel Hempstead,<br>Herts. |
| Watts, Blake, Bearne and Co. | Courtney Park,<br>Newton Abbot,<br>Devon. |
| Wengers Ltd. | Etruria,<br>Stoke-on-Trent,<br>Staffordshire. |